Women's Caring

Feminist Perspectives on Social Welfare

second edition

edited by

CAROL BAINES
PATRICIA EVANS
SHEILA NEYSMITH

Toronto   Oxford   New York
OXFORD UNIVERSITY PRESS
1998

Oxford University Press
70 Wynford Drive, Don Mills, Ontario M3C 1J9
http://www.oupcan.com

Oxford New York
Athens Auckland Bangkok Bogotá Buenos Aires Calcutta Cape Town
Chennai Dar es Salaam Delhi Florence Hong Kong Istanbul
Karachi Kuala Lumpur Madrid Melbourne Mexico City Mumbai
Nairobi Paris São Paulo Singapore Taipei Tokyo Toronto Warsaw

and associated companies in
Berlin Ibadan

Oxford is a trade mark of Oxford University Press

Canadian Cataloguing in Publication Data

Main entry under title:

Women's Caring: feminist perspectives on social welfare

2nd ed.
Includes bibliographical references and index.
ISBN 0-19-541302-4

1. Social problems - Sex differences. 2. Sex role. 3. Women - Attitudes.
4. Caring - Sex differences. 5. Feminism. I. Baines, Carol. II. Evans,
Patricia M. (Patricia Marie), 1944- . iIII. Neysmith, Sheila.

HV541.W65 1998   362'.042   C98-931184-8

Design: Max Gabriel Izod
Copyright © Oxford University Press Canada 1998

1 2 3 4 — 01 00 99 98

Contents

❦

Contributors

Jane Aronson is Associate Professor in the School of Social Work, McMaster University. Her research and writing are concerned with how social policies and discourses on the family, the state, need, and dependence shape women's paid and unpaid caring labour as well as women's experiences of relying on the care of others.

Carol Baines is Professor at the School of Social Work, Ryerson Polytechnical University, Toronto. Her research interests and publications focus on the history of women in the professions, social work history, and child welfare.

Patricia Evans is Associate Professor in the School of Social Work, York University. She writes in the area of women and the welfare state, with a particular focus on single mothers, work, and welfare. She is the co-editor of *Women and the Canadian Welfare State* (1997).

Evelyn Ferguson is Associate Professor in the Faculty of Social Work, University of Manitoba. Her research and writing interests include feminist approaches to social policy with a focus on day care, particularly gender and parental involvement. She has two school-age children.

Usha George, Assistant Professor at the Faculty of Social Work, University of Toronto, studied in India, the United States, and Nigeria. Her teaching, research, and writing interests are in the areas of immigrant adaptation, anti-racist and culturally competent social work, and gender in development and community practice. She was instrumental in the development of the Anti-Racism, Multiculturalism and Native Issues Centre at the Faculty of Social Work.

Sue McWatt is a graduate of the Faculty of Social Work, University of Toronto. For a number of years she has been involved with immigration and refugee issues, especially as they are experienced by women of colour. She is currently engaged in social development work in Nepal.

Janet Mosher, Associate Professor in the Faculty of Law, University of Toronto, is cross-appointed to the Faculty of Social Work and is Director of the combined LLB/MSW program at the University of Toronto. Her research has examined the conditions of women who are abused in their intimate relationships and women's poverty.

Sheila Neysmith is Professor at the Faculty of Social Work, University of Toronto. Her research and writing examine women's caring labour in both its paid and unpaid forms. She is currently policy and practice editor of the *Canadian Journal on Aging/La Revue canadienne du vieillissement*.

Marge Reitsma-Street is Associate Professor in the Faculty of Human and Social Development at the University of Victoria. Her past experiences as a social worker in correctional centres informs her continuing critique of juvenile justice policies. She is co-editor of *Changing Lives: Women in Northern Ontario* (1996).

Karen Swift is Associate Professor at the School of Social Work, York University. Her research on women's issues focuses on child welfare policy and practices. She is the author of *Manufacturing 'Bad Mothers'* (1995).

Preface

The work women do in looking after others takes place in the home, in the workplace, and in the community. But wherever this work occurs, it is usually undervalued and frequently invisible. In this book, we trace the implications of women's caring work, recognizing the significance of class and race in structuring the resulting inequities. We believe that a perspective on caring helps to articulate the complex nature of this work and reaches beyond the traditional divisions of paid and unpaid labour. A caring perspective also reveals the ambiguities and contradictions that pervade women's relationship to the welfare state and the realities they experience as they negotiate social services. The issues we explore are critical to the fields of social work and women's studies, and are also highly relevant to those individuals teaching, working, and studying in the fields of nursing, education, and child care.

When the first edition of this book was published in 1991, attention to women's work as 'caring' labour was in its early stages. Since then, the literature has expanded, the debates have developed, and the future of the Canadian 'welfare state' is far more perilous than we could have imagined seven short years ago. The second edition attempts to capture these changes through four new essays (Chapters 1, 4, 7, and 10) and extensive revisions to most of the others.

Women's Caring represents the work of a number of women, but we offer it as more than a collection of individual essays. Both the first and second editions have benefited from the lively discussions that have taken place, over time and in varying combinations, among the 10 women who are represented in this book. We owe a very large debt of gratitude to our authors. Each one has used her expertise and research to enrich the literature on caring and social welfare, and helped to move our own thinking further along. In the interval between the first and second editions, a research network, headed by Sheila Neysmith and funded by the Social Sciences and Humanities Research Council of Canada, helped to further these conversations and support the research of a number of us.

Other individuals have played an important role in guiding this second edition to press. Euan White of Oxford University Press made the initial suggestion and provided excellent advice throughout the process. Grateful thanks go to Fran Morphy, who produced the proverbial silk purse in the final stages of the manuscript, and to Richard Tallman, once again, for his excellent editing. Special thanks to our families, who helped, and cared, in so many tangible and intangible ways.

Carol Baines
Pat Evans
Sheila Neysmith

Toronto, February 1998

Part One

Perspectives on Caring

Women's Caring:
Work Expanding, State Contracting

CAROL T. BAINES, PATRICIA M. EVANS, AND SHEILA M. NEYSMITH

INTRODUCTION

Caring refers to the physical, mental, and emotional activities and effort involved in looking after, responding to, and supporting others. In our society, much of this work is done by women in varying forms throughout their lives. It is done as mothers, daughters, and wives in the context of individual relationships, in the community as volunteers, through the professions as nurses, social workers, and teachers, and as low-wage workers in hospitals, child-care centres, and home-care services. The persons who receive care are usually those we view as dependent, and include children, people with physical, intellectual, or psychiatric disabilities, and the frail elderly. However, within the family, the cared-for may also include able-bodied men.

The work of caring encompasses a range of activities that can take place in a variety of locations, including one's home, other people's homes, and the workplace. Care may be provided in the context of paid employment or undertaken on an informal basis, usually (but not always) without pay (Jenson, 1997). The gendered division of caring labour reflects economic and power relationships. In the home, this division of labour creates a socially constructed dependency that, paradoxically for women, is frequently the consequence of providing care to others, rather than the outcome of receiving care (Graham, 1983). What is common to caring labour, however, is that it is highly gendered and typically viewed as the responsibility of women. In addition, as Thomas (1993: 652) explains, care work, whether paid or unpaid, involves a relationship that 'is defined in terms of ties or bonds signifying degrees of personal familiarity and obligation.'

There is no paternal equivalent to the concept of 'maternal' bonding that has fuelled the ideology of motherhood, an ideology that helps to equate 'problem' children with a mother's neglect (Mandell, 1988). Likewise, while some men do care for elderly and disabled relatives, they do not take on the primary responsibility in the numbers that women do. Moreover, when men take on this care, they are viewed as exceptional and are likely to receive more services from the formal sector than women (Allen, 1994; Guberman, 1988; Stoller, 1992). As well, the profile of the poorly paid care workers and the 'caring' professionals of social work, teaching, and nursing is overwhelmingly female, jobs in which 'the "woman's touch" has been formally incorporated into the job specification' (Graham, 1983: 16).

Although the caring role is sharply gendered, it plays out in various ways in the lives of women who, after all, occupy a range of social locations. The price paid for caring, for example, is highest for low-income women who must absorb the costs without the buffer that babysitting, cleaning, and other supplementary services provide. Race also influences the structure of caring responsibilities. Immigration regulations, for example, allow some women into Canada on the condition that they provide paid caregiving to children in other people's families. This often means that these women have to make arrangements to have their own children cared for by female kin in their country of origin. The structures of caregiving and the available options, then, play out differently for women, according to class and ethno-racial position.

Finally, caring practices are influenced by the politics of globalization, changing economies, and the devolution of nation-states. The priority assigned to deficit reduction by Canadian governments means that the welfare state is undergoing a radical transformation. Many of the traditional services of the welfare state have been directed either to those who require care or to supplement the care provided by kin. The downsizing that occurs as services are shed, relocated into the commercial or non-profit sectors, or moved, by default, back into the family, all have very sharp and particular impacts on women.

This book contributes to a Canadian perspective on women's caring. The individual chapters cover a variety of topics, but all document the ways in which the social organization of caring structures women's opportunities and can impose significant costs and consequences. The chapters critique the assumption that caring is a female mandate, an assumption that continues to underpin policies, programs, and professional practice. Each author draws upon her own area of expertise to explore the caring labour of women, women who are differently positioned by class and race and who work in a variety of settings.

The first section of the book develops theoretical and historical perspectives on women's caring and considers issues of race, class, and poverty. Part Two documents some of the realities of caring in women's lives and explores their implications, recognizing that these realities vary by social location. Part Three focuses on specific policies and examines how they shape gendered caring expectations. All chapters demonstrate how the welfare state reinforces women's caring, explore the implications of its dismantling for the caring labour done by women, and consider proposals for alternative approaches. Authors assess these alternatives in terms of their effects on women as caregivers and care receivers in various sectors of Canadian society. Proposals for change start from the premise that it is necessary to restructure the current division of caring responsibilities.

In this opening chapter we explore the analytic dimensions of women's caring and discuss four central themes that articulate the perspective we write from and provide some common foundation for the analyses that follow. We also identify the major challenges that must be confronted if we are to reconstruct the current and inequitable division of caring work.

DIMENSIONS OF WOMEN'S CARING

The use of the term 'caring' signals not only the reality that this work is frequently invisible and usually undervalued, but that it also takes place in the context of relationships in which the norms of obligation, responsibility, and feelings of affection and resentment intertwine. Our concern is to ensure that this relational aspect is integrated into a conceptual understanding of the use and value of women's reproductive labour in a capitalist economy. Over a decade ago, Gillian Pascall (1986: 71) identified the need to develop an 'analysis . . . which can take seriously both the emotional and material understandings of caring and why women do it.'

While the notion of caring is often viewed as incorporating both 'labour' and 'love' (Finch and Groves, 1983), the extent to which affection is actually intertwined with activity should not be assumed (Leira, 1994). The assumption that they are inseparable can call into question the integrity of a woman's caring *about* when she no longer cares *for*. This is illustrated in the reaction towards mothers who are perceived as neglectful, and the guilt experienced by individuals who relegate the care of their frail elderly and disabled relatives to institutions. This conflating of caring for and caring about is not limited to familial caregiving. Foster mothers, nurses, or home-care workers who press for better pay in order to care *for* are likely to be suspected of not caring adequately *about*. Similarly, to conceptualize caring as a 'labour of love' minimizes the influence of normative obligations and the absence of alternatives that may bind individuals to care for even in the absence of caring about.

Carol Thomas (1993) identifies seven analytic dimensions common to all concepts of caring. Her typology highlights the variability that can exist within each of the seven dimensions and provides a useful departure point for discussing the different emphases reflected in the caring literature. The first dimension Thomas identifies is the *social identity of the carer*. While gender is its common characteristic, this identity is frequently further delineated by a familial (e.g., wives, mothers) or an occupational role (e.g., home help, social worker). Class and race are also characteristics that differentiate carers, although they are not mentioned by Thomas, perhaps because they remain underdeveloped in the literature, an issue we return to later in the chapter. The *social identity of the cared-for* is the second dimension and the overwhelming theme reflected in the literature is that those who receive care are typically constructed as 'dependent' (e.g., children, frail elderly). Writers from the disability movement have underlined the need to include attention to issues as they relate to the cared-for rather than to continue the almost exclusive emphasis on the carer (Morris, 1993).

The third dimension of caring is the *nature of the interpersonal relationship* between the carer and cared-for. This relationship may reflect ties of family or friendship, or incorporate structured obligations that exist when caring work is delivered through services (Thomas refers to this as a 'contingent' caring relationship). The *nature of care* provided comprises the fourth dimension. The type of care that is emphasized may be associated with a 'feeling' state (affection/emotion), an 'activity' state (physical work, tasks), and often as both (caring *for* and caring *about*; caring as 'labour' and 'love'). The fifth dimension concerns the *social domain* of a caring relationship and reflects the traditional dichotomies of public/private, informal/formal.

When care is discussed in the literature, it tends to be identified with one location only, often with the implicit assumption that this is the only type of care. The early literature, for example, focused exclusively on kin-based caregiving. As Thomas points out (1993: 52), despite claims to be comprehensive, the conceptualization of care is more often 'domain specific' and confined to issues that relate to informal *or* formal care. The sixth dimension involves the *economic character of the care relationship* and whether care is provided on a paid or unpaid basis. While this dimension is frequently assumed to parallel the public/private distinction, this is not always the case. Informal caring is not always unpaid (nannies, babysitters), nor is caring in the public domain necessarily undertaken for pay (voluntary work, for example). The seventh and final dimension of caring involves the *institutional/organizational setting*—the physical location, which may be the home, a hospital, or community clinics.

While Thomas's analytic dimensions are helpful in revealing the complex conceptual layers of care, it is also important not to 'deconstruct' the notion so completely that the commonalities are simply obscured by the differences. The concept of caring is not without its difficulties, and has been criticized as theoretically underdeveloped (Thomas, 1993; Graham, 1993). It has spawned a large and diverse, and frequently fragmented literature that tends to reflect the concerns and interests of individual academic disciplines and specific professional orientations. These include feminist debates about the legitimacy and helpfulness of an 'ethic of care' (Tronto, 1993; Gordon, 1996; Clement, 1996; Larabee, 1993; Bowden, 1997), the 'burden of care' literature that documents the nature and costs of kin caring (for a review of relevant research and theory, see Hooyman and Gonyea, 1995: 139–53), the professional literature (see, for example, Phillips and Benner, 1994), and the social policy writing that focuses on the distribution of formal and informal care. None the less, we find the concept of caring of considerable value in helping us to move beyond the assumptions that underpin the traditional dichotomies of women's work: paid/unpaid, public/private, and formal/informal. These categories do not easily encompass the situation of live-in domestic caregivers, mothers at home caring for children while on paid leave, or volunteer workers in a range of community-based services. The terms 'domestic labour' and 'unpaid work' reflect the language of the market and do not adequately reflect the personal dimension that characterizes much of the work women do. In 1996, for the first time, the Canadian census asked questions about women's unpaid work and divided it between 'housework' and 'caregiving'.

The caring perspective has also been criticized for its potential to reify the very work that has helped to entrap women. Underlining the importance of an affective dimension in the context of an analysis rooted in gender may, however inadvertently, serve to essentialize to women the work of caring labour. As Houston (1990: 118) comments, 'The current conventions governing gender relations not only resist significant change, but they can resist it in the ethic's own terms—in the name of caring.' We take this critique seriously but are not persuaded that ignoring the relational aspect of the 'people work' women do helps to further either an analysis of or resistance to what has perhaps more aptly been termed 'compulsory altruism' (Land and Rose, 1985). We have not found a perspective as useful in unravelling this type of work that is so prominent in the lives of women and has served as such an important site of exploitation, as well as satisfaction. It also provides a helpful way of understanding the inequities that women experience across spheres and sectors, while appreciating that these inequities are not experienced equally. A caring perspective allows us to explore the social construction of obligation in Canadian society, the benefits that accrue to particular individuals and sectors, and the harms that are visited on others.

DEVELOPING SERVICES TO PROVIDE CARE: CHANGING DISCOURSES, PERSISTING PROBLEMS

As the twentieth century unfolded, the early private voluntary services were gradually incorporated into an expanding public service structure. By mid-century these services were characterized by hierarchical bureaucracies in which women, in most cases, provided direct services while men quickly filled the managerial ranks. By the end of the 1980s, social services were struggling to contend with the fundamental challenges posed by a rapidly declining commitment to state-provided services and the emerging models that reflected a mixed economy of welfare. This mixed economy includes an effort to increase all forms of privatization by ensuring a voluntary sector in which agencies compete for low-cost delivery, encouraging the growth of commercially provided services, and placing an even greater reliance on women in households to provide care (Rekart, 1993). Over time, there have been important and discernible shifts in the discourse surrounding caring services, but the problems of inadequate provision, the structural disadvantage of women in formal and informal care, have all remained remarkably persistent.

Providing care is presented as the *raison d'être* of health and social services. Many services target persons with transitory needs who are viewed as on their way to becoming independent, contributing members of society. These include services to children, individuals in acute-care hospitals, and adults who require short-term treatment. However, many people, such as those with chronic illnesses or with physical or mental impairments, need long-term care to accomplish the basic activities of daily living. The young and temporarily disabled were the client base upon which teachers, nurses, therapists, and social workers developed their professional models of practice. As Carol Baines discusses in Chapter 2, the success of several traditionally female occupations in articulating skills and specifying interventions with such client groups has allowed them to lay claim to a knowledge and expertise that formed the basis for demands for better wages and working conditions. While professional social workers have gained more status, front-line caregivers such as child-care workers, homemakers, and residential workers remain among the lowest paid. Many of these workers belong to the most disadvantaged groups in our society, immigrant women and women of colour (Neysmith and Aronson, 1997). It is ironic that these poorly paid front-line care workers were the last women to benefit from a decade of pay equity legislation in Ontario, and only after they mounted a successful court challenge.

The vision of 'community care' as an alternative to institutionally based care for physically and developmentally handicapped persons has opened up the debate about who is responsible for ensuring that such persons receive the care they need. When the need for care is ongoing, just how are the boundaries between public and personal responsibility drawn? Although everyone recognizes the negative effects of institutionalization, the move to deinstitutionalize was fuelled primarily by the rising costs associated with such a model.[1] The limited availability of community-based services today is an important reminder that recognizing the problematic nature of a service does not ensure that an alternative will be developed.

The burgeoning literature on caregiving during the 1980s and 1990s might well lead one to dub it 'the age of the carer'. From a small feminist literature that was truly on the margins of social policy, the carer quickly came to be the focus of an extensive body of research. The growing discourse around informal carers was a pivotal ingredient in what came to be seen as a burgeoning caring crisis. In the process, the debate underwent several transformations that will affect women. One is the now regular reminder that men do caring labour, too—10 per cent of men versus 15 per cent of women reported doing regular caregiving for the elderly in 1996 (Statistics Canada, 1997). Secondly, informal caregiving has become normalized in research and theory. For example, caring and its effects are frequently conceptualized as a career with fairly predictable stages that professionals need to understand in order to anticipate interventions (see, for example, Aneshensel, Pearlin, Mullan, Zarit, and Whitlatch, 1995). On the other hand, the gendered nature of caring remains quite visible in some texts (Dwyer and Coward, 1992; Hooyman and Gonyea, 1995; Neal, Chapman, Ingersoll-Dayton, and Emlen, 1993) as well as in articles that appear in feminist and mainstream journals. The growing visibility of caring has been accompanied by an acceptance of it as a 'normal' family responsibility, albeit with particular consequences for women. This is worrisome. Old women become the social problem, rather than how we organize and deliver health and social services (Gibson, 1996). The demands placed on women's caring and the lack of support and recognition it receives affect the relationship between those women providing care and those in need of it. The devaluation of caring, coupled with its invisibility, places those who are cared for, whether family members or clients of service organizations, in a precarious position of socially created dependency. In other words, discussions of the burden of caring are as applicable to those receiving care as those providing. Both operate under conditions where options are extremely limited (Aronson, 1990; Barry, 1995; Hochschild, 1995). Thus, it is not caring that is the problem but the social conditions under which it occurs. A feminist approach to caring seeks to provide an analysis of the ideological context that shapes the relationship between those being cared for and those providing the informal and formal care, and identifies the strategies that will expand women's choices and control over their lives.

OUR PERSPECTIVE, OUR THEMES

The chapters in this book focus on substantive areas where caring occurs, documenting and discussing its effects on various groups of women and suggesting changes in programs and policies that would improve the lives of women. In these arenas we see how the social relations of caring are understood, valued, and practised within Canadian society. In this section, we highlight several themes of particular significance to issues of caring and social welfare. We hope that this discussion helps readers to understand our location in the debates about women and caring.

1. *Why is caring viewed as woman's 'natural' responsibility?* There is nothing inherent about the work of caring that 'belongs' to women. The reasons that women have been society's 'carers' are not to be found in biological or anatomical differences between the sexes, nor can the explanations be located in any 'womanly' innate disposition towards connectedness or 'relational' rather than 'rational' thinking. Carol Gilligan (1982: 160) explored apparent differences in the moral development of girls and boys, suggesting that female 'identity is defined in a context of relationship and judged by a standard of responsibility and care.' Her work has been subject to considerable debate and interpretation since its publication. In fact, the literature on caring generally has often been criticized for its inattention to issues of power and for its potential to support an essentialist view of caring. While important insights resonate through the 'different voice' that Gilligan's work helped to reveal, we reject a cultural or relational feminism that essentializes caring to women and valorizes it as an inherently superior value and a basis for a more humane society (Card, 1990).

By emphasizing the congruence of caring in women's lives, rather than its contradictions and consequences, caring is too readily perceived as an embedded part of women's identity. This ignores the fact that the caring women do has been forged under terms and conditions that were not of their choice (Scaltas, 1992). Conflating care with women's identity also sets the stage for an extremely negative image of women who do not fit this script by never opting for or by actually rejecting caring work. The reification of caring is apparent in popular discourse that emphasizes the emotional rather than the material aspects of care. To equate 'caring' with selfless, never-ending, and uncomplaining 'giving' virtually obliterates the constraints, costs, and consequences that fall so heavily on women. This orientation underlies policies that lodge responsibility for others with women and limit programs to supporting women rather than redistributing responsibility for caring.

Our views about why so much of the caring work devolves on women stem from approaches that recognize that the current construction of caring labour results, primarily, from the organization of relations in a capitalist and patriarchal society. In referring to current debates about the nature and relations of women's paid and unpaid work, Pat Armstrong and Hugh Armstrong (1990: 97–8) comment: 'They have been heavily influenced by the critiques of both marxists and non-marxists, as well as by changes in women's work. They have revealed the interpenetration of the so-called private and public spheres of the economy, the importance of sex divisions to developing an understanding of class divisions, the impossibility of explaining production without reference to reproduction.' A materialist perspective emphasizes the importance of structural constraints, which does not mean that the significant influence of familist ideology or gen- der-role socialization is ignored. But it does suggest that ideas and attitudes, on their own, do not cause women to be held primarily responsible for care, but rather the interaction of structures, material conditions, and ideology. It is also important to understand that women's caring is not simply shaped by these forces—women also affect the relations, locations, and structures of caring. Marge Reitsma-Street in Chapter 5 highlights these themes in her discussion of the resulting costs for young women who fail to conform to the expected femi- nine role and their strategies of resistance.

2. *How can we understand differences in the experiences of caring?* The previous section suggested that it was problematic to essentialize women's caring—to val- orize it and to assume that it is work that comes 'naturally' to women. Equally problematic is the tendency, rarely expressed but frequently implicit, to 'univer- salize' caring and to assume that women share similar experiences. Gender is only one aspect of women's identity and cannot be properly understood in isolation from other signifiers of location, including class, race, and sexual orientation. By ignoring important differences of social location, the carer is implicitly con- structed as 'mainstream'. It is the interrelationships among these locations that help to shape the expectations and implications of caring for specific women. The caring issues that confront White middle-class women were not, and are not, the same as those confronting women who are not White and/or middle class. Class, frequently intersecting with race, helps to structure whether a woman provides only informal care, or whether she is likely to be poorly paid by someone else to provide care. Usha George traces the connections between race, class, and gen- der in Chapter 4 and provides an important perspective on the issues of caring for women in the South Asian community.

White feminists identify the family as a central arena of economic and power relationships, but the forces of historic and systemic racism have meant that many women of colour struggle to 'build and maintain families in which to give and receive care' (Graham, 1993: 466). For many poor immigrant women, the choice has been low-paying jobs, often caring for dependent individuals outside their own familial circle (Daenzer, 1993). Research on domestic workers has doc- umented the oppressive conditions that frequently characterize this work (Arot- Koc, 1992; Calliste, 1991) and this issue is explored in relation to Filipina 'nan- nies' by Sue McWatt and Sheila Neysmith in Chapter 10. Another example is provided by home-care workers, frequently women of colour, who move into a type of work closely related to traditional domestic work. Racism is often appar- ent when elderly clients and their families respond to a home-care worker as if she were a domestic servant. Black family life need not be idealized to recognize that a certain equality exists that stems from having to survive the oppression of living in a racist society. Thus, as Nasir (1996: 19) comments, many women of colour must overcome the structural constraints that have made the ideology of 'servant' more salient than that of 'carer' in a long tradition of paid work. She reminds us that feminists 'universalize' experience when we forget that 'feminist' applies only to one part of our identity.

Exploring the past, Linda Gordon (1994) and Molly Ladd-Taylor (1994) observed that US professional women were unable to unite with their poorer sisters to press for changes that would enable women to assume rights as citizens, independent of their status as mothers. While White social welfare foremothers accepted the dominant ideology of their social position, Black women leaders pursued different avenues for change. The history of Black women's experiences in caring has reflected their greater commitment to collective caring at the familial, kinship, neighbourhood, and community levels. African-American and African-Caribbean communities have recognized that caring for children is more than a biological responsibility. It is shared by 'other mothers'. The communal responsibility assumed by women-centred networks in African-American neighbourhoods has been well documented (Hill-Collins, 1992). The presence of Black women's networks also spawned political activism in Canada and the United States, and in the nineteenth century Black Canadian women were pressing for equity in educational resources (Bristow, 1994; Daenzer, 1997). For instance, while social work leaders such as Julia Lathrop in the US fought for widows' pensions for poor White women, Black women activists underscored the need and right for Black women to work and thus fought for day-care programs, schools, and institutional reform that recognized this fact (Ladd-Taylor, 1994).

Class is another important area of difference that frequently intersects with race and is also a dimension of inequality that is underdeveloped in the caring literature (Arber and Ginn, 1992). Class helps to structure whether a woman is positioned only as an informal carer, or whether she is likely to be poorly paid, or relatively well paid, by someone else to provide care. Poor women, particularly, use social services, although the services they seek are frequently required on behalf of children, husbands, and other relatives. The care mothers on social assistance give to their children at home is increasingly subject to scrutiny, and at the same time their caring responsibilities are obliterated in the context of increasing calls for workfare. The connections between poverty and caring are taken up by Patricia Evans in Chapter 3, while Karen Swift, in Chapter 8, reveals how the contradictions in the caring mandate of the child welfare system are played out in the lives of women who are deemed 'neglectful'.

Although the critical importance of class and race is gaining more attention in the caring literature, there has been little effort to address the types of concerns raised by disability activists who reject the socially constructed dependency image that permeates the long-term care services they use. The literature on informal carers comes under particular critique for the separation it makes between 'women' (who do not include the 'disabled') and 'dependent' people (who are not distinguished by gender). Jenny Morris (1993) suggests that this problematic dichotomy arises because the writers themselves identify only with providing care and do not imagine themselves as individuals who might need care. The fact that the voice of the 'cared-for' is beginning to be heard is largely due to the work of the disability activists. Similarly, analyses by lesbians and gay men that challenge assumptions about family and caring relationships are conspicuously absent from much of the discourse on caring. Both the informal and formal care literature assumes heterosexist domestic arrangements. Considering the history of wage discrimination that faces all women, elderly lesbian couples are likely to be poorer than heterosexual couples. Taken together this will make it more difficult for partners to provide and receive care from one another (Graham, 1993). In summary, issues of caring and gender refract very differently when experienced and explored through the lenses of women in different social locations. Glenn (1992: 31) comments, 'By not recognizing the different relationships women have had to such supposedly universal experiences as motherhood and domesticity, they [feminists] risk essentializing gender—treating it as static, fixed, eternal, and natural. They fail to take seriously as a basic premise of feminist thought, that gender is a social construct.'

3. *Where can 'good' care take place?* Caring takes place in a variety of locations, as the chapters in this book illustrate. Evelyn Ferguson, in Chapter 9, highlights the variety of formal and informal, paid and unpaid arrangements that constitute 'child care', while Sheila Neysmith, in Chapter 11, explores the implications of different forms of care for the frail elderly and their carers. In this book, we wish to avoid the tendency either to focus on women's domestic labour exclusively or to assume that informal care by a family member provides a preferable location for care to take place. The literature on aging was marked throughout the 1980s by an emphasis on the costs of care to kin in what is sometimes termed the 'burden of care' discourse. The documentation of unpaid caring costs was of course important and legitimate but it also had the unintended effect of placing elderly women (and men) as the locus of a 'family problem', in addition to neglecting those situations in which women do caring work as paid labour. We reject a public discourse that asserts that the 'best' care occurs outside a cash nexus. The assumption that paid care is somehow inferior is apparent in public images where elderly people, for example, are often depicted receiving care within the bosom of their families. This ignores the vulnerable position of many people in their own homes. It also provides an implicit but powerful critique of the families who 'fail' to care, and diminishes the legitimacy of care choices by individuals who may prefer formal to informal care, at least with respect to some aspects of their care. Such images also ignore the research cited in several chapters of this book, which documents the importance that child-care and home-care workers attach to the relational aspects of their caring work. Both poor care and good care occur across a variety of settings, whether paid or unpaid, as the chapters in this book illustrate. The entanglement of caring for and caring about is not eliminated simply because caring is paid for.

Although much of the literature continues to reflect an emphasis on informal care, expanding attention is given to paid caring work. Women are the principal providers of care delivered through commercial firms, by non-profit organizations, and in publicly funded institutions providing services for children, people with disabilities, and frail elderly persons. The pattern in which poorly paid women provide care to vulnerable people has been evident throughout the period of development and expansion of health and social services in Canada. The most common reason young women give for wanting to enter the 'caring professions' is to help others; indeed, nursing, social work, and teaching have recognized this in their recruitment efforts.

4. *Caring is a collective responsibility.* Traditionally, the 'welfare state' has been integrally connected to women's caring work, although the relationship has been neither simple nor straightforward. Services and benefits have, at times and for some women, supported and supplemented their caring work but they have also reinforced their obligations to care. Many social welfare policies and programs, for example, are rooted in the assumption that women are primarily responsible for the care of family members: the mother is the usual focus for intervention in child welfare; the wife tends her aging spouse; the daughter is called on to care for elderly parents. Programs are routinely assessed in terms of their impact on families, even though families are made up of individuals and what is good for the family may not be equally good for all of its members. Jane Aronson takes up these themes in Chapter 6 and highlights the stresses and strains on both aging mothers and caregiving daughters. Janet Mosher in Chapter 7 reveals how women's efforts to protect themselves and their children from violence are not recognized when the policies ignore the caring commitments and economic dependence of women in families.

The welfare state has been an important source of jobs for women, but typically the jobs have been as poorly paid child-care workers, nursing attendants, and homemakers. Social services provide employment opportunities, but they also control and limit women's options, especially women who are disadvantaged by class or race. The problematic aspects of women's relationship to the state increase dramatically in the context of the radical dismantling taking place as the services and benefits of the welfare state downsize, privatize, and disappear. We are now confronting public discourses that, at worst, regard the idea of collective responsibility as essentially illegitimate or, at best, subordinate it to fiscal 'realities'. Governments have been successful in convincing Canadians that the debt problem is of 'crisis' proportions that resulted from excessive spending on redistributive programs that can no longer be afforded (for challenges to this view, see Cohen, 1997; McQuaig, 1995). As it is particularly women's caring work that is intensified as services are cutback, it is not surprising that in Canada, as elsewhere, cuts to social spending are typically accompanied by neo-conservative praise for family-based care and the creation of moral panic about the destruction of 'the family' (Pateman, 1992: 231; Luxton, 1997: 23).

An important theme in every chapter of this book is the way that caring work can be accomplished without reproducing and perpetuating gender inequality.

We argue that caring is everyone's work, and to achieve this requires a redistribution in the responsibilities assigned to women, to men, to states, and to markets. And yet, as we approach the end of this century, the public services that provide care are forced to downsize and an appeal to social responsibility appears to have little purchase in contemporary debates.

PATHWAYS AND POSSIBILITIES

At this moment in time caring in our society is not the same for all women, although it does affect the quality of women's lives in very different ways from that of men. Policies directed at diminishing the inequalities women face in the labour market will have little effect, except for a privileged few, unless there are changes in their domestic and child-care responsibilities that take into account the interacting forces that arise from disparities of class, gender, race, ethnicity, sexual orientation, and disability. The central challenge is to find ways to promote social change and a more collective responsibility towards caring for others. In the concluding part of this chapter we address four questions: What are the implications as the state restructures and retreats from public caring? Can caring be organized in ways that do not exacerbate inequities? Can we shift from individual care to collective care? What strategies can be used to promote social change?

1. *What are the implications as the state restructures and retreats from public caring?* With major cutbacks in public services, it is difficult to be optimistic about the future. For women, there are perhaps more reasons for pessimism. The downsizing and privatizing of essential services intensify the strains on women's caring. Pressures are being experienced with respect to child care, home care, and a variety of other support services as services become more difficult to access. In Alberta, the provincial government attempted to cut back on kindergarten provision, but ultimately had to back down because of public pressure. In health care, across the country, procedures formerly offered in hospitals are now expected to be accomplished at home. The evidence is accumulating that hospital cutbacks have sharp impacts on the quality of care provided and increase the stress on the mostly female health care staff (Armstrong and Armstrong, 1996; White, 1997). For care providers in a variety of settings, the prospect of low wages, more clients, and job insecurity ensures a less caring environment.

The privatizing of services is accompanied by the increased individualization of social problems and an erosion of a community conscience and responsibility. Images of 'welfare moms', 'crack babies', 'child abusers', and 'intergenerational poverty' dominate the media and fuel a conservative ideology and a 'get tough' approach that justifies attacks on the welfare state. Child welfare services are focused on women's failure to care rather than the provision of services that enhance the capacity of families to provide care. This has been highlighted in media attention to infant deaths, where mothers and social workers (generally women) are berated for their failure to protect children within the child welfare service. For example, in late 1997, a 19-year-old mother and her Children's Aid Society worker in Toronto were both charged with criminal negligence after the death of her five-week-old baby in a hostel in which the mother and child were both residing. The fact that this infant was premature and discharged from the hospital in the care of a young, homeless mother points to inadequate provisions. Yet these failures are not emphasized; rather, the message conveyed to the public is that more and better trained social workers can ferret out the 'child abuser'. The fact that many women and children remain victims of poverty and violence fails to excite or unite the community to assume collective responsibility and action. While individualism has always permeated Canadian social policy, it has intensified as the state restructures and the public accepts the view that social services that have been supportive to women in need are no longer necessary. If interdependence, rather than independence, became the central tenet of what defines citizenship, caring for others would be recognized as a social provision and supported through the state.

Health care in Canada is generally viewed as the distinctive unifying force that contributes to a view of our country as a gentler, a more 'caring' society than our neighbours to the south. Despite the widespread acceptance of health care as a right, there are clear indications of erosion. Cutbacks and rationing of specialist services show signs of a two-tier health service where those with the ability to pay can purchase services not available to low-income individuals (Armstrong and Armstrong, 1996). The adoption of such solutions to control rising health care costs reinforces inequities and threatens the security of elderly persons, children, and individuals with disabilities who require ongoing care.

None the less, as we suggested earlier in this chapter, welfare state provisions have been very problematic for women. Brodie (1995: 10) comments:

> nostalgic welfarism puts feminists in the paradoxical position of having to defend the same welfare state that they had previously, and with good reason, criticized for being an agent of social control and for being patriarchal, classist and racist. The postwar welfare state was always an ambiguous resource for women; even though it is now fading into history, it was never the endpoint in the evolution of state formation for women.

The challenge is immense. How do we reconfigure services in ways that meet needs, respect diversity, and redress inequities? The first step, and we hope that this book contributes to the process, is to make more explicit the analysis. Challenging family ideology and underscoring the contradictory forces that exist in women's lives are highlighted in the chapters that follow. As feminists and social workers, we recognize the importance of caring to our profession and to our society but we need also to acknowledge the accompanying exploitation of women and develop alternative channels that substitute for the care we expect women to provide. This leads us to the second challenge.

2. *Can caring be organized in ways that do not exacerbate inequities?* As the state withdraws its support from public services, can we expect a more woman-friend-

ly workplace? By changing the workplace, we can set the stage for increasing the caring responsibilities for men. We begin by suggesting that caring cannot simply be seen as women's work. That caring must be shared between men and women seems obvious, but it must also be seen as more than a 'family' responsibility. This means that two areas need to be central to policy discussions and commitment. Child-care services must be available as a given rather than a series of temporary and strategic arrangements that individual mothers patch together as best they can. This is hardly novel, and we simply add our voices to the many that have called for a national child-care strategy. The ideas are there; political will is not.

The second area is to develop employment policies that support the caring responsibilities of Canadian men or women, 50 per cent of whom reported that caring responsibilities affect their paid work (Statistics Canada, 1997). This means that employers would need to ensure that their practices do not penalize those who assume family obligations and that men and women have equal freedom and responsibility in decision-making about who does what in caring. The provision of services and caring-friendly workplaces are necessary but not sufficient conditions to achieve an equitable distribution of caring. Even at the apex of the Swedish welfare state, the availability of well-developed public care services had not significantly shifted the gendered responsibilities for ongoing child care (Leira, 1993). In Sweden, as Jane Jenson (1997: 183) comments, 'the male breadwinner model is weak, but the female caregiver model is hegemonic.' Only 1 per cent of Canadian parents claiming parental leave under Employment Insurance are fathers. As Bettina Cass (1994: 114) suggests, 'Women's dependence . . . is not a problem for public policies, but rather the problem resides in men's independence.'

We have no illusions that such policies will be even more difficult to realize than the elusive goal of a national child-care policy. Today, restructuring discussions are limited to reorganizing strategies that cut costs rather than rethinking how employment might be radically restructured to incorporate the multiple dimensions of people's lives. This suggests to us that there can be no single, unitary solution. The problems of caring do not confront all women in the same way; the solutions have to be diverse.

3. *How might we shift from individual responsibility to a collective commitment to care?* In fighting the cutbacks that are devastating former levels of benefits and services, most feminists do not intend to reproduce the 'old' models of social welfare that, as we have suggested, have been problematic for women. So as women seek simultaneously to maintain and transform social services, a commitment to a collective responsibility for care is essential. A greater degree of mutuality in relationships and collective co-operation are identified as a keystone to redistributing the costs and benefits among men, women, markets, and states. Many feminists suggest, for example, that an ethic of care emphasizing interdependence and responsibility must be integrated into the highly individualized, rights-oriented approach that underlies our traditional conceptions of justice (Young,

1992). Incorporating an ethic of care into social welfare means that individuals cannot be separated from the relationships that influence how they make decisions and what decisions they make. It means identifying and making visible the social relations embedded in decisions that involve obligation and responsibility. This would entail, for example, ensuring that decisions that allocate services and resources to the care of vulnerable adults are not made on a series of rule-based criteria, in isolation from the particularities of their situation. Decisions must take into explicit account the fact that 'needs' cannot be assessed in the absence of a range of alternatives. Similarly, adequate weight has to be given to a care recipient's own preferred options for care. In other words, the first question must *not* be how much care can family members provide? Socially created dependency will only be eradicated when care receivers, as well as care providers, have real choices and are core players in the policy development process (Baldwin and Twigg, 1991). The development of policies, programs, and practices must pay attention to the realities that caring is highly gendered, it can be classed as inferior because women do it, and the caring women do is frequently not done under conditions of their choice (Clement, 1996).

The first step towards such a policy framework would be the recognition that public services providing care for vulnerable individuals must be available as part of the rights of social citizenship. Child care and long-term care are two policy arenas in which the needs of young children, the frail elderly, and those with severe disabilities seem never to make it beyond rhetoric about supporting families. Recognizing that the welfare of children and adults with physical or cognitive limitations is a collective concern would move beyond bolstering the stretched resources of 'family' to ensuring that policies are enacted to promote the quality of life of all Canadian citizens no matter what the configuration of the households within which they live. For instance, the September 1997 federal Speech from the Throne suggested that a national home-care policy could be a response to communities struggling with the effects of hospital restructuring. If implemented, legislation similar to the Canada Health Act would be required to ensure that funding provided to the provinces was accompanied by a commitment to national standards of accessibility.

We offer no simple panaceas, nor grand solutions, to the resolution of women's caring responsibilities, but we believe a starting point is the recognition that the provision of care in our society is a collective responsibility and that many voices must be heard in devising alternative approaches. This goal is not innovative or radical, but operationalizing it takes creativity as well as political commitment. Examples are available that do challenge the ideology of competition, individualism, materialism, and rational thinking that underpins much of Canadian social policy. The holistic approach of Aboriginal communities to healing, for example, emphasizes the importance of wellness, harmony, and a collective response. This is captured in a statement included in the recent report from the Royal Commission on Aboriginal Peoples (Canada, 1996: 612):

Among the most important aspects of cultural difference is the emphasis still placed on the collectivity in Aboriginal society—that is, the importance of family, clan, community and nation; the importance of the collective to an individual's sense of health and self-worth; the conception of the individual's responsibility to the collective and of the collective's responsibility to care for and protect its most vulnerable members; the importance of collective rights and collective action. While much of contemporary social policy is geared to the individual—providing welfare to those who are eligible, training to the unemployed—we need to understand that the problems of the relationship cannot be resolved by a narrow focus on individual-level problems and solutions. The importance of the collective, of collective rights and responsibilities, must be recognized.

The spirit of such an approach is beginning to be reflected in a variety of projects. For example, a project in Newfoundland attempts to change the way that offenders, victims, and the community respond to violence by providing decision-making conferences that involve a range of participants. These conferences make it possible for family members and community agencies to move from allocating care solely to mothers to include other members of the family, community, and state (Burford and Pennell, 1995). This type of program affirms, confronts, and mobilizes a more collective approach to caring for persons experiencing abuse or violence.

4. *How might we organize to promote social change?* Feminists organizing over the past three decades have been engaged in a process of consciousness-raising, education, lobbying, and coalition-building. Transforming a White, middle-class movement into one that is more inclusive is an ongoing struggle. As we approach the millennium, the challenge for those in what are referred to today as the 'caring professions' is to reach out and join forces with many groups, particularly those who are marginalized in the political process. Economic restructuring is creating a job market of part-time and contract work among both women and men that is dividing communities even more sharply into the 'haves' and 'have nots'.

The restructuring of the economy has meant that the jobs of many White men are taking on the characteristics that have long characterized the paid work of women, in general, and of men and women of colour, in particular. The 'feminization' of the labour market (Armstrong, 1996) is an example of the way in which gender is 'everywhere and nowhere' (Brodie, 1995: 76), causing some to argue that gender is disappearing as a nexus for political action, and the politics of class and race become more vigorous and relevant. Rather than obliterating gender as an important axis of inequality, it seems to us, these observations point to the necessity for broad-based coalitions around specific issues. The challenge is to develop mechanisms that allow diverse groups to align despite their profound differences in approaches to addressing the structural inequities in Canadian society. Indeed, it is likely that activists share many goals, commonalities that are not immediately apparent when looking at only the explicit objectives of an organization. This was highlighted by research on gay/lesbian, feminist, peace, labour, and anti-poverty/urban activists in British Columbia. This study found that such groups seemed to share a vision of a caring society organized around a commitment to economic equality and welfare (Carroll and Ratner, 1996: 422–3). A similar range of activist groups have organized the 'Days of Action' events in a number of Ontario cities in protest against the neo-liberal politics of the Harris government. As Mouffe (1993: 87) points out, feminism embraces emancipation, representation, democracy, and equality.

Coalitions representing a broad range of interests are essential if we are to challenge the precepts and practices of a neo-liberal paradigm that portrays the complete subordination of the rights and claims to social citizenship to the 'natural and inevitable' forces of a globalized market economy. However, while rejecting a universalizing and/or essentializing view of women, all of the various chapters in this book also illustrate the salience of feminist analyses and the directions they suggest for feminists organizing for change. While women's caring has been articulated and experienced as women's responsibility, the challenge is to incorporate a wide spectrum of players to arrive at more equitable solutions to the needs of all members of Canadian society.

NOTE

1. For an excellent review of the various threads of the aging population and long-term care costs debate, see the *Canadian Journal on Aging* (1995); for a review of the situation in the US, see Estes et al., 1993.

REFERENCES

Allen, S.M. 1994. 'Gender Differences in Spousal Caregiving and Unmet Need for Care', *Journal of Gerontology: Social Sciences* 49, 4: S187–95.

Aneshensel, C., L. Pearlin, J. Mullan, S. Zarit, and C. Whitlatch. 1995. *Profiles in Caregiving: The Unexpected Career*. San Diego: Academic Press.

Arber, S., and J. Ginn. 1992. 'Research Note—Class and Caring: A Forgotten Dimension', *Sociology* 26, 4: 619–34.

Armstrong, P. 1996. 'The Feminization of the Labour Force: Harmonizing Down in a Global Economy', in I. Bakker, ed., *Rethinking Restructuring: Gender and Change in Canada*. Toronto: University of Toronto Press: 29–54.

Armstrong, P., and H. Armstrong. 1990. *Theorizing Women's Work*. Toronto: Garamond.

Armstrong, P., and H. Armstrong. 1996. *Wasting Away: The Undermining of Canadian Health Care*. Toronto: Oxford University Press.

Aronson, J. 1990. 'Old Women's Experiences of Needing Care: Choice or Compulsion?', *Canadian Journal on Aging* 9, 3: 234–47.

Arot-Koc, S. 1992. 'In the Privacy of Their Own Homes: Foreign Domestic Workers as Solution to the Crisis of the Domestic Sphere in Canada', in M.P. Connelly and P. Armstrong, eds, *Feminism in Action: Studies in Political Economy*. Toronto: Canadian Scholars' Press: 149–74.

Baldwin, S., and J. Twigg. 1991. 'Women and Community Care: Reflections on a Debate', in *Women's Issues in Social Policy*. New York: Routledge: 117–35.

Barry, J. 1995. 'Care-need and Care-receivers: Views from the Margin', *Women's Studies International Forum* 18, 3: 361–74.

Bowden, P. 1997. *Caring: Gender-Sensitive Ethics*. London and New York: Routledge.

Bristow, P. 1994. 'Whatever you raise in the ground you can sell it in Chatham: Black women in Buxton and Chatham, 1850–1865', in P. Bristow, D. Brand, L. Carty, A. Cooper, S. Hamilton, and A. Shadd, eds, *We're Rooted Here and They Can't Pull Us Up: Essays in African Canadian Women's History*. Toronto: University of Toronto Press.

Brodie, J. 1995. *Politics on the Margin: Restructuring and the Canadian Women's Movement*. Halifax: Fernwood.

Burford, G., and J. Pennell. 1995. 'Family Group Decision-Making: An Innovation in Child and Family Welfare', in J. Hudson and B. Galaway, eds, *Child Welfare in Canada: Research and Policy Implications*. Toronto: Thompson Educational Publishers.

Calliste, A. 1991. 'Canadian Immigration Policy and Domestics from the Caribbean: The Second Domestic Scheme', in J. Vorst, ed., *Race, Class, and Gender: Bonds and Barriers*. Toronto: Garamond Press and the Society for Socialist Studies: 136–68.

Canada. 1996. Royal Commission on Aboriginal Peoples. *Looking Forward, Looking Back. Volume 1. Final Report*. Ottawa: Minister of Supply and Services.

Card, C. 1990. 'Caring and Evil', *Hypatia* 5, 1: 101–8.

Carroll, W., and R. Ratner. 1996. 'Master Frames and Counter-Hegemony: Political Sensibilities in Contemporary Social Movements', *Canadian Review of Sociology and Anthropology* 33, 4: 407–35.

Cass, B. 1994. 'Citizenship, Work, and Welfare: The Dilemma for Australian Women', *Social Politics* 1, 1 (Spring).

Clement, G. 1996. *Care, Autonomy and Justice*. Oxford: Clarendon.

Cohen, M. 1997. 'From the Welfare State to Vampire Capitalism', in P. Evans and G. Wekerle, eds, *Women and the Canadian Welfare State: Challenges and Change*. Toronto: University of Toronto Press: 28–67.

Daenzer, P. 1993. *Regulating Class Privilege: Immigrant Servants in Canada, 1940s–1990s*. Toronto: Canadian Scholars' Press.

Daenzer, P. 1997. 'Challenging Diversity: Black Women and Social Welfare', in P. Evans and G. Wekerle, eds, *Women and the Canadian Welfare State: Challenges and Change*. Toronto: University of Toronto Press: 269–90.

Dwyer, J., and R. Coward, eds. 1992. *Gender, Families and Elder Care*. Newbury Park, Calif.: Sage.

Estes, C., J. Swan, and Associates. 1993. *The Long Term Care Crisis: Elders Trapped in the No-Care Zone*. Newbury Park, Calif.: Sage.

Finch, J., and D. Groves, eds. 1983. *A Labour of Love: Women, Work, and Caring*. London: Routledge and Kegan Paul.

Gibson, D. 1996. 'Broken Down by Age and Gender: The "Problem of Old Women" Redefined', *Gender and Society* 10, 4: 433–48.

Gilligan, C. 1982. *In a Different Voice*. Cambridge, Mass.: Harvard University Press.

Glenn, E. 1992. 'From Servitude to Social Work: Historical Continuities in the Racial Division of Paid Reproductive Labor', *Signs* 18, 1: 1–43.

Gordon, L. 1994. *Pitied But Not Entitled: Single Mothers and the History of Welfare*. New York: Free Press.

Gordon, S. 1996. 'Feminism and Caring', in S. Gordon, P. Benner, and N. Noddings, eds, *Caregiving: Readings in Knowledge, Practice, Ethics, and Politics*. Philadelphia: University of Philadelphia Press: 256–77.

Graham, H. 1983. 'Caring: A Labour of Love', in Finch and Groves, eds, *A Labour of Love*.

Graham, H. 1993. 'Social Divisions in Caring', *Women's Studies International Forum* 16, 5: 461–70.

Guberman, N. 1988. 'The Family, Women and Caring: Who Cares for the Carers?', *Resources for Feminist Research* 17, 2: 37–40.

Hill-Collins, P. 1992. 'Black Women and Motherhood', in B. Thorne and M. Yalom, eds, *Rethinking the Family: Some Feminist Questions*. Boston: Northeastern University Press.

Hochschild, A.R. 1995. 'The Culture of Politics: Traditional, Post-Modern, Cold-Modern and Warm-Modern Ideals of Care', *Social Politics* 2, 3: 331–46.

Hooyman, N., and J. Gonyea. 1995. *Feminist Perspectives on Family Care: Policies for Gender Justice*. Thousand Oaks, Calif.: Sage.

Houston, B. 1990. 'Caring and Exploitation', Review Symposium, *Hypatia* 5, 1 (Spring): 115–19.

Jenson, J. 1997. 'Who Cares? Gender and Welfare Regimes', *Social Politics* 4, 2 (Summer): 182–7.

Ladd-Taylor, M. 1994. *Mother-Work: Women, Child Welfare, and the State, 1890–1930*. Urbana: University of Illinois Press.

Land, H., and H. Rose. 1985. 'Compulsory Altruism for Some or an Altruistic Society for All?', in P. Bean, J. Ferris, and D. Whynes, eds, *In Defence of Welfare*. London: Tavistock.

Larabee, M., ed. 1993. *An Ethic of Care: Feminist and Interdisciplinary Perspectives*. New York and London: Routledge.

Leira, A. 1993. 'The "Woman-Friendly" Welfare State?: The Case of Norway and Sweden', in J. Lewis, ed., *Women and Social Policies in Europe: Work, Family and the State*. Aldershot, Hants, and Brookfield, Vt: Edward Elgar: 49–71.

Leira, A. 1994. 'Concepts of Caring: Loving, Thinking, and Doing', *Social Service Review* 68, 2: 185–201.

Luxton, M. 1997. 'Feminism and Families: The Challenge of Neo-Conservatism', in M. Luxton, ed., *Feminism and Families: Critical Policies and Changing Practices*. Halifax: Fernwood: 10–26.

Mandell, N. 1988. 'The Child Question: Links Between Women and Children in the Family', in N. Mandell and A. Duffy, eds, *Reconstructing the Canadian Family: Feminist Perspectives*. Toronto: Butterworths: 49–81.

McQuaig, L. 1995. *Shooting the Hippo: Death by Deficits and Other Canadian Myths*. Toronto: Penguin.

Morris, J. 1993. 'Feminism and Disability', *Feminist Review* 43: 57–70.

Mouffe, C. 1993. *The Return of the Political.* London and New York: Verso.

Nasir, S. 1996. '"Race", Gender and Social Policy', in C. Hallett, ed., *Women and Social Policy: An Introduction.* London: Prentice-Hall/Harvester Wheatsheaf: 15–30.

Neal, M., N. Chapman, B. Ingersoll-Dayton, and A. Emlen. 1993. *Balancing Work and Caregiving for Children, Adults, and Elders.* Newbury Park, Calif.: Sage.

Neysmith, S., and A. Aronson. 1997. 'Working Conditions in Home Care: Negotiating Issues of Race and Class in Gendered Work', *International Journal of Health Services* 27, 3: 479–99.

Pascall, G. 1986. *Social Policy: A Feminist Analysis.* London: Tavistock.

Pateman, C. 1992. 'The Patriarchal Welfare State', in L. McDowell and R. Pringle, eds, *Defining Women: Social Institutions and Gender Divisions.* Cambridge: Polity Press: 223–45.

Phillips, S. and P. Benner, eds. 1994. *The Crisis of Care: Affirming and Restoring Caring Practices in the Helping Professions.* Washington: Georgetown University Press.

Rekart, J. 1993. *Public Funds, Private Provision: The Role of the Voluntary Sector.* Vancouver: University of British Columbia Press.

Scaltas, P. 1992. 'Do Feminist Ethics Counter Feminist Aims?', in E. Cole and S. Coultrap-McQuin, eds, *Explorations in Feminist Ethics: Theory and Practice.* Bloomington: University of Indiana Press: 15–26.

Statistics Canada. 1997. *1996 General Social Survey. Cycle 11—Social & Community Support: Initial Data Release.* Ottawa.

Stoller, E. 1992. 'Gender Differences in the Experiences of Caregiving Spouses', in J.W. Dwyer and R.T. Coward, eds, *Gender, Families and Elder Care.* Newbury Park, Calif.: Sage: 49–64.

Thomas, Carol. 1993. 'De-Constructing Concepts of Care', *Sociology* 27, 4: 649–69.

Tronto, J. 1993. *Moral Boundaries: A Political Argument for an Ethic of Care.* New York: Routledge.

White, J. 1997. 'Health Care, Hospitals, and Reengineering: The Nightingales Sing the Blues', in A. Duffy, D. Glenday, and N. Pupo, eds, *Good Jobs, Bad Jobs, No Jobs: The Transformation of Work in the 21st Century.* Toronto: Harcourt Brace: 117–42.

Young, I. 1992. 'Recent Theories of Justice', *Social Theory and Practice* 18, 1: 63–79.

2

Women's Professions and an Ethic of Care

CAROL T. BAINES

One of the major contradictions facing women who enter the so-called women's professions of nursing, social work, and teaching is, according to Barbara Finklestein, the need to be 'saints, fools or sentimental idealists' (Finklestein, 1989: 94). As the end of the 1990s approaches, these professions are for the first time facing competition as women flock to the more prestigious 'traditionally male' professions of law, medicine, and engineering.[1] While the increased options may signal greater equality, part of the explanation for this change can be found in the way the women-dominated professions have been undervalued and under-rewarded. The reality may be that women have begun to believe that the work they do in these fields has little value (Daniels, 1987; Finklestein, 1989).

Through a historical perspective, this chapter analyses the influence of an ethic of care on the evolution of social work, nursing, and teaching. It focuses on women's caring in the public sphere, emphasizing the ways in which caring has shaped the public role of women and the division of labour in these occupations. Two main themes emerge: firstly, the relationship between maternal feminism and caring; secondly, the tension women have experienced in combining caring and professionalism.

In the 1970s and 1980s, historians of women identified maternal feminism as the underlying ideology that spurred the movement of women into the public sphere during the first wave of feminism. Determined to play a useful role in a society in flux, women transferred the values and caring functions they had learned and practised within the home and the community to new fields of work. The paradox was that, although maternal feminism provided women with a rationale to work outside the home and served to unite women, it also reinforced the traditional role of women as caregivers. Women today continue to struggle with reconciling the contradictions in exercising their right to autonomy and equality without abandoning an ethic of care.

The second theme examines the experiences of women in social work, teaching, and nursing as they began to model their work on the male professions of medicine and law. Professionalization, as it materialized in the late nineteenth century, was a process in which White, middle-class males carved out new roles and ultimately obtained a monopoly for their services. Critiques of professionalization suggest that although specialized knowledge and expertise are characteristics attributed to the professions, the key element is social power (Melosh, 1989). In contrast, the women who entered the women-dominated professions emphasized an ethic of service or care that on the surface replicated the 'traditional' view of women as nurturers (Glazer and Slater, 1987; Kinnear, 1995). Yet this was not explicitly acknowledged or understood. Service to society and an ethic of care constrained women in the professions who had assumed that meritocracy and new fields of work would provide them with equal opportunities. Kinnear (1995), in her study of professional women in Manitoba, has also pointed out that married women in the professions experienced particular conflict. A model wife placed the needs of her husband and family before her career aspirations.

A review of the literature, which examines the movement of women from the private world of the home to the public sphere, reveals a range of different interpretations. Cott (1977) has argued that, initially, interpretations focused on women as victims oppressed by the rigid definition of women's domestic status. A subsequent perspective suggested that women took advantage of participating in the public sphere and increased their satisfaction as well as their opportunities. A third interpretation argues that women developed a subculture, a sisterhood, and a solidarity attributed to women's own motivations as much as to impositions of male society.

The argument I wish to make follows the latter interpretation. As women moved into the public sphere to engage in caring activities, they were, as Carroll Smith-Rosenberg (1985) has articulated, more than actors in a male play. They seized the opportunities society presented and carved out a place for themselves as women, different and separate from men. Some women worked in separate female organizations and gained collective strength; some accepted their subordinate status; others attempted to be the equivalent of the modern-day superwoman.

What follows is only a brief examination of the history of women in nursing, social work, and teaching. It attempts to increase our understanding of the way a commitment to an ethic of care framed the experiences of women in these fields but also constrained their opportunities as the surge to professionalize took hold. The chapter begins with a discussion of maternal feminism and social reform at the turn of the century. It is followed by an examination of the links between an ideology of caring and maternal feminism as it unfolded in social work, nursing, and teaching. The third section explores how professionalization based on a male ethos and a traditional division of labour clashed with a feminine ethos of caring. Women were expected to care about and for their clients, while men in these professions assumed authority for the management and leadership. The final section presents some possible resolutions to the issues of women's caring and professionalism.

MATERNAL FEMINISM, CARING, AND SOCIAL REFORM

In the late nineteenth century, a 'new woman' graced the Canadian landscape. Determined to play a part in the changing society, middle- and upper-class women moved into the public sphere. Some women found positions as teachers in the newly emerging public school system, while other women became involved in voluntary charity work in the fledgling health and welfare services. The care of dependent children, the establishment of health services for poor women, the education of the young, and the abolition of alcohol were some of the issues women began to address (Kealey, 1979).

However, the public work women performed was not, in fact, new work. It was an extension of the work women previously had carried out in the home. In caring for the sick, the aged, and the young, women developed skills that they recognized were essential to transfer to the public sphere. As part of the reform movement, women were determined to extend their caring roles to the larger society and male reformers were only too willing to use the labour of women to complete their vision of a new Canadian society. The 'grand mission of mothering' articulated by Lady Aberdeen, the first president of the National Council of Women, revealed the extent to which women accepted the reality that they were responsible for caring about and for dependent groups (Roberts, 1979). Maternal feminism ensured the transformation of women's caring into public caring, as Linda Kealey (1979: 7) underlines when she defines maternal feminism as:

> the conviction that woman's special role as mother gives her the duty and the right to participate in the public sphere. It is not her position as wife that qualifies her for the task of reform, but the special nurturing qualities which are common to all women, married or not.

While this provided women with a rationale to move into the public sphere, it was also reinforced by the complex set of forces that spawned a movement for social reform.

During the latter part of the nineteenth century, Canada was confronted with pressing political and social issues. Family and community were affected by such factors as the integration of immigrants, the introduction of machine technology, factory labour and trade unions, and the availability of transportation. Ontario, in particular, was undergoing a transition from a rural to an urban society and families were experiencing its economic and social impacts. Accompanying these signs of a developing industrial society were the corresponding problems of city slums, delinquent children, child labour, infant mortality, unemployment, poor sanitation, public health concerns, and the evil effects of 'drink' (Brown and Cook, 1974).

While these problems were facts of life for working-class families and impinged on all family members, women usually bore the brunt of these difficulties. Coping with illness and death, the care of their children, poor nutrition, unsanitary milk supplies, and, perhaps most of all, the need for women to supplement meagre family incomes took an incredible toll on women's lives.

In contrast, middle- and upper-class women were experiencing increased affluence and leisure time and a declining birth rate. These factors fostered the growth of women's organizations and clubs. It was not surprising that these women, well schooled in the importance of Christian stewardship, responded to the trouble of their working-class sisters. An urban and economic transformation, a demand for a response to the problems facing an industrial society, and a changing conception of what women were able to do all contributed to the shaping of new institutions and laid the groundwork for the welfare state.

The Church, the most important institution in Canada at the turn of the century, played a critical role in shaping the movement for reform and the entry of women into the public sphere. Part of the explanation for the Protestant church-es' interest in reform was the realization that individual salvation no longer seemed relevant in a society confronted with massive social problems. By the late nineteenth century, Darwin's theory of evolution, the ascent of science in gener-al, and the historical criticism of the Bible were seriously undermining the authority of the Church (Cook, 1985). Many theologians came to conclude that Christianity could no longer be based on faith alone. The 'social gospel' move-ment developed in response to this conundrum and reinforced the idea that Christianity was a social religion, concerned with the Kingdom of God in this world. By making the Church more socially responsive and creating a new mis-sion—social regeneration—liberal Protestants believed that the scientific and historical criticism of the Bible could be ignored and the significance of religion in people's lives maintained (Cook, 1985).

Implicit in the move towards regeneration was the recognition that the Church needed the agency of 'Christian women' if it were to embark on a pro-gram of social evangelism (Austin, 1890: 33). Given the reality that women, over time, have been the most active supporters of the Church, this was hardly sur-prising. However, it is too simplistic to claim that women were conscripted to carry out a mission of reform created by male leaders. Women themselves recog-nized the need to transpose their vision of a more caring society into the creation of services for women and children.

Agnes Maule Machar, for instance, an active participant in the social gospel movement, was 'one of the most gifted intellectuals and social critics of the late nineteenth century' (Cook, 1985: 186). The author of many works of fiction and poetry, Machar became a strong advocate of translating the ethical teachings of Christ into social reform. Concerned about the conditions of industrial labour, she urged middle-class women to respond to the needs of their poorer sisters. Her description of Christian social action, which epitomized a maternal approach to reform, was that it should be 'earnest, active and practical' (Cook, 1985: 187). This approach became the hallmark of women's reform efforts in Canada as well as in the United States (Scott, 1984; McDowell, 1982).

In summary, the reform work of women had the following elements: (1) women enacted their caring mission not as individuals but as members of women's organizations—women were able to do in concert things that would be difficult to do alone (Scott, 1984: 266); (2) women instituted new services and careers for women; (3) the targets of their reform efforts were typically poor women and children; and (4) women accepted subordinate and traditional roles under the aegis of the clergy.

Although maternal feminism was in many respects a narrow, biological, and conservative view of women's caring role, it empowered women to work in hos-pitals, church-based social services, and schools and fostered a feminine con-sciousness and the solidarity of women (Mitchinson, 1977; Freedman, 1979). Not only did women refine their domestic skills, they learned and developed new skills that changed their view of themselves. They became more autonomous and independent and were exposed to social and educational opportunities that had previously been denied. Although women were often working in tandem and under the leadership of middle-class Protestant, Anglo-Saxon business and professional men, this replication of the familial division of labour was, for the most part, not seen as problematic.

WOMEN AND CARING IN SOCIAL WELFARE

The history of women in social welfare in Canada has tended to centre on the work of White, Protestant, upper middle-class volunteers who have been considered the foremothers of the twentieth-century social worker. Despite the considerable labour expended by the early volunteer, she has been represented in the literature by the disparaging image of the 'Lady Bountiful'. In this respect, class was considered a more important dimension for analysis than gender and the feminist concerns underpinning the work of women's organizations were not identified until the 1970s. Committed to moral reform and rescue work, women's organizations focused on the needs of women and children. As the following examination of five women's organizations reveals, women transferred their private caring into the public sphere.

The easiest avenue for women to enter the public sphere was through the Women's Missionary Societies (WMS). These organizations, regardless of religious denomination, enabled women to take responsibility for public caring without affecting their primary caring role within the family. The phenomenal growth in membership is an indication of its importance as an outlet for women's social and educational aspirations. In 1882, the Methodist WMS had 900 members and supported two missionaries; by 1916, its membership had soared to 44,135 supporting 120 missionaries (Mitchinson, 1977: 309). The WMS also became a vehicle for the development of a sense of sisterhood and collectivism that fostered its missionary and maternal feminism goals. The refusal of all but the Anglican WMS to become an auxiliary to male missionary societies attests to the value women placed on a separate female organization. And although part of their motivation was evangelism, the needs of poor women and children in Canada and abroad awakened the feminine consciousness of the WMS (Mitchinson, 1977). It also sparked their interest and frequently led to women's involvement in other social service endeavours.

An example of a women's organization that became an offshoot of the WMS was the Wimodausis Club (Wives, Mothers, Daughters, Sisters) of Toronto, a group of upper-class women formally constituted in 1906. Like other women's charitable groups, the Wimodausis Club began by providing food, clothing, and health supplies, along with moral and financial support, to poor women and children in downtown Toronto. In 1915, they decided to concentrate on the welfare of children and formed a permanent partnership with the Earlscourt Children's Home (ECH), a Methodist institution established as an emergency resource for single-parent families in 1913.

The goal of the Wimodausis women was to make ECH one of the finest 'professional' institutions in Canada serving the need of poor children from fragmented families. From 1915 until 1948, they were responsible for fund-raising, a building campaign, and policy directions, as well as for assisting in the direct work of the Home (Baines, 1994). As such, their work entailed both the private (domestic) and public (funding) operations of the Home. But as expected of women, they formally deferred to a small group of Methodist men, and the assets and properties of the Home remained vested with the Church (Baines, 1990).

The survival of ECH, until the late 1940s, as an entirely privately funded organization was due to the caring labour of unpaid Wimodausis members and a dedicated group of poorly paid workers under the direction of Hattie Inkpen, a Methodist deaconess. Mrs Mason, the president of the Wimodausis Club in 1926, expressed their commitment to a maternal feminist mission in this way: 'It is work that particularly appeals to women, for here we find something greater than individual motherhood, that sublimation of the Mother spirit that opens the heart to all little children' (Baines, 1988: 35).

An ideology of caring about and for poor children sustained the Wimodausis Club and the Earlscourt Children's Home. By engaging in charity work, this group of upper- and middle-class women gained an understanding of themselves as builders of a more caring community. Yet what was equally important, but not acknowledged, was the success they achieved in raising money, managing Earlscourt, building networks, and developing a sense of autonomy and an appreciation of their own abilities. The self-sacrifice implied in caring fostered their own humility and subordinate status.

One of the largest networks of women's organizations that reinforced traditional views about women and the family and yet embarked on energetic policy initiatives to improve the lives of young women was the work of the Young Women's Christian Association (YWCA). From 1870 to 1894, 14 YWCAs were formed across Canada, with a national association established in 1893 (Mitchinson, 1977: 282). The work of caring about and for young working women was based on an awareness that the social and economic environment was not a nurturing place for women. However, their approach to change was not directed at the workplace. Rather, it was a woman's need for a suitable home that captured the impulse of reform-minded YWCA women.

Inevitably, the good intentions of the YWCA reformers were frequently patronizing and evoked sharp criticism from some of the young women. The concerns of upper- and middle-class women for their poorer working sisters were coloured by a limited understanding of how gender and class intersected in their lives. None the less, they were successful in drawing attention to the needs of young working women.

Gradually, reforms directed at promoting protective labour legislation, social hygiene measures, street patrols, and even trade unions for women found their way onto the agenda of the Y (Pedersen, 1987). The vision of reform involved the building of a prototype all-purpose YWCA facility that provided residential accommodation, a library, a kitchen, a cafeteria, classrooms, and a gymnasium and swimming pool. It was to be a 'woman's refuge from an inhospitable male environment and a base from which they could attempt to modify that environment in the interests of women' (Pedersen, 1987: 227). To gain public support for young women, the Y members appealed to other women's organizations. The YWCA became a meeting place for women's clubs, and in return women's groups like the Woman's Christian Temperance Union (WCTU), the WMS, the Wimodausis, and the Imperial Order of the Daughters of the Empire made financial contributions to the YWCA.

However, the networks of support that had furnished resources for the early YWCA activities proved insufficient to build a modern YWCA. Public caring and the YWCA's vision of a women's centre depended on the financial support of the male business community. Influenced by the successful fund-rasing campaigns mounted by the Young Men's Christian Association, the YWCA developed a strategy that ensured the co-operation of businessmen. Using slogans such as 'Building Today for the Womanhood of Tomorrow', the YWCA capitalized on the thrust for efficiency, sound business management, and prevention, the buzz words of professional and business men (Pedersen, 1987: 234).

The dependence of women's organizations like the YWCA on male philanthropy had mixed results. It helped to legitimate the myth that a shared sense of community existed and that men cared about the needs of young working women (Pedersen, 1987). But the reliance of the YWCA on support from the business community reinforced a division in public caring—men's caring was manifested in providing financial support; women's caring continued to be linked with serving others and self-sacrifice—and YWCA workers have remained among the most lowly paid of social workers.

A further example of a women's group demonstrating an ethic of care was the Big Sisters Association of Toronto and its attention to delinquent girls. With the passing of the Juvenile Delinquent Act in 1908 and the subsequent changes to the care and control of delinquent children, a Juvenile Court judge suggested that the Local Council of Women establish a Big Sister Organization (Robinson, 1979). Motivated by maternal feminist goals, their conception of caring included both personal goals for the individual girls as well as a vision of a society that was to be more protective of young girls.

By providing supportive relationships such an organization could guide young girls in trouble and protect them from further crime and imprisonment. The work of the Big Sisters expanded to include advocacy for improved housing, schooling, recreational services, decent wages, and a more protected home environment. An ethic of caring depended on changes in policy. The constant pull between the need to provide personal counselling services and more political reforms was exemplified in Mrs Sydney Small's address to the annual meeting in 1920:

> Some day, society will realize the unwisdom and folly of allowing any children to be born and bred in conditions of poverty, ignorance and preventable disease. In the meantime, it is our privilege and duty to help adjust these little starved lives to a fuller measure of health and happiness which should have been their heritage, and which has been denied them. (Robinson, 1979: 46)

The Big Sisters, as the need for their service mushroomed, were also confronted with the necessity of compromising their caring activities in the interests of ensuring support from the male-dominated Federation of Community Services. Instructed by the Federation to refrain from endorsing women candidates in municipal elections who supported their reforms, the Big Sisters felt compelled to comply. However, they vehemently resisted the suggestion that they should amalgamate with the Big Brothers. The Big Sisters recognized that the interests of men were quite different and that their mission could be best achieved through a separate women's organization.

The women's organization that achieved the greatest success in the political field was the WCTU. It was founded in 1874 by Mrs Letitia Youmans, a widowed school teacher from Picton, Ontario. The belief that the social problems facing Canada were linked to the evils of drink led to the conclusion that the cause of poverty was intemperance. J.J. Kelso's assertion that three-quarters of child neglect cases were the result of alcohol centred the work of the WCTU on 'removing the cause, rather than remedying the evils' (Mitchinson, 1977: 153). This took the WCTU women along a path directed at legislative changes to promote prohibition and the introduction of a temperance education program in the public schools (Mitchinson, 1977). To this extent, the members of the WCTU represented a more militant brand of maternal feminists, and women's issues remained central to their mission. In advocating for higher education for women, the employment of women as factory inspectors, doctors, and teachers, child protection legislation, reformatories for juveniles, a hospital for women, and the establishment of cottage homes for children rather than large barrack-style institutions, the key to their conception of reform was the need 'to make the whole world more home-like than when we found it' (Mitchinson, 1977: 174). Or as Youmans opined: 'Who would say it was unwomanly or unladylike to plead for our children?' (Mitchinson, 1977: 153). In sum, the reforms of the WCTU were couched in familiar themes: service and caring for others.

In this pre-professional period, the unpaid work of women as members of voluntary organizations, coupled with the poorly paid work of church deaconesses and social service workers, expedited the development of services for poor women and children through city missions and fledgling social service organizations (Mitchinson, 1987). These institutions assumed a range of social service roles as they attempted to put in place a feminine vision of a caring society. In promoting an ethic of care, women were fund-raisers, managers, planners, and policy-makers as well as providers of concrete services to poor women and children. A maternal mission of service and a feminine consciousness united these women as they formed networks of support and alliances. But the contradiction was that it was viewed as women's natural work and therefore remained relatively invisible and unvalued.

Social welfare concerns also included the health needs of the poor, as the founding in 1875 of the Hospital for Sick Children in Toronto attests. Raising funds, managing the institution, and caring for the patients offered women the opportunity of playing a prominent role in health care (Morrison, 1971).

However, the most significant role women occupied in the health field was nursing.

CARING AND THE HEALTH CARE SYSTEM

Nursing has also been confronted with the contradiction inherent in a field of work based on both labour and love. Prior to industrialization, women had been responsible for the caring and healing of sick members within their families. The first European settlements in Canada had included women who were members of French nursing sisterhoods and who provided health care. Unlike their nursing counterparts in Great Britain, who were members of the servant class, French nursing sisters came from all walks of life, were viewed as highly competent, and were given responsibility to provide for the medical needs of the community. A French nursing order founded the first Canadian hospital, the Hôtel Dieu in Quebec City, in 1639; the Grey Nuns, another order, have been credited with the introduction of district nursing to other parts of Canada (Coburn, 1974).

The training of nurses in Canada and the United States adopted the model established by Florence Nightingale in the 1860s in England. Nightingale's primary goals were to eliminate the menial nature of nursing and to increase its professional nature (Kerr and MacPhail, 1988; McPherson, 1996). Training for nursing became not only a preparation for an occupation, it was character training for life. Moral development, proper behaviour both within the hospital and outside, loyalty, order and discipline, and hierarchical control by a nursing matron who considered the hospital a home all became a part of the culture of a nurse's training (McPherson, 1996). Uniforms and badges exemplified the military nature of hospital life and reflected the status and position of the different levels of nursing education (Reverby, 1988).

Nightingale's vision of nurses as independent and confident women who would define a clear role for themselves in the hospital hierarchy was not without its contradictions. Just as opportunities for women had been strengthened by the establishment of separate women's colleges in the United States, nursing sought to create a culture that would enhance the competence and autonomy of women. However, others have argued that it was the place where 'women learned to be girls' (Reverby, 1988: 57). It reinforced the subordination of nursing and defined nursing as a respectable occupation distanced from its working-class roots. Efficiency, discipline, deference to superiors and doctors, and the standardization of procedures limited initiative and independence, and reinforced the male-dominated medical hierarchy. However, as McPherson (1996) has pointed out, nurses were not simply victims: they participated in the creation of the emerging health care system.

The advent of hospitals and the institutionalization of health services accentuated a division of labour that allocated the 'curing' role to men, with women relegated to the maternal tradition of 'caring' (Reverby, 1988). Nurses were responsible for aseptic conditions, good nutrition, and meticulous aftercare (Keddy, 1986). In the early years of modern health care, nurses carried out a range of tasks. Along with doing the drudgery and cleaning, they were expected to be nurturing and caring to sick individuals. An ethic of service and altruism committed to the public good underpinned the work of nurses (Kerr and MacPhail, 1988). However, as Charles Rosenberg (1981) has pointed out, efficiency, centralized control over the workforce, and scientific medicine were the ideological influences that shaped the American hospital, and physicians became the key players in health care. Professionalization meant that medicine needed to be identified as a science, and hence rigid criteria and accreditation standards were developed to gain the prestige and credentials needed for medical practice to be seen as a 'masculine' profession and distanced from the unorthodox female practice of home medicine. Creating a culture of like-minded educated men was crucial to the development of a medical monopoly. Yet the organization of the hospital depended on a cadre of disciplined nurses to uphold the authority and primacy of the physician. None the less, as skilled workers, nurses' position in the hospital hierarchy was superior to that of orderlies and housekeeping staff. Thus, nursing's place in the health care system reflected a division of labour based on class as well as gender. By the 1920s, nursing had emerged as a woman's occupation that offered employment in three arenas: hospitals, private duty, and public health. Gender was a strong unifying force, as was the relatively homogeneous ethnic background (White, Anglo-Saxon, and French-Canadian) of nurses (McPherson, 1996).

CARING AND TEACHING

Teaching as women's work, particularly elementary teaching, had its roots in a maternal caring ethic. Women teachers were expected to uphold the domestic virtues of the home and transmit these to the broader community through the education of the young (Graham, 1974). For most of the eighteenth and nineteenth centuries, most children in rural Canada were educated at home or in small private schools, and many of their teachers were women (Prentice, 1977). Given a rudimentary knowledge of the three Rs, girls and boys were taught domestic and agricultural skills, respectively.

Beginning with private institutions and followed by partially supported government schools, schooling as an institutional force began to take root in the mid-nineteenth century. In 1846, with the appointment of Egerton Ryerson as the Superintendent of Schools in Ontario and the enactment of the Common Schools Act in 1848, free public schooling was gradually put in place. The passing of the Ontario Schools Act in 1871 made school attendance compulsory for children aged 7 to 12 for four months of the year, and this greatly accelerated the feminization of teaching (Graham, 1974; Prentice, 1977).

Alison Prentice (1977) has attributed the involvement of women in public school teaching to three factors. Firstly, the introduction of public schooling was accompanied by the desire to make education more efficient through consolidating schools and grouping pupils by age. This gave the more experienced teachers responsibility for the higher grades, and women could be employed at a much

lower wage to handle the elementary levels. Secondly, advocates of public schooling, the 'school promoters', came to believe that women were suitable for the job.
In 1865, Ryerson reflected the essence of maternal feminism in his statement
that women were 'best adapted to teach small children, having as a general rule,
most heart, most tender feelings, most assiduity, and in the order of Providence,
the qualities best suited for the care, instruction and government of infancy and
childhood' (cited in Prentice, 1977: 54). The third factor that accelerated the
feminization of teaching came from women themselves. The lack of alternative
careers and the opportunity to work outside the home were motivating factors for
women to become teachers. Teaching, although originally compared to work as a
domestic servant, offered more status and higher wages than other women's
work.

By the third quarter of the nineteenth century, women comprised the majority of elementary teachers in Canada and a distinct division of labour was evident
within the school system. Men taught in the higher grades and acted as principals and superintendents while women were relegated to a female ghetto of offering nurture and care to the youngest children. And not surprisingly, women
teachers were paid considerably less. In 1861, the average salary for a male
teacher in Ontario was exactly twice the salary paid to a woman (Prentice, 1977).
Despite the apparent widespread acceptance of their subordinate status, some
women objected to the undervaluing of their work. However, for the most part,
women teachers did not articulate the inequities until the end of the nineteenth
century.

PROFESSIONALIZATION AND CARING

The creation of social work, nursing, and teaching as new fields of work for
women broadened the horizon of middle- and upper-class women and provided
upwardly mobile working-class women an alternative to factory or domestic
work. For some women, these career opportunities became an alternative to marriage. Although women were re-enacting their caring roles, which typified service to others, and despite the subordinate status of these jobs, such opportunities also provided women with a growing sense of power and competence.
Women as social service workers, volunteers, nurses, and teachers collectively uti-
lized the ideology of maternal feminism to participate in a new society. By adopting an argument that stressed the difference between men and women, a broadly based women's movement was created and was successful in gaining the vote
in 1917. United by an ethic of caring that replicated their traditional work within the family, women could comfortably criticize masculine society without
threatening the social order. However, the stress on male-female differences also
reinforced a biological argument that would be difficult to overcome as women
in these newly created occupations moved towards professionalization and the
increased ghettoization within these professions that accompanied it.

The process of professionalization, which began in the late nineteenth century in Canada, greatly accelerated during the first two decades of the twentieth

century. The new occupations of social work, nursing, and teaching must be understood within the context of the changing political and social environment. In the early twentieth century, Canada was faced with a burgeoning population, the settlement of the western provinces, immigration, urbanization, and industrial development. Yet mixed with the remnants of nineteenth-century idealism was the fear that Canada lacked a sense of purpose and direction for its economic and moral development as a nation (Owram, 1986).

Canada's involvement in World War I, reflecting both idealism and imperialism, was seized as an opportunity to bring the nation together. By the end of the war, however, Canadians were no longer sure that the patriotic ideals that had united them during the war would live up to their promise. The carnage of the war and the loss of life, which touched the majority of English-speaking Canadian families, raised serious concerns about whether the survival of a British way of life was worth the means. Both the Wartime Elections Act, which disenfranchised recent foreign immigrants, and conscription were difficult to understand in light of the idealism so apparent in the pre-war period (Owram, 1986).

Given this tumultuous set of events, new solutions were required. Although the Church and women had played an instrumental role in building new organizations to ameliorate the ills of society, the role of the state in legislating conscription and the granting of the vote to women appeared to open the door for greater state involvement in social affairs. Yet the social and moral values that held society together had to be preserved (Owram, 1986). Bliss (1968) has argued that once the state used its influence to conscript wealth for the war effort, reformers came to believe that a stronger state would be able to mobilize wealth for the construction of a new social order. A combination of voluntary, religious-based social services and government support would usher in the hopes for a unified, socialist, and Christian society.

In the 1920s, a new reform élite, made up of male, middle-class social scientists, frequently educated at Chicago, Harvard, or Oxford, upheld the ideals of efficiency and social stability. A male ethos reflected the belief that a rational and scientific approach was essential for the eradication of social problems. Owram (1986) has suggested that professionalism and secularism, characteristic objectives of the new reformers, were intended to free these reformers from the moral reform movement. This altered the participation of women because maternal feminism was linked to moral reform. Although women would continue to form the majority of the front-line workers in the health, education, and welfare sectors, their influence in policy and government agencies was marginal. Owram (1986) and Carol Bacchi (1983) have both argued that the women's movement was weakened by a loss of momentum after gaining the vote. In any event, the partnership forged between the social gospel movement and women's organizations was seriously eroded, as the new professional élite included few women and non-Anglo-Saxons in its ranks.

The recognition that professionalism has reflected a male ethos has been argued by a number of scholars who have examined the experience of women within the professions. Hearn (1985) has linked professionalization to patriarchy and traces the evolution of the 'semi-professions' of nursing, teaching, and social work. He points out that men first gained a monopoly within the traditional professions and then gradually assumed control of the semi-professions. As men took over the management and leadership of these professions, a culture developed that affirmed male-centred values of order, efficiency, and a hierarchical division of labour.

Glazer and Slater (1987) have also argued that a male ethos has made women's entry and participation into the professions difficult. They suggested that 'successful professionals were objective, competitive, individualistic and predictable; they were also scornful of nurturant, expressive and familial styles of personal interactions.' One of the further differences identified by Glazer and Slater (1987: 229) was that, for the most part, men in the professions first emphasized expertise and the creation of a monopoly for their work. Only after this was established were they concerned about the 'greater social good'.

Those women who were successful in breaking the barriers of entry into the professions expected that, by emulating a male ethos of professionalism, meritocracy would prevail. However, the gaining of professional credentials did not establish a level playing field. In Kinnear's (1995: 18) view, 'The history of women in the professions is partly the story of how the conventions were challenged, reinforced and subverted.' Not surprisingly, compared to their working-class sisters, women professionals considered themselves fortunate and had little choice but to accept their roles as token women in a man's world.

Social work, nursing, and teaching all laid down their roots during the nineteenth-century urban reform movement and were based on a maternal ethic of care and duty. In the post-World War I period, these professions attracted the majority of women pursuing post-secondary education (Prentice et al., 1988). However, too often, this was regarded as a stepping-stone to women's main career: marriage. As a result, the development of a strong core of career women in these fields was limited. Yet, each of the three professions sought to replicate a male ethos of professionalization as they began to formalize their training programs. The tensions between caring and professionalization increased and succeeding generations of women social workers, nurses, and teachers have had to struggle with this.

PROFESSIONALIZATION AND SOCIAL WORK

Historians of social work in both the United States and Canada have focused considerable attention on social work's pursuit of professional status. That professionalization was the motivation of the leaders in social work has been well documented. The significant milestone generally noted in the literature occurred in 1915 at the National Conference on Charities and Corrections when Abraham Flexner in a plenary address argued that social work had no specific area of expertise or knowledge and therefore lacked the necessary attributes for a profession. In the subsequent decades of the twentieth century, social work leaders have earnestly and consistently pursued professionalization (Struthers, 1987a; Ehrenreich, 1985).

The developing interest in adopting a more scientific approach to social problems fostered the growth of social work education in Canada. The social service program at the University of Toronto, established in 1914, had its roots in the Department of Political Economy and was predicated on the belief that social work should be a masculine activity. Sara Burke (1996) has argued that the Toronto program was initiated to challenge the growing involvement of women in social work. However, despite its mission, Toronto did not succeed in attracting large numbers of men to the fields. From 1914 to 1938, Toronto graduated 53 men compared to 478 women (Burke, 1996: 93). What it did succeed in doing, however, was to create a climate where the administration of the profession would remain in the hands of male graduates, a division of labour that has continued to dominate the field (Gripton, 1974; Kenyon, 1997). The marriage between university scholarship and applied social service work at the University of Toronto was thus fraught with gender dimensions from the onset.

Complicating the issue of professionalization was dissension about social work's mission. The leaders of the program at Toronto were committed to idealism as a way of solving social problems. In contrast, many of the women and men working in the fledgling social work community looked to their US counterparts and leaders in casework to provide the cornerstone for the profession. The 'medical' model, with its emphasis on investigation, co-ordination, and efficiency, offered the hope that this would provide social work with a distinct body of knowledge (Lubove, 1977).

The biggest challenge facing social work in its pursuit of professionalization was its identification with the image of the 'Lady Bountiful', dispensing charity to poor clients. As early as 1927, Dr Helen Reid, a Montreal social work educator, reflected the importance of identifying with a male scientific model. In her address to the Canadian Conference on Social Work, Reid categorized two groups of women in social work: female philanthropists and volunteers, whom she described as traditionalists, obstructionists, and sentimentalists, and the 'new scientific woman', the expert social worker committed to economy and efficiency (Rooke and Schnell, 1982). Reid was also raising some of the issues around class. Social service work, as it became a paid occupation, provided new opportunities for middle-class men and women. Volunteers have continued to be perceived in a sentimental, patronizing, and trivial way and not well understood. Daniels (1988), in her study of outstanding upper-class women volunteers in the United States, has pinpointed the invisible nature of volunteer labour and our inability to conceptualize it because it is considered caring rather than work.

However, despite the conscious attempt to distance social work from its maternal/volunteer/charity/heritage, it continued to be viewed as women's work and linked to 'social motherhood' with low status and low pay (Ehrenreich, 1985). For women social workers, the paradox was that they were viewed as nurturers and emotional beings confined to caring for others. Since women were perceived to be ideally suited for offering direct services, men, as Struthers

(1987a) has pointed out, were needed to fill the more élite administrative positions. Social work, although largely made up of women, became a profession under the control of men.

Charlotte Whitton's comment, that 'the boys have discovered it [social work] now', symbolized a deliberate strategy that had begun in the 1930s and continued in the post-World War II period, as schools of social work turned their attention to recruiting men into the profession and to lengthening professional training (Struthers, 1987a). Many women, including Whitton and Ethel Dodds Parker, had advocated the importance of attracting capable men to assume administrative roles. The sex-segregation within social work was also replicated in fields of practice. Women were deemed more suitable to work in the fields of child and family welfare and medical social work, while men were more likely to be working in welfare councils, corrections, and social policy.

Some women did not fit this stereotype. Charlotte Whitton exemplified a woman who openly confronted the subordination of women in social work. She, however, did not articulate her feminist concerns until the 1940s, when her career in social work ended abruptly with her dismissal from the Canadian Welfare Council. As she examined the salary inequities for women in occupations such as teaching, nursing, and social work, Whitton concluded that social work was the most discriminatory (Struthers, 1987b). A decade later Dr Elizabeth Govan fought to ensure that she would receive compensation equal to her male colleagues at the Canadian Welfare Council (Struthers, 1987a; Baines, 1997). Both Whitton and Govan resisted the stereotype of women in social work. They fought and played leadership roles within the profession, but they were viewed as combative and encountered difficulties in their careers. And unlike most women in social work, their areas of expertise were social policy, administration, and history.

In the US, Bertha Reynolds, another well-known female social work educator and the Associate Director of Social Work at Smith College, also experienced difficulties in her career. Reynolds tried to develop a theoretical and practical approach to social work education that integrated a commitment to service and a concern for social justice with the individualistic casework method. Disturbed by the overwhelming economic problems that impinged on family life in the 1930s, Reynolds supported left-wing causes and the efforts of young radicals intent on organizing the poor. But the merging of Marxism with Freudianism was not part of Smith College's grand plan for social work education and Reynolds's activism placed her in a vulnerable position. She was not prepared to compromise her principles and in 1938, when she was forced to resign from Smith, Annette Garrett, her successor and a leading casework educator, suggested to Reynolds that she should have been more willing to subordinate herself to the male director—'The politic thing would have been to ask for his advice and to cultivate him much more' (Glazer and Slater, 1987: 198). The tragedy of Reynolds's departure from Smith was more than a personal one. She conceptualized social work practice in a holistic way and recognized the importance of forming coalitions with the poor to effect social change. From her perspective, the cared-for should be partners in social work's mission.

Govan also argued that social work needed to combine social policy and case-work practice. Her experience in Third World countries led her to a much broad-er view of social work and its relationship to volunteers and other workers. However, women such as Govan, Whitton, and Reynolds lacked collegial sup-port. This is an important factor identified by Kinnear (1995) in her study of women in different professional occupations in Manitoba. Women social work-ers in the middle and latter part of the twentieth century, unlike the first gener-ation of women in social work, did not have the same network of support from unpaid women workers or colleagues from other disciplines. The move to pro-fessionalize was accompanied by specialization, and social workers wanted to dis-tance themselves from the volunteers, district nurses, and deaconesses who had provided many of the early social services in Canada. Without the support net-work that had accompanied the creation of separate female institutions, women in social work were particularly dependent on the approval of male superiors.

The dominance of men in the more lucrative administrative positions of lead-ership, so well documented by Struthers (1987a), has continued to characterize social work. Although approximately 70 per cent of the profession are women, they remain concentrated in the lower-paying direct service positions committed to an ethic of caring about and for marginal populations (Struthers, 1987a; Kenyon, 1997).

PROFESSIONALIZATION AND NURSING

A brief look at the history of nursing also reflects the tensions that developed as nursing education advocated professionalization as a means to achieve both sta-tus and autonomy (Baumgart and Larsen, 1988). A commitment to service cou-pled with a nurse's subordinate status to a physician in an increasingly complex hierarchical division of labour presented severe obstacles to nurses who were interested in professionalization.

Nursing as a career was greatly enhanced by the influenza epidemic in 1918 in which 50,000 Canadians died (Prentice et al., 1988). As hospital nursing began to replace private duty and public health nursing as the principal field of employ-ment, nurses began to wrestle with a problem that continues to challenge them—the lack of autonomy in their work.[2] Home and private duty and public health nursing had produced a 'Jill of all trades' who experienced considerable satisfac-tion and independence in her work despite the long hours and hard work. By 1920, however, the entrepreneurial role of nurses declined as pressures to staff hospitals increased, and physicians' criticisms of public health and private duty nurses intensified (Keddy, 1986).

As hospitals became the principal employer of nurses, on-site programs for nursing training were initiated. Like early social work education, most of the classes for nurses were taught by men, in this case, male physicians. The real training for nurses, however, occurred on the job. The apprenticeship model pro-vided hospitals with the free labour of student nurses who spent 12 to 14 hours a day caring for patients. In return, nurses received room and board and a small stipend, approximately $8 to $10 per month. While some historians point out the exploitative nature of nurses' training and labour, it also fostered strong networks of support and affection among nurses.

A culture of nursing education emphasized service, dedication, and self-sacrifice, the traditional attributes of caring women (Baumgart and Larsen, 1988). Fear of the erosion of this service commitment became the strongest argument made by the 'traditionalist' nurses as advocates for professionalization surfaced. Composed of 'angels of mercy', the voices of tradition argued, 'Nursing is not merely a profession—it is a vocation; not merely a gainful occupation, but a ministry' (Melosh, 1989: 673). According to this view, technical skills and the acquisition of knowledge were secondary to the skills of intuition and empathy that were crucial to its caring mission. In contrast, those in favour of professionalism emphasized objectivity, technique, and efficiency and, moreover, attempted to eradicate the image of the self-sacrificing nurse. With this, it was thought, higher status and wages would follow.

The ensuing conflict between traditionalists and professionalists was largely played out through different conceptions of nursing education. Proponents of professionalism pushed for an academic program for nursing education centred in the universities. In 1920, the first degree program was established at the University of British Columbia, followed a few years later by McGill and the University of Toronto (Coburn, 1974). However, university training in nursing accentuated the internal tension within the field. In Canada in 1932, the Weir report recommended that responsibility for nursing education should be transferred to educational institutions (Baumgart and Larsen, 1988). This and subsequent reports on nursing education failed to change the hospital-based training model until the 1960s, when community colleges across Canada began to assume responsibility for nursing education.

Melosh (1982), in her study of American nursing, has contended that hospital-trained nurses considered a degree program as a direct devaluation of the basic skills associated with nursing on the job and detrimental to the cultural milieu that was essential for the socialization of a nurse. Despite different perspectives, the reality was that many working-class women entering nursing could not afford a five-year university program. As well, physicians were not interested in the elevation of nursing training and generally supported the continuation of the three-year hospital apprenticeship model for nurses.

As health care became more specialized, the forms and levels of personnel increased and exacerbated the development of a rigid and hierarchical division of labour within nursing. The internal dissension created by competition among different fields of practice and types of training proved to be formidable barriers to unifying and strengthening a nursing mandate (Coburn, 1974). In addition, an influx of nurses from the Caribbean and other countries produced racial and ethnic tensions (McPherson, 1996). By creating its own hierarchy, a hierarchy committed to efficiency and organizational goals, the nascent profession found that a sense of sisterhood or an analysis of nurses' subordination was difficult to achieve. Unfortunately, as Melosh (1982) has suggested, advocates of the university model failed to identify ways to bridge the gap between hospital- and university-trained nurses.

The nurses who wished to buy into 'professionalism' failed to recognize that its essence reflected a male culture. In replicating the élitism associated with male professions, the fight for nurses to become 'professional' was centred on licensing and registration. Theoretical knowledge and technical skills, and 'women's caring', were seen as opposites and the complexities involved in melding the two were not understood (Reverby, 1988).

The mission of service and caring that had shaped the formation of nursing as a field became a source of both strength and oppression. Baumgart and Larsen (1988) have argued that, as with other women's work, caring as part of a nursing mandate has been constrained by understaffing and by the priority given to the more technical aspects of medical care. Concurrent with this view, Reverby (1988) concluded that nurses lacked the power to implement their vision of an ethic of care. Nurses have also failed to see how caring was shaped not simply by women's psychological identity but by the social and political context in which nursing developed. It was a duty to care directed by a male medical hierarchy, not an ethic of care in which nurses would be able to make more autonomous judgements about the kind of care patients should receive.

In the last two decades, issues of nursing autonomy and rights have intensified. The unionization of nurses has promoted a greater consciousness and Canadian nurses are voicing their concerns and aspirations. As well, the creation of the nurse practitioner in the 1990s that has extended the practice and scope of nursing, particularly in poorly served health care areas, is a step for nurses in gaining more autonomy and authority for their work. The changes in nursing and the health care system have presented both opportunities and tensions. These tensions point to the need to examine the contradictions and continuities that shape nursing and extend our analysis to include not only gender and class, but also how racism and homophobia affect the options of who takes up nursing as a career (McPherson, 1996).

PROFESSIONALIZATION AND TEACHING

In an examination of teaching as a profession, Finklestein (1988) presents a rather discouraging perspective on teaching as a field of women's work in the United States. She is saddened by the reality that her daughter's commitment to children 'has led her to the courthouse rather than to the schoolhouse door'. Questioning why young women are choosing law over teaching, Finklestein examines the way in which teaching as a women's career has been undervalued in the last 100 years. As she traces the evolution of teacher training, Finklestein demonstrates how the emphasis shifted from the preparation of rural elementary teachers to the preparation of secondary school teachers, principals, and the teachers of teachers.

Women teachers, like nurses and social workers, were also limited in their ability to control the profession or to achieve equality. According to Finklestein, the explanation for this is found in efforts to professionalize teaching and a gradual acceptance of the male university research model. Despite the ways in which training for teaching has opened the doors and minds of women, they continued to be regarded as intellectually inferior. Elementary school teaching was undertaken by women and rooted in practice. In contrast, the men who made up the ranks of the secondary schools and administration were expected to wrestle with a formal academic program of educational theory. Learning through classroom practice teaching continued to be downgraded in the twentieth century as teacher training programs were lodged within the university. Thus, the experiences women gained from the day-to-day world of practice were devalued.

Differences over the way teachers should be prepared for their role were also evident in Canada. Ryerson had advocated training for teachers in the middle of the nineteenth century, but this was not easily attained. By 1875, a quarter of the teachers in Ontario were graduates of the Toronto Normal School, which first offered a training program for teachers in 1847. Ryerson's interest in upgrading teaching through the development of the Normal School was a direct attack on the county model schools, an alternate form of teaching preparation for candidates who had one or two years of high school. Given three months of training, under the supervision of a qualified teacher, graduates received a third-class teaching certificate enabling them to teach in their own county. The issue of what constituted appropriate training for teaching in Ontario was not resolved until 1971, when all teachers, including those in the elementary system, were required to have a degree.

Women teachers, like social workers and nurses, have also been marginalized. In 1981, less than 10 per cent of women in teaching were employed at the secondary level while over 80 per cent were in the elementary schools (Prentice et al., 1988: 372). Not only did women face discrimination in the areas of teaching, women in Manitoba were also limited by differential pay scales, the marriage bar, appointments to administrative positions, and differential support from teachers' associations (Kinnear, 1995). The argument that men received higher salaries as they were expected to support a wife proved to be hard to swallow when single men were paid at the same rate as their married colleagues. Denied the status that Ryerson envisioned, women as teachers have turned to the trade union movement to achieve solidarity and to work towards collective rights.

Collective action was a strategy women teachers entertained much earlier. In 1918, for instance, the Saskatoon Women's Teachers Association was established to develop their own strategies to speak for their constituency. Aware that women teachers received less pay, had lower status, were generally regarded as intellectually inferior, less adept at using discipline, and not administratively prepared, Saskatoon women teachers realized that their interests would not be represented by men's teaching associations. The SWTA, as one of the largest teaching organizations in Saskatchewan, went on to become a strong political organization that fought for higher wages for women and objected to the policy prohibiting married women from teaching. It was also successful in encouraging the employment of women as principals (Kojder, 1986).

A less militant women's organization existed in Ontario with the establish-ment, in 1918, of the Federation of Women Teacher Associations of Ontario, which fought for the rights of women teachers. However, perspectives that favoured the identification of teaching with the trade union movement were in conflict with the middle-class aspirations of professionalism. The FWTAO was also faced with the contradiction experienced by women trained to assume self-sacrificing roles yet determined to enhance and gain greater autonomy over their work (Graham, 1974). Efforts to support the professionalization of teaching have been an ongoing strategy of professional organizations. Interestingly, in the 1950s, as Manitoba teachers advocated higher qualifications, a more stringent code of ethics, and greater solidarity, male teachers questioned how a female-dominated occupation could be a profession and called for the recruitment of men into teaching. Despite the attempt to defeminize teaching, teachers in Canada are largely women and, indeed, the majority of professional women are in teaching-related positions (Kinnear, 1995: 126).

CONCLUSION

There is no easy way for women to resolve the contradiction of maintaining an ethic of care at the same time as they seek to have more autonomy and equality within the caring professions. The answer does not lie in either a glorification of caring or a repudiation of professionalism. Rather, we must begin with an under-standing of how caring and professionalism have defined the work of women in these fields of work. Both have reinforced a gendered division of labour and both must be examined.

Professionalism, as it has been implemented, has not and will not be the panacea advocated by leaders in the fields of nursing, social work, and teaching. Expectations that equality and increased status would gradually prevail as men entered fields traditionally filled by women have proven to be false; nor have efforts to professionalize along the male model created gender-free systems of meritocracy. As this journey into the past reveals, women's experiences in the pro-fessions have been different from men's. Some women have resisted complete domination and developed strategies to ensure more influence. Both Reverby (1988) and Melosh (1989) argue that women's experience in nursing made them aware of the limits to their autonomy, one of the first requirements for change. In the last decade, nurses have made a strong case for more input into the health care system, but their vulnerability in the restructuring of health care that has characterized the last decade has been felt by the large number of nurses who have lost their positions.

For the most part, women in social work have been more conservative than their sisters in nursing and teaching, and they have tended to work towards equal-ity in a more individualistic way. However, feminist critiques in social work are beginning to uncover the experiences of women as professionals and clients and these critiques provide a starting point for collaboration and consciousness-rais-ing.[3] Women are no longer prepared to internalize or accept individual responsibility for their subordination or the discrimination they have experienced. Feminist critiques have been bolstered by the voices and experiences of women from minority groups who are refusing to remain on the margins.

A final point presents a formidable barrier to change in nursing, social work, and teaching: the presence of these occupations in large bureaucratic organizations. Women, as direct service professionals in these organizations, have had limited autonomy, control over their work, and influence in policy and resource allocation. Hierarchical divisions—whether men and women, the caregiver and the cared-for, the administrator and the direct service worker, the professional and the volunteer, the principal and the teacher, the doctor and the nurse, the theoretician and the practitioner—all reflect differences in power, esteem, and autonomy. Dichotomies of this nature ensure rigid role definitions and organizational structures that fail to uncover the complexities and solutions involved in arriving at a collective responsibility for caring. Changes need to be centred on examining and altering the internal structures of the professions, the state organizations in which they are embedded, and the barriers that prevent the advancement of women (Kinnear, 1995).

That changes may well benefit men in these fields needs to be emphasized. No longer can we assume that the model professional has a wife at home to handle domestic and caring labour. As Daniels (1987) has argued, the invisible work that women do as homemakers, mothers, and volunteers must be recognized and shared in the interests of creating a caring community. The danger is that women themselves have begun to devalue their unpaid work, in the home and the community. And when it becomes paid work, as evident in the above review, its value is only marginally higher. For those women in the professions who attempt to carry two careers, the price is often very high. Women may model and emulate successful men, but as super-women they do not produce change.

NOTES

1. From 1971 to 1987, the number of women in engineering increased from 1.2 per cent of the total graduates to 12.2 per cent; in law, from 9.94 per cent to 46.7 per cent; and in medicine, from 12.8 per cent to 41.7 per cent. See Statistics Canada, *Women in Canada: A Statistical Report*, 2nd edn, Cat. 89–503E (Ottawa: Ministry of Supply and Services, Feb. 1990), 55.
2. In 1943, the CNA estimated that 14,000 of its membership were employed in hospitals and public health and 6,000 nurses were engaged in private duty work. See McPherson, 1996.
3. See, for example, Nan Van Den Bergh, ed., *Feminist Practice in the 21st Century* (Washington: National Association of Social Workers, 1995).

REFERENCES

Austin, B.F., ed. 1890. *Woman: Her Character, Culture and Calling*. Brantford, Ont.

Bacchi, C.L. 1983. *Liberation Deferred: The Ideas of the English-Canadian Suffragists, 1877–1918*. Toronto: University of Toronto Press.

Baines, C.T. 1988. *Women's Reform Organizations in Canada 1870–1930: A Historical*

Perspective. Working Papers on Social Welfare in Canada, #26, Faculty of Social Work, University of Toronto.

Baines, C.T. 1990. 'From Women's Benevolence to Professional Social Work: The Case of the Wimodausis and the Earlscourt Children's Home, 1902–1971', Ph.D. thesis, University of Toronto.

Baines, C.T. 1997. 'Elizabeth Govan, an Outsider in Her Own Community', paper presented at the annual meeting of the Canadian Association of Schools of Social Work, St John's, Nfld.

Baumgart, A.J., and J. Larsen, eds. 1988. *Canadian Nursing Faces the Future: Development and Change.* Toronto: C.V. Mosby.

Bliss, M. 1968. 'The Methodist Church and World War I', *Canadian Historical Review* 49 (Sept.).

Brown, R.C., and R. Cook. 1974. *Canada, 1896–1921: A Nation Transformed.* Toronto: McClelland & Stewart.

Burke, S.Z. 1996. *Seeking the Highest Good: Social Service and Gender at the University of Toronto, 1888–1937.* Toronto: University of Toronto Press.

Coburn, J. 1974. '"I See and Am Silent": A Short History of Nursing in Ontario', in J. Acton, P. Goldsmith, and B. Shepard, eds, *Women at Work 1850–1930.* Toronto: Canadian Women's Educational Press.

Cook, R. 1985. *The Regenerators: Social Criticism in Late Victorian English Canada.* Toronto: University of Toronto Press.

Cott, N. 1977. *The Bonds of Womanhood.* New Haven: Yale University Press.

Daniels, A.K. 1987. 'Invisible Work', *Social Problems* 34 (Dec.).

Daniels, A.K. 1988. *Invisible Careers: Women Civic Leaders From the Volunteer World.* Chicago: University of Chicago Press.

Ehrenreich, J.H. 1985. *The Altruistic Imagination: A History of Social Work and Social Policy in the United States.* Ithaca, NY: Cornell University Press.

Finklestein, B. 1989. 'Conveying Messages to Women: Higher Education and the Teaching Profession in Historical Perspective', *American Behavioral Scientist* 32, 6 (July-Aug.).

Freedman, E. 1979. 'Separatism as Strategy: Female Institution Building as American Feminism 1870–1930', *Feminist Studies* 5, 3.

Glazer, P.M., and M. Slater. 1987. *Unequal Colleagues: The Entrance of Women into the Professions, 1890–1945.* New Brunswick, NJ: Rutgers University Press.

Graham, E. 1974. 'School Marms and Early Teaching in Ontario', in J. Acton, P. Goldsmith, and B. Shepard, eds, *Women at Work 1850–1930.* Toronto: Canadian Women's Educational Press.

Gripton, J. 1974. 'Sexism in Social Work, Male Takeover of a Female Profession', *The Social Worker* 42: 78–89.

Hearn, J. 1985. 'Patriarchy, Professionalization and the Semi-Professions', in C. Ungerson, ed., *Women and Social Policy.* London: Macmillan.

Kealey, L. ed. 1979. *A Not Unreasonable Claim: Women and Reform in Canada, 1880s–1920s.* Toronto: Women's Educational Press.

Keddy, B. 1986. 'Private Duty Nursing Days of the 1920s and 1930s in Canada', *Canadian Woman Studies* 7, 3: 99–103.

Kenyon, G. 1997. 'Gender and Income Among Ontario Social Workers: The Source of Disparity', paper presented at the annual meeting of the Canadian Association of Schools of Social Work, St John's, Nfld.

Kerr, J., and J. MacPhail. 1988. *Canadian Nursing Issues and Perspectives*. Toronto: McGraw-Hill Ryerson.

Kinnear, M. 1995. *In Subordination: Professional Women 1870–1970*. Montreal and Kingston: McGill-Queen's University Press.

Kojder, A.M. 1986. 'In Union There is Strength: The Saskatoon Women's Teachers Association', *Canadian Woman Studies* 7, 2 (Fall).

Lubove, R. 1977. *The Professional Altruist: The Emergence of Social Work as a Career, 1880–1930*. New York: Atheneum.

McDowell, J.P. 1982. *The Social Gospel in the South: The Women's Home Mission Movement in the Methodist Episcopal Church, 1886–1939*. Baton Rouge: Louisiana State University Press.

McPherson, K. 1996. *Bedside Matters: The Transformation of Canadian Nursing, 1900–1990*. Toronto: Oxford University Press.

Melosh, B. 1982. *'The Physician's Hand': Work, Culture and Conflict in American Nursing*. Philadephia: Temple University Press.

Melosh, B. 1989. '"Not Merely a Profession": Nurses and Resistance to Professionalization', *American Behavioral Scientist* 32, 6 (July-Aug.).

Mitchinson, W. 1977. 'Aspects of Reform: Four Women's Organizations in 19th Century Canada', Ph.D. thesis, York University.

Mitchinson, W. 1987. 'Early Women's Organizations and Social Reform: Prelude to the Welfare State', in A. Moscovitch and J. Albert, eds, *The Benevolent State: The Growth of Welfare in Canada*. Toronto: Garamond.

Morrison, T.R. 1971. 'Child-Centred Urban Social Reform in Late 19th Century Ontario', Ph.D. thesis, University of Toronto.

Owram, D. 1986. *The Government Generation: Canada Intellectuals and the State, 1900–1945*. Toronto: University of Toronto Press.

Pedersen, D. 1987. '"Building Today for the Womanhood of Tomorrow": Businessmen, Boosters and the YWCA, 1870–1930', *Urban History Review* 15, 3 (Feb.).

Prentice, A. 1977. 'The Feminization of Teaching', in S.M. Trofimenkoff and A. Prentice, eds, *The Neglected Majority*. Toronto: McClelland & Stewart.

Prentice, A., et al. 1988. *Canadian Women: A History*. Toronto: Harcourt Brace Jovanovich.

Reverby, S. 1988. *Ordered to Care: The Dilemmas of American Nursing, 1850–1945*. Cambridge: Cambridge University Press.

Roberts, W. 1979. '"Rocking the Cradle for the World": The New Woman and Maternal Feminism, Toronto, 1877–1914', in L. Kealey, ed., *A Not Unreasonable Claim: Women and Reform in Canada, 1880s–1920s*. Toronto: Women's Educational Press.

Robinson, H. 1979. *Decades of Caring: The Big Sister Story*. Toronto: Dundurn Press.

Rooke, P.T., and R.L. Schnell. 1982. 'Rise and Decline of North America's Protestant Orphanage as Woman's Domain, 1850–1930', *Atlantis* (Spring).

Rosenberg, C. 1981. 'Inward Vision and Outward Glance: The Shaping of the American Hospital 1890–1914', in D.J. Rothman and S. Wheeler, eds, *Social History and Social Policy*. New York: Academic Press.

Scott, A.F. 1984. *Making the Invisible Woman Visible*. Urbana: University of Illinois Press.

Smith-Rosenberg, C. 1985. *Disorderly Conduct*. New York: Alfred A. Knopf.

Struthers, J. 1987a. '"Lord Give Us Men": Women and Social Work in English Canada, 1918–1953', in A. Moscovitch and S. Albert, eds, *The Benevolent State: The Growth of Welfare in Canada*. Toronto: Garamond.

Struthers, J. 1987b. 'A Profession in Crisis: Charlotte Whitton and Canadian Social Work in the 1930s', in A. Moscovitch and J. Albert, eds, *The Benevolent State: The Growth of Welfare in Canada*. Toronto: Garamond.

3

Gender, Poverty, and Women's Caring

Patricia M. Evans

Women comprise half of the world's population but perform nearly two-thirds of all the work hours, receive only one-tenth of the world's income, and own less than one-hundredth of the world's property. (UN figures, cited in Gunderson and Muszyski, 1990: 31)

INTRODUCTION

Women are more likely to be poor than men, and the phrase 'the feminization of poverty' was coined to capture this vulnerability. Women's poverty, however, should not be interpreted as a recent phenomenon because poor women have always out-numbered poor men. This chapter explores the reasons for the enduring nature of women's poverty, highlighting the contribution made by the gendered division of labour and the particular responsibilities women have for providing care to others. In addition, social assistance and retirement benefits are assessed for their adequacy in redressing the high poverty rates of single mothers and elderly women.

Women's poverty frequently reflects their biographies as caregivers, and it is not surprising that the women who are most likely to be poor are single mothers and elderly women living on their own. The undervaluing of women's work in the home and in the labour market results in inadequate incomes for a large proportion of single mothers who are without the financial support of a traditional male 'breadwinner'. The disadvantageous relationship between gender and employment accumulates over a lifetime to produce low pensions, and the poverty of many older women can be regarded as the economic legacy of their caregiving. Not all caregivers are poor, and not all poor women are caregivers. However, as Hilary Graham (1987: 223) commented more than a decade ago: 'Poverty and caring are, for many women, two sides of the same coin. Caring is what they do; poverty describes the economic circumstances in which they do it.'

To explore the relationship between women's poverty and women's caring, the competing demands of the 'family ethic' and the 'work ethic' are examined. Mimi Abramovitz (1988, 1996) uses the term 'family ethic' to refer to a traditional and patriarchal ideology that assumes a heterosexual family and delegates to women the principal responsibility for caring for family members, helping to marginal-ize the work they do in the labour market. While the hold of the family ethic on women may appear much looser now than in earlier periods, the realities of women's lives and a resurgence of a family values discourse suggest that its influence continues to be powerful. The norms that underlie the work ethic are also extremely influential and reflect a capitalist economic structure that privileges the work done in the public and 'productive' market and renders invisible the work women do in the home. Self-sufficiency is rewarded and 'dependency' is penalized, and both are defined only with reference to economic criteria. This chapter uses the concepts of the family ethic and the work ethic to explore their contradictory influences on the links between women, poverty, and caregiving, and examines their impact on the social policies designed to address women's poverty.

Women's poverty, although frequent, is not random. Race intersects with gender to ensure that Aboriginal women and women of colour are almost twice as likely to be poor than other women (Statistics Canada, 1995: 146, 162). Nor does the family ethic operate identically across all women. Black women, for example, have a long and prominent history of paid employment, including domestic work for White middle-class women (Kemp, 1994: 14). The image and reality of Caribbean women as family breadwinners reflect 'a long history of colonialism, slavery, and neo-colonial economic patterns' (Henry, 1994: 60). Women with severe disabilities are also more likely to be poor than those with no disabilities. They may receive care from others, but they are also caregivers. Single mothers with disabilities, for example, find it extremely difficult to locate affordable housing that is both accessible and accepts children (National Council of Welfare, 1990). Although caring may be incorporated in a range of ways into the lives of different women, caring and poverty are, for many women, intimately connected.

The Canadian landscape has altered dramatically through the 1990s. The prospects for individuals locating stable full-time employment are rapidly diminishing as a variety of non-standard forms of employment proliferate, including part-time, temporary, and self-employment. In response to a changing, globalized economy, Canadian governments have focused on deficit reduction and cuts to social spending. As a result, the contours of the welfare state are retracted at the very time that they urgently need expansion. This has profound consequences for women. It is women who are more likely than men to use social services, and the public sector has been a very important source of women's employment. The downsizing of the Canadian welfare state and the impacts on women's access to services and employment illustrate, in a particularly stark way, the connections between women's paid and unpaid work (Luxton and Reiter, 1997).

This chapter opens with an exploration of the demographic profile of women's poverty. The consequences of assuming that caring belongs to women are considered in the second section and include work interruptions, low pay, economic reliance on a male partner, and the undervaluing of women's work within the home. The third and fourth sections address, in turn, the situations of single mothers and elderly women, groups who most clearly illustrate the links among poverty, gender, and caring. The chapter concludes with a discussion of the general directions for, and the difficulties of, change.

THE MEANING AND MEASUREMENT OF WOMEN'S POVERTY

The assumption that women's primary role is in the home and that economic dependence on a man is 'natural' has meant that women's particular vulnerability to poverty was slow to gain recognition. When Canada, along with the United

Kingdom and the United States, 'rediscovered' poverty in the late 1960s, men's poverty was in the forefront. The 1971 Report of the Special Senate Committee on Poverty selected a photograph of an elderly man for its cover and devoted only two of its 200 pages to issues of maternal employment and child care. Even the radical alternative report of the time emphasized male poverty (Adams et al., 1971). The 1970 Status of Women Report (Canada, 1970), however, documented the prevalence of poverty among women as one of its most unexpected and important findings.

Poverty is typically measured through a 'poverty line', an indicator of income used to separate the poor from the non-poor. Statistics Canada's unofficial poverty line is set in relation to the amounts that Canadians typically spend on food, clothing, and housing. As a result, it is not simply a 'subsistence' measure of need but reflects some attention to community standards. In keeping with general use elsewhere, Statistics Canada's poverty line is adopted throughout this chapter, but it should be borne in mind that it produces one of the least generous of poverty lines in use in Canada (Ross, Shillington, and Lochhead, 1994). Although Statistics Canada began to report data on the distribution of low income in 1971, not until 1980 were data published on the overall numbers and distribution of poverty by sex in addition to household type.

The shares of poverty attributed to adult women and men during selected years, 1980–95, are shown in Table 1. The table indicates that throughout the 15-year period, women were disproportionately represented in the ranks of the poor. Women accounted for 58–61 per cent of all adult poverty during these years, while men's share ranged from a low of 39 per cent to a high of 42 per cent. However, women's proportion of total adult poverty has declined somewhat in the 1990s, a decline that reflects the sharper impact of the recent recession on men's unemployment. Although the likelihood of women's poverty actually increased during the 1990s, men's increased more, and so their share of total poverty grew.

Table 1: Poverty Rates, Women as % of All Poor Adults, 1980–1995

Year	% Women	Year	% Women
1980	59.6	1988	60.6
1981	59.6	1989	60.5
1982	58.3	1990	60.0
1983	57.9	1991	58.8
1984	58.2	1992	58.3
1985	58.5	1993	58.2
1986	58.3	1994	58.3
1987	58.7	1995	56.9

Source: Calculated from National Council of Welfare, *Poverty Profile 1995* (Ottawa: NCW, Spring 1997), Table 17.

Despite the small change in the 1990s, what emerges clearly from Table 1 is that the phrase 'the feminization of poverty' does not accurately describe women's poverty over this period, a poverty that is characterized more by stability than by change. Reference to the feminization of poverty may help to mask the reality that women have *always* been poor in greater proportions than men. It is the continuing and disproportionate nature of their poverty that is of such striking concern.

Figure 1 illustrates the likelihood of poverty in 1980 and 1995 for four groups of women: married women with children under the age of 18, single mothers with children under the age of 18, women under the age of 65 living on their own, and women living on their own who are 65 years and older. As Table 2 indicates, the risk of poverty for married women has increased from 9 to 13 per cent, while the rates have remained remarkably stable for single mothers and women under the age of 65 who are living on their own. In contrast, and as a result of improved income support programs, elderly women living on their own have experienced a clear decline in their poverty rates over the 15-year period.

Figure 1: Poverty Rates for Women, 1980 and 1995

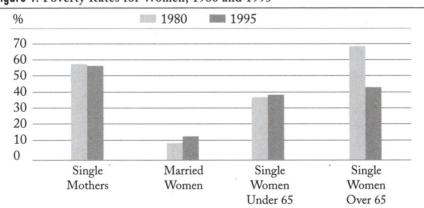

Source: National Council of Welfare, *Poverty Profile 1995* (Ottawa: NCW, Spring 1997), Table 6 and Graph D.

While the data presented above help to reveal the overall profile of women's poverty, the assumptions that underpin the data collection also help to obscure some important features. Married women's poverty is encompassed in a measure that assumes household financial resources are equally available to all its members, who are all equally poor or non-poor. Millar (1996), in reviewing the evidence, suggests that only about one in five couples jointly pool their resources in the way that the concept of family income implies. Women may well live in a non-poverty household but have access to only a poverty share of those resources. In addition, the type of family poverty that is measured is based on the traditional heterosexist model. Gay/lesbian families and extended families are not counted as family households.

Poverty lines are useful to indicate the extent of progress in combating poverty over time, but they are woefully inadequate reflectors of an experience that encompasses so much more than simply a lack of income. Poverty also carries with it a sense of powerlessness, exclusion, and stigma. A woman from northern Ontario comments: 'My son even said that the kids at school said he had germs because he was poor. And he asked me if he had germs. I had to tell him he did-n't and those kids were being cruel. It hurts when your kids come home hurting because we are poor' (quoted in Kauppi and Reitsma-Street, 1996: 213). At the same time, poor single mothers may feel both 'better off and worse off'. Although their income drops significantly, their control over it increases, as a single mother from Nova Scotia explains: 'we might be poorer now than before my husband left . . . but at least I know that there is money coming in regularly . . . and I don't have to worry about him spending it all after work' (cited in Gunderson and Muszynski, 1990: 12).

Women's poverty was in the closet in the 1970s and in the 1980s the door was slightly ajar. By the 1990s, women's poverty was no longer news. However, as we approach the end of the century, it continues to present significant challenges to the traditional ways of understanding its causes, consequences, and solutions.

FEMINIST LINKS: WOMEN'S POVERTY AND WOMEN'S WORK

Low wages and occupational segregation have long been recognized as hallmarks of women's labour force participation, but the explanations for these labour market disadvantages have differed. Orthodox economic models focus on the 'supply' side of the labour market and the characteristics of the individual as a major source of disadvantage. The theory of 'human capital' suggests that women's low pay reflects their reluctance to invest in training and other employment-enhancing activities because they expect that the pay-offs will be diminished by their domestic obligations. Women's employment decisions, therefore, represent a rational estimate of a variety of costs and benefits. In attempting to explain why single mothers 'choose' work or welfare, these models consider such factors as likely wages, costs of child care, and the level of available welfare benefits. Other perspectives, however, look to the labour market, the 'demand' side, for an explanation of employment disadvantage. Structural explanations, such as dual labour market theory, seek to understand the processes at work in the labour market that create barriers between 'good' jobs and 'bad' jobs and disproportionately consign particular groups, notably women and people of colour, to the lowest paid and least stable employment (Phillips and Phillips, 1993).

These frameworks for understanding women's poverty and their employment disadvantage provide, at best, only cursory attention to the impact of women's unpaid labour in the home. Orthodox economic models do not question the assumptions that give primacy to women's role in the household, and these models systematically undervalue their work both at home and in the paid workforce. However, structural explanations that pay attention to the operation of the labour market but group women with other disadvantaged groups have little to say about the particular processes that identify women as targets for discrimination. As Pat Armstrong and Hugh Armstrong (1990: 63) point out, a dual labour market approach 'does not tell us why clerical work is a secondary rather than a primary job, nor why the Irish no longer do the least attractive jobs but women still do.' It also does not explain why gender and race intersect to ensure that women of colour are so much more highly concentrated in lower-paid and insecure jobs than White women. Of the 93 per cent of the workers in Metro Toronto homes for the aged who are women, for example, more than half are Black (Das Gupta, 1996: 8).

Feminist frameworks understand women's poverty as the result of the intersecting processes of the family ethic and capitalism that designate men as the primary workers in the public world and women as the primary workers in the private domain of the household. The separation of the roles of men and women, the dichotomy between the public and private, spills over into the valuation of skills in the labour market. As Ruth Buchanan (1995: 6) points out, in discussing secretarial work: 'One could describe it as the ultimately "flexibly specialized" job; requiring multitasking, multiskilling, organization, discretion and so forth. Yet, perhaps because it occasionally looks not unlike the multiskilling required by domestic labour, it is generally not identified as a skilled labour job.' An analysis of women and poverty must be based on an understanding of the interrelationship between the labour women do in the home and their employment in the workplace.

The assumption that women are primarily caregivers and men are economic providers also affects women's earning capacities in important ways. Women's lower earnings reflect, in part, time spent out of the labour market engaged in caregiving responsibilities. However, over and above this direct impact, the gendered division of responsibilities and the lack of value attached to women's work contribute in important ways to the segregation and general devaluation of the work women do in the labour market. These direct and indirect effects of caregiving on women's employment will be examined in turn.

CAREGIVING AND EMPLOYMENT: DIRECT AND INDIRECT IMPACTS

Perhaps the most obvious, well-documented, and uncontroversial impact of women's caring is that they are much more likely than men to work part-time and to interrupt employment to take care of family members and the household. In 1994, for example, 26 per cent of employed women worked part-time, in comparison to 9 per cent of men. While roughly similar proportions of men and women worked part-time because that was all they could find (34 and 37 per cent, respectively), women were more than 10 times as likely as men to report that personal or family responsibilities precluded full-time employment (12.3 per cent vs 0.9 per cent) (Statistics Canada, 1995: 74). And when they are employed, women, on average, lose more than a working week a year for personal and family responsibilities. Men, by comparison, lose less than a day (Akyeampong, 1995). Although children are the most visible beneficiaries of women's care, women, as Sheila Neysmith discusses in Chapter 11, also carry a great deal of responsibility for dependent adults. A 1996 Statistics Canada survey, for example, found that employed women were 50 per cent more likely than employed men to be caregivers to individuals with chronic health problems or disabilities (Lipovenko, 1997).

There is broad agreement that discrimination is a significant factor in the gap between men's and women's wages, although estimates of its impact vary and there is no consensus about what precise factors are to be considered discriminatory. However, it is generally agreed that women pay a greater 'price' for their household responsibilities than can be justified on purely economic grounds. Occupational segregation and non-standard employment are other factors that contribute to women's low wages and increase their vulnerability to poverty.

The gendered division of labour is also sharply reflected in the continuing concentration of women's work in particular occupations. This segregation has persisted in spite of important occupational changes in the labour force and efforts to remove barriers to women's employment. Throughout time and across cultures, a lesser value is assigned to the work identified as 'women's work', regardless of its contribution or its complexity. Indeed, occupational segregation has been found to be a more important factor than education or work experience in explaining the male-female wage gap (Gunderson and Muszynski, 1990: 92).

Much of the work women do in the labour market continues to mirror their work in the household and incorporates a significant component of personal service. In 1994, more than 70 per cent of employed women were located in occupations related to teaching, health, clerical work, sales, and service (Statistics Canada, 1995). Women have made gains in their labour force participation rates, the wage gap has narrowed, and women have increased their representation in some male-dominated occupations, although typically at the bottom of the hierarchy. However, the restructuring of the labour market that is occurring in the context of globalization is 'feminizing' the labour market (Armstrong, 1996). The number of women's jobs is growing while the traditional forms of employment for men are decreasing and men's work looks increasingly like women's work. As a result, some of the decrease in the wage gap is accounted for by the lowering of men's wages rather than real improvement in the wages of women. Men are also making greater inroads into some of the relatively well-paid jobs where women predominate. Pat Armstrong (1996) depicts these deteriorating conditions of men's employment as 'harmonizing down in a global economy'.

A long-standing justification for women's segregation into insecure and low-paid employment was that women worked for 'pin money' and wanted to be able to enter and exit the labour market with ease. However, the shift from full-time permanent employment to part-time, casualized work results from employers, not employees, attempting to increase their 'flexibility' (Jenson, 1996). Despite the increase in the number of single mothers and the growing evidence that the earnings of married women are an important factor in keeping families out of poverty (Schellenberg and Ross, 1997), women's paid work continues to be generally marginalized and wage equity difficult to achieve. Initially conceived as 'equal pay for equal work' and now as 'equal pay for work of equal value,' wage equity has been particularly elusive for women of colour. Despite higher levels of education, women of colour who work full-time for a full year earn $1,400 less a year than other women (Statistics Canada, 1995: 138).

Viewing men as breadwinners and significant players in the 'public market-place' has important consequences for women. As we have seen, women's work in the labour market consistently has been underpaid and women's work in the household remains hidden in the private domain, despite estimates that its economic value is the equivalent of between one-third and one-half of the GNP (Pupo, 1997). Thus, the gendered division of labour helps to structure women's economic vulnerability, both at home and in employment. Efforts to improve the economic position of women through strategies that begin and end at the workplace door can only have a limited impact.

WOMEN IN POVERTY

The observation that a woman is frequently 'only a man away from poverty' highlights the inadequate incomes of the increasing number of women who do not have access to the earnings of a male partner. The remainder of the chapter focuses on two groups of women for whom the gendered assumptions of caring have resulted in an extremely high risk of poverty—single mothers and elderly women living on their own. The impact of the family ethic and the work ethic on their poverty is explored, and the income security policies that impose gendered and conflicting expectations about employment and family responsibilities are examined.

A Profile of Single Mothers

Single mothers represent a diverse group of women who live with at least one dependent child but separately from the father of the child. Single mothers may be separated, divorced, widowed, or they may never have lived with the father of their child. This latter group includes young mothers as well as those older mothers who opted for single motherhood, sometimes with the help of new reproductive technologies. Single mothers also come from a variety of ethno-racial backgrounds, although the forces of colonialism and racism have meant that Aboriginal women and Black women are more than twice as likely as their White counterparts to be single mothers (Lindsay, 1992).

Canadian single-mother families are growing. Between 1973 and 1991 they increased from 8 per cent to 14 per cent of all women with children under the age of 18. However, as Dooley's (1995: 42–3) research indicates, an important part of this increase reflects the fact that fewer women now marry *and* have children. As a result, single mothers, as a proportion of women as a whole, increased from a modest 5 per cent in the early 1970s to 7 per cent in the early 1990s. The current proportion of single mothers is not at an all-time high, although concerns aired in the media are likely to make us think otherwise. More than 50 years ago, almost one in seven Canadian families was headed by a single parent, but for different reasons; there have been important changes in the pathways to single parenting. Forty-five years ago more than 60 per cent of single mothers were widowed; in 1991, the majority were separated and divorced, and widows accounted for less than one in four of single mothers (Lindsay, 1992). In what has been termed a 'moral panic' about single mothers, the problem of their poverty has been submerged and lone mothers themselves are constituted as the problem (Roseneil and Mann, 1996). While a longitudinal study that interviewed 150 single mothers and their children at three different points between 1987 and 1994 did not support this problem profile, Carolyne Gorlick (1995) did find that change was characteristic of their lives. For example, at the first interview, fully 86 per cent of single mothers reported that a housing move followed their separation, and an additional 61 per cent had also moved between the second and final interviews. These moves, some of which were associated with improved housing, involved the overwhelming majority of children in changing schools and/or friends.

What has not changed in the lives of Canadian single mothers over the years is their very high risk of poverty. Single mothers are more likely to be poor than any other group. Between 1980 and 1995, the proportion of poor single mothers has ranged from a low of 53 per cent in 1989 to a high of 63 per cent in 1984. In 1995, more than half (57 per cent) of single mothers lived in poverty. In contrast, the highest rate of poverty reported for single fathers was 34 per cent, in 1993. Just over one in 10 (13 per cent) of husband-wife families with children under the age of 18 were poor in 1995 (National Council of Welfare, 1997).

The single mother's exceptional vulnerability to poverty can be attributed to three factors: barriers to earning an adequate income, inadequate levels of child support, and low social assistance benefit rates. The barriers to adequate earnings—unemployment, low pay, occupational segregation, and increasing forms of non-standard work that confront all women in the labour market—make it extremely difficult for single mothers to earn an income that brings their households above the poverty line. In addition, as Evelyn Ferguson discusses in Chapter 9, the availability of adequate and affordable child care is extremely limited, despite the fact that some single mothers may be given priority for child-care spaces. Secondly, income from child support payments is frequently non-existent, and when available, usually inadequate. Using data from 1990, Statistics Canada (1995: 90) estimated that only one in five single mothers received child support, and when it was received, it accounted for less than one-fifth (18 per cent) of household income. Finally, many single mothers must rely on provincial social assistance programs for financial support, and all provinces provide an income to single mothers and their dependant(s) that fails by a wide margin to lift them out of poverty. In 1995, provincial social assistance benefits to single mothers ranged from a low of 50 per cent to a maximum of 75 per cent of the poverty line (National Council of Welfare, 1997). The likelihood of single mothers receiving adequate benefits has been eroded by the 1996 Canada Health and Social Transfer (CHST), which drastically reduces the federal contribution to the costs of social assistance and removes any incentive for provinces to provide better benefits because the federal transfer is the same whether they spend a lot or a little. In addition, the new Child Tax Benefit will not help women on social assistance because increases in benefits are targeted to the 'working poor'.

These facts, however, do not reveal very much about either the effect of the severe and continuing pressures that many single mothers experience or the anxiety and guilt that accompanies the fear that they may not be able to provide adequately for their children and themselves. This ability has been significantly compromised in the 1990s as a number of provincial governments have actually cut social assistance benefits. In 1995, for example, the Ontario government reduced social assistance benefits by a Draconian 22 per cent. Terri, a victim of these cuts and a single mother with three children aged 7, 11, and 15, describes the impact:

> I have been eating very little, and have gone whole days without food so I can feed my children. They are starting to notice that I am not eating, and have tried to give me their food. . . . They wear ragged jeans and shoes and they have inadequate winter clothes. I know they will be very cold in winter, and I am helpless to keep them warm. . . . I worry that their health will deteriorate due to lack of proper nutrition. . . . My little girl will probably never reach her full growth potential. She is small for her age, and I can see that she has been losing weight. (cited in Ontario Social Safety Network, 1997: 60)

Ann, a single mother of two girls, ages 6 and 8, speaks of the insecurity and fears she and her children experience:

> I am afraid and scared about what the future holds for us. . . . But I am afraid that we are going to have to move again. They will have to say goodbye again to the friends they've made and to our neighbours. . . . I am scared that I won't have enough money to feed my girls at school or at home. Right now, we eat a lot of pasta because it is cheap. I only eat at supper to save the food for my girls. I am going to end up disconnecting my phone. Then, how am I going to get a job if potential employers can't reach me? If things really get bad, I am going to have to decide what to cut next—gas, hydro, water or heat? What's next? (cited in Ontario Social Safety Network, 1997: 20)

It is hardly surprising that single mothers are disproportionately represented in the ranks of the food bank users (Daily Bread Food Bank, 1989). They are also vastly overrepresented in their involvement with the child welfare system. This should not surprise us, given its focus on 'mothering' and intimate close connections between the construction of 'neglect' and problems of poverty, issues that Karen Swift explores in Chapter 8.

The Competing Demands of the Family Ethic and the Work Ethic

A recurring theme throughout this book is the contradictory demands made on women, and this is particularly evident in social assistance policies. Social assistance represents the 'lower' track of the two-track income security system and it is disproportionately comprised of women who claim social assistance benefits on the basis of income and as wives and mothers. Men traditionally have been more likely to benefit from social insurance on the basis of entitlements related to employment and their 'breadwinner' role (Evans, 1997; Scott, 1996). Social assistance has been shaped by the family ethic and the work ethic, and single mothers have been subject to their conflicting requirements. Over time, the dictates of social assistance programs for single mothers have ebbed and flowed between their emphasis on the work ethic and the family ethic—at times single mothers have been viewed as 'mothers', as 'mothers *and* workers', and more recently, as 'workers, *not* mothers' (Evans, 1995b).

Mothers' Allowance legislation, enacted in a number of provinces between 1916 and 1920, established, for the first time, eligibility to a regular, if meagre, allowance to single mothers in economic need. Assumptions about which mothers were 'deserving' of the benefit excluded many categories of single mothers. Ontario's statute of 1920, for example, did not include women who were either unmarried mothers or the wives of prisoners. In the beginning, single mothers with only one child were not eligible because it was assumed that they could, or should, support themselves (Kierstead, 1925: 21). Finally, before the allowance was granted, the mother was scrutinized to ensure that she was a 'fit and suitable person' to care for her children. The influence of the family ethic is apparent in the types of paid work that were considered appropriate and the concern to exclude women and children whose husbands should be providing for them, even if they were not.

The family ethic continues to dictate a breadwinner-dependent homemaker model of the family for social assistance purposes. For example, a single mother is typically not able to claim social assistance if she is living with a man, even when he is under no legal obligation to support her or her children. The only exception is in Quebec, where a woman may live with a man for a year before he is obliged, for the purposes of social assistance, to provide financial support. Ontario operated a similar rule, but based on a three-year co-residency, from 1987 until it was abolished by the newly elected Progressive Conservative government in 1995. In contrast, the principles that underlie family law assume that as far as possible and as soon as possible, a woman is to be self-financing upon the dissolution of a marriage (Mossman and MacLean, 1997).

The family ethic has not operated in isolation; the work ethic has also had an important influence on programs to provide financial assistance to single mothers. A primary motivation for Mothers' Allowance was to provide an alternative to full-time maternal employment, but part-time work, particularly of the domestic variety (e.g., taking in laundry or sewing), was positively encouraged in the early days to diminish the 'pauperizing' potential of the allowance. Following World War II, when the needs of the returning male workforce dictated the return of the women to their homes, even part-time employment for single mothers on social assistance was discouraged (Ontario Ministry of Community and Social Services, 1984).

In the 1960s, partly spurred by the incentives provided by the establishment of the Canada Assistance Plan in 1966, programs to increase women's 'employability' began to make their appearance. The discourse, but not the reality, emphasized notions of opportunity and choice, as limited financial incentives were instituted and services expanded. These included a variety of measures to encourage paid work and reflected both the 'carrot' and the 'stick', such as education and training, subsidized child care, financial incentives, and lowering or cutting off benefits. Beginning in Ontario in the late 1980s, the ambivalence between the view of single mothers as mothers and single mothers as workers began to shift perceptibly towards their role as workers. A 1988 Ontario report from a task force struck to recommend changes to provincial social assistance exempted single mothers from employment expectations, but suggested that if enough did not make the 'right' choice—i.e., employment—this exemption should be reconsidered (Ontario Ministry of Community and Social Services, 1988). In other provinces, single mothers were not usually exempted in legislation, but they often were in practice.

In the late 1980s and throughout the 1990s, single mothers on social assistance have been subject to cutbacks in benefits and increased work requirements. Alberta's policy is the most stringent and now deems a single mother 'available for work' when her youngest child is six months old. Manitoba used to exempt single mothers with children under 18 from work requirements; a recent change lowered the age to seven. In the current period of retrenchment, single mothers on social assistance are increasingly targeted for employment as enthusiasm for 'workfare' encompasses those with children as well as those without (Evans, 1995a). This supports the thesis that motherhood is an increasingly devalued activity within capitalism and patriarchy (Silva, 1996).

The assumption that single mothers are *either* employed *or* relying on social assistance oversimplifies the complex patterns that social assistance and employment weave in the lives of many single mothers as they negotiate the competing demands of the labour market and their work at home. The National Council of Welfare found that 46 per cent of poor single mothers reported earnings in 1995, while 68 per cent reported income from social assistance. This clear overlap between work and welfare is reinforced by a study in Ontario that found that 28 per cent of single mothers on social assistance worked full- or part-time (Ornstein, 1995: 57). But employment does not necessarily equate with exit from social assistance, and a significant minority who leave social assistance will return (Evans, 1987; Barrett, 1994: 1). Annette, a former fast-food worker, explained why she left a program designed to supplement the low wages earned by single mothers: 'I had worked 55 hours a week for seven months. . . . I'd work three or four shifts if I had to.' However, when her mother who cared for her children moved, Annette had to cut back on her hours: 'And then it got a lot harder and then I lost my job. My boss just got fed up, and I got fired' (cited in Bancroft and Vernon, 1995: 47). A survey by the National Anti-Poverty Organization reported that half of the single mothers in training programs had to leave because of child-care problems (CLMPC, 1990: 141).

As Katherine Scott (1996: 8) argues, 'the "sanctity of motherhood" no longer shields women from the market; rather a new vision of "gender-neutral worker-citizen" has emerged.' This gender-neutral version of Canadians also underlies the retirement income system, the focus of the next section.

THE POVERTY OF OLDER WOMEN

Canada's elderly represent one group for whom there has been real progress in reducing poverty: between 1980 and 1995, the incidence of poverty among older people was cut in half, from 34 per cent to 17 per cent (National Council of Welfare, 1997: 13). Progress is particularly evident in the situation of older couples, who in 1995 had the lowest incidence of poverty (8 per cent) among all types of families (National Council of Welfare, 1997: 33). However, elderly women living on their own did not fare nearly as well as their male counterparts over this period, and the gender gap actually increased. Women's rates fell from 68 per cent to 43 per cent, while elderly men living on their own fell from 58 per cent in 1980 to 21 per cent in 1995. Thus, when the poverty rates fall, the experience of being poor continues to fall disproportionately on women. As Alan Walker (1992: 176) suggests, 'gender is one of the clearest lines along which the economic and social experience of old age is divided.'

The poverty of older women is not primarily a problem of aging. The high risk of poverty in older women results from the social construction of women's caregiving responsibilities, its material consequences, and the related labour market inequalities we examined earlier in this chapter. And because of the systemic nature of wage discrimination and occupational segregation, all women are affected, not only those who have depended on a male breadwinner or who have withdrawn from the labour market to provide care to family members. As Sheila Neysmith (1984: 17) observed years ago: 'Poor old women are not exotic plants that live in the special conditions of retirement—rather, poor old women are perennials, their roots are laid down in youth, their poverty merely comes into full flower in later life.'

But, unlike flowers, the poverty of older women does not fade or wilt. Autonomy, dignity, and health are all the more difficult to retain in the face of poverty. As women age, they do not cease their caring activities and simply become care receivers rather than care providers. While elderly women spend about half the amount of time that elderly men do in formal volunteer work (Statistics Canada, 1997: 119), they spend more time in informal labour. For example, women over the age of 65 spend about 25 per cent more time in household work than elderly men, and they are also more likely to provide assistance to other seniors (Statistics Canada, 1997: 92, 128).

The poverty of older women, like the poverty of single mothers, reflects the contradictions of the family ethic and the work ethic. The impact of the family ethic is most evident in the lives of elderly women, who have generally spent less time in the paid workforce than younger women. The family ethic, however, also exerts a powerful influence on middle-aged women who, even if currently employed, may well have spent earlier periods of their lives at home raising children. Many of these women will retire in poverty (Townson, 1995). And, unless the direct and indirect barriers to women's employment and wage equity disappear, today's cohort of younger women, despite employment histories that mirror those of men, will continue to carry a higher risk of poverty into their old age. The next section explores how the work ethic and the family ethic, operating through the retirement income system, play a significant role in the poverty of older women.

Income Support for the Elderly: Multiplying Inequality?

The reasons why poverty so frequently accompanies women's aging in Canada can be explored by unravelling the three tiers of the retirement income system and assessing the extent each layer contributes to, or counteracts, women's disadvantage. These tiers consist of government non-contributory benefits, publicly funded pensions, and private pensions. The first tier, government benefits, provides elderly Canadians with a basic guaranteed income that does not depend on their employment record, although it does discriminate against recent immigrants.[1] It is this tier of publicly funded income support that has caused the poverty rates among the elderly to fall so significantly.

The cornerstone age-related benefit is Old Age Security (OAS), which in September 1997 provided a monthly benefit of $405. Once a universal benefit, its actual value to seniors began to vary in 1989, when it was first considered taxable income. The federal government also administers the Guaranteed Income Supplement (GIS), an income-tested, sliding-scale monthly benefit. In 1997, the maximum GIS supplement was $314 for an individual and $628 for a couple.[2] In 1995, 39 per cent of elderly Canadians received a full or partial GIS and almost 80 per cent of single recipients are women (National Council of Welfare, 1996).

Because the OAS and GIS do not depend on employment history, this tier provides a particularly important source of income for elderly women. In 1994, these two benefits accounted for 40 per cent of the total income of elderly women, in contrast to 22 per cent of the income of elderly men (Statistics Canada, 1997: 108). In addition to the income-tested GIS, a third federal benefit discriminates according to marital status and clearly embodies the family ethic. The Spouse's Allowance is available to low-income spouses or widows (and widowers) aged 60–4 who are therefore not yet eligible for OAS in their own right. Spouse's Allowance clearly reflects the assumptions and attitudes of the family ethic and is not available to low-income men or women between 60 and 64 who have never married, those who are divorced or separated, or same-sex couples. Half of the provinces and both territories also provide income-tested benefits to the elderly that supplement the OAS and GIS.

The first layer of the retirement income system, income-tested government benefits, is considerably more important for women than for men, and is the only part of the income support system for the elderly that does not reinforce women's disadvantage. None the less, in 1995, the income of an elderly woman relying on the combined value of the OAS, GIS, and provincial supplements fell between $2,550 and $5,550 below the poverty line, depending on where she lived (National Council of Welfare, 1996). The 1996 federal budget announced that beginning in 2001, the OAS and GIS will be combined into a new Seniors Benefit that is estimated to increase benefits by a very modest $10 a month per household. Unlike the current benefits, the Seniors Benefit will be based on family rather than individual income. This is a significant departure from current practice and will mean that women who spent most of their lives as homemakers will not receive a benefit in their own right. Even women who have spent much of their lives in employment may be ineligible for the benefit, or receive a partial benefit, because of their husband's income. As Monica Townson (1996: 6) suggests, 'In an environment when we are trying to encourage women's autonomy and to protect women who must take time out of the paid work force to raise their families, the acceptability of income testing based on family income is certainly questionable.'

The second layer of income support for the elderly comprises the employment-related Canada/Quebec Pension Plan (c/QPP). Instituted in 1966, this social insurance program provides retirement, disability, and survivors' benefits and is funded entirely through employer and employee contributions. In September 1997 the maximum monthly pension payable was $737. As the benefit levels vary according to earnings and time spent in employment, they reflect and reinforce the disadvantaged position of women caused by the accumulated effects of low-wage, part-time, and discontinuous employment discussed earlier. In 1996, for example, women received CPP benefits that averaged 56 per cent of the benefits paid to men (National Council of Welfare, 1996: 26). The survivor's benefit is particularly important to married women, the majority of whom will outlive their spouses. Nine out of ten (89 per cent) recipients of the survivor's benefit are women (National Council of Welfare, 1996: 20). There is also a provision that helps to reduce women's disadvantage by allowing her to 'drop out' periods of child-rearing from the total of lifetime earnings, which is in turn used to calculate the retirement pension. There are also recent benefit-sharing and credit-splitting provisions when marriages end. Changes recently announced to CPP include increases in contributions, a slight lowering of the annual maximum benefit, more restrictive conditions for disability benefits, and a 30 per cent decrease in the one-time-only death benefit, of particular importance to elderly women. In addition, the level of income exempted from contributions, which is currently indexed, will be frozen, placing a disproportionate burden on low-income and part-time workers who will pay a greater proportion of their earnings in contributions (Prince, 1997). These changes will increase the relative importance of private pensions, the layer of the income retirement system that is least helpful to women.

Private pension schemes, the third and final layer of the retirement income system, actually magnify some of the problems identified in the public pension scheme. Women, so frequently employed in poorly paid and low-status jobs, are much less likely than men to be covered by private pensions. In 1992, for example, 43 per cent of employed women, compared to 52 per cent employed men, were covered by private pension plans (Townson, 1995: 37). Women tend to work in small businesses in retail and wholesale and in other non-unionized environments. In addition, part-time workers, disproportionately women, are much less likely than full-time employees to be covered by private pensions (Townson, 1995: 39). Private pension plans must now incorporate survivor benefits of at least 60 per cent of the benefits paid to the contributor unless both spouses waive this entitlement. Historically, the public sector was much better served by private pensions than the private sector. Given the decline in the public sector, it is very likely that private pension coverage for women will also decline.

Thus, both the public and private employment-related income benefits for the elderly serve to perpetuate into old age the inequalities that women experience throughout their lives. And the increasing number of men who are out of the labour market or employed in low-paid or unstable jobs will also benefit less from employment-related programs, a disadvantage that reflects the inequities of class. However, the interaction between class and gender places a particularly dispro-portionate burden on women. While women's entitlement to c/QPP is formally equal to men's, the consequences of the family ethic on women's employment produce significant inequities. The additional employment discrimination expe-rienced by women of colour only multiplies these inequalities. The Seniors Benefit and the changes proposed to the c/QPP will not improve the position of women. The Seniors Benefit will erode the importance of women's past contri-butions in the home and in the workplace in the determination of their future income, while announced cuts will decrease the value of the c/QPP as a public, employment-related pension. In the absence of full equity in the labour market, and in the context of economic restructuring, women must necessarily lose out in a policy direction that places increasing emphasis on private-sector pensions.

DEFEMINIZING POVERTY

This chapter has explored the connections between women's poverty and women's responsibilities for caring and examined the implications of the family ethic and the work ethic. The family ethic directly affects women's earnings by limiting their availability for paid work. The work ethic, buttressed by the fami-ly ethic, emphasizes a market-based and gender-blind 'productivity' that dis-counts the significance of women's work in the labour market and devalues its importance in the home. The relationship between the family ethic and the work ethic is reflected in social welfare policies, and this chapter has suggested how these policies, at best, fail to redress effectively women's economic vulnerability and, at worst, reinforce the poverty of single mothers and elderly women. In social assistance, policies are becoming increasingly gender-blind as single moth-ers become an important focus of workfare. In elderly benefits, the formal equal-ity in entitlement has not addressed, and cannot address, the inequities women experience in the labour market. Adequately paid work is becoming more and more critical to women's economic survival at a time when, in the global econo-my, it is more difficult to obtain. This final section considers the dilemmas and potential for change.

Feminists agree on the significance of unpaid labour in continuing women's subordination, although there is vigorous debate regarding what should be done about it. The controversy centres on whether an emphasis on sameness or differ-ence provides a better route to gender equality. At one end of the spectrum are those who fear that to acknowledge difference will further entrench the damag-ing demarcation between the public and private spheres. Those more prepared to recognize difference argue that the pursuit of a form of gender equality that requires women to live like men is no less problematic than the status quo. As Anne Phillips (1992: 222) suggests, 'feminists will continue to debate and dis-agree over how far the inequality stems from the difference, and how far the dif-ference can or should be eliminated.' Others suggest that the opposition of equality and difference is part of the problem and that their interdependence must be recognized.

Proposals for homemakers' 'pensions' and the related concept of homemakers' 'wages' and caregiver 'allowances' are put forward from time to time as a constructive way to recognize the significance and value of women's household labour. The objective of homemakers' pensions is to extend pension coverage to women while they are at home caring for dependants, thus entitling them to an improved economic position when they are older. The goal of homemakers' wages, in contrast, is to provide some type of cash payment to adults (almost always women) who are currently home with dependants (usually children). Homemakers' pensions and wages, although appealing to some, raise important dilemmas. These include the creation of inequities between women in employment who have caregiving responsibilities and those who work full-time in the home, and the favouring of one-earner families over two-earner families at the same level of income. As Jane Millar (1996: 63) points out, such proposals may increase women's independent access to income benefits but they also reduce the chances of independent income through paid work. The economic position of women will not be altered fundamentally through strategies that simply recognize the value of a woman's labour in the home but pay little attention to her position in the labour market. Similarly, her economic independence will not be secured by attending to labour market inequities without addressing the reality of the caregiving that must be accorded to children and some adults. However, equity in the allocation of caring responsibilities will require, as Sheila Neysmith outlines in Chapter 11, changes in ideology about the family ethic, a shift towards more collective values, and a more vigorous role for the state. Clearly, these are not on the near horizon, and we are immersed in a climate inflected with a renewed interest in 'family values', a shift towards individualism, and governments' commitment to deficit reduction through cuts to social expenditures. Despite the difficulties there may be in imagining increased benefits and services, it is essential to identify some directions that should be pursued, and the pitfalls to avoid, if we are to reduce the economic vulnerability of specific groups of women.

Firstly, in the absence of an equitable distribution of caregiving responsibilities and equal access to resources, it is necessary to recognize that formal models of equality are likely to be harmful to women. Their limitations were apparent in the examination of the c/QPP, which reproduces in its benefits the inequities women confront in the labour market. Similarly, the problematic ways in which women's financial and legal protections may be eroded through family law reforms intended to promote 'equal treatment' after a marriage ends are well documented (Mossman and MacLean, 1997). It is essential that changes truly operate to women's advantage. Resources are better directed towards improving child care rather than pressing for a homemakers' pension or wage, which may tend to reinforce, rather than to mitigate, women's economic disadvantage. The exclusive assignment of caring responsibilities to women is the issue, not simply whether or not payment is accorded to this work.

Secondly, policies must explicitly acknowledge women's 'complex allegiances and claims' (Lewis, 1986: 97) and maximize choices and options. In turn, this means a careful and sensitive evaluation of social policies for their impact on different individuals and different family forms. Income benefits may favour the breadwinner family or the two-earner family, and may use the individual or the family unit as the basis for claims. Canadian social welfare, in common with other liberal welfare states, relies heavily on the breadwinner model of the family, which assumes that the father provides economic support to his family and that the mother is available to provide care to family members. We saw this most clearly in operation of the 'man in the house' rule, which dictates that a single mother can be on social assistance only as long as she does not live with a man. Social policies based on the breadwinner model will reinforce women's economic dependency. The changes planned for the Seniors Benefit, transforming it from an individual to a family-based income-tested benefit, will undercut some of the improvements that might have been anticipated from the increasing prominence of employment in the lives of younger, married women. Without accompanying changes, however, entitlements based on individual claims will not alleviate poverty among older women, as the discussion of the c/QPP illustrated. And there are class implications in such a policy direction. Individual entitlements that favour the two-earner family conflict with the goal of income redistribution.

Thirdly, it is important to assert the claims of women to paid employment, but we must also recognize that equity in the workplace must be accompanied by efforts to make work in the labour market and caring labour more compatible. This entails employers accepting that many of their employees (women and men) have caring responsibilities for others; as well, the state must be seen to have a critical part in the active sharing of care. As Evelyn Ferguson's chapter illustrates, Canadian social policies have recognized relatively little responsibility for child care. Avoiding public responsibility for the caring work done by women in families constructs the problem as 'private troubles', advantaging families with resources to purchase child care. Maternity leave provisions and the 10 weeks of parental leave available under Employment Insurance are, in comparison to most European countries, characterized by limited coverage, the low level of earnings replacement, and a relatively short duration of benefits (Baker, 1995).

Sweden's approach to women's employment and child care provides perhaps the most attractive existing model that has 'constructed a distinctive equal opportunity strategy by grafting the right to make a claim on the basis of difference onto a policy based on equal treatment' (Lewis and Åström, 1992). In their efforts to attract women into the labour market in the early 1960s, the Swedish government recognized the need to make paid work more compatible with women's child-care responsibilities. The resulting policies include a generous and flexible parental leave policy and a universal and heavily subsidized child-care system that reflects Sweden's rejection of the view that the care of young children is largely a private and family responsibility. But it is still overwhelmingly mothers who take advantage of parental leave and there is a shortage of child-care spaces, making it more difficult for women to opt for remaining in employment. Although the Swedish model has created significant improvements for women, Lewis and Åström (1992: 61) suggest that it also represents a 'cautionary tale' because women remain entrenched as the primary carers and, despite a very narrow wage gap between men and women, the labour market remains highly segregated, partly because of these policies. In addition, it has not been particularly successful in changing assumptions of the 'good' employee or the profile of what constitutes a career path. Although interruptions in employment histories are legally protected and compensated generously, the ideal of the traditional full-time-plus commitment to work remains intact and those using these hard-fought-for policies suffer in comparison to those who do not have to use them.

In the Canadian context, the immediate struggle may have less to do with expanding services and benefits than with being more focused on the protection of what we have and on vigorous opposition to the cutbacks to the public services that provide women with an important source of employment and an important resource for child care and elder care. These services, after all, make paid work possible. Pragmatically, this suggests the importance of child care, although its limits must be situated in a political and economic context. As Schellenberg and Ross (1997: 14) suggest, women's labour market poverty 'is not simply an issue of access to the paid labour force that can be neatly resolved by providing women with affordable child care. It is also an issue of how labour market activity—and consequently, paid or "socially useful" activity—gets defined.'

In the light of the global economy, strategies for full employment become only more critical, albeit more difficult, to advance. The dramatic cuts imposed by the neo-conservative agenda have also accentuated the significance of race and class, placing women of colour and those who are poor in double and triple jeopardy. The reassertion of the importance of class in a retrenched political economy and the continuing force of systemic racism also serve as reminders of the important common interests held by a wide variety of social movements. There are no easy solutions to resolving the problems of women's (and men's) economic vulnerability and marginalization, but the costs of failing to do so have never been higher.

NOTES

1. The 1996 budget contained eligibility restrictions. New immigrants do not qualify for full benefits until they have lived in Canada for 10 years.
2. The cut-off level for eligibility for a partial GIS benefit in September 1997 was a monthly income of $1,368 for an individual and $2,065 for a couple.

REFERENCES

Abramovitz, M. 1988. *Regulating the Lives of Women: Social Welfare Policy from Colonial Times to the Present.* Boston: South End Press.

Abramovitz, M. 1996. *Under Attack, Fighting Back: Women and Welfare in the United States.* New York: Monthly Review Press.

Adams, I., W. Cameron, B. Hill, and P. Penz. 1971. *The Real Poverty Report.* Edmonton: Hurtig.

Akyeampong, E. 1995. 'Missing Work', *Perspectives* 7, 1 (Spring): 12–15.

Armstrong, P. 1996. 'The Feminization of the Labour Force: Harmonizing Down in a Global Economy', in I. Bakker, ed., *Rethinking Restructuring: Gender and Change in Canada.* Toronto: University of Toronto Press: 29–54.

Armstrong, P., and H. Armstrong. 1990. *Theorizing Women's Work.* Toronto: Garamond.

Baker, M. 1995. *Canadian Family Policies: Cross-National Comparisons.* Toronto: University of Toronto Press.

Bancroft, W., and S. Vernon. 1995. *The Struggle for Self-Sufficiency: Participants in the Self-Sufficiency Project Talk About Work, Welfare, and Their Futures.* Vancouver: Social Research and Demonstration Corporation, Dec.

Barrett, G. 1994. 'The Duration of Income Assistance Spells in British Columbia', Department of Economics, University of British Columbia.

Buchanan, R. 1995. 'The Flexible Woman: Gendered Implications of Post-Fordist Narratives', Feminism and the Law Workshop Series, Faculty of Law, University of Toronto, 8 Nov.

Canada. 1970. *Royal Commission on the Status of Women in Canada.* Ottawa: Information Canada.

Canadian Labour Market and Productivity Centre (CLMPC). 1990. *Report of the CLMPC Task Forces on the Labour Force Development Strategy.* Ottawa: CLMPC.

Daily Bread Food Bank. 1989. 'The Kids are Hungry', Toronto: Daily Bread Food Bank.

Das Gupta, T. 1996. *Racism and Paid Work.* Toronto: Garamond.

Dooley, M. 1995. 'Lone-Mother Families in Canada and Social Assistance', in M. Dooley, R. Finnie, S. Phipps, and N. Naylor, *Families Matter: New Policies for Divorce, Lone Mothers, and Child Poverty.* Toronto: C.D. Howe Institute: 35–104.

Evans, P. 1987. 'A Decade of Change: The FBA Caseload, 1975–1986', report prepared for the Ontario Social Assistance Review Committee, June.

Evans, P. 1995a. 'Linking Welfare to Jobs: Workfare, Canadian Style', in P. Evans, L. Jacobs, A. Noël, and E. Reynolds, *Workfare: Does It Work? Is It Fair?* Montreal: Institute for Research on Public Policy: 75–104.

Evans, P. 1995b. 'Single Mothers and Ontario's Welfare Policy: Restructuring the Debate', in J. Brodie, ed., *Women and Canadian Public Policy.* Toronto: Harcourt Brace: 151–71.

Evans, P. 1997. 'Divided Citizenship? Gender, Income Security, and the Welfare State', in P. Evans and G. Wekerle, *Women and the Canadian Welfare State: Challenges and Change.* Toronto: Unviversity of Toronto Press: 91–116.

Gorlick, C. 1995. *Taking Chances: Single Mothers and Their Children Exiting Welfare.* Ottawa: National Welfare Grants, Human Resources Development.

Graham, H. 1987. 'Women's Poverty and Caring', in C. Glendenning and J. Millar, eds, *Women and Poverty in Britain.* Brighton: Wheatsheaf: 221–40.

Gunderson, M., and L. Muszynski, with J. Keck. 1990. *Women and Labour Market Poverty.* Ottawa: Canadian Advisory Council on the Status of Women.

Henry, F. 1994. *Caribbean Diaspora in Toronto: Learning to Live with Racism*. Toronto: University of Toronto Press.

Jenson, J. 1996. 'Part-time Employment and Women: A Range of Strategies', in I. Bakker, ed., *Rethinking Restructuring: Gender and Change in Canada*. Toronto: University of Toronto Press: 92–108.

Kauppi, C., and M. Reitsma-Street. 1996. 'Women and Poverty in Northern Ontario', in M. Ketchnie and M. Reitsma-Street, eds, *Changing Lives: Women in Northern Ontario*. Toronto: Dundurn Press.

Kemp, A. 1994. *Women's Work: Degraded and Devalued*. Englewood Cliffs, NJ: Prentice-Hall.

Kierstead, W. 1925. 'Mother's Allowances in Canada', *Canadian Congress Journal* 4, 7 (July): 27–9; 4, 8 (Aug.): 21–3.

Lewis, J. 1986. 'Feminism and Welfare', in J. Mitchell and A. Oakley, eds, *What is Feminism? A Re-examination*. New York: Pantheon.

Lewis, J., and G. Åström. 1992. 'Equality, Difference, and State Welfare: Labor Market and Family Policies in Sweden', *Feminist Studies* 18, 1: 59–87.

Lindsay, C. 1992. 'Lone-Parent Families in Canada', Target Groups Project. Statistics Canada: Minister of Industry, Science and Technology, cat. 89–522E, Dec.

Lipovenko, D. 1997. 'Caregiving taking toll, survey finds', *Globe and Mail*, 20 Aug.

Luxton, M., and E. Reiter. 1997. 'Double, Double, Toil and Trouble . . . Women's Experience of Work and the Family in Canada, 1980–1995', in P. Evans and G. Wekerle, *Women and the Canadian Welfare State: Challenges and Change*. Toronto: University of Toronto Press: 197–221.

Millar, J. 1996. 'Women, Poverty and Social Security', in C. Hallett, ed., *Women and Social Policy*. Hertfordshire: Harvester Wheatsheaf: 52–64.

Mossman, M., and M. MacLean. 1997. 'Family Law and Social Assistance Programs: Rethinking Equality', in P. Evans and G. Wekerle, *Women and the Canadian Welfare State: Challenges and Change*. Toronto: University of Toronto Press: 117–41.

National Council of Welfare. 1990. *Women and Poverty Revisited*. Ottawa: NCW, Summer.

National Council of Welfare. 1996. *A Pension Primer*. Ottawa: NCW, Summer.

National Council of Welfare. 1997. *Poverty Profile 1995*. Ottawa: NCW, Spring.

Neysmith, S. 1984. 'Poverty in Old Age: Can Pension Reform Meet the Needs of Women?', *Canadian Woman Studies* 5, 3 (Spring): 17–21.

Ontario Ministry of Community and Social Services. 1984. 'One-Stop Service'. Report of the Joint Steering Committee. Toronto: Publications Ontario.

Ontario Ministry of Community and Social Services. 1988. *Transitions*. Report of the Social Assistance Review Committee. Toronto: Publications Ontario.

Ontario Social Safety Network. 1997. *Reality Cheque: Telling Our Stories of Life on Welfare in Ontario*. Toronto: Ontario Social Safety Network.

Ornstein, M. 1995. *A Profile of Social Assistance Recipients in Ontario*. Toronto: Institute for Social Research, York University, June.

Phillips, A. 1992. 'Feminism, Equality and Difference', in L. McDowell and R. Pringle, eds, *Defining Women: Social Institutions and Gender Divisions*. Cambridge: Polity Press: 205–22.

Phillips, P., and E. Phillips. 1993. *Women and Work: Inequality in the Canadian Labour Market*, 2nd edn. Toronto: James Lorimer.

Prince, M. 1997. 'Lowering the Boom on the Boomers: Replacing Old Age Security with the New Seniors Benefit and Reforming the Canada Pension Plan', in G. Swimmer, ed., *How Ottawa Spends: 1997–98*. Ottawa: Carleton University Press: 211–34.

Pupo, N. 1997. 'Always Working, Never Done: The Expansion of the Double Day', in A. Duffy, D. Glenday, and N. Pupo, eds, *Good Jobs, Bad Jobs, No Jobs: The Transformation of Work in the 21st Century*. Toronto: Harcourt Brace: 144–65.

Roseneil, S., and K. Mann. 1996. 'Unpalatable Choices and Inadequate Families: Lone Mothers and the Underclass Debate', in E. Silva, ed., *Good Enough Mothering? Feminist Perspectives on Lone Motherhood*. New York: Routledge: 191–210.

Ross, D., R. Shillington, and C. Lochhead. 1994. *Canadian Fact Book on Poverty*. Ottawa: Canadian Council on Social Development.

Schellenberg, G., and D. Ross. 1997. *Left Poor by the Market: A Look at Family Poverty and Earnings*. Ottawa: Canadian Council on Social Development.

Scott, K. 1996. 'The Dilemma of Liberal Citizenship: Women and Social Assistance Reform in the 1990s', *Studies in Political Economy* 50 (Summer): 7–36.

Silva, E. 1996. 'The Transformation of Mothering', in E. Silva, ed., *Good Enough Mothering? Feminist Perspectives on Lone Motherhood*. New York: Routledge: 10–36.

Statistics Canada. 1995. *Women in Canada: A Statistical Report*, 3rd edn. Ottawa: Minister of Industry, Aug. 1995.

Statistics Canada. 1997. *A Portrait of Seniors in Canada*, 2nd edn, cat. no. 89–519–XPE. Ottawa: Minister of Industry, Feb.

Townson, M. 1995. *Women's Financial Futures: Mid-Life Prospects for a Secure Retirement*. Ottawa: Canadian Advisory Council on the Status of Women, Apr.

Townson, M. 1996. *Our Aging Society: Preserving retirement incomes into the 21st Century*. Ottawa: Canadian Centre for Policy Alternatives, Jan.

Walker, A. 1992. 'The Poor Relation: Poverty Among Older Women', in C. Glendinning and J. Millar, eds, *Women and Poverty in Britain: The 1990s*. New York: Harvester Wheatsheaf: 176–92.

4

Caring and Women of Colour:
Living the Intersecting Oppressions of Race, Class, and Gender

Usha George

Discussions of caring rarely appear in the literature on women of colour. In an annotated bibliography of research on South Asian women from 1972 to 1992 (Naidoo, 1994) I found no reference to caring. Historically, the absence of scholarly interest in how caring affects the lives of women of colour can be attributed to both practical concerns and theoretical issues. At a practical level, the immediate settlement and adaptation needs of immigrant women of colour directed research and programming priorities to issues of employment, housing, language training, and access to health and community services. Theories of immigrant adaptation and ethnic identity in the context of multicultural Canada have framed much of this work. More recently, major discourses in race/ethnicity, class, and gender have also focused attention on structural inequalities that define the lives of most immigrant women and limit their participation in Canadian society. Women's unpaid labour within their homes and communities has received very little systematic attention.

The absence of discourse, however, does not mean that caring is not an issue for women of colour. In many of the informal discussions women have among themselves, caring surfaces as an important aspect of their new lives in Canada. For some women, caring assumes new dimensions that are made visible as they are no longer able to afford the household help that was available in their home countries. For others, the double days of paid and unpaid work are a continuation of earlier patterns with the added strain of surviving in a foreign country. These discussions reveal important class, racial, and gender disparities that shape the lives of immigrant women as well as women in other segments of Canadian society. In the following section, I argue that the absence of caring in theory and policy is influenced by two factors: a normative context that limits public discussions on caring and confines it to the private realm; and the fear of what is called cultural racism.

The normative context refers to the prevailing cultural ideals about women's roles and responsibilities. For example, in the South Asian community, the normative context includes the fear of public scorn that follows a woman who is not perceived as a good wife, mother, and daughter-in-law, as well as housekeeper and hostess. The label 'too westernized' is often used to refer to women who choose to ignore cultural prescriptions, and is used in a pejorative way. Thus, many women are reluctant to enter into public debates about the distribution of caring responsibilities in their communities. None the less, as issues of wife abuse and elder abuse are made visible by women of colour, a discussion of the burdens and benefits of caring may develop that will highlight the experiences of South Asian women.

Stereotyping by the dominant culture, or cultural racism, is a genuine fear in the consciousness of most women of colour, who know they are minorities in a predominantly White society. Cultural racism promotes an image of difference that, while no longer assumed to be rooted in biological characteristics, is contained in dominant and pervasive negative images about the language, religion, traditions, and ethnic origin of 'minority' groups (Wieviorka, 1997). Cultural racism has several dimensions: (1) it denies to those who believe in the uniqueness of their cultural heritage a language in which to give expression to ethnicity; (2) it rejects the possibility that a community can express its unique identity 'within a public discourse of equality and civic integration' (Modood, 1997: 158); and (3) it blocks the exploration and discussion of ethnicity 'while seeking, at the same time, to oppose racist stereotyping and public expression of contempt, as well as right-wing "culturalist" constructions of identity' (Modood, 1997: 158).

In this chapter, I present the intersecting oppressions of race, gender, and class as a framework for understanding how caring is experienced by women of colour. The chapter is divided into four sections: the first section reviews current theoretical attempts at explicating relationships among race/ethnicity, class, and gender. These analyses highlight the way in which 'immigrant', 'visible minority', and 'women of colour' are constructs of the Canadian state. I argue that such labels are a racist society's attempt to deal with difference. The second section examines the experience of caring among immigrant women of colour. The third section explores South Asian family structures and the demands placed on women and their caring labour. The chapter concludes with a discussion of the policy context and directions for research as women of colour try to balance the challenges of paid and unpaid labour in Canada.

IMMIGRANT, VISIBLE MINORITY WOMEN, AND WOMEN OF COLOUR AS SOCIAL CATEGORIES OF RACE

Who is a woman of colour? The delineation of women of colour in Canada is both a social and political process (Ng, 1991b; Ralston, 1988; Szekely, 1990; Bannerji, 1993; Estable and Meyer, 1989). In theory, the term 'immigrant women' embraces every woman born outside Canada. In practice, however, it refers to women of colour, women from Third World countries, and women who do not speak English (Ng and Estable, 1987: 11). The label 'immigrant woman' is applied to women of colour regardless of whether or not they have been born in Canada (Szekely, 1990). The terms 'ethnic' and 'immigrant' are also used interchangeably (Ng, 1996). The Canadian state has had a major role in defining 'immigrant' and 'visible minority women'. Carty and Brand (1993) and Leah (1995) argue that they prefer the term 'women of colour' because it moves beyond skin colour and emphasizes a common experience of systemic discrimination. As such, the term captures the essence of being non-White and minority (Leah, 1995).

Race refers to a socially constructed hierarchical division of people based on phenotypical characteristics (Henry, 1995; James, 1996). In contrast, the most common indicators for ethnicity are descent, common cultural values and customs, common religion, and a shared feeling of belonging to the same group (Isajiw, 1974). In this chapter, however, like Ng, I use race and ethnicity interchangeably to 'draw attention to their socially, ideologically and politically constructed character' (Ng, 1996: 14). Race and ethnicity are extremely complex constructs both in substantive content and in their ideological implications.

Canadian conceptualizations of the intersecting relationships among race/ethnicity, class, and gender recognize the multiple identities and oppressions experienced by women of colour (Szekely, 1990; Bannerji, 1993; Ng, 1991a, 1995b; Calliste, Dei, and Belkhir, 1995; Leah, 1995; Agnew, 1996; Das Gupta, 1996). Common to all is a conception of the social construction of race/ethnicity, class, and gender, which is created and changed through changes in the relations of production.

Citing the efforts of feminists such as Juteau-Lee and Roberts (1981), Ng (1995) argues that gender, race/ethnicity, and class are three different, yet overlapping systems of domination. She calls for a different conceptualization, one that treats these 'as *social* relations which have to do with how people relate to each other through productive and reproductive activities (Ng, 1991b: 16). She points out that class and ethnic relations are constituted from a need for domination and control, which in Canada is prompted by a capitalistic system and neo-colonial immigration policies. Bannerji (1996) adds that any attempt to understand the intersecting effects of sexism, classism, and racism in Canada must be set in the historical context of a nation where English-French relations are the central defining discourse, where both Aboriginal rights and policies of multiculturalism are seen as marginal because they focus on 'others' outside of these dominant groups.

Calliste, Dei, and Belkhir (1995) and Dei (1995), as well as Leah (1995), outline a clearly Canadian attempt to integrate race, gender, and class within mainstream academic discourses across disciplines. In what is called 'integrative antiracism', incorporating a multicentric and holistic understanding of human experience, this approach argues for the centrality of race in the exploration of the relational aspects of social differences. Race becomes a *point of entry* through which other intersecting forms of oppressions, such as class, gender, and sexual orientation, are examined. In this framework, racism is about power wherein skin colour becomes the identifier in hegemonic evaluations of human differences (Dei, 1995).

Whichever label is used, immigrant women, women of colour, and visible minority women are not homogeneous categories, and they reflect diverse cultural, linguistic, and religious backgrounds. They may include women who are Chinese, African, South Asian, Caribbean, Latin American, Southeast Asian, and Korean. They come from countries with different resource bases and different historical and contemporary experiences with slavery, colonialism, neo-colonialism, capitalism, and democracy.

This diversity of origins makes terms such as 'South Asian' problematic (Ralston, 1988, 1991), as South Asians come from India, Pakistan, Bangladesh, and Sri Lanka, as well as from Africa and the Caribbean, and all have distinct identities. India, for example, has 18 different languages and many different religions, such as Hinduism, Christianity, Islam, Zoroastrianism, Buddhism, Jainism, and Parsi. It seems virtually impossible to capture commonalities among these groups (Naidoo, 1985a; Agnew, 1996). None the less, it could be argued that the common experience of colonialism, life in the same region in Asia, and cultural similarities outweigh their differences and provide a common basis for understanding the experiences of these women in Canada (Das Gupta, 1994). Women of colour are automatically assigned immigrant and minority status because of their skin colour. Ethnicity, as an indicator of class (Cassin and Griffith, 1981), along with culturally ascribed gender role expectations generate intersecting and multilayered oppressions in the lives of women of colour (Szekely, 1990; Dua, 1992; Ralston, 1988, 1991; Das Gupta, 1994, 1996; Agnew, 1996).

As mentioned earlier, theory and research on women of colour focus mostly on race/ethnicity, gender, and class in the context of structural factors, and 'the family', as an institution of oppressive social relationships, has generally escaped critical scrutiny. In fact, mainstream feminist perspectives on the family as a site of patriarchal oppression have been challenged by many women of colour. In Canada, much of the research on caring and women of colour was done outside the family, in the caring professions. For example, Head's (1986) study of discrimination in the nursing profession and Calliste's study of the immigration of Caribbean nurses to Canada (1993) focused on nursing as a caring profession in the public sphere. In Chapter 10, McWatt and Neysmith examine the experiences of nannies who care for children who are not their own. These observations are not to claim that one area of research is superior to the other, but rather to point out that concepts and research change their name and location when the entry point is race.

CARING AND WOMEN OF COLOUR: NORMATIVE CONTEXTS AND IMMIGRANT EXPERIENCES

In spite of rejecting cultural explanations of immigrant behaviour, we must recognize the value placed on caring and the motivations for caring among communities of colour. Most studies on the normative context of family/kin caring come from outside Canada. Deeply entrenched values, usually shaped by religion, are at the core of the normative context of caring. While it can be argued that many of these values are shared with White mainstream society, the overwhelming support for and justifications of these values, based on cultural and religious norms, distinguish the context of caring in communities of colour.

For example, when caregivers in Korea were asked to list their motivation for caregiving, responses fell into nine categories (Sung, 1994): respect for parent, filial responsibility, care with sacrifice, filial sympathy, harmonization of family, compensation for unaccomplished family matters, desire to repay, religious belief, love for parent, and other forms of filial motivation. The values of filial piety and multigenerational cohabitation provide the moral basis for family-centred parent care in Korea (Sung, 1991). Sung (1990) identified four salient motives for the practice of filial piety: respect, responsibility, harmonizing family, and sacrifice. Filial piety can be seen as a form of recognition of what parents gave during the years they were bringing up their children. Thus, among Korean families in the United States, intergenerational relations remain very strong long after immigration. Not surprisingly, the preferred source of help in dealing with anticipated problems among older people was one's spouse or children (Koh and Bell, 1987). The influence of Confucianism in Asian cultures, with its emphasis on filial piety and the importance of the individual in relation to others (Yee, 1992), is undoubtedly a major factor in maintaining the strength of these norms.

The ideals of co-operation and family loyalty, which require that family obligations take precedence over personal interests, are basic to all South Asian communities. These generate strong emotional bonds and an acute sense of interdependence among parents, siblings, and children (Shaw in Elliot, 1996; Gannon, 1994). The concepts of karma (destiny) and dharma (duty), which are fundamental to Hinduism, are essential to understanding Asian Indian families, whether they are Hindu, Muslim, or Sikh (Almeida, 1996). People from India, Pakistan, Bangladesh, and Sri Lanka belong to these religions. The Hindu belief in the cycle of life, transmigration of souls, and reincarnation emphasizes that each person is judged on the basis of his/her accumulated bad and good deeds (Gannon, 1994; Welty, 1970). Miller (1994) suggests that the concept of dharma in Hindu religion is inextricably connected to the view of self. Dharma denotes moral duty, code of conduct, right action, and inherent character. Miller's research among Hindu Indians in the United States reveals a duty-based interpersonal moral code as opposed to the individual-based moral code of Americans. For example, the values that South Asian women model for their children are: respect, tolerance, sharing, and helping (Naidoo, 1985a). In fact, Naidoo's study (1985b) of religion and ethnicity among South Asians concluded that feelings of respect for older people were cultural rather than religious. Such research is important not only for understanding the changing context of caring in the lives of South Asian women but because these types of studies highlight how the ethics of care and ethics of justice debate referred to in Chapter 1 of this volume are culturally bound.

The distinction between individually oriented and duty-based moral codes parallels the distinction between individualistic and collectivistic cultures. The duty-based moral code found among Indians may also be found among other cultures with collectivist orientations. For example, various researchers have shown that an emphasis on helpfulness and obligations to kin is found among Hong Kong and mainland Chinese, Tibetan Buddhist monks, Nigerian and Pakistani Muslims, and rural populations in Honduras, Kenya, and Papua New Guinea. Similar to Hindu Indians, Chinese populations also treat interpersonal responsibilities as natural, with the Confucian concept of *jen* depicting love and benevolence as innate (Miller, 1994). Similar value systems, albeit from different sources, exist among Blacks, Hispanics, and Salvadorans in the United States

(Cox and Monk, 1990; Gelfand, 1989). Black and Hispanic families in the US express filial obligations and motivations as their underlying value for caring (Cox and Monk, 1990). Regardless of changes in their lives due to immigration, older Salvadoran refugees continue to believe in filial responsibility. In a study of Hispanic families in the US there was unanimous agreement that it was the responsibility of children to provide care and support to parents in their old age (Gelfand, 1989). In a Toronto study, women from five ethnocultural communities (Spanish-speaking, Afghan, Somali, South Asian, and Caribbean) indicated that caring for aged parents must be provided by the family, whereas 'mainstream women' saw a need for state provision of care (Weber, 1994):

> They should be looked after with great love. They should enjoy the care and assistance they need. They should be looked after by their own children; not by nurses, senior's centres or homes for the elderly and sick. (words of an Afghan woman, Weber, 1994: 96)

> They have done their part and deserve respect. It takes a lot of patience but the old start by looking after the young and the young look after the old later on. It is the natural law of life and looking after the elderly is part of our culture. (words of a Caribbean woman, Weber 1994: 96)

However, it is important to recognize that disjunctures exist between normative contexts and practical experiences. Cultural beliefs and actual supportive behaviour need not be congruent (Rosenthal, 1986). In spite of the publicly acclaimed value given to caring, such obligations are demanding for many immigrant women. Concepts such as 'women in the middle' (Weber, 1994) and 'sandwich generation' never adequately captured the experiences of immigrant women. Immigration is stressful and immigrant families face a multitude of problems in their settlement process. Finding jobs, housing, coping with children in the new surroundings, adapting to a new culture, to name but a few pressures, are tremendous burdens on newcomers. Multigenerational living arrangements are sought to avoid financial problems. Yet the women in these households are expected to do the housework, the child care, and the servicing of family members.

In a study of immigrant women who have young children at home and are primary caregivers for elderly relatives sharing the same household, Slonim-Nevo et al. (1995) concluded that caregiver strain in such three-generation situations seemed to result from a combination of both universal and immigrant-specific components. The four variables they found that related to caregiver strain were: the health condition of the elderly person, the amount of care provided by caretakers, the psychological condition of the children in the family, and length of time since arrival to the new country. Moreover, in multigenerational families, there were tensions around issues of control of children and the authority of older parents. Women's relationships within and outside of their families suffered as a result of caregiving responsibilities. While some used formal care such as respite services, nursing homes were seen as totally inappropriate because of the stigma attached to them.

Gelfand and McCallum's (1994) study of caregiving in seven major ethnic groups (Croats, Greeks, Jews, Italians, Lebanese, Turks, and Vietnamese) that migrated to Australia seems to capture the contradictions that immigrant women face. Studies reveal the importance of both culture and immigration, but across groups, caregiving is mainly the responsibility of women; husbands played only limited roles. Ethnic women in Toronto also point out that it is they who become the caregivers. Men are only marginally involved in the daily provision of care (Weber, 1994). Immigrant women share the gendered experience of caring with other groups of Canadian women. However, as the following section highlights, the resulting demands on women's caring labour vary by their social location.

CARING AND SOUTH ASIAN WOMEN IN CANADA

In this section, I discuss the family structures and patterns of caring that exist within the South Asian community in Canada, the community with which I am most familiar. No study has been done specifically on caring. However, by bringing together the literature and my own understanding, I will try to draw out the ways in which the interconnecting dynamics of race, gender, and class shape the issues of caring for South Asian women. This mode of analysis moves away from monocausal explanations that disaggregate the effects of race from those of gender and class, or treat them as additive rather than interactive. 'It recognizes not only that women's experience is specific to their class, ethnic, and "racial" positions in particular historical periods, but that women, because they are located in a range of social divisions, have a range of identities' (Elliot, 1996: 72).

The realities of caring in the lives of South Asian women cannot be understood outside of an analysis of the immigration experience that positions them as women of colour. Within this new location a value system, which is almost prescriptive in the caring mandate it assigns to women, where family is the locus of personal attachments, and where caring is a holistic, lifelong activity, takes on dimensions that were not so costly to women in their country of origin.

Asian gender and family structures, even though highly differentiated due to language, cultural, and religious variations, have certain underlying similarities (Elliot, 1996). In the 1950s and 1960s, the ideal rural South Asian family was characterized by patrilineality, three-generation patriarchal households, and hierarchical ordering of relationships between genders and within/between generations (Ballard in Elliot, 1996). Even though many changes have occurred in family structures due to immigration, South Asian family structures in the new world are characterized by both change and continuity. For example, in the United Kingdom, where there are large numbers of South Asian immigrants, identification with various elements of Asian life, such as collectivism, the strength of religious traditions, and the integrity of Asian cultures, over the years has preserved and perpetuated traditions along with changes prompted by new ways of life (Ballard in Elliot, 1996: 50).

In Canada, there are also indications that old and new co-exist in terms of cultural values, practices, and family patterns (Ames and Inglis, 1976; Adams, 1977;

Chekki, 1988; Naidoo, 1992; Ralston, 1988, 1991; Das Gupta, 1994). For example, children are encouraged to be competitive to obtain a university education that can open up possibilities for good jobs in the Canadian labour market, but they are expected to uphold and practise traditional South Asian values of filial and family obligations.

The value system of the South Asian community in relation to family and gender is characterized by a strong sense of community, dense social networks, and an emphasis on familial relations (Das Gupta, 1994; Ralston, 1991). Selflessness, deference, service (Gannon, 1994; Welty, 1970), respect, tolerance, obligation, duty, sacrifice, and compromise (Filteau, 1980) are held in high esteem. Traditional patriarchal notions assign supportive and sustaining functions to women (Gill, 1995). Caring is seen as part of a woman's ethical and moral self that is devoted to the larger family group (Khosla, 1981). Generally, marriage is for life. Hindu marriage emphasizes identity, not equality, and a woman's role is to continue the chain of life—there is pride in the roles of wife and mother (Gannon, 1994). Indian family structure supports the privileged treatment of men (Dhruvarajan, 1992; Gannon, 1994) and gender ideology dictates that men are to be looked after by women (Ralston, 1988, 1991).

For South Asian women, and perhaps for most women of colour, caring is a lifelong activity. Throughout their lives women will care for family members. As young girls growing up, they fill in for their mothers. As wives, they are expected to provide care not only for their husbands but also for their in-laws and even members of the extended family. Men may assist when the care receivers are their fathers. Women's caring responsibilities increase once they have children. Even when the children become adults, women still perform caring tasks for them; in fact, caring is an essential ingredient of motherhood. Most adult women live with their parents until marriage—to move out before marriage would reflect negatively on the women in the family. When children get married, daughters follow their husbands; sons may stay in the same household. When grandchildren are born, caring for them by older women is routine. Women's participation in the labour force, and any volunteer commitments they may have, in no way reduces the foregoing expectations. Many of the volunteer tasks women take on in cultural or religious organizations revolve around various caring tasks. Even when their class status allows them the privilege of help in the house, overall responsibility for caring rests with women. In all, culturally defined gender roles dictate the nature and content of women's caring labour.

The persistence and change in South Asian women's patterns of caregiving described above cannot be separated from their experiences as immigrants to Canada. The racialized, gendered, and capitalistic structures of Canadian society exacerbate pressures of everyday living. The process of immigration has been, and continues to be, a stressful experience for most South Asian women (Ralston, 1988, 1991; Das Gupta, 1994; George and Ramkissoon, 1998). Early immigration policy was clearly discriminatory in terms of race/ethnicity and gender (Bolaria and Li, 1988). South Asian women were not allowed to accompany their husbands to Canada until 1919. Even after that, there was considerable discrimination in immigration processing, as it was stipulated that people of 'non-assim-ilative race' should not be allowed to immigrate to Canada (Matas, 1996). Post-World War II immigration policy saw a considerable change in formal and prac-tical access to rights and privileges by South Asians (Buchignani, 1979). The immigration process introduced in 1976, which distinguishes between family class and economic class immigrants and refugees, has resulted in more equitable treatment for South Asians.

At the time of the 1991 census (1996 census data on ethnicity are not avail-able at the time of writing), there were 543,000 South Asians in Canada. This makes them, along with Chinese (666,000) and Blacks (540,000), one of the three largest minority ethnic groups in Canada. There is an expected increase of 110 per cent between 1991 and 2001 (Metropolitan Toronto Planning Division, 1995). Statistics Canada (1996) has projected, on the basis of medium-growth assumptions, that by the year 2000 there will be over 470,000 South Asians liv-ing in Ontario alone, accounting for 8 per cent of the population of that province.

Most South Asian women enter Canada via the family class category, which allows spouses, unmarried siblings, and parents to join the 'head of the family'. 'Canadian returned' bachelors enjoy high prestige in their countries of origin, and therefore these men are able to enter into arranged marriages with women from upper-class families in their home countries (Ralston, 1988, 1991). Under the point system for economic class immigration, applicants are selected from 'among the skilled, educated, resourceful and heavily anglicized middle class' (Buchignani, 1979: 56). Thus, a high proportion of the South Asian women who enter Canada, in either the economic or family class categories, have upper-class origins. However, as discussed earlier, because of the social construction of immi-grant and visible minority women, most of these women are 'reassigned' in terms of their class position as they enter a highly racialized and gendered labour mar-ket (Szekely, 1990). For most South Asian immigrant women, getting a paid job or generating an income is essential for the sustenance of their families. However, their class of origin does not provide them with any security in the Canadian social structure.

South Asian women's experiences in the Canadian labour market are mediat-ed by cultural imperialism, racism, and gender oppressions (Aggarwal, 1987, 1990; Khosla, 1983; Rajagopal, 1988; Dhruvarajan, 1992; Das Gupta, 1996). Barriers to participation in the labour market include the existence of negative stereotypes in many workplaces about women of colour, as well as refusals to rec-ognize educational qualifications obtained outside of North America. These bar-riers have the effect of relegating South Asian women to employment positions considerably beneath their qualifications and abilities. Many women who are successful in obtaining employment outside the home find themselves the sole breadwinners because their men have not been able to obtain jobs (Cassin, 1979; Gill, 1995). There is, however, no subsequent reduction in caring responsibilities. Rather, these women shoulder the double burden of being sole breadwinners and primary caregivers. The transfer of gender myths from the home culture to domestic life in Canada is very pervasive (Ralston, 1988, 1991).

At the same time, however, South Asian women experience new forms of patriarchal relations. Not only are jobs dominated by deference to men's needs, but traditional gender norms ensure that men are unchallenged by South Asian women in Canada. Bhachu (1991) argues that South Asian women create their own reality in the context of their new experiences. There are also indications of changes in values held by South Asian women in Canada (Naidoo, 1988). Guzder (1992), Mangalam (1985), and Qureshi (1980), for example, highlight the tensions arising from significant value shifts by South Asian women in Canada. 'Burden of care' is a topic of discussion at informal gatherings of South Asian women, and in many cases this has a therapeutic effect on women experiencing high stress levels. There is also evidence that the traditional patterns of elder care in India are eroding (Desai and Bhalla, 1978). Massive changes that accompany industrialization and modernization have not been favourable to aged persons' expectations of care. Young people may pay lip service to traditional values of deference to old people but the practice is often far from the reality (Desai and Bhalla, 1978). Although the next generation will see increasing numbers of elderly South Asians moving into independent households, this is likely to be limited in the foreseeable future, as most elderly immigrants do not have the financial means to establish separate residences.

RESEARCH AND POLICY CONTEXT IN CANADA: EXCLUSIONARY OR INCLUSIVE?

As suggested at the beginning of this chapter, the caring experiences of women of colour have received little attention in research. The overlap of domestic responsibilities, labour market experiences, and changes and continuity in obligation and task performance need more thorough scrutiny. In South Asian communities, caring is seen as a very private and highly gendered activity, a family matter to be handled with great discretion. Women of colour generally have not articulated the stresses they undergo as a result of the caring and domestic responsibilities they carry as they try to balance the demands on their paid and unpaid labour. Nevertheless, it is safe to predict that the focus of future research, the questions asked, and the conceptualization of issues will differ from those dominating the literature today. For women of colour, research into paid caring work is important because most of them are in the lowest strata of the labour market. Even for those who work as professionals, such as registered nurses, the differential impact of downsizing and restructuring on their jobs needs to be examined within a framework that uses 'otherness' as a point of entry if this differential impact is to be understood.

The multiple caring responsibilities carried by women who live in immigrant communities limit their participation in planning activities that have policy outcomes affecting their well-being. A good example can be found in the development of long-term care policy by the Ontario provincial government. In my observations of several information sessions and a workshop conducted during the development of this policy, there was virtually no participation from women of colour. Yet there is ample evidence showing that women of colour, or ethno-racial minorities, face barriers in accessing health and social services (Reitz, 1995; Henry et al., 1995). These barriers include lack of information on services, lack of understanding by service providers of cultural and linguistic needs, discrimination, and prejudice. For example, in a study on volunteer caregiving, key informants from ethnoracial communities had to point out that respite care, in the recipients' primary language, was essential if it was to meet the needs of families in their communities (Ministry of Citizenship, 1994).

Rhetoric to the contrary, the welfare of family caregivers has not been an important component of North American social policy (Aronson, 1990; Calasanti and Zajicek, 1993). Policy debates in the future will need to focus on providing guidelines for programs that accommodate the needs of all caregivers—by eliminating distinctions in the work done by men and women at home and in the labour market, by de-gendering caring responsibilities, by enacting supportive workplace policies, and by providing formal support services. All programs will need to guarantee not only equality of access, but also equality of outcome. This means that an institutional rather than residual approach to policy formulation is essential to respond to the continuum of caring responsibilities that shape the lives of women of colour. In other words, caring should be treated as an integral part of the policy discourse that surrounds such major institutions as the family and the economy. Finally, it must be recognized that Canada is a racist society. Thus, anti-racist and anti-discriminatory criteria have to be integrated into policies and programs. Inclusive policies and programs require more than goodwill; they require continuous monitoring and evaluation to assess their effectiveness.

REFERENCES

Adams, B. 1997. 'Ugandan Asians in Exile: Household and kinship in the resettlement crisis', *Journal of Comparative Family Studies* 8, 2: 167–78.

Aggarwal, P. 1987. 'Business as usual in the factory', *Resources for Feminist Research* 16, 1: 42–3.

Aggarwal, P. 1990. 'English classes for immigrant women: A feminist organizing tool', *Fireweed* 30: 94–100.

Agnew, V. 1996. *Resisting Discrimination: Women from Asia, Africa and the Caribbean and the Women's Movement in Canada.* Toronto: University of Toronto Press.

Almeida, R. 1996. 'Hindu, Christian, and Muslim Families', in M. McGoldrick, J. Giordano, J. Pearce, eds, *Ethnicity and Family Therapy.* New York: Guilford: 395–423.

Aronson, J. 1990. 'Women's Perspectives on Informal Care of the Elderly: Public Ideology and Personal Experience in Giving and Receiving Care', *Ageing and Society* 10: 61–84.

Ames, M., and J. Inglis. 1976. 'Tradition and Change in British Columbia Sikh Family Life', in K. Ishwaran, ed., *The Canadian Family*, rev. edn. Toronto: Holt, Rinehart and Winston of Canada: 77–91.

Bannerji, H. 1993. *Returning the Gaze: Essays on Racism, Feminism and Politics.* Toronto: Sister Vision Press.

Bannerji, H. 1996. 'On the Dark of the Nation: Politics of Multiculturalism and the State of "Canada"', *Journal of Canadian Studies* 31, 3: 103–28.

Bhachu, P. 1991. 'Culture, ethnicity and class among Punjabi Sikh women in 1990s Britain', *New Community* 17, 3: 401–12.

Bolaria, B., and P. Li. 1988. *Racial Oppression in Canada.* Toronto: Garamond Press.

Buchignani, N. 1979. 'South Asian Canadians and the Ethnic Mosaic: 1885–1930', *Canadian Ethnic Studies* 11, 1: 48–68.

Calasanti, T., and A. Zajicek. 1993. 'Bringing in Diversity: Toward an Inclusive Theory of Retirement', *Journal of Aging Studies* 7, 2: 133–51.

Calliste, A. 1993. 'Women of "Exceptional Merit": Immigration of Caribbean Nurses to Canada', *Canadian Journal of Women and the Law* 6: 85–102.

Calliste, A., G. Dei, and J. Belkhir. 1995. 'Canadian Perspective on Anti-Racism: Intersection of Race, Gender and Class', *Race, Class and Gender* 2, 3: 5–10.

Carty, L., and D. Brand. 1993. 'Visible Minority Women: A Creation of the Canadian State', in Bannerji, ed., *Returning the Gaze*: 169–81.

Cassin, A.M., and A. Griffith. 1981. 'Class and Ethnicity: Producing the Difference that Counts', *Canadian Ethnic Studies* 23, 1: 109–29.

Chekki, D. 1988. 'Family in India and North America: Change and continuity among the Lingayat families', *Journal of Comparative Family Studies* 19, 2: 329–43.

Cox, C., and A. Monk. 1990. 'Minority Caregivers of Dementia Victims: A Comparison of Black and Hispanic Families', *Journal of Applied Gerontology* 9, 3: 340–54.

Das Gupta, T. 1994. 'Political Economy of Gender, Race and Class: Looking at South Asian Immigrant Women in Canada', *Canadian Ethnic Studies* 26, 1: 59–73.

Das Gupta, T. 1996. *Racism and Paid Work.* Toronto: Garamond.

Dei, G. 1995. 'Integrative Anti-Racism: Intersection of Race, Class and Gender', *Race, Gender and Class* 2, 3: 11–30.

Desai, K., and R. Bhalla. 1978. 'Social Situation of the Aged', *Institute of Social Sciences* (Bombay).

Dhruvarajan, V. 1992. 'Conjugal power among first generation Hindu Asian Indians in a Canadian city', *International Journal of Sociology of the Family* 22, 1: 1–33.

Dua, E. 1992. 'Racism or Gender?: Understanding oppression of South Asian Canadian Women', *Canadian Woman Studies* 13, 1: 6–10.

Elliot, F. 1996. *Gender, Family and Society.* London: Macmillan Press.

Estable, A., and M. Meyer. 1989. *A Discussion Paper on Settlement Needs of Immigrant Women in Ontario.* Ottawa: Canadian Advisory Council on the Status of Women.

Filteau, C. 1980. 'The role of the concept of love in the Hindu family acculturation process', K. Ujimoto and G. Hirabayashi, eds, *Visible Minorities and Multiculturalism: Asians in Canada.* Toronto: Butterworths: 289–99.

Gannon, M., and Associates. 1994. *Understanding Global Cultures: Metaphorical Journeys through 17 Countries.* Thousand Oaks, Calif.: Sage.

Gelfand, D. 1989. 'Immigration, Aging and Intergenerational Relationships', *Gerontologist* 29, 3: 366–72.

Gelfand, D., and J. McCallum. 1994. 'Immigration, the Family and Female Caregivers in Australia', *Journal of Gerontological Social Work* 22, 3–4: 41–59.

George, U., and S. Ramkissoon. 1998. 'Race, Gender and Class: Interlocking Oppressions in the Lives of South Asian Women in Canada, *Affilia* 13, 1: 102–19.

Gill, D. 1995. 'Changes in the Breadwinner Role: Punjabi families in transition, Canada', *Indian Journal of Canadian Studies* 4: 30–40.

Guzder, J. 1992. 'South Asian women: Psychological issues related to assimilation', in R. Ghosh and R. Kanungo, eds, *South Asian Canadians: Current Issues in the Politics of Culture*. New Delhi: Shastri Indo-Canadian Institute: 105–13.

Head, W. 1986. *Black Women's Work: Racism in the Health System*. Toronto: Ontario Human Rights Commission.

Henry, F. 1995. 'Perspectives on Racism', in F. Henry, C. Tator, W. Mattis, and T. Rees, eds, *The Colour of Democracy*. Toronto: Harcourt Brace: 13–59.

Isajiw, W. 1974. 'Definitions of Ethnicity', *Ethnicity* 1: 111–24.

James, C. 1996. 'Race, Culture and Identity', in C. James, ed., *Perspectives on Racism and the Human Services Sector*. Toronto: University of Toronto Press: 15–35.

Juteau-Lee, D., and B. Roberts. 1981. 'Ethnicity and Femininity: (d')après nos experi-ences', *Canadian Ethnic Studies* 13, 1: 1–23.

Khosla, P. 1981. 'The changing familial role of South-Asian women in Canada: A study in identity transformation', in *Asian Canadian Symposium V: Conference Proceedings*. Halifax.

Khosla, P. 1983. 'Profiles of working class East Indian women', *Fireweed* 16: 43–8.

Koh, J., and W. Bell. 1987. 'Korean Elders in the United States: Intergenerational Relations and Living Arrangements', *Gerontologist* 27, 1: 66–71.

Leah, R. 1995. 'Anti-Racism Studies: An Integrative Perspective', *Race, Gender and Class* 2, 3: 105–22.

Managalam, J. 1985. 'Post-immigration adjustment of India's immigrants in Canada: A case study', *Population Review* 29, 1–2: 95–112.

Matas, D. 1996. 'Racism in Canadian Immigration Policy', in C. James, ed., *Racism and the Human Services Sector*. Toronto: University of Toronto Press.

Metropolitan Toronto Planning Division. 1995. *Key Facts*.

Miller, J. 1994. 'Cultural Diversity in the Morality of Caring', *Journal of Comparative Social Science* 28, 1: 3–39.

Ministry of Citizenship, Ontario. 1994. *Volunteer Caregiving*. Toronto.

Modood, T. 1997. 'Difference, Cultural Racism and Anti-Racism', in P. Werbner and T. Modood, eds, *Debating Cultural Hybridity: Multicultural Identities and the Politics of Anti-Racism*. London: Zed Books.

Naidoo, J. 1985a. 'Contemporary South Asian Women in the Canadian Mosaic', *International Women's Studies* 8, 4: 338–50.

Naidoo, J. 1985b. 'The South Asian Experience of Aging', *Multiculturalism* 8, 3: 3–6.

Naidoo, J. 1988. 'Between East and West: Asian Indian Women in Canadian Society', keynote address, Effective Participation of Women in Canadian Society conference, Kitchener, Ont.

Naidoo, J. 1992. 'Between East and West: Reflections on Asian Indian Women in Canada', in R. Ghosh and R. Kanungo, eds, *South Asian Canadians: Current Issues in the Politics of Culture*. New Delhi: Shastri Indo-Canadian Institute: 81–90.

Naidoo, J. 1994. *Research on South Asian Women in Canada: Selected Annotated Bibliography 1972–1992*. Waterloo, Ont.

Ng, R. 1991a. 'Constituting Ethnic Phenomenon: An Account from the Perspective of Immigrant Women', *Canadian Ethnic Studies* 13, 1: 97–107.

Ng, R. 1991b. 'Sexism, Racism, and Canadian Nationalism', in J. Vorst, ed., *Race, Class, Gender: Bonds and Barriers*. Toronto: Garamond: 12–26.

Ng, R. 1996. *Politics of Community Services: Immigrant Women, Class and State*. Halifax: Fernwood Publishing.

Ng, R., and A. Estable. 1987. 'Immigrant women in the labour force: An overview of present knowledge and research gaps', *Resources for Feminist Research* 16, 1: 29–33.

Qureshi, R. 1980. 'The family model as a blueprint for social interaction among Pakistani Canadians', paper presented at Canadian Symposium on Asian Canadians and Multiculturalism, Montreal.

Rajagopal, I. 1988. 'Obasan's "Silent Warriors": Urban immigrant women in Canada', in K. Ujimoto and J. Naidoo, eds, *Asian Canadians: Research on Current Issues*. Guelph, Ont.: University of Guelph Press: 103–27.

Ralston, H. 1988. 'Ethnicity, Class and Gender among South Asian Women in Metro Halifax: An Exploratory Study', *Canadian Ethnic Studies* 20, 3: 63–83.

Ralston, H. 1991. 'Race, Class, Gender and Work Experience of South Asian Immigrant Women in Atlantic Canada', *Canadian Ethnic Studies* 23, 2: 129–39.

Reitz, J. 1995. *A Review of the Literature on Aspects of Ethno-Racial Access, Utilization And Delivery of Social Services*. Toronto: Multicultural Coalition for Family Services.

Rosenthal, C. 1986. 'Family Supports in Later Life: Does Ethnicity Make a Difference?', *Gerontologist* 26, 1: 19–24.

Slonim-Nevo, V., J. Cwikel, H. Luski, M. Lankry, and Y. Shraga. 1995. 'Caregiver burden among three-generation immigrant families in Israel', *International Social Work* 38, 2: 191–204.

Statistics Canada. 1996. *Projections of Visible Minority Population Groups, Canada, Provinces and Regions, 1991–2016*. Ottawa.

Sung, K.T. 1990. 'Study of Filial Piety: Ideals and Practices of Family Centered Parent Care', *Gerontologist* 30, 5: 610–17.

Sung, K.T. 1991. 'Family Centered Informal Support Networks of Korean Elderly: The Resistance of Cultural Traditions', *Journal of Cross-Cultural Gerontology* 6, 4: 431–47.

Sung, K.T. 1994. 'A Cross-Cultural Comparison of Motivations for Parent Care: The Case of Americans and Koreans', *Journal of Aging Studies* 8, 2: 195–209.

Szekely, E. 1990. 'Immigrant Women and the Problem of Difference', *Women and Well-being* 3: 125–37.

Weber, G. 1994. *Celebrating Women, Aging and Cultural Diversity*. Toronto: The Arthur Press.

Welty, P. 1970. *The Asians: Their Heritage and Their Destiny*. New York: J.B. Lippincott.

Wieviorka, M. 1997. 'Is It So Difficult to be an Anti-Racist?', in P. Werbner and T. Modood, eds, *Debating Cultural Hybridity: Multicultural Identities and the Politics of Anti-Racism*. London: Zed Press.

Yee, B. 1992. 'Elders in South East Asian Refugee Families', *Generations* 16: 24–7.

Part Two

Living the Realities of Care

5

Still Girls Learn To Care: Girls Policed To Care

MARGE REITSMA-STREET

INTRODUCTION

When Dell was 18, she participated in a survey on the development of delinquency and conformity in siblings. Dell admired her grandmother for being a doctor. But she wondered why her grandmother told her 'to put everyone ahead of yourself' while her grandfather stressed that Dell should 'try to do what I wanted to do' (Reitsma-Street and Offord, 1991). Dell's confusion about these two different messages for adolescent girls illustrated troublesome questions about caring for others and caring for oneself (Gilligan et al., 1990; Holmes and Silverman, 1992). What does it mean 'to put everyone ahead'? While putting others ahead, how can girls pay serious attention to trying 'to do what they want to do'? What influences the balance between putting others ahead and doing what you want to do? What costs are there, and to whom, if girls focus on putting others ahead? What is the price they pay if they try to do what they want to do? For instance, Mies (1989: 55) questions what will happen to the 're-creation of living relations' among males and females when females pursue the type of autonomy idealized in our culture as self-determination.

Each chapter in this book wrestles with these questions, using different data, areas of interests, and groups of women. This chapter focuses on adolescent girls. The chapter looks at the essential caring lessons girls learn, the costs of these lessons, and how girls are socialized and policed to care for others. The data from a study of delinquent and non-delinquent sister pairs provide the major source for analysing the development of caring in adolescents.[1] The second source includes historical and contemporary research on delinquent and non-delinquent girls in the Western industrialized world and, in particular, Canada.

The central arguments set forth in this chapter are that girls learn to care in certain prescribed ways and to bear the costs of caring, and that they are also *policed to care and to bear the costs*. Although girls may want to develop a range of ways to care, they are pressured subtly and coercively to care for others in particular ways, especially for boyfriends, fathers, and children, *more than* for themselves. The evidence is clearest in the lives of girls who more obviously challenge the prescribed expectations, in word and especially in deed. The more a girl fights against how she is expected to care for others and for herself, the greater the costs she is likely to bear. Sadly, the most serious cost is in the constriction of her already limited opportunities to care for herself and her loved ones. Because caring is so important to delinquent and non-delinquent girls alike, the risk of losing limited opportunities to care effectively constrains the development of alternative ways to care for self and others. The chapter ends with a discussion on directions for change, including resistance to limits on caring, recovery of strengths, and new ways to teach a healthier approach to caring to young girls.

Using information generated in part from delinquent girls may appear an odd source for understanding the development of caring in adolescent girls. Very few girls commit serious crimes of injury. Birth cohort studies and retrospective self-report surveys indicate that between 2 per cent and 5 per cent of girls have had any contact with the police or been charged in youth court for a crime, mostly minor, before the age of 18. Despite modest increases in the past decade in official charges against girls, especially against Native, Black, and minority girls, in industrialized countries, fewer than 20 per cent of charges in youth courts are against girls (Beikoff, 1996; Canadian Centre for Justice Statistics, 1996: Table 3; Chesney-Lind and Shelden, 1992: 12, 21; Pedersen and Wichstrom, 1995: 553).

The older literature concludes that those few girls who are convicted of crimes are quite different from non-delinquents in their relationships, personality, experiences, education, and behaviours (Cowie et al., 1968; Felice and Offord, 1975; Konopka, 1966; Konopka, 1976; Widom et al., 1983). This concept of difference is challenged in this chapter, and in other recent research. There are important commonalities among girls, despite significant diversity in deviant behaviours and the constraints of class, race, and health. The data from the sister study, presented in the next section, solidly ground several commonalities in the development of caring in girls. The commonalities refer to what is occurring often in the daily lives of the girls, such as the familiar events and pressures that affect them, as well as their feelings and choices. Common lessons about caring shared by delinquent and non-delinquent girls presented in this chapter include: (1) women are the primary providers of emotional and physical care; (2) adolescent females learn a very restrictive notion of what self-care means; and (3) boyfriends become the primary recipients or objects of care. Thus, ideas about the commonalities that exist in the development of caring in adolescence are strengthened by evidence from girls whose public behaviour is most divergent.

The study of young females in conflict with the law adds another important contribution to understanding the development of caring in girls. Feminist criminology helps us to see more clearly the depth of regulation, policing, and sanctioning that affects girls as they negotiate meaning, relationships, and survival in their daily lives (Artz, 1994; Baines and Alder, 1996; Cain, 1989; Schur, 1984). Control of deviance in females is pervasive in all aspects of life, with criminal justice sanctions and correctional processes on the end of a continuum of controlling devices (Comack, 1996; Chesney-Lind and Shelden, 1992; Reitsma-Street, 1991). Analysing the lives of delinquents helps to reveal more clearly the range of costs borne by girls as they learn the traditional lessons of caring and the costs of challenging those lessons.

THE SISTER STUDY

The sister study was part of a larger research project on the development of delinquency and conformity in pairs of siblings. Between 1978 and 1981 the files of 638 mostly Caucasian girls and 1,292 boys who were referred to Ontario correctional, mental health, and social service agencies were reviewed to identify sibling pairs who met the criteria of minimal age differences, shared early upbringing, and definite differences in delinquency and agency contact. In each pair, one of the siblings had been convicted in youth court for delinquent activities and had used social services extensively, while the other sibling was free of judicial convictions and had minimal service contacts.

Twenty-six sister and 45 brother pairs who met the criteria agreed to engage in: (1) a four-hour semi-structured life history interview focused on their experiences in and perceptions of health, home, school, work, and relationship interactions; (2) short parental telephone interviews about the youths' early life; (3) birth, school, and agency record reviews; and (4) two standard instruments to estimate educational achievement and cognitive abilities (Reitsma-Street et al., 1985).

The parent-sibling study used the logic and procedures of a quantitative hypothesis testing survey, including univariate and multivariate matched-paired statistical analyses of over 250 variables (Reitsma-Street et al., 1985). The analysis of the quantified variables, however, did not adequately help me to understand the development of delinquency and conformity in girls. Furthermore, much of the data had not been analysed, especially the semi-structured questions and the interviewers' rich field notes. Thus, in 1985 I received permission to use the data for a doctoral thesis on the sister pairs. This time the logic and procedures of a qualitative multicase study were used, including purposive sampling, examination of themes, the constant comparative analysis of the themes in depth, and the search for negative cases (Reitsma-Street and Offord, 1991).

The theme of commonality, rather than of difference, emerged from my study of sisters. Of most relevance to women and caring were the core commonalities—these revolved around how the sisters learned to care for themselves and for others, the costs they bore for caring, and how they were policed to conform to expectations about caring. These commonalities, or as the biologist (Hubbard 1981: 291) eloquently states, 'the similarities that tie us together', are developed in the subsequent sections. The fictitious names for the sisters have been chosen to help readers remember the distinction that originally divided the sisters and to illustrate that commonalities are grounded in the experiences of both delinquents and non-delinquents. Thus, those names beginning with a 'D', like Dell whose words opened this chapter, are the delinquent siblings; those with an 'N' are the non-delinquent sisters.

LEARNING TO CARE: THE LESSONS

1. *Females as care providers.* The sisters learned early that females, young and old, are the major providers of care. Spontaneously, repeatedly, and specifically the sisters reported that they received far more care from females than they did from males. The sisters said they had lunch, sang, lived with, shopped, learned about money and getting along with others, looked for help, and above all spent time with and talked with females. While peers primarily consisted of sisters and close friends, adult females included aunts, babysitters, neighbours, mothers of friends,

a homeroom teacher, a guidance teacher, and several social workers. Despite dissatisfaction with some mothers who did not act like 'a *real* mother who is quiet, caring and understanding', the sisters saw mothers, stepmothers, or grandmothers as the most important sources for companionship, advice, learning, and a home.

The sisters certainly did things, ranging from fishing to planning burglaries, with fathers and other males. Some of the sisters appreciated fathers 'putting a roof over our heads and giving us food' or, as Nasya said, 'my father helped me overcome shyness.' But the sisters spoke far more of indifference from males who were not around or too busy, of the absence of affection and conversation, and of the physical and sexual violence they experienced from males inside and outside the home.

The caring received and given by the sisters can be categorized into two dimensions, which are identified in the literature as: (1) *love and affection about others* that is made up of the emotional work needed to create, enrich, and maintain human relationships; and (2) *labour and help for others*, which includes the daily domestic work to meet the basic necessities of life (Hochschild, 1989; Finch and Groves, 1983).

Caring, as expressed in love and affection, was emphasized more in the sisters' comments. That is, they were more conscious of wanting to give and to receive this element of caring. All the sisters spoke of talking as an important activity—all wanted to understand others and be understood. They seemed to understand that communication is essential to achieving a sense of intimacy, well-being, a foundation for making decisions about what is important in life. For instance, Nola felt that the school social worker listened and wanted to help her: 'She understood me like a friend; she wanted to find out what I wanted, and to help me; turn me on to good things.'

The labour of caring was evident in frequent references to the concrete forms of aid they received—a good meal, a safe place to live—especially if a girl could not stay in the parental home. At the same time the girls showed care for others by performing such tasks as child care and housework, helping mothers tend to a sick husband, or assisting in the store. From other women the sisters learned the skills of housekeeping as well as the more joyous skills such as singing, 'the gift of gab, communicating with people in public, enjoying jewellery'. Although the sisters frequently reported that these types of caring activities were routinely done by the women in their lives, they were not aware of their importance or the energy that went into the labour aspect of caring.

Not only did the girls report that the females in their lives were the primary providers of affection and help, but they also saw themselves as giving affection and help to others. As early as late childhood, and definitely by adolescence, both delinquent and non-delinquent sisters reported their responsibilities for supervising children, doing housework, and, when able, providing money and a place to stay to those who needed it. The most important people they cared for included their own or other people's children, boyfriends, then parents and siblings, and to a lesser extent other relatives, peers, and at times strangers. For example, Nasya earned money by babysitting regularly and stayed at home after her mother's suicide to take care of the household for her father. Dolly ran away from the physical abuse of her father and then kept house for an older boyfriend with whom she committed many burglaries. Natalie also spent much energy in caring, as the following paraphrase of her words illustrates: 'I took care of myself as of age eight; I also tried to take care of my brother and sister, because mom had lost interest. I just feel responsible for Darcy; I don't want anything to happen to her.'

2. *Learning to look nice and to be nice.* The sisters first learned that women were the major providers of care for others and that they were expected to do likewise. But they also learned not to provide such care to themselves, except in a very restricted sense. The goal of self-care was not directed at meeting present personal needs or planning for their future welfare. Rather, the sisters reported that they learned primarily to care for their physical appearance in order to look nice and to avoid actions that prompted labels such as 'tomboy' or especially 'tramp' or 'prostitute'. Thus, the focus in caring for themselves was on developing distinctive physical features and personality, conceptualized in the literature as the making of the Western *feminine* female (Wolf, 1990). Education, individual interests, or job opportunities can be developed as long as they enhance, or at least do not seriously impede, the pursuit of femininity.

Nicci, for example, reported that she learned very early 'to dress nice, cook a lot, be a lady, be petite'. Darcy tried to be more like her grandmother, who was 'sweet, mellow, there when needed', and less like her mother or herself, that is, 'hyper, lying, irritable, and tricky, trying to evade everything'. Nasya wanted to be like her mother and her babysitter Cleo. Both were very nice, as she summed up in these remarks:

> Mom is able to get along with people. She makes friends easily. Basically she is soft spoken, and gives any help that is wanted. She's there whenever I needed her.

> Cleo, my babysitter, was soft-spoken and understanding. She takes me out for supper. We get along together and talk. From Cleo I learned to get along with others.

The sisters still tried to put energy into activities that attended to their own needs and aspirations and reflected a broader understanding of caring for themselves. All the sisters reported repeated attempts to pursue their schooling despite disruptions, failures, and boredom. Many spoke of extensive participation, enjoyment, and skill in sports or recreational interests—whether pruning trees, earning a black belt in martial arts or a Grade 8 piano certificate, going to parties and travelling to new cities, singing musicals with an aunt, or writing for the school paper. Earning money and planning for a future job, sometimes even a non-traditional job such as a diesel mechanic or a cowhand, were also included in the sisters' attempts to pay attention to their needs.

The delinquent girls were more likely than their non-delinquent sisters to report that they fought against giving priority to looking nice and being nice. Sometimes they tried to dress 'like a tomboy' and to avoid wearing dresses. Sometimes they swore and talked loudly and explored physical fighting as a way

to meet their needs. The delinquent sisters were far more likely than their conforming sisters to explore their own interests and sexuality without adult permission: for instance, they spoke of travelling, of learning to use birth control and to
experiment with lesbian relationships. Also, the delinquent sisters pursued
excitement and fun more frequently than their siblings and rebelled against abusive, unjust, or unpleasant situations because they wouldn't 'take it'. Mothers, and
a few fathers, were more likely to remember the delinquent girls as 'pesty', bois-
terous, running everywhere, moving furniture at the age of two, and not wanting
to go shopping. In contrast, the non-delinquent sisters, such as Naomi, were
more often remembered by parents as 'quiet, shy, and good'.

It is interesting that the non-delinquent siblings sometimes reported admiration, even envy, of the delinquent sisters' struggles to develop their own personality, interests, and appearance beyond looking and being nice. For example,
although Nola said her sister Dawn was stubborn, spoiled, and wanted everything, Nola also expressed admiration: 'Dawn used to fight all the time with me
and others. I like Dawn's guts and I know she had more guts than me.'

But, by late adolescence, both delinquent and non-delinquent sisters had
learned to restrict the care of themselves primarily to looking and being nice, and
above all to not 'making a fuss'. For example, Deborah still loved fighting physically and verbally, but she said she was 'learning from mom to *hold it all in, and
to cry like her*'. The following words from Darcy poignantly capture how a girl
learns to restrict her care of herself to looking and being nice. Darcy had finished
her stay in a training school, returned to live at home, and had enrolled in college for upgrading. She stopped wearing boy's clothes and learned that she could
not do what boys do. Instead, she sums up the prescription of what looking after
oneself means for girls: 'I am learning to stop being selfish, and to think of others, and to like myself. I am learning to be passive, but also to get out of my shell.
I am learning that if I stay at home, be good, all will be okay.'

3. *Boyfriends as the primary object of caring.* In their first lesson on caring, girls
learn to see other females and themselves as the major providers of caring. The
second lesson is to restrict the care of themselves to an emphasis on personal
appearance and appropriate demeanour. Successfully learning these two lessons
makes it possible to learn the third lesson: a singular focus on making and maintaining a relationship with a boyfriend.

By mid-adolescence, if not sooner, all the sisters had made or were systematically seeking a steady, encompassing relationship with a boy. With only one
exception, the sisters engaged in relationships with boys who were older. Before
the age of 20, all the sisters had experienced sexual relations with males. Sexual
activity rarely occurred outside the context of romantic love or the possibility of
a committed relationship with a boyfriend.

A number of sisters, including Nicci, Dolores, Deborah, Nora, Nadine, and
Natalie, clearly stated that they judged their happiness by their ability to attract
boys. They worked to encourage a steady relationship with a boy, which might
lead to an engagement. Spending time with boys was essential, even if this meant
skipping school or not pursuing their own interests. For example, Natalie remem-

bered that she first became interested in boys at age 10. She was pleased that losing weight brought her more boyfriends. By the age of 12 she was visiting boyfriends about once per week, and went steady by age 15 with a boy who was three years older. Natalie reported feeling 'comfortable with guys but not without'. The breakup with her first boyfriend was accompanied by a clinically diagnosed depression and by leaving school.

Some girls, such as Dawn and Darcy, had less romantic views about making a boyfriend the primary object of their caring. Dawn's relationships were shadowed by 'horrible' thoughts and feelings about her father, her brother, and other males from whom she suffered serious physical abuse, rape, and indifference. But she also wanted to live in a decent place and to provide a home for foster kids, which she thought she could do through getting a boyfriend. Her terse, angry story is replete with attempts to attract a boyfriend:

> I was engaged to two men whom I met in court. When I was in jail, I wrote to one who also was in jail. When I got out, I asked to marry him, but no answer. In London, I lived with and got engaged to another man. He tattooed my name on his body. But, don't know where he is now; he left me in the air. Now I stay with Paul; he works; I take care of the house. There is a chance I might be pregnant now.

Caring for a boyfriend can mean a relationship that includes affection, friendship, and excitement. Unfortunately, learning to care for a boyfriend is likely to produce other outcomes and be at the expense of caring for oneself in a broader way or for other females who provide care. These costs are explored in a subsequent section. Before doing so, however, we need to place the findings from this study within a broader context. In brief, the lessons learned by the sisters, whether delinquent or not, are all too familiar when one examines the conditions of girls' lives in the past and in the present.

LEARNING TO CARE IN OTHER RESEARCH ON GIRLS

Findings that suggest that females are the major providers of care may appear trite. It is so obvious, and commonplace—yet so invisible. It is almost embarrassing to admit that during the first year of analysis in the sister study I did *not* attach significance to the finding that it was women who primarily provided the love and labour of caring in the sisters' lives. Rather, I was following the more usual method of sorting through the sisters' separate relationships with their fathers versus their mothers and then relationships with their adult friends versus their peers. I found both delinquent and non-delinquent sisters were not closely connected to their fathers and quite ambivalent about their mothers, but I did not see how this pattern or any other in the girls' relationships contributed to either delinquency or conformity.

When a gendered approach to understanding relationships was introduced into the analysis, I began to see clear, strong patterns that promoted conformity: females were the primary providers of care and females were judged on their ability to care—through creating, enriching, and maintaining relationships, especially with one boyfriend. Understanding the development and invisibility of caring mostly by females, whether they keep or break the law, and the way this female monopoly is maintained remains central to feminist scholarship (Chodorow, 1978; Barrett and McIntosh, 1983; Brodie, 1996; Sommers, 1995; Swift, 1994).

Learning to restrict the care of oneself to looking nice and being nice is a lesson learned over and over by girls. Compared to 50 years ago (Brenzel, 1983; Dyhouse, 1981), the contemporary conception of acceptable nice girls may be expanding somewhat to include pluck and strength. In their review of two decades of empirical and theoretical work on California adolescent subcultures the Schwendingers wrote: '[Girls] are under great pressure to organize their personalities around themselves as objects that are valued as sexually attractive things' (1985: 167). In the 1990s, physical beauty and compliant femininity remain very important to girls, especially in adolescence. Attention to emotional needs, economic independence, birth control, and protection from AIDS and physical abuse may be important, but not priorities (Cain, 1989; Child Welfare League of Canada, 1996; Foster, 1988; Holmes and Silverman, 1992; Kostash, 1987; McRobbie, 1991; Pyke, 1996).

Besides learning to look and be nice, female adolescents learn to make boyfriends their major object of caring. This lesson found in the sister study may not be inevitable, but it remains pervasive for girls, delinquent or not, and for girls of all races (Gagnon and Langelier-Biron, 1982; Hudson, 1983; Kostash, 1987; McRobbie, 1991). For many, especially poorer girls, caring for a boyfriend who may become a husband is the chief means of getting away from parents, becoming an adult, and establishing a home of one's own (Cain, 1989; Davies, 1984). In her study of 249 West Indian, Caucasian, and Asian girls in four working-class schools in England, Sharpe (1976: 302) comments that 'the idea of finding true love with Mr. Right is always the primary goal and the key to everlasting happiness.' In ground-breaking studies on the development of girls in the 1980s and 1990s, Carol Gilligan and her colleagues explore how even very privileged, mostly White girls comply with sacrificial, selfless caring about idealized 'relationships' defined through the 'male voice' at the expense of a myriad of reciprocal authentic relationships (Gilligan et al., 1990; Brown and Gilligan, 1992: 7, 24, 30).

Learning these lessons about how to care, and for whom, imposes high costs on girls. The next section describes these costs, illustrated with data from the sister study and other research. A subsequent section concludes with the argument that girls do not simply learn to bear these costs; rather, they are policed or pressured to do so.

THE COSTS OF CARING

The first major cost is that in learning the skills and attitudes needed to care for others, girls seriously restrict the development of their own interests and independence. Daisy was aware of this, for though she valued the way her mother 'showed me to care for someone', she did not want to dedicate her whole life to children and a husband, only to find out that, like her mother, she would be 'left out'. To continue caring for a boyfriend meant that sisters not only restricted their own interests, but also gave less emphasis to their caring relationships with others, especially females. For instance, Dolores commented: 'I used to like sports and movies. But now I act differently. I changed my friends from girlfriends to a boyfriend who does drugs. We just hang around, with his boyfriends and their girls.'

Sisters reported changing their educational and recreational activities, or their preparation for future work, to spend time with their boyfriends, listen to them, admire them, and run errands for them. Dallas worked hard to get a driver's licence when she was just 16, to rent her own apartment, and to think 'things out on my own'. But her boyfriend moved in and life began to revolve around his parties, drinking, and friends. The shift in caring was most prominent if a sister lived with a boyfriend or became pregnant. By the age of 14, Naomi had narrowed her interests to focus on caring for her boyfriend, who later became her husband, and then extended her caring to the children she bore. At the time of the interview Naomi still lived with her parents, minded the children, and listened to the baseball and shop talk of her husband. In a final example from the sister study, a probation officer noted that Dee had 'settled down', demonstrated by the fact that she had 'no time for any actions, including antisocial ones, other than caring for her son'.

The costs for girls who care for others more than themselves is documented in studies of girls growing up 50 to 100 years ago (e.g., Jephcott, 1942; Dyhouse, 1981; Gordon, 1988) and those born in the last decades (e.g., Breines, 1992; Brown and Gilligan, 1992; Sharpe, 1976). The cost of negating their own interests means, for example, a reduction in time available for study and for play (Holmes and Silverman, 1992; Propper, 1979). It means that helping and caring for others comes before thinking of oneself. McRobbie and McCabe (1981: 4) poignantly sum up the cost of emphasizing the care of others while restricting the care of self: 'Growing up for girls is little more than preparation for growing old prematurely.' Twenty-five years later girls are still struggling with the cost of caring for others. At a recent national workshop on 'the girl child' a bright 17-year-old girl said:

> I like school. I like to cook. I like to take care of my friends and boyfriend, but he doesn't help much and it isn't fair. It is hard to have a boyfriend and prepare for a job. What can I do? I don't want to lose him. (Child Welfare League of Canada, 1996)

Another cost of the restricted lessons female adolescents learn about caring is inattention to personal basic health needs. A girl learns to take care of her physical appearance and acquire the necessary social skills to look nice and be nice. If she learns this lesson well, she may attract and keep a boyfriend. But with this focus, a girl does not learn how to seriously care for and care about the needs of her body, especially in its capacity to experience pleasure or to produce children. In the sister study, Nicci loved to be treated like a lady, and was adored by a boy who 'made me feel good, made me happy, got on his knees to do anything for me'. But Nicci felt confused and betrayed by her experiences with boys: she endured forced sex at a party, was impregnated by her adoring boyfriend, and then had to deal with the pressure either to get an abortion or to quit school.

Surveys of adolescents indicate that as many as two-thirds do not use contraception, especially in the first few instances of sexual intercourse. In the past decade, the use of condoms has increased, but this is not part of every sexual encounter among young teens: only 45 per cent of randomly surveyed adolescent girls (compared to 57 per cent of boys) used condoms in their most recent sexual encounters (Galt, 1997). Those girls with least exposure to explicit sex education or AIDS prevention and with higher risk of economic dependence on men are finding it difficult to demand that partners use condoms every time. Neither are pregnancy rates decreasing for girls of disadvantaged backgrounds or those without post-secondary education. With the lessons of caring concentrated on looking nice and being nice, girls too often find their bodies and spirits pay the price of sexual assault, HIV infection, unwanted pregnancy, and inadequate birth control, as well as miscarriages and abortions (Scott, 1996; Baines and Alder, 1996; Foster, 1988; Herold, 1984; Orton and Rosenblatt, 1986). Kostash (1987: 175), in her study of a cross-section of 50 Canadian girls, captures the apprehension that accompanies this bodily cost:

> Suddenly her body is no longer at her own disposal but has become a zone where others have competing interests—parents and boyfriends and social workers and ad agencies—a territory liable to a whole series of catastrophes: diseases, pregnancy, rape, abortion.

This apprehension about physical vulnerabilities in their reproductive capacity and on unsafe streets fuelled heated debates among the 107 youth at a Canadian symposium on young women. Fortunately, anger at the costs and ideas for change also emerged (Canadian Advisory Council on the Status of Women, 1992).

In addition to restriction of interests and neglect of their bodies, the girls also risk poverty and dependence. Pat Evans, in Chapter 3, explores this in detail as it affects adult women. For many women the seeds of their economic dependency are sown in adolescence. Despite attempts to advance their education and job skills, the sisters in the sibling study had trouble preparing for economic independence, or even interesting work. The importance of caring for their appearance and demeanour, and the focus on the care for others, especially boys, too often interfered with or interrupted their schooling and job preparation.

Canadian surveys completed during the 1980s and 1990s found that young girls wanted and expected to combine education, marriage, motherhood, and paid work, but their aspirations were threatened by the harsh realities in which girls try to earn a living and care for themselves and others (Baker, 1985; Holmes and Silverman, 1992; Robertson, 1990). Pink ghettos and poor pay, steady unemployment rates between 20 per cent and 30 per cent especially for girls of colour, cuts to universal services and child care, and drastic cuts in welfare rates, special assistance, and eligibility to youth under 18 years old make girls even more vulnerable to poverty or dependence on others for food and shelter (Cain, 1989; Kauppi and Reitsma-Street, 1996; National Council of Welfare, 1997).

In the sister study, Nora revealed her desire to be both a mother and vice-president of her company, and not to be dominated like her mother. But to her dismay she found that her husband earned more on unemployment insurance than she did working. Linda Davies's (1984) two-year participant-observation study of girls in a large, comprehensive London, England, school found that working-class girls saw the major route out of the parental home and into the adult world as being through caring for a boyfriend and minding his house and children. Unfortunately, by turning marriage into a route to freedom and by not finishing school, the girls de-skilled themselves for the paid labour force. In her study of New York girl gangs Anne Campbell (1984: 266) paints a bleak picture of the economic price girls can pay for their lessons in caring: 'But in the end, gang or no gang, the girls remained alone with their children, still trapped in poverty and in a cultural dictate of womanhood from which there was no escape.'

Adequate, steady income and safe housing remain illusive dreams for many females, young and old, those who keep and those who are caught breaking the law (Carrington, 1996; Comack, 1996; Oliker, 1995; Stacey, 1990). Worse, economic contributions and longer working hours have seeped into what is expected of a caring, nice girl. Girls are learning that caring for self and others may mean working for money in order to buy nice clothes, keep up with the group, get ahead, and contribute to the family (Baker, 1985; Holmes and Silverman, 1992; Robertson, 1990). Girls in poor families have always worked in unpaid and paid jobs to help the family. For higher profits, sometimes they take the risks associated with stealing, prostitution, and selling drugs. More often girls earn low, erratic incomes from boring jobs in factories and doughnut shops (Bell, 1987; Gordon, 1988; Comack, 1996). Working for pay at a young age and preparing for paid work in the future, no matter what financial resources and *without giving up any of the other responsibilities for caring labour*, intensifies expectations of girls and takes even more time and energy from exploring alternative ways of caring for self and others. In a Canadian study of 1,603 representative girls under age 17, 56 per cent report working for pay; 16-year-olds work on average 10.7 hours per week. Girls say they find pleasure in the money and peer contact they gain from their jobs, but they also find their jobs unrewarding and routine, and worry about fewer hours for school work (Holmes and Silverman, 1992).

The costs of economic vulnerability and long working days for females of all backgrounds and races are rooted in a key conundrum. By caring for others more than for self in their early years, girls risk not being able to care for themselves or those they love in later years. Without the skills, education, and time to find a job in an economy geared to hire males before females and to pay males better, girls have a hard time earning enough money to help feed, clothe, and shelter themselves or their loved ones. Paradoxically, focusing on a boyfriend's care usually means risking personal economic vulnerability. But the focus becomes necessary because a relationship with a male who earns a satisfactory income is the major hope most girls have for minimizing the impact of economic vulnerability in our contemporary world.

POLICED TO CARE

If learning the lessons of caring is so costly for girls, why do they pay these costs of constricted independence and physical as well as economic vulnerability? Why are not other ways to care developed to decrease the costs, and to increase the capacity to care for self and others? Why is change so difficult? Under what conditions can caring lessons change and caring costs decrease?

These questions have fuelled some feminist scholarship of the past two decades. One particularly helpful perspective comes from feminist criminologists who examine why laws and punishment in the criminal justice system are, on one hand, so harsh towards certain behaviours such as running away and prostitution, but on the other hand, so indifferent to most of the deviant behaviour and needs of girls (Carrington, 1996; Chesney-Lind and Shelden, 1992; Reitsma-Street, 1991). This contradiction is captured in the phrase 'policed to grow up good' (Cain, 1989).

The concept of policing pulls together the evidence that girls are more than encouraged and socialized to learn their lessons of caring and to pay the attendant costs; rather, *they are policed to learn their lessons*. Policing, or what Donzelot (1979: 8) defines as the 'techniques of regulation', includes the subtle, helpful pressuring and monitoring of behaviours and attitudes that are built into daily norms and interactions. Policing also includes, however, the stronger pressures of regulations and sanctions inherent in laws, policies, and programs. Drawing from the literature, with illustrations from the sister study, I describe three levels of policing, beginning at the subtle, informal level and ending with the obvious, less frequent formal level of policing embodied in the criminal justice system. The three policing levels pressure girls to restrict their experimentation with alternative ways to care in order to avoid risking even further restrictions on their already limited opportunities to care for self and others.

The first level of policing is the most common and the most effective. This is the judgement of a girl's reputation (Alder and Baines, 1996; Breines, 1992; Hudson, 1983; Schur, 1984). Every study on female adolescents speaks to the pervasive, daily assessment of whether a girl's clothes, appearance, personality, enthusiasms, speech, associations, and actual or imputed sexual activity are acceptable (Kostash, 1987; Davies, 1984; Shacklady-Smitt, 1978; Sharpe, 1976; Wilson, 1978; McRobbie, 1991). The assessment examines whether a girl cares enough about herself in the right way to get and keep a boyfriend, and eventually to acquire a decent husband and the associated status and economic rewards.

For instance, in a study of 100 English girls from various backgrounds, Sue Lees (1989) found that even in the 1980s the vague, fluid, but potent use of the term 'slag' effectively policed girls to minimize any behaviours that may lead to this label and to being dropped by a boy. No girl wanted to be called a slag, or a 'slut', 'wench', 'tramp', or to be described as 'loose', terms used in other studies.

Unfortunately, the only way to avoid being tagged is to become a loner or by having a steady relationship with a boy. More recently, Brown and Gilligan (1992) found similar forces continue to affect even White, privileged girls in an all-girls school. During the five years of their study, they found the 'perfect girl' pattern: as they entered their teens girls became quiet, worked hard at grades and sports, and became 'involved in increasingly complicated and futile attempts to be always nice and kind, never mean or rude'. To avoid being called 'bad', 'mad', or 'selfish', girls had to bury themselves in school and other activities that did not involve boys (Brown and Gilligan, 1992: 195).

The second level of policing is the extensive, albeit intermittent, use of physical force or the threat of force, mostly by males to vent frustration, to settle conflict, to get sex, and to maintain dominance over girls. The primary policers at this level are chiefly the males that girls know well—fathers, brothers, relatives, teachers, neighbours, and spiritual advisers. The most common places where the violence occurs are the everyday spaces of home, school, and work. Girls speak of the restrictions they feel every day, every night, and everywhere about what they can and cannot do (Comack, 1996; Committee on Sexual Offences, 1984; Johnson and Sacco, 1995).

Although not a secret any longer, this second level of policing remains powerful, and deadly. Many of the girls in the sister study spoke of their fear and hatred of the sticks, screams, taunts, wandering hands, and sometimes rapes and beatings of fathers, grandfathers, uncles, boyfriends, and occasionally mothers. The extensiveness of this level of policing is the focus of Chapter 7 by Janet Mosher.

No study or event, however, so vividly captures the deadly impact this intermittent, interpersonal violence has on females as the 1989 Montreal massacre of 14 young female engineering students. The young women were separated from the male teacher and male students in the class and gunned down by Marc Lépine. A torrent of anguish, fear, and denial erupted in homes, on the airwaves, and in papers across the nation and continent (Malette and Chalouh, 1991). Many, mostly men, saw Lépine as a deranged person, acting individually. Many, mostly women, felt and argued that this man who killed the female students and then himself expressed the common fears and rage about young women who want to build bridges, make money, and do more than take care of others. 'Before destroying the brains that so disturbed him, Lépine shouted "You are feminists!"' (Bibeau, 1989/1991: 43). Stevie Cameron anguished over the continued policing of our girls: how they must be taught to be so careful, and yet they remain at risk: 'Fourteen of our bright and shining daughters won places in engineering schools, doing things we, their mothers, only dreamed of. That we lost them has broken our hearts; what is worse, is that we are not surprised' (Cameron, 1989/1991: 161).

Public regulations, administrative interventions, and judicial sanctions act as the third and most obvious level of policing. Laws reinforce and supplement the intermittent violence and the daily assessments of their reputation experienced by girls. Girls risk complaints from parents, arrests and sentences from judicial representatives, and treatment in correctional centres (before the 1980s) or medical and treatment establishments (in the last two decades). If caught committing an infraction or delinquency, however small or serious, girls learn that their behaviours and motivations will be measured primarily against a male standard of femininity. A girl may steal to get clothes, run away from sexual abuse, try drugs to escape boredom, sell sex because prostitution pays more than selling doughnuts, or strangle an abusive partner. But these behaviours are not seen in the context of a society that limits how girls can care for themselves and their loved ones, and restricts avenues of protest against these limitations. Instead, behaviours such as hanging around in the streets and malls, swearing loudly, running away, selling sex, being truant from school, breaking curfew, sleeping with more than one male, fighting and not getting along with parents, or generally behaving unseemly or obscenely are all interpreted by parents, teachers, and lawmakers as signs of disturbances in the girl's personality, especially her identity as a girl. *She needs help, protection, or correction to act more like a normal girl* (Baines and Alder, 1996; Byles, 1980; Chesney-Lind and Shelden, 1992; Lerman, 1984; Petrie, 1986; Schwartz et al., 1984; Parent, 1986).

In the sister study, Dolly and her boyfriend committed over 20 home burglaries. Burglary is a serious crime against property. But the judge argued that Dolly was simply following her boyfriend and thus was not really culpable of the burglaries. The judge, therefore, gave Dolly a light sentence—she was banned from living in British Columbia. However, when Dolly made her own decision to run away from a residential treatment centre and thus break one condition of her probation order, she was treated much more harshly and sent to a training school. In the sister study, the most serious judicial responses were reserved for running away from home and truancy from school, not for crimes against persons or property.

In the past, most of the infrequent delinquencies by girls were ignored and the personal needs of convicted female delinquents were treated indifferently with minimal services—unless a girl's behaviour violates standards of femininity or no male in her household takes responsibility for her care and behaviour (Langelier-Biron, 1983: 70; Geller, 1987). Up to 60 per cent of girls admitted to Canadian correctional institutions before the 1980s were admitted for status offences (Bertrand, 1979: 142; Weiler, 1978; Nease, 1966; Hatch and Faith, 1989–90: 443, 449). Status offences, such as running away, incorrigibility, truancy, prostitution, or other sexual immoralities, were often not considered offences if committed by boys.

An aim of the federal 1985 Young Offenders Act (1985) was to decrease the discriminatory, inadequate, and unfair treatment against Canadian delinquent girls purportedly spawned by interpretations of the old 1908 Juvenile Delinquents Act (Reitsma-Street, 1991). The Young Offenders Act (YOA) made the age of responsibility uniform across the provinces. Girls 12 to 18 years of age appear in youth courts, while those under 12 are dealt with under child welfare legislation; those 18 and over (and those over 14 for whom a transfer application is successful) go to adult criminal courts. Status offences can no longer be used as reasons to charge a girl. Determinate minimal sentences replaced indeterminate sentences, with three years of custody as the maximum sentence for serious offences. A litany of rights in the YOA aimed to ensure fair, due process for boys and girls alike. Also, youth were now to be held accountable in part for their actions and were not considered by the courts as misdirected or in need of protection (Reitsma-Street, 1993). As in other countries, now the 'deed', not the 'need', drove the Canadian juvenile justice system (Beikoff, 1996; Cain, 1989; Chesney-Lind and Shelden, 1992; Pedersen and Wichstrom, 1995).

It cannot be assumed that the YOA has reduced the sexist regulation of girls; this question is currently under study. It is known, however, that contrary to expectations, charges and convictions have not dropped from before to after the YOA for either boys or girls. Despite the decriminalization of status offences and the decline in population of young people, more charges are being laid against females and more females were appearing in youth courts in the late 1980s and early 1990s than in the years before the law was changed in 1985 (Reitsma-Street, 1993). It is also known that pre-trial detention has increased quite dramatically for both sexes and that the use of lawyers and the length of time between charge and conviction have increased substantially. Time spent in custody seemed to decrease after 1985, but the subsequent YOA amendments of 1986, 1991, and 1995 increased maximum sentences from three to five years, and then to 10 years. Neither the number or rates of females sentenced to custodial sentences have decreased as had been hoped. Nor has the use of alternative sentences increased, although there have been modest exceptions (Caputo and Bracken, 1988; Carrington and Moyer, 1994; Corrado and Markwart, 1994; Reitsma-Street, 1990; Reitsma-Street, 1993; Trépanier, 1986).

As occurred before the YOA, girls charged with crimes continue to endure various forms of discrimination and inappropriate services in Canada and elsewhere. In January 1990, two of the four girls who died in a fire in a Montreal secure-custody facility were there only because they had been charged with truancy. The girls were in the secure-custody facility because alternatives were not available (Collister and Scott, 1990: A5). In 1997, the secure-custody beds for girls have virtually disappeared from northeastern Ontario. Girls are shipped south to the women's reformatory in Brampton. Compared to White youth, those of colour, male and female, face the deepest discrimination in Canada and elsewhere. They are more likely to be arrested, detained, and sentenced to custody, even after offence seriousness and social factors are taken into account (Beikoff, 1996: 21; LaPrairie, 1993; Wordes et al., 1994).

Most worrisome is the steady strengthening of punitive regulations in the justice arenas (and in other arenas, like social assistance). I have mentioned the obvious increase in maximum sentence from three to 10 years for youth convicted of serious violent crime. But the intensification of policing through the use of regulations and laws can be stealthy. For example, an apparently innocuous new offence was incorporated into the 1986 amendments to the Young Offenders Act to help officials ensure that youth complied with the range of dispositions under the YOA. Section 26 reads: 'A person who is subject to a disposition . . . and who wilfully fails or refuses to comply with that order is guilty of an offence punishable on summary conviction.'[2] This section 26 provision, also called 'failure to comply with the YOA', was added to the older offences of non-compliance with the administration of justice, like 'failure to appear in court' or 'escape from custody'.

Before section 26 was passed in 1986, less than 5 per cent of all charges against girls were for offences against the administration of justice. By the 1990s, it was apparent that there was an explosive use of the administrative offences, including section 26. These non-compliance administrative offences bring serious repercussions to the girls. Over one-quarter of the female cases in secure and open custody in Ontario during 1991 had been sentenced on non-compliance charges, and 30 per cent of girls charged in Toronto courts for non-compliance were sentenced to custody (Doob and Meen, 1993; Reitsma-Street, 1993). In 1994–5, 28 per cent of young female cases in all the Canadian provinces were heard in court for offences against the administration of justice (Canadian Centre for Justice Statistics, 1996). Although the rate of similar charges against boys has also steadily increased since 1985, the male rate is lower than for girls, hovering around 20 per cent.

In brief, judicial laws, regulations, and sanctions make up the third level of policing that works to keep girls in their place. Even when the severity of offence and criminal record are taken into account, girls face earlier and harsher sentences if they are not 'respectable' or strongly tied to a parental or marital home in which a male will take responsibility for restricting the girl's conduct (Beikoff, 1996; Chesney-Lind and Shelden, 1992; Kruttschnitt, 1982). With few exceptions, interventions for convicted female delinquents are minimal and inadequate, but they are not benign. There are frequent referrals for home investigations and counselling, repeated gynaecological examinations, intense perusal of sexual history, and a strong emphasis on retaining relationships with biological families. There is minimal vocational training; the focus is on poorly paid service jobs in cosmetology and housekeeping, and on good mothering or volunteer services (Ackland, 1982; Alder and Baines, 1996; Davidson, 1982; Geller, 1987; Kersten, 1989; Pyke, 1996; Reitsma-Street, 1991). These specific practices have not abated over the years, as one might have expected with the greater consciousness of sexism and discrimination and the repeal of overtly sexist legislation. Sadly, the new laws of the 1990s, with their increased punitive sanctions and decreased support for well-being, continue to constrain girls. Exploring alternatives to traditional ways of caring is not getting easier, although the directions for change are emerging more clearly.

DISCUSSION

Girls bear costs for the way they are expected to learn to care. These costs include limits in their available energy for personal development, minimal control over their bodies, and economic vulnerability. But it is not easy to explore other ways to care. Girls are policed to accept these costs. The daily judgements made on their reputation, the intermittent violence experienced in intimate relationships, and the severe, albeit infrequent coercive interventions by public agencies for unfeminine behaviours all pressure girls to learn the traditional lessons of caring and to discourage searching for new ways to care.

Compliance, endurance, and resignation to the lessons and policing are not just the strategies of yesterday. Unfortunately, struggles for change rarely go beyond anger, personal rituals, escapism, and martyrdom (Alder and Baines, 1996; Cain, 1989; Connell et al., 1982; Davies, 1984; Hall and Jefferson, 1975; McRobbie, 1991). Hemmed in by the towering constraints of class and racism that appear once again to menace more girls every day, girls in the 1990s struggle to negotiate their daily, complex encounters (Buettner, 1994; Canadian Advisory Council, 1992).

The majority of girls still believe that 'boys are girls' destiny because boys are girls' livelihood' (Cain, 1989: 9). *Thus, girls feel they cannot afford not to attract a boy.* The economic realities and the perspectives of most males about heterosexual relationships mean that girls must be 'just girls' to get a man, and thus have some chance of having a decent place to live, status, legitimate children, and some opportunities to get ahead. A girl learns quickly that to be different or bad is not to be more like a boy, with the attendant privileges, or to be regarded as a more rounded person, an individual, or maybe a new breed of girl. Rather, she learns that she risks not even being 'just a girl'. Losing her gender, a girl may well miss the chance to sign up for the unfair gender contract (Worrall, 1989: 79) in which she provides domestic, sexual, and personal caring for others, particularly a man, in return for some opportunities to be cared for by others. In brief, the high costs of deviation police girls to continue paying the costs for the way they care for others and themselves.

If a girl deviates too far from what is expected, she risks losing her reputation and gender, possibly a school year, and personal liberty. She may lose the potential economic benefits of a relationship with a male earner. But she also risks disruption in what she values most: caring for herself and others, and being cared for by others. Ostracism from friends, disruption in contact with parents and children, and loneliness are very high costs (Comack, 1996; Llewellyn, 1980; Sommers, 1995). Covering up their voices and feeling self 'slipping away in relationships' are at the heart of the loneliness most girls feel as they learn the lessons of becoming a female adolescent, even if privileged and educated. Brown, Gilligan, and their collaborators wept as they understood how girls become silenced by adult women and men. Standing at the edge of womanhood, girls begin to speak about themselves, about their thoughts and feelings, as something that might be endangered or jeopardized:

> If they speak their strong feelings and thoughts—that is, if they bring themselves fully into relationships—they risk losing their relationships because no one will want to be with them; yet if they do not speak—if they take themselves out of relationship for the sake of 'relationships'—they lose relationships that are genuine or authentic. (Brown and Gilligan, 1992: 165)

As we near the next century, understanding the need for change is growing, as is the value of exploring alternatives that build on the actual experiences of girls, their mothers, and their grandmothers. Change starts with girls and adult women listening to and learning from the resistance of girls to the lessons of caring. By resistance I mean the sustained use of routines, discourse, and actions that oppose and modify the 'dailiness' or immediate circumstances in which a person or group lives. Resistance is not a unitary concept and is not confined to a few people or places. There are many sites to contest, to express discontent, and to build alternatives. Several aspects or approaches to resistance should be considered: 'not taking it', pursuing power, building mutuality, and creating new strengths.

There is the resistance of 'not taking it'. Darcy used these words to sum up her stance to the abuse, injustice, indifference, and confusion in her world and her willingness to break rules to get something else. This type of resistance includes straightforward opposition to expectations, rules, and demands and some form of gentle, rude, or violent refusal. Girls in the sister study exemplified this type of resistance in their attempts to have fun, to get away, to find the answer, and to search for a better life for themselves.

In a study of three Boston child welfare agencies over an 80-year period Gordon (1988) found examples of girls who tried to resist the repeated demands for sexual and domestic services from males in their homes by, for instance, refusing to do housework, running away to a religious order, or escaping to the streets and getting paid for their sexual services. From her study of two Puerto Rican girl groups, Campbell (1987: 464) describes resistance as rejection of certain oppressive aspects of race, class, and gender. 'She is Puerto Rican but neither provincial nor un-American. She may be poor but her life is neither drab nor criminal. She enjoys her femininity but rejects passivity and suffering.' Breines (1992: 23) explores how even young, White, privileged girls kept protesting the ambivalences and contradictions that their gender bred them to. The rebelliousness was like 'dry tinder ready for the spark of revolt'. Cain (1989: 17) conceptualizes this approach to resistance as the 'circuitous strategies for salvaging autonomy'. This approach to resistance emphasizes the need to take better care of self—to put more value on one's own needs, interests, and desires (Gordon, 1988: 242).

Another aspect of resistance is the active search for power, or what Davies (1984) conceptualizes as the ability to alter the course of events and to create possibilities where none existed before. In the sister study, Diane and Daphine, two girls convicted for many delinquencies, were the most articulate and conscious in their development of strength and power in order to do more things for themselves and others they cared about. Although they worried they were ugly and not ladylike, they also resisted the pressures to act just like a girl. Moreover, they valued strength and consciously pursued it in its physical, intellectual, and emotional dimensions. Diane was proud that 'it took six men to hold me' in a fight, and she admired a female social worker because 'she had the power to do things'. Daphine felt she could learn and do anything, and was very pleased she 'beat 14 guys when I wrote the test for the Armed Forces'.

Many girls do not seem very clear about what they wish to create with this fledgling strength and power. What is clear is that girls are searching for the power to create the 'space for change' (Brophy and Smart, 1985: 17), so they can learn to name, explore, enjoy, expand, and construct alternative ways to care for themselves and others, and to make their own mark on the world (Canadian Advisory Council, 1992; Holmes and Silverman, 1992; McRobbie, 1991; Robertson, 1990). For five years Brown and Gilligan kept coming back to listen to the voices of 100 young girls, ages 7 to 16. What did they hear?

> . . . signs of self-silencing or capitulation to debilitating cultural norms . . . and signs
> of political resistance, times when people struggle against abusive relationships and
> fight for relationships in which it is possible for them to disagree openly with others,
> to feel and speak a full range of emotions. (1992: 30)

Girls pursue power in areas of intimacy, such as in relations with friends, in the struggle against physical violence from loved ones, and in control over reproductivity. In the sister study, Deborah finally decided her boyfriend was making the important decisions about the use of drugs and school and that this was not good for her. Therefore, upon leaving training school she resisted building her life around one boy and resumed her earlier interests in the theatre, outrageous dressing, and caring for close female friends. Survey and qualitative research shows that girls, delinquent or not, identify healthier relationships or 'making connections' as top priorities (e.g., Canadian Advisory Council, 1992; Child Welfare League of Canada, 1996; Holmes and Silverman, 1992; Gilligan et al., 1990; Sommers, 1995). Finding strength to pursue these humane connections without sacrificing sexual orientation or racial pride is particularly strong among lesbians and girls of colour (O'Brien, 1994).

Another arena of resistance occurs as a protection against economic vulnerability and the pursuit of economic independence. From the sister study completed in the early 1980s we learn that one-quarter of the girls aspired to non-traditional jobs. If they are successful, they may earn at least some money to support their struggle for a space to change. By the 1990s, the majority of girls, delinquent or not, report working for pay or looking for work. They want vocational training and good jobs, although most still find paid work in services and in part-time jobs (Canadian Council on Social Development, 1996: 24; Holmes and Silverman, 1992; Pyke, 1996).

Searching for mutuality or building supportive relationships is an approach to resistance that minimizes the damage of problematic daily life and maximizes the protection of others. Girls try to take care of each other, like Natalie protecting her younger sister from her father's belt or running to her friend's mother for some loving and fun. Gordon (1988), for example, found girls went to child welfare agencies for help when the father began to molest a younger sister. Brown and Gilligan found that their 100 girls 'remain on the lookout for others with whom they can be safely seen and with whom they can safely speak' (1992: 168). Better relationships with friends and families were the top concerns, major topic of discussion with peers, and priority for change in the Canadian survey of 1,603 representative girls, with drugs, school, and environment ranking lower (Holmes and Silverman, 1992: 75, 78, 81).

The Girl Guides, an organization that works exclusively with young girls, reaches 10 per cent of Canadian girls. Despite ambivalence around feminism, there is a growing awareness of sexism and the lessons and costs girls face just because they are girls. Currently, leaders are facing complex challenges and charges of being anti-male. But the Guides organization is reaffirming its commitment to pro-female principles and a single-sex organization in the face of court challenges by men wishing to become leaders:

> Most significant is the view that the Girl Guide movement is a 'safe place' for them to be together, to attempt to learn new skills without fear of failure, and to talk about issues of interest and concern to them. Unlike their experiences in a co-ed setting, the girls and women did not fear exclusion or ridicule, and genuinely valued and enjoyed the company of other girls and women in this all too rare all-female environment. (Varpalotai, 1994: 20)

Aptheker (1989) conceptualizes resistance as more than spaces to protest, to find power, or to build mutual strength. Basing her work on an extensive review of the art, songs, life stories, and needlework of generations of women of all races, Aptheker speaks of the resilient and persistent efforts of women to refuse to tolerate oppressive situations and ugliness by salvaging, coping, building, and putting up a struggle to celebrate and to strengthen 'connections between people in the family, at work, and in the community' (Aptheker, 1989: 178–80). She argues that the attention women give to singing, celebrations and rituals, bake sales, pretty curtains, mutual aid, working at double jobs to keep their children in school and out of the mines, or making something out of nothing is a form of resistance—despite the appearance of compliance—to *what men define as important in life*. For instance, Alice Walker, the Black author, writes of the way her mother always found time for her flower garden, no matter how poor they were or how long she had to work. In her *Revolutionary Petunias and Other Poems*, Walker (1973: 70) captures the resistance in caring for beauty:

> Rebellious. Living.
> Against the Elemental Crush.
> A Song of Color
> Blooming Gloriously
> For its Self.

The most exciting new work in the 1990s describes how girls and women are redefining caring relations. Brown and Gilligan (1992) worked with themselves and collaborators to stop 'hiding in expectations of goodness and control' with each other and the girls they were researching. They experimented with disagreement, risks, and authentic relations within a supportive, knowledge-seeking environment. Duffy speaks of 'learning as a subversive activity' in a Toronto woman-centred alternative school (1994: 33). Teachers, and students as young as nine years old, reflect on how they do things and how they could be done differently, using co-operative models, co-evaluation, vigorous physical education, and individual pacing of learning. Olafsdottir (1996) argues that systematic alternatives are needed in caring lessons by age five. The work groups in junior kindergarten need to be segregated by sex so neither sex feels the humiliation of learning new skills in areas already monopolized by the other sex. Thus, the lack of power, individual attention, assertiveness, and risk-taking that girls experience is addressed in the pedagogy of 'dare training', lessons in mistakes, and a balanced response to pain, blood, and disagreements.

In the 1995 Platform for Action developed at the 4th United Nations Conference on Women in Beijing, China, the rights of the 'girl child' and her potential as a future leader became a critical area of concern (Child Welfare League, 1996). It is a tall challenge for a girl to learn to care for herself, her future children, and her community in less destructive ways. This is an unfair burden, however, unless adult women and men learn to listen to girls as they resist the current discriminatory, silencing world they grow up in (Vanstone, 1996). Adults need to change their lessons about what is caring and to stop policing girls into constrictive, hurtful ways of caring.

It is possible and has started. Far more research and redeployment of resources are needed to understand the varieties of resistance and the conditions under which resistances flourish best so alternative ways for girls to care for themselves and others can emerge. The girls in the sister study, and delinquent and non-delinquent girls in other research, see that females are the major providers of caring. Those few sisters who found nourishing relationships with adult women seemed more likely to resist the hurtful costs of caring—by learning to care better for themselves, to celebrate life, and to find some space for alternatives. Their courage and creativity suggest directions for change. The tasks and love of caring for self and others can be enriched and the costs decreased. Shall we start in our relations with each other as adult women, and with five-year-old girls?

NOTES

1. Thanks to Dr David R. Offord for permission to use the sister data from the McMaster University 'Comparison of Hard-to-Serve Adolescents and Their Siblings' study, and for years of insightful suggestions. The financial assistance of the Ontario Ministry of Community and Social Services, the Laidlaw Foundation, Laurentian University Research Funds, and 'Changes in the Conditions that Shape Caring Labour' SSHRC Strategic Research Grant helped in the collection of data and supported me while I was writing the findings.

    For further information on the original sibling survey, see Reitsma-Street et al. (1985), and on the sister study, see Reitsma-Street and Offord (1991). All but one of the 26 sister pairs were Caucasian. The average age of the delinquents was 16.9 while the non-delinquent sisters averaged 19—one-third of them first-born. The questions and analysis took into account differences in age and birth order. Four-fifths of the parents were English-speaking, and 75 per cent of the families had more than three children. Names and identifying details about the girls from the study have been changed. Quotes are taken from the record made of all the interviews, records, tests, and summary data available on 12 of the 26 sister pairs (24 girls) theoretically selected for intense qualitative analysis (Reitsma-Street, 1988). The quotes accurately reflect what the interviewers wrote to capture a girl's response to open-ended questions, or her spontaneous comments to structured questions in the 80-page interview schedule. Occasionally I changed syntax and grammar.

2. Section 26, Young Offenders Act, 1980–81–82–83, c.110; amended by c. 32, Bill C-106, passed by the House of Commons, 27 June 1986.

REFERENCES

Ackland, J.W. 1982. *Girls in Care: A Case Study of Residential Treatment.* Hampshire, England: Gower.

Alder, C., and M. Baines, eds. 1996. . . . *And When She Was Bad? Working with Young Women in Juvenile Justice and Related Areas.* Hobart, Tasmania: National Clearinghouse for Youth Studies.

Aptheker, B. 1989. *Tapestries of Life: Women's Work, Women's Consciousness, and the Meaning of Daily Experience.* Amherst: University of Massachusetts Press.

Artz, S. 1994. 'Violence in our schools and the violent school girl', in H. Coward, ed., *Anger in Our City: Youth Seeking Meaning.* Victoria: University of Victoria, Centre for Studies in Religion and Society: 1–68.

Baines, M., and C. Alder. 1996. 'Are girls more difficult to work with? Youth workers' perspectives in juvenile justice and related areas', *Crime and Delinquency* 42, 3: 467–85.

Baker, M. 1985. *What Will Tomorrow Bring? A Study of the Aspirations of Adolescent Women.* Ottawa: Canadian Advisory Council on the Status of Women.

Barrett, M., and M. McIntosh. 1983. *The Anti-Social Family.* London: Verso.

Beikoff, L. 1996. 'Queensland's juvenile justice system: equity, access and justice for young women?', in Alder and Baines, eds, 1996: 15–24.

Bell, L., ed. 1987. *Good Girls/Bad Girls: Sex Trade Workers and Feminists Face to Face.* Toronto: Women's Press.

Bertrand, Marie-Andrée. 1979. *La Femme et le Crime.* Montréal: L'Aurore.

Bibeau, J. 1989. 'Murders and misogyny', *Le Devoir*, 9 Dec.; reprinted and translated in Malette and Chalouh, eds, 1991: 43–4.

Breines, W. 1992. *Young, White, and Miserable: Growing Up Female in the Fifties.* Boston: Beacon Press.

Brenzel, B. 1983. *Daughters of the State: A Social Portrait of the First Reform School for Girls in North America, 1856–1905.* Cambridge, Mass.: MIT Press.

Brophy, J., and C. Smart, eds. 1985. *Women-in-law: Explorations in Law, Family and Sexuality.* London: Routledge & Kegan Paul.

Brodie, J., ed. 1996. *Women and Canadian Public Policy.* Toronto: Harcourt & Brace.

Brown, L.M., and C. Gilligan. 1992. *Meeting at the Crossroads: Women's Psychology and Girls' Development.* New York: Ballantine.

Buettner, E. 1994. 'Book reviews of *Fashioning the Feminine: Girls, Popular Culture and Schooling; Young, White, and Miserable*; and *Young, Female, and Black*', *Signs* 20, 1: 180–4.

Byles, J.A. 1980. 'Adolescent girls in need of protection', *American Journal of Orthopsychiatry* 50, 2: 264–78.

Cain, M. 1989. 'Feminists transgress criminology', in M. Cain, ed., *Growing Up Good: Policing the Behaviour of Girls in Europe.* London: Sage.

Cameron, S. 1989. 'Our daughters, ourselves', *Globe and Mail*, 8 Dec.; reprinted in Malette and Chalouh, eds, 1991: 159–61.

Campbell, A. 1984. *Girls in the Gang: A Report from New York City.* Oxford: Basil Blackwell.

Campbell, A. 1987. 'Self definition by rejection: The case of gang girls', *Social Problems* 34, 5: 451–66.

Canadian Advisory Council on the Status of Women. 1992. *Young Women Speak Out: 1992 Symposium Report.* Ottawa.

Canadian Centre for Justice Statistics. 1996. *Youth Court Statistics, 1994–95.* Ottawa, catalogue 85–522–XPB.

Canadian Council on Social Development. 1996. *The Progress of Canada's Children.* Ottawa.

Caputo, Tullio, and Denis C. Bracken. 1988. 'Custodial dispositions and the *Young Offenders Act*', in J. Hudson et al., eds, *Justice and the Young Offender in Canada.* Toronto: Wall & Thompson: 124–43.

Carrington, K. 1996. 'Offending girls: rethinking intervention regimes', in Alder and Baines, eds, 1996: 7–14.

Carrington, P.J., and S. Moyer. 1994. 'Interprovincial variations in the use of custody for young offenders: A funnel analysis', *Canadian Journal of Criminology* 36, 3: 271–90.

Chesney-Lind, M., and R.G. Shelden. 1992. *Girls: Delinquency and Juvenile Justice.* Pacific Grove, Calif.: Brooks/Cole.

Child Welfare League of Canada and Ontario Association of Children's Aid Societies. 1996. 'The Girl Child', Canada's Children . . . Canada's Future Conference. Ottawa, 26 Nov.

Chodorow, N. 1978. *The Reproduction of Mothering: Psychoanalysis and the Sociology of Gender.* Berkeley: University of California Press.

Collister, E., and S. Scott. 1990. 'Girls' parents demand inquest', *Montreal Gazette*, 23 Jan.: A5.

Comack, E. 1996. *Women in Trouble: Connecting Women's Law Violations to their Histories of Abuse.* Halifax: Fernwood.

Committee on Sexual Offences against Children and Youths (R.F. Badgley, chairman). 1984. *Sexual Offences Against Children*, 2 vols. Ottawa: Minister of Supply and Services.

Connell, R.W., D.J. Ashenden, S. Kessler, and G.W. Dowsett. 1982. *Schools, Families and Social Division.* Sydney: George Allen & Unwin.

Corrado, R.R., and A. Markwart. 1994. 'The need to reform the YOA in response to violent young offenders: Confusing, reality or myth?', *Canadian Journal of Criminology* 36, 3: 343–78.

Cowie, J., V. Cowie, and E. Slater. 1968. *Delinquency in Girls.* London: Heinemann.

Davidson, S., ed. 1982. *Justice for Young Women.* Seattle: New Directions for Young Women.

Davies, L. 1984. *Pupil Power.* London: Falmer Press.

Donzelot, Jacques. 1979. *The Policing of Families*, trans. Robert Hurley. New York: Pantheon Books; originally published, 1977.

Doob, A.N., and J.M. Meen. 1993. 'An exploration of changes in dispositions for young offenders in Toronto', *Canadian Journal of Criminology* 35, 1: 19–30.

Duffy, M.A. 1994. 'Linden lore: Images of a new educational model for young women', *Resources for Feminist Research* 23, 3: 32–6.

Dyhouse, C. 1981. *Girls Growing Up in Late Victorian and Edwardian England.* London: Routledge & Kegan Paul.

Felice, M., and D.R. Offord. 1975. 'Girl delinquency', in R. Cavan, ed., *Readings in Juvenile Delinquency*, 3rd edn. Philadelphia: J.B. Lippincott.

Finch, J., and D. Groves, eds. 1983. *A Labour of Love: Women, Work and Caring.* London: Routledge & Kegan Paul.

Foster, S. 1988. *The One Girl in Ten: A Self Portrait of the Teen-age Mother.* Washington: Child Welfare League of America.

Gagnon, R., and L. Langelier-Biron. 1982. *Les filles en marge.* Rapport No. 6. Groupe de Recherche sur L'Inadaptation Juvenile, Université de Montréal.

Galt, V. 1967. 'U.S. Study cites teens' need for parental involvement', *Globe and Mail*, 10 Sept.: A1.

Geller, G.R. 1987. 'Young women in conflict with the law', in E. Adelberg and C. Currie, eds, *Too Few to Count.* Vancouver: Press Gang Publishers: 113–26.

Gilligan, C., N. Lyons, and T. Hammer, eds. 1990. *Making Connections: The Traditional Worlds of Adolescent Girls at Emma Willard School.* Cambridge, Mass.: Harvard University Press.

Gordon, L. 1988. *Heroes of Their Own Lives.* New York: Viking.

Hall, S., and T. Jefferson. 1975. *Resistance Through Rituals: Youth Subcultures in Post-War Britain.* New York: Holmes and Meier.

Hatch, Alison, and Karlene Faith. 1989–90. 'The female offender in Canada: A statistical profile', *Canadian Journal of Women and the Law* 3, 2: 432–56.

Herold, E.S. 1984. *Sexual Behavior of Canadian Young People.* Markham, Ont.: Fitzhenry & Whiteside.

Holmes, J., and E.L. Silverman. 1992. *We're Here, Listen to Us! A Survey of Young Women in Canada.* Ottawa: Canadian Advisory Council on the Status of Women.

Hochschild, A., with A. Machung. 1989. *The Double Shift: Working Parents and the Revolution at Home.* New York: Viking.

Hubbard, R. 1981. 'The Emperor Doesn't Wear Any Clothes: The Impact of Feminism on Biology', in D. Spender, ed., *Men's Studies Modified.* New York: Pergamon Press.

Hudson, A. 1983. 'The welfare state and adolescent femininity', *Youth and Policy* 2, 1: 5–13.

Jephcott, A.P. 1942. *Girls Growing Up.* London: Faber & Faber.

Johnson, H., and V. Sacco. 1995. 'Researching violence against women: Statistics Canada's national survey', *Canadian Journal of Criminology* 37, 3: 281–304.

Kauppi, C., and M. Reitsma-Street. 1996. 'Women and poverty in Northern Ontario', in M. Kechnie and M. Reitsma-Street, eds, *Changing Lives: Women in Northern Ontario.* Toronto: Dundurn Press: 213–23.

Kersten, Joachim. 1989. 'The institutional control of girls and boys', in M. Cain, ed., *Growing Up Good.* London: Sage.

Konopka, G. 1966. *The Adolescent Girl in Conflict.* Englewood Cliffs, NJ.: Prentice-Hall.

Konopka, G. 1976. *Young Girls.* Englewood Cliffs, NJ.: Prentice-Hall.

Kostash, M. 1987. *No Kidding: Inside the World of Teenage Girls.* Toronto: McClelland & Stewart.

Kruttschnitt, C. 1982. 'Respectable women and the law', *Sociological Quarterly* 23 (Spring): 221–34.

Langelier-Biron, Louise. 1983. 'The delinquent young girl: A non-entity?', in R.R. Corrado, M. LeBlanc, and J. Trepanier, eds, *Current Issues in Juvenile Justice.* Toronto: Butterworths: 61–72.

LaPrairie, C. 1993. 'Aboriginal women and crime in Canada: Identifying the issues', in E. Adelberg and C. Currie, eds, *In Conflict with the Law: Women and the Canadian Justice System.* Vancouver: Press Gang: 235–46.

Lees, Sue. 1989. 'Learning to love: Sexual reputation, morality and the social control of girls', in M. Cain, ed., *Growing Up Good.* London: Sage: 9–37.

Lerman, Paul. 1984. 'Child welfare, the private sector and community-based corrections', *Crime and Delinquency* 30, 1: 5–38.

Llewellyn, Mandy. 1980. 'Studying girls at school: The implications of schooling', in R. Deem, ed., *Schooling for Women's Work.* London: Routledge & Kegan Paul.

McRobbie, A. 1991. *Feminism and Youth Culture: From 'Jacki' to 'Just Seventeen'.* London: Macmillan Education.

McRobbie, A., and R. McCabe. 1981. 'Introduction', in McRobbie and McCabe, eds, *Feminism for Girls.* London: Routledge & Kegan Paul.

Malette, L., and M. Chalouh, eds. 1991. *The Montreal Massacre*, trans. M. Wilderman. Charlottetown: Gynergy.

Mies, Maria. 1989. 'Self-determination: The end of a utopia', *Resources for Feminist Research* 18, 3: 51–6.

National Council of Welfare. 1997. *Welfare incomes 1995.* Ottawa.

Nease, Barbara. 1966. 'Measuring juvenile delinquency in Hamilton', *Canadian Journal of Criminology and Corrections* 8, 2: 133–45.

O'Brien, C. 1994. 'The social organization of the treatment of lesbian, gay and bisexual youth in group homes and youth shelters', *Canadian Review of Social Policy* 34: 37–58.

Olafsdottir, M.P. 1996. 'Kids are both girls and boys in Iceland', *Women's Studies International Forum* 19, 4: 357–69.

Oliker, S.J. 1995. 'The proximate contexts of workfare and work: A framework for studying poor women's economic choices', *Sociological Quarterly* 36, 2: 251–72.

Orton, M., and H. Rosenblatt. 1986. *Report #3: Adolescent Pregnancy in Ontario.* Hamilton, Ont.: McMaster University School of Social Work.

Parent, C. 1986. 'Actualités et bibliographics: La protection chevalresque ou les représentations masculines du traitement des femmes dans la justice pénale', *Déviance et Société* 10, 2: 147–75.

Pedersen, W., and L. Wichstrom. 1995. 'Patterns of delinquency in Norwegian adolescents', *British Journal of Criminology* 35, 4: 543–62.

Petrie, C. 1986. *The Nowhere Girls*. Aldershot, Hants, England: Gower.

Propper, Alice. 1979. 'The relationship of maternal employment and sex to adolescents' parental relationship', in I. Ishwaran, ed., *Childhood and Adolescence in Canada*. Toronto: McGraw-Hill Ryerson.

Pyke, J. 1996. 'Young women in the Australian vocational training system', in Alder and Baines, eds, 1996: 97–104.

Reitsma-Street, M. 1988. 'Female Delinquency and Conformity in Adolescent Sisters', doctoral diss., University of Toronto.

Reitsma-Street, M. 1990. 'Implementation of the *Young Offenders Act*: Five Years Later', *Canadian Social Work Review* 7, 2: 136–58.

Reitsma-Street, M. 1991. 'A review of female delinquency', in A. Leschied and P. Jaffe, eds, *The Young Offenders Act Revolution*. Toronto: University of Toronto Press: 248–90.

Reitsma-Street, M. 1993. 'Canadian youth court charges and dispositions for females before and after implementation of the Young Offenders Act', *Canadian Journal of Criminology* 35, 4: 437–58.

Reitsma-Street, M., and D.R. Offord. 1991. 'Girl delinquents and their sisters: A challenge for practice', *Canadian Social Work Review* 8, 1: 11–27.

Reitsma-Street, M., D.R. Offord, and T. Finch. 1985. 'Pairs of same-sexed siblings discordant for antisocial behavior', *British Journal of Psychiatry* 146: 415–23.

Robertson, H. 1990. *A Cappella: A Report on the Realities, Concerns, Expectations and Barriers Experienced by Adolescent Women in Canada*. Ottawa: Canadian Teachers' Federation.

Schur, E.M. 1984. *Labeling Women Deviant*. New York: Random House.

Schwartz, I.M., M. Jackson-Beeck, and R. Anderson. 1984. 'The "hidden" system of juvenile control', *Crime and Delinquency* 30, 3: 371–85.

Schwendinger, H., and J. Schwendinger. 1985. *Adolescent Subcultures and Delinquency*, research edn. New York: Praeger.

Scott, K. 1996. *The Progress of Canada's Children 1996*. Ottawa: Canadian Council on Social Development.

Shacklady-Smitt, L. 1978. 'Sexist assumptions and female delinquency', in C. Smart and B. Smart, eds, *Women, Sexuality and Social Control*. London: Routledge & Kegan Paul.

Sharpe, S. 1976. *Just Like a Girl*. Harmondsworth, Middlesex: Penguin.

Sommers, E.K. 1995 *Voices from Within: Women Who Have Broken the Law*. Toronto: University of Toronto Press.

Stacey, J. 1990. *Brave New Families—Stories of Domestic Upheaval in Late Twentieth-Century America*. New York: Basic Books.

Statutes of Canada. 1908. *An Act Respecting Juvenile Delinquents*. 7–8 Edward VII, c.40.

Statutes of Canada, Revised. 1985. *An Act Respecting Young Offenders*, c. Y-1.

Swift, K. 1994. *Manufacturing Bad Mothers*. Toronto: University of Toronto Press.

Trépanier, Jean. 1986. 'La justice des mineurs au Québec: 25 ans de transformations (1960–1985)', *Criminologie* 19, 1: 189–214.

Vanstone, S. 1996. 'Young women and feminism in Northern Ontario', in M. Kechnie and M. Reitsma-Street, eds, *Changing Lives: Women in Northern Ontario*. Toronto: Dundurn Press: 325–34.

Varpalotai, A. 1994. '"Women only and proud of it!": The politicization of the Girl Guides of Canada', *Resources for Feminist Research* 23, 1–2: 14–23.

Walker, Alice. 1973. 'The nature of this flower is to bloom', in Walker, *Revolutionary petunias and other poems*. New York: Harcourt Brace Jovanovich.

Weiler, K. 1978. 'Unmanageable children in Ontario: A legal review', in H. Berkley et al., eds, *Children's Rights*. Toronto: Ontario Institute for Studies in Education: 59–77.

Widom, Cathy Spatz, Faith S. Katkink, Abigail J. Stewart, and Mark Fondacaro. 1983. 'Multivariate analysis of personality and motivation in female delinquents', *Journal of Research in Crime and Delinquency* 21, 3: 277–90.

Wilson, Deidre. 1978. 'Sexual codes and conduct: A study of teenage girls', in C. Smart and B. Smart, eds, *Women, Sexuality and Social Control*. London: Routledge & Kegan Paul.

Wolf, N. 1990. *The Beauty Myth*. Toronto: Vintage Books.

Wordes, M., T.S. Bynum, and C.J. Corley. 1994. 'Locking up youth: The impact of race on detention decisions', *Journal of Research in Crime and Delinquency* 31, 2: 149–65.

Worrall, Anne. 1989. 'Working with female offenders: Beyond "alternatives to custody"', *British Journal of Social Work* 19: 77–93.

6

Dutiful Daughters and Undemanding Mothers: Constraining Images of Giving and Receiving Care in Middle and Later Life

JANE ARONSON

In Canada, as in comparable economic and social welfare jurisdictions, it is commonly estimated that up to 90 per cent of the care of old people is provided informally, largely in the context of families (Ontario Ministry of Community and Social Services et al., 1991: 4). The rest, only about 10 per cent, is supplied by formal health and social services. In the world of informal care in families, women—typically wives, daughters, and daughters-in-law—tend to be the care providers and, by virtue of women's longer life expectancy, it is predominantly women, especially in older age groups, who are the care receivers.

This chapter addresses the way in which this largely taken-for-granted pattern of care actually unfolds in women's lives in contemporary Canada and with what consequences for their welfare. I focus particularly on the unfolding of this pattern in the context of giving and receiving care in mother-daughter relationships. The accounts of women in studies of caregiving and receiving are penetrated and constrained by dominant images and ideologies concerning the family, gender relations, and old age. Particularly striking in women's experiences are how seemingly remote social policies—in the form of limited public supports and care and images of their scarcity—pressed them into difficult and unwanted relations of dependence and obligation. In the 10 years since this study was done, we have seen continuing retreat in formal or public provisions for the care of elderly people and significant erosion of previous understandings of people's entitlements to health and social security. Families, and especially women within them, are expected to do more and social programs to do less as governments respond to the declared imperatives of deficit reduction, privatization, and enhancement of marketplace competition (Armstrong and Armstrong, 1996; Brodie, 1996). Thus, if the women described in this chapter struggled with the tensions of family care relations 10 years ago, it is likely that they and women in comparable circumstances today struggle to an even greater degree.

As an area for exploring the complexities of women's caring, societal responses to the needs of elderly people who are ill, disabled, or frail are an especially fruitful context. For one thing, care of elderly people is an area that has received a fair amount of attention over the last 20 years. There is, therefore, a substantial amount of material to draw upon and consider, and patterns can be clearly identified in the tone and content of government activity and public debate. Secondly, practices, ideas, and beliefs about meeting the needs of old people touch the lives of a great many people. The aging of the population means that most of us will have elderly relatives and friends, at least some of whom will need support of one kind or another. Some will require very heavy physical care, but most will need what Lewis and Meredith (1988: 32) term 'semi-care' and Hasselkus (1988: 686) terms 'anticipatory' and 'protective' caregiving—in other words, a mix of practical support and invisible emotional work. We therefore have direct experience of thinking about our own or our families' relationships with and obligations towards elderly parents or relatives, their expectations or wishes in relation to us, and the place of collective provision for their welfare. Furthermore, we can now all reasonably expect to grow old ourselves. Thirdly, exploration of the care of old people in families (daughters and daughters-in-law assisting mothers and mothers-in-law being the most common intergenerational care relationships) provides an opportunity for understanding women's experiences on both 'sides' of care relationships and, thus, for thinking about ways of meeting people's needs that value and enhance the interests and welfare of both care providers and care receivers. With this object in view, Lynne Segal's important question about the challenge for feminism in the future serves as the focus for the chapter: 'How do we provide for the needs of all, and not at the expense of women?' (1987: 242).

To explore this overarching question and to consider how needs for care can be met under conditions that are nourishing, fair, and unexploitative for both receivers and givers, I build here on data drawn from a qualitative study I carried out in urban southern Ontario (Aronson, 1988). The 32 women who participated in in-depth interviews described themselves as either aging women who had adult daughters and were concerned about the future or as daughters of such women. They ranged in age from 35 to 85. I located them through provincial organizations of teachers and retired teachers. All of them had worked outside the home as school teachers at some point in their lives, none were poor, and almost all were White and Canadian-born. The participants' accounts of their experiences constitute both descriptions of individual situations and life histories and 'points of entry' into the wider social and ideological processes that frame them (Smith, 1986: 7).

This sample presents both limits and opportunities for exploring women's caring in the context of long-term care for elderly people. Firstly, in terms of methodological considerations, it is clear that the participants were a relatively privileged group in terms of social class and race. Caution is therefore needed in generalizing from their experiences to the realities of women in different social locations. At the same time, though, their relative privilege gives us a glimpse at women giving and receiving care in, theoretically, quite favoured and well-supported circumstances. For example, study participants' class positioning and economic circumstances afforded them particular choices and entitlements: some of the older women I interviewed could afford to pay for cleaning or for other needed supports or 'extras' to sustain themselves at home; caregiving daughters in the sample had more flexibility in organizing their time (for instance, to accompany their mothers to medical appointments or to take off time in an emergency) than would their counterparts in jobs that have fewer protections or benefits than teaching. Further, middle-class, English-speaking, Canadian-born women such as these study participants generally face fewer barriers than working-class women, immigrant women, or women of colour in claiming their entitlements and negotiating their pathways through the array of public institutions that make

up long-term care for older people. That caring still proved to be tense and problematic for this sample of women is, therefore, especially noteworthy and sober-
ing.

At a broader conceptual level, it is important to recognize that this study's
focus on women's caring in mother-daughter relationships gives us only a partial
image of the totality of women's caring in the arena of long-term care. It leaves
out women's paid caring as well as women's unpaid caring in relationships other
than nuclear family/intergenerational ties. I began this study of mothers and
daughters in the mid-1980s, buoyed by the gathering stream of feminist work on
caring that challenged the social policies and the rhetoric of community care that
simply took for granted the 'naturalness' and availability of family care (Finch and
Groves, 1980, 1983; Graham, 1983; Neysmith, 1981; Waerness, 1984). This
important body of critical work made visible the ways in which such policies and
their assumptions disadvantage women in families and in the labour market and
curtail their entitlements and opportunities as citizens. Generated in reaction and
resistance to public policies deemed regressive and unfair to women in families,
this critique kept a fairly narrow focus on women's care within nuclear family ties.

Only with hindsight is it apparent that this strategic focus overlooked the
experiences and possibilities of women's caring in other relational contexts, for
example: in family ties that extend more broadly than those characteristic of
White, Western, middle-class family forms; and in lesbian relationships, friendships, and communities that lie outside the orbit of heterosexual kinship ties
(Graham, 1993). Caregiving and receiving in contexts such as these, which are
not structured by narrow images of family obligation or by family obligation at
all, represent possibilities of care and connection worked out on different, potentially less coercive bases from which we might envision constructive alternatives
for the future (Aronson, forthcoming; Ahmad and Atkin, 1996; Callwood, 1986;
Carpenter, 1994). Later in the chapter, these possibilities are addressed as we
consider future directions for knowledge-building and practice and as we set the
experiences of the mothers and daughters presented below in their full social
context.

As a backdrop for positioning and exploring participating mothers' and
daughters' accounts, a brief review follows of the present pattern of care of old
people and of emerging trends in health and social policy.

PATTERNS IN THE CARE OF OLD PEOPLE: MATERIAL ARRANGEMENTS AND RESOURCES AND THEIR UNDERLYING ASSUMPTIONS

Publicly provided services for old people in need of care or support include a
range of health and social services: different types of congregate care (e.g., homes
for the aged, nursing homes, chronic care facilities' day centres) and a mix of services and resources intended to support people in their own homes (e.g., homemakers, visiting nurses, meals-on-wheels). With the exception of specialized
medical interventions, all these services can be provided informally—they have a
high degree of what has been termed 'substitutability' (Arber et al.,1988). The

boundary between formal and informal care is thus a very permeable phenome-non and the division is set in such a way that government services remain very much in the background.

Over the last decade, governments have been retreating further and further into this background. Dominant images of imminent fiscal crisis and public debt reduction have been used to justify cutbacks in all social programs (Battle and Torjman, 1995; Cooper and Neu, 1995; Lightman and Baines, 1996). With the introduction of the Canada Health and Social Transfer, the federal government has relinquished its role in framing and enforcing national standards in health care. Provincial governments, responsible for the delivery of health care, are thus able to renege on previously understood commitments as they preoccupy them-selves with balancing budgets.

In the long-term care arena, this preoccupation generates a number of trou-bling and regressive trends. Broadly, responsibility for the care and support of elderly people is being shifted from the public sphere of government attention to the private sphere of families and informal ties and to the realm of private care markets that can, of course, only be accessed by those with the ability to pay. We see public institutional care being reduced, but without a matching transfer of funds to public community-based services (Armstrong and Armstrong, 1996; Rosenthal, 1994). In community or home-based care, we see managerial approaches built on 'thin' (Hochschild, 1995) definitions of need and market-place images of efficiency that are more suited to assembly-line production of goods than to the delivery of personalized care (Aronson and Neysmith, 1997). Governments are simultaneously encouraging the development of private care markets and, within the shrinking domain of public care, moving towards fun-der-provider splits and the structuring of internal markets (Armstrong and Armstrong, 1996; MGEU, 1996). Allocation of the shrinking public resources available is not, of course, a random process. Research and the observations of service providers suggest consistently that they are introduced either when infor-mal caregivers, usually female kin, are non-existent or unavailable or, more typi-cally, when informal care arrangements have been so overtaxed as to break down, rather than on a truly shared or supportive basis (Aronson, 1992a; Walker, 1985).

At the time of writing, long-term care in Ontario contains elements of all these currents of instability and government retreat. A provincial commission formed to restructure health services is in the process of closing hospital and institutional beds, while the provincial government is proposing to shift respon-sibility for home-based care from the jurisdiction of the province to the jurisdic-tion of municipalities. In this highly disorganized environment, there is no clear assurance that additional funding for home-based care will actually be made available. In the media and in the protests of seniors' groups and coalitions of advocacy groups, we hear with mounting frequency of the human costs, risks, and inequities generated in this climate (Harman, 1997; Henderson, 1997; Weintraub, 1995). In effect, those who are disabled or frail are left increasingly to their own devices: if they have any informal sources of support—regardless of their quality or suitability—they are pressed to rely on them; if they can afford to do so, they may pay privately for support or care; or, their needs may simply go unmet.

In this straitened climate, public services and programs for the elderly rest ever more heavily on the informal sector—largely on the care provided by women in families. This pattern of intervention is legitimated by the ideology of familism—by the assumption that 'the family' is the proper locus of care for frail elderly people (and others deemed dependent) and that care can and should be moved 'closer to home' (British Columbia Royal Commission on Health Care and Costs, 1991). Political rhetoric and written policy are couched in language that implies the 'naturalness' of family ties and obligations to older kin, for example: 'Generally, family and friends provide the most effective support for older persons' (Ontario Office for Senior Citizens' Affairs, 1986: 10); 'Professional services should be used to enhance and supplement, not replace, family support services' (Ontario Ministry of Community and Social Services, 1991: 8). Writing from Alberta, Dacks et al. (1995: 276) characterize this process as 'the reprivatization of nurturing', noting how women's work is transferred from the public to the private domain, from visibility to invisibility.

The interests of women, either as providers or receivers of care, are seemingly not a central concern as this 'reprivatization' is accomplished by a range of health and social policies. Female family caregivers are the object of policy interest only in the sense that their work is recognized as crucial to the present organization of care. Thus, we see social programs intended to shore up their efforts and help them to carry on caring. Such programs as caregiver support groups and respite care serve to provide minimal short-term relief, but with the intention of sustaining the present division of care rather than changing it or asking whether it is in women's best interests to be, effectively, pressed into caregiving.

Just as women carers are of policy interest as a critical supply of unpaid caring labour, rather than as complete persons with aspirations and needs of their own, so it seems that the welfare of frail or disabled old people themselves is not, either, at the centre of debate about the care of the elderly. Inattention to old people's perspectives renders them passive participants in care arrangements, as if the objects rather than the subjects of the circumstances of their aging (Aronson, 1990). Looking at elderly women in particular, their lack of control in determining the conditions of their aging can be understood as one element of the systematic and lifelong disadvantage they experience in a culture that favours youth, independence, and masculinity. The small amount of research that exists on elderly women's realities suggests, unsurprisingly, that the experience of needing assistance can often be tense and problematic (Evers, 1981, 1985) and, indeed, that our understanding of the very idea of 'need' is poorly developed (Aronson, 1992b).

While women's interests as givers or receivers of care are seldom accorded primacy in policy-making, in the academic literature, the media, and public debate caregivers come into focus considerably more than do care receivers. Women located in the disability rights movement articulate with increasing clarity how commonly this erasure of those deemed 'dependent' occurs and take to task the tendency of feminist analyses of caring to be aligned, implicitly, with caregivers rather than with those who receive care (Morris, 1995). Research in the social sciences generally has tended to contribute to this divisive conceptualization by segmenting the life course into static stages and sets of interests. Images of 'intergenerational conflict' and the 'old age dependency burden' are more commonly heard in public discourse than are images of reciprocity and solidarity between generations (Binney and Estes, 1988; Johnson, 1995). In relation to women and care of old people, we see these divisive conceptualizations in the tendency to frame caregivers' and receivers' interests in oppositional terms as givers or takers (Briar and Ryan, 1986) or 'us and them' (Morris, 1993).

My interest in studying mothers *and* daughters was prompted by a concern to break down this problematic construction of givers and takers, which was, predictably, not reflected in the realities of my study sample. More than half of the older women I interviewed had cared for their own elderly mothers in the past. Exploration of their experiences as both caregivers and receivers counters the tendency in the literature to focus on fixed life stages and underscores, rather, the continuity of gender identity and caring over time. The biographies of two of these women are presented below. Their experiences illustrate sharply the degree to which women's lives are shaped by their care for and overlapping commitments to others. Their accounts also suggest how their caregiving experiences influenced their thoughts and feelings about receiving care in later life. After briefly addressing the patterned realities of women's life course that their experiences typify, I will explore how the assumptions and values embedded in social policies and public debate, discussed above, unfold and translate into women's lives as mothers and daughters engaged in care relationships. From the case material, I go on to discuss aspects of this process of translation over the life course, elaborating key issues by introducing the accounts of other women who participated in the research.

GIVING AND RECEIVING CARE OVER THE LIFE COURSE: MRS C AND MRS S

Mrs C

Mrs C is 66, a widow, and has a son and two daughters, all living in the Toronto area. She lives alone in the family home and has a number of chronic health problems: heart condition, post-cancer treatment complications, and impaired mobility. She continues to drive a car and is quite self-sufficient with some outside help: home care provides assistance with cleaning; she pays someone to do the heavy garden work; she attends a foot clinic; and she has a GP whom she likes. She is in regular phone and visiting contact with her children, especially her daughters, whom she describes as supportive and helpful with 'the incidentals'. She 'feels sorry' for an older friend who has no children.

Mrs C went into teaching when her children were all in elementary school, prompted by her husband's unemployment. Her salary became crucial as he grew increasingly disabled as a result of diabetes. Shortly after Mrs C finished her teacher training, her mother's health deteriorated; Mrs C felt her mother was overprescribed tranquillizers and, as a result, became mentally slow and confused. Mrs C contemplated having her mother come to live with her, but with a full-time job, a sick husband, and small children she decided this would be too much. Instead, for a period of time she ran two households. She tried to limit the amount of time she gave to her mother, feeling torn and concerned to devote proper attention to her husband and children.

As her mother's condition worsened, she realized that she 'couldn't handle everybody' and, very reluctantly, organized her mother's admission to a nursing home. She resented that her brother, her only sibling, was uninvolved in this, partly because he lived outside Toronto and partly because his wife kept her in-laws at a distance. Mrs C recalled upsetting weekly visits to her mother and the poor care provided in the nursing home. She expressed guilt at the memories and reflected that: 'I should have sued them, but I didn't have enough energy to take it on.'

Over the next few years, Mrs C's husband had to give up work completely and her children married and left home. In Mrs C's late fifties, her mother died, and shortly afterwards she had to retire because her husband required constant care. She regretted retiring and, for a time, tutored children privately at home because it brought her so much satisfaction. However, her own health then deteriorated and, as a result, her husband was admitted to a chronic care hospital where he died three years before the time of the interview.

Talking of her current situation, Mrs C was determined to stay in her own home and to be as independent as possible. While sometimes expressing a fierce independence and anger at the poor treatment meted out to old people, Mrs C also expressed some fears and uncertainty about her future. She acknowledged that her children were helpful and supportive and described their lives as busy and successful. Recognizing their limitations, she recognized her own a generation before:

> As my son said to me at one point, 'Mum, I'll come and help you as much as I can, but my first obligation's to my own family—you know, to my wife and children.' And I thought that was kind of callous . . . and then I thought afterwards: I did the same thing, you know, with my mother.

She explained that she made a point of not asking her daughters for too much, trying to pace her requests so as not to exceed their capacities. They did not talk about the future and she did not want to share her anxieties with them. She likened herself to her mother, whom she described as 'too proud' to say what she needed or was concerned about. Her mother's indirectness had irritated her, but now she felt she understood it. It was, thus, a matter of pride to Mrs C to be as independent as possible and not to expose her needs or concerns.

Mrs S

Mrs S is a 74-year-old divorced woman who lives alone in an apartment in Toronto and has a daughter who lives about an hour's drive away. Mrs S enjoyed the early years of her retirement. However, at 70 she had a heart attack followed by surgery and a caution from her doctor to be very careful. In the year or two before the interview, she had given up driving, hired someone to do housework, and no longer took the kinds of trips and vacations that she had enjoyed previously. She expressed anxiety about the future, concerned that she might be unable to manage alone in her apartment and frightened particularly at the prospect of dying alone. Her experiences of being hospitalized and of a local seniors' centre that she had 'tried' once left her with a distaste for 'being herded together'.

Mrs S had left her husband when their daughter was an infant, taking her back to her parental home in northern Ontario where she began working as a teacher. When her daughter left home and moved to Toronto, Mrs S followed some years later, found a teaching job, and established friendships and ties centred on her local church. When her daughter's first marriage ended, she and her small daughter lived with Mrs S for some years. After her daughter remarried and moved to the suburbs, Mrs S's mother—by then a widow and becoming frail—sold her home and stayed with Mrs S and her two sisters on a rotating basis for six months or a year at a time.

Mrs S saw it as unremarkable that her mother would stay with her and remembered, gratefully, her helpfulness to her when she had left her husband. She also recalled, with some guilt at talking about it, the tensions that her mother's long visits introduced into her life—the lack of privacy at home, the constraints on her social life—and how she tried to put limits on their duration. As her mother's health deteriorated, she went into a local home for the aged for a period, but she hated it because she so disliked 'being ruled' by other people. She eventually became confused and spent her last years in a hospital near one of Mrs S's sisters in another province. She had died only a few months before the interview.

Mrs S spoke to her daughter several times a week and described her, her son-in-law, and granddaughter with great affection. After Mrs S's heart attack, her daughter had raised the possibility of Mrs S going to live with them, but the plan did not materialize because of her son-in-law's objections. Mrs S noted, 'We didn't make a big thing of it. You know, it's a good stand to take because they [parents] can cause trouble.' She thought that her own mother's stays with her 'could have changed my mind about things'. Mrs S and her daughter had not spoken of the future since that time. She described herself as 'an ostrich', wanting to keep her head firmly in the sand and not to talk about the future. Recognizing her daughter's busy life, she asked for little help. She sometimes asked a friend favours of certain kinds, but hated to be 'dragging on people' and would sooner go without whatever it was she wanted. Summing this up, she said,

> Once in a while, I get kind of depressed, low-spirited, and I miss them, not seeing them. I think: 'Oh, grow up, will you! You know, they can't be running over here at night to see me after their work.' But I feel that they're doing all they can do. And I don't want to be one of these possessive mothers that just . . . will act the martyr or . . . play dependent, you know, at all. I like to be able to live my own life and see them in a nice social way.

Mrs S said that she would not share her dark moods or sense of loneliness with her daughter because it would make her feel ashamed.

In Mrs C's and Mrs S's biographies, we can identify certain patterned forms that characterize the life course for women. Recalling herself as a young woman, Mrs C represents the 'woman in the middle' described by Brody (1981). She is set in the midst of competing commitments to her mother, her children, her sick husband, and her job. Evident in her account is the sheer hard work of juggling responsibilities and managing paid work, running two households, and responding to other people's needs—she is 'swamped' by caring for and about those around her.

Mrs S's biography introduces another reality of women's caring over the life course—that women are caring for elderly parents for much longer periods and at later times in life than ever before. Because of increased life expectancy, generations of women in families can expect to have longer overlapping biographies than ever before (Hagestad, 1986) and to experience care relationships of increased duration. Mrs S's mother depended on staying with her for periods over a stretch of almost 20 years. She had died at the age of 99 a few months before I met Mrs S, who was then herself 74 years old.

The profile of 'women in the middle' (Brody, 1981) has highlighted the complex commitments that characterize women's lives. The term has captured well the notion of women's activities in relation to others. However, it has tended not to include aspects of women's orientation to themselves—their own needs and aspirations. Remembering her mother's long visits, Mrs S minded that her presence meant that she saw friends less. In discussing the years she had cared for her mother, her reluctant retirement, and the inability to devote more time to her work, Mrs C communicated regret at opportunities for self-development and advancement that she had forgone. Both spoke of their guilty feelings at voicing these regrets. Because caring is understood as an other-directed activity and a central feature of female identity, raising such self-directed concerns as these is not easy for women (Jordan et al., 1991). These self-directed issues are, none the less, part of the landscape of realities into which caregiving expectations fall in women's lives.

Women's reluctance to raise individual concerns accords with Allatt and Kiel's (1987) observations that ideas about the life course and the interrelationships of individual and family time have been very different for women and men. For women, there is a systematic entanglement or fusion of individual and family time—a pattern well illustrated by Mrs C's and Mrs S's life experiences. Men's life trajectories, on the other hand, are thought of in terms of the public domain and their life transitions are relatively unfettered by the concerns of family time, e.g., household organization, the care of children and dependants. The challenge, then, is 'to unshackle our conceptualizations of women's life experiences from the family life cycle' (Allatt and Kiel, 1987: 1).

Turning to later life stages, Mrs C and Mrs S introduce characteristic features of older women's realities. Both experience significant chronic health problems that, in different ways, limit their activities and prevent them from looking after themselves alone. Both were in a position to purchase services that they needed and, thus, could exercise a degree of choice and self-determination that is not the privilege of the majority of older women. None the less, both felt apprehensive about how they would manage if their health worsened and alluded to fears about the future of which they seldom spoke. While feeling well connected in terms of friends and social ties, both mentioned a narrowing of horizons in terms of social activity that they expected to become even narrower with time.

These, then, were the realities of Mrs C's and Mrs S's lives: complex process-es of juggling and balancing commitments in a very broadly defined 'middle' period, and, in the later period they were just entering, a growing awareness of constraints on their activities and the possibility, if not the reality, of increased dependence. In the next section, we look beyond this descriptive picture to con-sider the ways in which prevailing beliefs and dominant expectations of women, old age, family life, and public policy are reflected in women's experiences over the life course. The experiences of Mrs C, Mrs S, and the other women I inter-viewed suggest considerable tension between their everyday realities and received social expectations and images about the appropriate conduct of mothers and daughters in middle and late life.

SOCIAL EXPECTATIONS: DUTIFUL DAUGHTERS AND UNDEMANDING MOTHERS

Like most of the women I interviewed, Mrs S and Mrs C took it for granted that, as a general rule, daughters should assist elderly parents in need of support. Assumptions were made at two levels: firstly, families were seen as an obvious support for elderly parents; and secondly, daughters were the logical caregivers within families. For example, two study participants in their fifties commented:

> I think it goes beyond a sense of duty. . . . I think I have a strong feeling that the world would be a better place if we had much stronger family relations, where it was expected and conformed to that parents lived with their daughters.

> I think it's our duty to do those things. . . . I think most people find it natural to do it. . . . you have to do certain things at certain stages of life.

Older respondents also reflected these assumptions about family ties and gender. One noted her 'good fortune' at having a daughter; others, like Mrs C, felt sorry for elderly friends who did not or who, worse, had no children at all. Qureshi and Walker (1989) have identified the normative processes that designate female rel-atives as carers of choice, giving empirical support to the now well-developed analyses of the association of femininity with caring (Graham, 1983; Tronto, 1993). Women who participated in my research found these patterns of caring so self-evident as to be unremarkable; as Qureshi and Walker observe: 'Norms need no explaining' (1989: 132).

Several women, like Mrs C, noted the absence of their brothers in the division of caring labour and were at pains to explain and justify their resentful feelings, which were, effectively, challenges to the normative ordering of responsibility and gender relations. A few others voiced guilty feelings about brothers and sisters-in-law who, because of geographical proximity, were more involved with their mothers than they were themselves. Again, their discomfort suggested recognition of dominant expectations about care and gender that were not being followed and therefore required explanation.

The general social expectation of daughters was, as understood by these women, to be dutiful and responsive to elderly parents. The general social expectations of old women have been less explored in the literature. We know that they occupy a marginal and disadvantaged social position (Cohen, 1984; Peace, 1986) but still know relatively little of their experiences of needing support. Mrs S, like other older women participating in the research, had an acute sense of how she should *not* behave. She was at pains to distance herself from old women who were 'possessive', 'dependent', or 'martyrish'. Another respondent referred with disdain to her daughter's mother-in-law, who was 'fearful' and 'demanding'. Thus, older women's accounts revealed a strong imperative to be independent and self-sufficient—echoing the often-heard wish 'not to be a burden' to anyone. The strength of this imperative to be independent motivated women not to 'impose' on their daughters and to 'let them live their own lives'.

These powerful images of 'dutiful daughters' and 'undemanding mothers' were further shaped and confirmed by encounters with formal health and social services. Speaking from the perspectives of daughters, many women referred to the lack of interest of their mothers' family doctors—people whom they rightly saw as pivotal in the formal care system. In the absence of interested and active GPs, women felt, as one said, 'I'm "it" then'—the only person feeling responsible for her mother's health and welfare and mindful of whatever future planning might be needed.

One woman described her frustrated efforts to make arrangements for her mother to get a homemaker when she was discharged home after a period in hospital. She noted how 'grudgingly' the hospital responded to her request and how little information was made available: 'I had to fight for it. I felt it should have been offered.' This woman's description of the 'fight' was accompanied by a long justification for her request for services—a justification that she had felt obliged to impress upon the hospital staff. It included a list of her commitments—to a demanding job, to three children, and to her husband—and her assertion of entitlement to public services:

> We're under pressure too . . . there really were limits. . . . It sounds really awful, but my mother's been a Canadian citizen for umpteen years and I pay a hell of a lot in income tax every year, my husband pays a hell of a lot every year, my sister and her husband pay . . . and now and then, when we need some short-term help, I don't think it should be difficult to find, I really don't.

That this assertion of entitlement felt 'awful' and was voiced with some difficulty suggests that—even for a woman with the advantages of being articulate, middle class, and White—it is not easy to assert claims for public support.

Experiences like these reveal how the division of care between formal and informal spheres, described above, actually shapes our ideas of 'dutiful' behaviour. Janet Finch's work on the social construction of obligations draws attention to these patterned processes, underscoring how public policies and institutional practices 'form part of the structure of constraints within which individuals conduct their own negotiations, restricting or expanding the range of alternatives available' (Finch, 1987: 162).

There has been less study of the way potential care recipients experience the restrictions imposed by social policies and programs. Just as grudgingly provided services communicate diminished entitlement for women in caregiving positions, so do they for older women. For example, despite their privileged class position, many older respondents felt they had weak claims upon public resources: 'We can't expect much'; 'There are so many of us now'; 'They just don't have the money, you see.' Such comments suggest the effectiveness of political rhetoric that has cast the elderly as an expensive burden on society (Johnson, 1995). In addition to having an uncertain sense of entitlement to public services, women also had low expectations, even fears, about the quality of the services available. Mrs C, for example, was apprehensive about the kind of care provided in institutions for old people—apprehensions informed by her observations of her mother's and friends' experiences. In the years since these interviews, public knowledge of the effects of cutbacks in health care can only serve to heighten such apprehensions (Harman, 1997; Weintraub, 1995).

To summarize, if we juxtapose these perceptions of entitlement and social expectation with the realities of women's situations at different life stages, we see some difficult tensions and contradictions. Women speaking of being caregiving daughters endorse, on the one hand, the general notion that daughters should help their aging parents, while, on the other, they often find themselves in the midst of competing commitments, feeling overextended and suppressed in terms of the pursuit of their own needs and objectives. Women speaking about the experience of growing older feel they should not be burdensome and should not impose on daughters, yet they recognize their need and are motivated to achieve security and confidence. These dilemmas were reinforced among the women I interviewed by their perceptions of public services that, by virtue of being unavailable, hard to obtain, unwelcoming, or of poor quality, did little to expand their options. Smith (1979: 141) captures the tension between powerful cultural expectations and everyday, lived experience that is central to these dilemmas when she notes 'how ideas and social forms of consciousness may originate outside experience, coming from an external source and becoming a forced set of categories into which we must stuff the awkward and resistant actualities of our worlds.'

In the next section, we will consider women's experiences of managing this tension, exploring how they 'stuff' their realities into dominant images of caregiving and receiving and with what consequences for their welfare.

MANAGING THE CONTRADICTIONS OF BEING DUTIFUL AND UNDEMANDING

Recognizing the different dilemmas that characterize women's experiences of caregiving and receiving accords closely with analyses of women's psychological development that underscore the degree to which concerns of personal integrity and identity change over the life course (Allatt and Kiel, 1987). Study participants' dilemmas were shaped by the combined impact of social expectations and predictable life events—in this instance, by images of family ties, gender, old age, and public and private responsibility, and by the health problems and losses associated with aging. The concerns of different life stages also evoke different strategies of negotiation—in Hanmer and Statham's terms, they call forth different 'survival behaviours' (1989: 96).

For women speaking from the viewpoint of daughters, the central contradiction they confronted lay between cultural expectations that they be caring and responsive to their aging mothers and their competing commitments to others, including themselves. While often wanting to be responsive and deriving satisfaction and pleasure from assisting their mothers, women's situations rested, none the less, on this underlying disjuncture. To manage the resulting tension, respondents spoke at length about how they tried to set limits on their supportive activities with their mothers—ways of 'drawing the line'. For example, Mrs C described how she decided against bringing her mother to live with her because she felt it was not in her children's best interests. When her children were small, she also limited the time she devoted to her mother. In a sense, having her mother admitted to a nursing home, despite feeling torn and guilty about it, was a way of limiting what she did. Similarly, Mrs S described how she took steps to limit the length of her mother's visits, encouraging or organizing her to move on to stay with one of her sisters, so that Mrs S could 'have some privacy' and 'get back to normal'.

Women articulated limits in terms of their time, space, competing commitments, energy, and emotion, sometimes offering complex justifications and explanations for their conduct. Whatever their form, their limit-setting consisted of efforts to preserve their integrity and self-determination, whether that meant securing some privacy, more time with husbands and children they felt they had neglected, the opportunity to see friends or become more engaged in work-related activity, or relief from tiredness. Several respondents spoke of the need to protect their own futures. For example, a divorced woman in her mid-fifties reflected on how important it was to her that her very frail and confused mother either receive extensive community services at home or go into an institution:

> If they'd forced me into that [sharing her home with her mother] I would have had to stop my development of a second career, which is going to help me in my retirement. I would've had to stop, you know, a lot of things that interest me and it would have interfered with my job to some degree, as well, so . . . it would have closed my life down, I think.

This awareness of the consequences of assuming responsibility for very substantial care of a mother echoes Finch and Groves's observation that for women in their middle years, accommodating their work lives to the care of elderly relatives can be 'a prelude to poverty in old age for the carer' (1980: 507).

The setting of limits emerged as a clear theme from older women's perspectives, too, though in rather different form. Their limits were expressed in terms of how much they would ask or accept from their daughters. Mrs C, for instance, explained how her requests for assistance were 'measured' in an effort not to lean too heavily on her daughters. Rather than ask too much of others, Mrs S noted that it was easier simply to go without. Such limits seemed to serve the central purpose of lessening older women's senses of dependence and indebtedness. For example, to fend off diminishment an older participant explained to me how her daughter and son-in-law helped her each week with shopping and laundry, then added hastily: 'And they don't make a big song and dance about it and I don't. I'm grateful and I let them know, but . . . you know, it's not "poor granny" or any of that at all, you know.' Older women often set limits in terms of their daughters' interests, effectively containing their demands to protect their daughters. One woman described her daughter's life—her work, her children, and her home life—and observed: 'I don't want to put any extra burdens on her. Because of her nature . . . she would assume responsibilities that perhaps she shouldn't . . . you know, take too much on herself, and I don't want her to do that.' Like others, this woman enjoyed her daughter's attentiveness and warmth and was comforted by it, yet she remained watchful and alert to the impropriety of overstepping her own sense of its bounds.

In setting limits on the ways they gave or received care, study participants seemed to be trying to manage and contain the tensions, noted above, between the realities of their situations and what they felt they 'should' do, that is, be 'dutiful daughters' or 'undemanding mothers'. The limits represented efforts to reconcile these valued images with, for caregivers, their busy, overcommitted lives and aspirations, and for women needing care, their real needs for assistance and a sense of confidence that they could manage their lives securely. Some of the resolutions achieved by the limits—for example, Mrs C conserving some energy by admitting her mother to a nursing home, or Mrs S maintaining her sense of integrity by doing without things rather than asking for help—may, indeed, have resolved some immediate tensions. However, such resolutions came at considerable costs and did not modify in any fundamental way the underlying tensions that women confronted in giving and receiving care.

THE COSTS AND TENSIONS OF CONFORMING TO EXPECTATIONS: GUILT AND SHAME

The costs of trying to conform to expected images of caregiving daughters and cared-for mothers were revealed sharply in the feelings that characterized women's experiences. Speaking as caregiving daughters, women consistently said they felt guilty in relation to their mothers. Many, like Mrs S, felt guilty at simply talking about the limits they set on the support they provided. Another respondent who was very involved with her frail widowed mother talked about her fatigue and the tension she felt at trying to mediate between her husband, children, and mother, then added: 'I shouldn't be either complaining about her or talking about her as if she's a burden . . . there's a fair amount of guilt to that.'

Women spoke also of their guilt at not doing enough for their mothers. The strength of their feeling seemed unrelated to how much care they actually provided or how affectionately they described their ties. Mrs C, for instance, felt guilty at being unable to 'cope' with the many demands on her and at admitting her mother to a nursing home. After describing her life—a full-time job, three children, and living an hour's drive from her mother—another participant, a widow, talked at length about feeling guilty that she could only help her mother out on weekends.

We can understand guilt as what has been termed a 'reflexive role-taking sentiment' (Shott, 1979: 1324). Such emotions are evoked by considering how oneself appears to others or to the generalized other. One regards and judges oneself as if through the eyes of an outside audience, generating an inner process of self-censorship; normative rules of conduct are internalized and levelled at the self. Shott (1979), Hochschild (1979), and others writing about the sociology of emotion reveal how feeling states signal this invisible process of social control. The account of a woman who had once contemplated bringing her mother over from Holland to live with her illustrated this complex process of self-control and self-critical internal dialogue. She had recognized that, had her mother come to live with her, her mother's needs for substantial care and the lack of compatibility in their interests and lifestyles would have constrained her significantly. She spoke of her ambivalence tearfully:

> So that's how I imagined it would be if I brought her over and yet I had such a *tremendous* guilt feeling . . . that it was a duty that I had to do . . . someone pointed out to me how much one's life is ruled by 'shoulds' and 'oughts' and I began to see what happened . . . and I knew it would be a sacrifice to my mother . . . but that was so ingrained in me at the time. I thought that was what I *really* believed. It's something that's very hard to escape.

This woman crystallized her internal struggle in relation to her mother in her account of a friend in a situation similar to her own. On the one hand, she noted with admiration that her friend was much better at setting limits on her support for her mother: 'She is *so* strong, she's able to say: "I do this much and no more. I have my own life to live and I have my duty to myself too".' On the other, she judged her friend harshly, thinking to herself: 'I'm surprised at your coldness, you know, you really ought to be more dutiful; you should understand your mother more.'

This woman's internal struggle typifies the dilemma between self-enhancement and self-sacrifice that is articulated in different ways in feminist analyses of women's psychological and moral development (Jordan et al., 1991; Tronto,

1993). It accords, too, with Mrs C's and Mrs S's difficulties in speaking of regrets about opportunities they had forgone for themselves when caught in a web of commitments to their mothers or their families. Despite general public assertions that women are entitled to autonomy and self-direction, exercise of such choices often conflicts with powerfully internalized imperatives to be responsive and caring in relation to others. To be self-directed and autonomous is to risk being thought 'uncaring'—a damning indictment in the context of dominant images of femininity and the socialization of lifetimes (Graham, 1983; see also Reitsma-Street, in this volume).

We have seen that the central dilemma experienced by the older women studied lay in trying to resolve the tension between the cultural imperative to be independent and undemanding and their wishes to feel secure and confident. Resolving this tension by limiting the demands they made on others or exercising care in the ways they asked for or accepted help meant that they adhered to the strongly felt value of self-sufficiency but at the cost of suppressing their own needs and concerns. Again, the feelings associated with these limit-setting strategies reveal the power and the consequences of cultural expectations placed on older women.

In their accounts of their situations, many of the older women recognized their precarious social status and their weak claims on both their families and public services. Mrs C's and Mrs S's biographies illustrate particularly acutely the interpenetration of these socially structured realities and feeling states—of the political and the personal, the public and the private. Mrs C noted that, as for her mother before her, pride motivated her not to let her daughters know the extent of her concerns for the future. Identified as another reflexive role taking emotion, Shott (1979: 1326) suggests that pride derives from knowing one has behaved in accordance with social expectations. Mrs C and her mother thus preserved their pride at the expense of not revealing their needs and, in so doing, excluded the possibility of having their needs met and anxieties allayed.

When I asked Mrs S what it would be like to tell her daughter about her anxieties and loneliness, she said she would feel ashamed. Shame represents the opposite of pride—a feeling provoked by recognizing that one's self is inadequate or disreputable. Mrs S thus fends off shame—the humiliation of her daughter or others knowing that she does not feel independent or secure—by not sharing her real concerns. As for Mrs C, there is, therefore, no possibility of her concerns being addressed or of her security being enhanced. Further to this, Mrs S distances herself from older women who do not live up to the undemanding ideal and are, rather, 'possessive' or 'martyrish'.

In summary, feelings of shame and guilt sustained women in their commitments to duty and to undemanding independence. For the women who participated in my research, these internalized processes of social control resulted in varying degrees of self-alienation (Mrs S is, for example, a very harsh critic of her own experience) and in the stifling of their aspirations for self-enhancement and security. The costs of struggling to conform were high.

THE FUTURE: POSSIBILITIES FOR MEETING NEEDS AND ENHANCING WOMEN

From the accounts of the women presented in this chapter, we have seen that the present pattern of care of old people offers mothers and daughters little room to manoeuvre: the minimal provision of acceptable public services, the general absence of men from responsibility for caring for others, and the ideological assumptions that underpin this division of care trap women in ties of dependency and obligation. In reflecting on this socially structured pattern of care, we can return to the question posed at the outset: 'How do we provide for the needs of all, and not at the expense of women?' (Segal, 1987: 242). Segal's question challenges us to move beyond analysis and critique to think about strategies to enhance the welfare of women like those who took part in the research reported here. With them in mind, we might strive towards changes that would: relieve women of the privately borne pressure to be dutiful and undemanding and permit them, rather, to give and receive care in ways that are in keeping with the particular nature of their wishes and capacities; foster in older women a sense of entitlement and confidence in articulating their needs without shame; and, in younger women, foster a sense of entitlement to pursue their own interests and development without a sense of guilt and inadequacy in relation to others. To strategize towards these visionary ends, it is important to look at both material and ideological barriers to their accomplishment—at both the design of practical possibilities for reshaping the boundaries and forms of care arrangements, and at ways of unsettling the cultural meanings of care, dependence, and gender relations that sustain the present division of care between men and women and between public and private spheres. In doing so, we can resituate this analysis of family-based care in the broader context of societal responses to the needs of those who are frail and disabled.

Turning first to the material aspects of women's situations in giving and receiving care within families, one approach to expanding their possibilities and enhancing their welfare would be to work towards more generous provision of formal services. Features of formal care that would be important to incorporate are increasingly explored and articulated. For example, we hear more of the need for flexible community care (Lewis and Meredith, 1988; Qureshi and Walker, 1989) and for sophisticated support services that recognize the complexities of receiving and giving care at home (Opie, 1992). We hear more, too, of the qualities of congregate care that might enhance people's sense of control and self-direction (Aronson, 1992b; Dalley, 1988; Willcocks et al., 1987).

Even as these emphases on 'thick' definitions of needs and on ideas for improved public care are generated, we find ourselves in a political climate antithetical to such developments—as matters of public policy, federal and provincial governments are seeking to reduce public services and, instead, to foster the growth of private care markets (Armstrong and Armstrong, 1996; Cooper and Neu, 1995). To justify these changes, it is commonly suggested that old people can best exercise choice and achieve greater control over the circumstances of their aging in the private market. Subjected to scrutiny, however, this claim proves hollow. Only those women with sufficient resources can choose to pay privately for services—a minority given the significant and growing proportion of old women who are poor (National Council of Welfare, 1997). More significant-ly, however, even when private means are available, the notion of consumer sov-ereignty is an ill-fitting model to apply to old people's need-meeting experiences (Aronson and Neysmith, 1997; Croft and Beresford, 1995; Tarman, 1989). Indeed, among the relatively privileged women who participated in the research reported here, the ability to pay for supportive services at home and the knowl-edge that relatively expensive institutional care would be affordable brought no sense of security or confidence. The structured disadvantage of being old and female and, actually or possibly, dependent proved more determining of their experiences than did their ability to engage in the private market.

For women caring in families, seeking formal help (whether private or public and whether generously or meanly provided) to meet their relatives' needs is not an easily made, practical decision. For Mrs C, for example, seeking formal care—a public nursing home—for her mother left her with a painful sense that she had failed in her duty. The Association of Carers, a lobby and support group of fam-ily carers in the UK, has identified the common reluctance of carers to seek or accept formal support (Briggs and Oliver, 1985). For many, the acceptance of outside help represents a failure to cope and to care, and the association of fem-ininity with caring renders the inability to cope a personal inadequacy (O'Connor, 1996). As a logical corollary to this, in the few instances where sub-jects' brothers assumed a more than usually significant role in supporting their mothers, women felt guilty and uneasy.

It is evident, then, that there are profound ideological barriers to exercising options for obtaining or sharing care when, in simple material terms, they might be available. Identifying and challenging these barriers is a crucial dimension of envisioning different ways of caring for old people that do not disadvantage women. Two particular facets of these ideological barriers emerged forcefully from the accounts of participants in my study: the power of prevailing imagery of family ties, and the degree to which the cultural importance of being dutiful and undemanding stifled women's articulation of stress or of complaint at their situations.

Permeating the accounts of the women who participated in my research were strong cultural images of proper family ties and women's place within them. As we have seen, women generally took it for granted that the family was the prop-er locus of care and that it was women's lot to be responsive to others and unde-manding for themselves. Contemporary social policy and the mounting retreat of governments from public service provision mean that we can expect these cul-tural images to become increasingly entrenched.

Exploration of the ways these cultural images unfold in women's lives has sug-gested, however, that they do not correspond with their actual experiences but instead provide ill-fitting forms into which their realities are pressed. The imagery of the family communicated in political rhetoric and policy and program planning implies a readily available pool of female care—both in terms of love and labour—and a population of elderly women ready to receive passively the support of younger female kin. We have seen, rather, women's recognition of the marginal claims of elderly women. Mrs C, for instance, recognized that marginality over three generations of women: she remembers her own limits when her mother needed support, recognizes her daughters' limits now, and, in response, asks little and conceals her needs. Among the women I interviewed, there was consistent recognition of the primacy of the nuclear family—of husbands and dependent children—and of the relatively weak and tenuous entitlement of elderly mothers. These realities do not accord with the comfortable imagery of the extended family and intergenerational relations that is assumed in the vocabulary of social policies and in the rhetoric of politicians committed to privatization at all costs.

Women's awareness of the lack of correspondence between this official vocabulary and their everyday realities and family lives was experienced privately. The women who participated in my research did not speak easily of the tensions they felt: for older women, the tension between wanting to feel secure and the imperative to be undemanding and, for younger women, the tension between wanting to be self-determining and wanting to be dutiful and caring of others. Unspoken, these dilemmas were experienced as personal struggles or failings. Speaking about them would occasion feelings of guilt and shame. Thus, as Mrs S and Mrs C illustrate, women concealed their concerns from their respective mothers and daughters and seldom shared them with their peers. In not sharing them, they did not, therefore, recognize their concerns as commonly experienced dilemmas and did not identify with other women in similar situations. This was especially true among older respondents like Mrs S, who, rather than identifying with other old women, tended to distance themselves from them. As relatively privileged women in fair economic circumstances and with paid employment histories, the women I interviewed might have been expected to chafe against the constraints of caregiving and receiving more than women accustomed to less autonomy in their lives. That they were silenced and their difficulties individualized sounds a very pessimistic note for the future.

We can understand the silence surrounding women's experiences of the costs and tensions of receiving care as the result of entrenched cultural beliefs about independence and individualism, proper family ties, and feminine behaviour. Like all effective ideologies, these images make the possibility of other patterns of care and need-meeting seem unthinkable or impossible and render the present pattern 'obvious' and 'natural'. Theorizing on the early stages of social movements suggests that, for individual experiences of stress or injustice to be tranformed into publicly expressed claims for change, it is necessary that people talk about and share their difficulties and come to develop a sense of collective consciousness and identity (Henley, 1986); the first step in making change and other possibilities thinkable is that they be speakable.

Among older women and among caregivers, we can certainly see some instances of emerging collective voice and activity. Organizations such as the Older Women's Network and the Raging Grannies represent efforts to make visible and to change the circumstances of women's aging. There is a growing literature of complaint and protest about the disadvantages that characterize women's life course and culminate in old age (e.g., MacDonald, 1984; Marshall, 1987; Sarton, 1988). In the UK, the Association of Carers presses the claims of family care providers in the public political arena.

Such examples of women acting in concert to bring questions of need-meeting and caring into public view are energizing and hopeful. However, within the broad arena of long-term care, there is also much to divide women. For example, the predominantly White, middle-class women who participated in my research would not have found themselves reflected among the paid care providers that populate institutional and home-based care for old people. This low-status labour force is drawn, increasingly, from the ranks of immigrant women and women of colour who have few occupational choices (Foner, 1994; Neysmith and Aronson, 1997). The degradation of their work in the public sector is increasingly documented (Armstrong and Armstrong, 1996; Aronson and Neysmith, 1996; MGEU, 1996; Weintraub, 1995). In the private sector, their employment conditions are likely to be even worse and even less accessible to public scrutiny.

Given the retreat of governments from the provision of public home care and institutional care, it is likely that middle-class women will come to rely more and more on the low-paid labour of women less privileged than themselves. It will be important that these structurally rooted conflicts are identified and challenged in the years ahead, and that we strive for care that is 'user-centered and worker-friendly' (Carpenter, 1994: 3). Without such an overarching analysis and vision, intersecting conflicts between paid and unpaid carers and care recipients and between women in different locations in terms of race and class will be seen as inevitabilities, rather than as the products of government retreat from responsibility for collective welfare and security. The Live-In Caregiver Program represents a particularly vivid example of government retreat that pits women against each other. As McWatt and Neysmith describe in Chapter 10, this program can be seen, bleakly, as Canada's national child-care strategy, so it might become Canada's long-term care strategy. As elderly people and their familes are pressed to seek private solutions to care needs as cheaply as possible, privately purchased live-in care providers may become more commonplace in the future. Already conceived to include home care of the disabled or elderly, the Live-In Caregiver Program will generate working conditions for elder care providers as exploitative as those experienced by child-care providers and domestic workers.

Challenging and fending off regressive developments such as these will be an important focus of activity in working towards Segal's vision of meeting the needs of all—and not at the expense of women. Equally important will be attention to alternative and innovative care arrangements—wherever they may be found—that are not locked into confining images of family care and that are nourishing for both those who need assistance and those who provide it. The small but growing literature on caring arrangements outside families makes an important contribution to expanding our thinking about the possibilities of alternative approaches to meeting people's needs when frail, disabled, or ill. For example, June Callwood (1986) chronicles the network of friends and community that formed to support an elderly single woman through illness. Such ties of friendship and community in women's lives are fragile and have been little examined because of the cultural primacy accorded to family ties and relations with men—hence, Callwood writes with a sense of both innovation and celebration. In a similar spirit, Chris Sinding (1994) describes a network of support that sustained a lesbian through breast cancer diagnosis and treatment. She notes network members' conscious efforts to avoid problematic relations of obligation, indebtedness, and isolation so often characteristic of family care. Because of lesbians' positioning, at least in part, outside heterosexual family ties, they are required to design supportive relations in relatively uncharted social spaces. While these spaces may be jeopardized and tense by virtue of the heterosexist cultural surround, they also present an opportunity to unsettle the rigidity of the discourse on family and community care (Aronson, forthcoming; Rich, 1989).

Feminist and post-modern analyses of language are illuminating the ideological underpinnings of this rigidity and its embeddedness in discussions of social policy. For example, Fraser and Gordon (1994) identify the ideological legacies of such commonplace terms and oppositions as 'dependence' and 'independence'. Women with disabilities know intimately the damage of these legacies and call attention to the revolutionary possibilities of care rooted in ties recognized as interdependent and reciprocal (Morris, 1995). Relatedly, social policy critics call for care arrangements structured in ways that are respectful and unexploitative of all participants and forged in political alliances of care users and paid and unpaid care workers (Carpenter, 1994). Such analyses offer some strategic guidance for the long-term project of meeting the needs of all—and not at the expense of women.

REFERENCES

Ahmad, W.I.U., and K. Atkin, eds. 1996. *'Race' and Community Care.* Buckingham: Open University Press.

Allatt, P., and T. Kiel. 1987. 'Introduction', in P. Allatt, T. Kiel, A. Bryman, and B. Bytheway, eds, *Women and the Life Cycle: Transitions and Turning Points.* London: Macmillan: 1–12.

Arber, S., G.N. Gilbert, and M. Evandrou. 1988. 'Gender, Household Composition and Receipt of Domiciliary Services by Elderly Disabled People', *Journal of Social Policy* 17, 2: 153–75.

Armstrong, P, and H. Armstrong. 1996. *Wasting Away: The Undermining of Canadian Health Care.* Toronto: Oxford University Press.

Aronson, J. 1988. 'Women's Experiences of Giving and Receiving Care: Pathways to Social Change', Ph.D. diss., University of Toronto.

Aronson, J. 1990. 'Old Women's Experiences of Needing Care: Choice or Compulsion?', *Canadian Journal on Aging* 9, 3: 234–47.

Aronson, J. 1992a. 'Women's Sense of Responsibility for the Care of Old People: "But Who Else Is Going To Do It?"', *Gender and Society* 6, 1: 8–29.

Aronson, J. 1992b. 'Are We Really Listening? Beyond the Official Discourse on the Needs of Old People', *Canadian Social Work Review* 9, 1: 73–87.

Aronson, J. forthcoming. 'Doing Research on Lesbians and Caregiving: Disturbing the Ideological Foundations of Family and Community Care', in J. Ristock and C. Taylor, eds, *Sexualities and Social Action: Inside the Academy and Out*. Toronto: University of Toronto Press.

Aronson, J., and S. Neysmith. 1996. '"You're Not Just in There To Do the Work": Depersonalizing Policies and the Exploitation of Home Care Workers' Labour', *Gender and Society* 10, 1: 59–77.

Aronson, J., and S. Neysmith. 1997. 'The Retreat of the State and Long-Term Care Provision: Implications for Frail Elderly People, Unpaid Family Carers and Paid Home Care Workers', *Studies in Political Economy* 53: 37–66.

Battle, K., and S. Torjman. 1995. *How Finance Re-Formed Social Policy*. Ottawa: Caledon Institute of Social Policy.

Binney, E.A., and C.L. Estes. 1988. 'The Retreat of the State and its Transfer of Responsibility: The Intergenerational War', *International Journal of Health Services* 18, 1: 83–96.

Briar, K.H., and R. Ryan. 1986. 'The Anti-Institution Movement and Women Caregivers', *Affilia* 1, 1: 20–31.

Briggs, A., and J. Oliver, eds. 1985. *Caring: Experiences of Looking After Disabled Relatives*. London: Routledge & Kegan Paul.

British Columbia Royal Commission on Health Care and Costs. 1991. *Closer To Home*. Victoria.

Brodie, J. 1996. 'Restructuring and the New Citizenship', in Isabella Bakker, ed., *Rethinking Restructuring: Gender and Change in Canada*. Toronto: University of Toronto Press: 126–40.

Brody, E.M. 1981. '"Women in the Middle" and Family Help to Older People', *Gerontologist* 21, 5: 471–80.

Callwood, J. 1986. *Twelve Weeks in Spring*. Toronto: Lester and Orpen Dennys.

Carpenter, M. 1994. *Normality Is Hard Work: Trade Unions and the Politics of Community Care*. London: Lawrence and Wishart.

Cohen, L. 1984. *Small Expectations: Society's Betrayal of Older Women*. Toronto: McClelland & Stewart.

Cooper, D., and D. Neu. 1995. 'The Politics of Debt and Deficit in Alberta', in Gordon Laxer and Trevor Harrison, eds, *The Trojan Horse: Alberta and the Future of Canada*. Montreal: Black Rose Books: 163–81.

Croft, S., and P. Beresford. 1995. 'Whose Empowerment? Equalizing the Competing Discourses in Community Care', in R. Jack, ed., *Empowerment in Community Care*. London: Chapman and Hall: 59–76.

Dacks, G., J. Green, and L. Trimble. 1995. 'Road Kill: Women in Alberta's Drive Toward Deficit Elimination', in G. Laxer and T. Harrison, eds, *The Trojan Horse: Alberta and the Future of Canada*. Montreal: Black Rose Books: 270–85.

Dalley, G. 1988. *Ideologies of Caring: Rethinking Community and Collectivism*. London: Macmillan.

Evers, H. 1981. 'Care or Custody? The Experiences of Women Patients in Long-Stay Geriatric Wards', in B. Hutter and G. Williams, eds, *Controlling Women: The Normal and the Deviant*. London: Croom Helm: 108–30.

Evers, H. 1985. 'The Frail Elderly Woman: Emergent Questions in Aging and Woman's Health', in E. Lewin and V. Oleson, eds, *Women, Health and Illness*. New York: Tavistock: 86–112.

Finch, J. 1987. 'Family Obligations and the Life Course', in A. Bryman, B. Bytheway, P. Allat, and T. Kiel, eds, *Rethinking the Life Cycle*. London: Macmillan: 155–69.

Finch, J., and D. Groves. 1980. 'Community Care and the Family: A Case for Equal Opportunities?', *Journal of Social Policy*, 9, 4: 487–514.

Finch, J., and D. Groves, eds. 1983. *A Labour of Love: Women, Work and Caring*. London: Routledge & Kegan Paul.

Foner, N. 1994. *The Caregiving Dilemma: Work in an American Nursing Home*. Berkeley: University of California Press.

Fraser, N., and L. Gordon. 1994, '"Dependency" Demystified: Inscriptions of Power in a Keyword of the Welfare State', *Social Politics* 1, 1: 4–31.

Graham, H. 1983. 'Caring: A Labour of Love', in Finch and Groves, eds, 1983: 13–30.

Graham, H. 1993. 'Social Divisions in Caring', *Women's Studies International Forum* 16, 5: 461–70.

Hagestad, G.O. 1986. 'The Aging Society as a Context for Social Life', *Daedalus* 115, 1: 119–39.

Hanmer, J., and D. Statham. 1989. *Women and Social Work: Towards a Woman-Centred Practice*. Chicago: Lyceum Books.

Harman, M. 1997. 'Stay Healthy!', *Canadian Pensioners Concerned, Seniors' Viewpoint* 23, 1: 5.

Hasselkus, B.R. 1988. 'Meaning in Caregiving: Perspectives on Caregiver-Professional Relationships', *Gerontologist* 28, 5: 686–91.

Henderson, H. 1997. 'Harris Tax Shuffle Deals a Blow to Seniors', *Toronto Star*, 25 Jan.

Henley, N.M. 1986. 'Women as a Social Problem: Conceptual and Practical Issues in Defining Social Problems', in E. Seidman and J. Rappoport, eds, *Redefining Social Problems*. New York: Plenum Press: 65–79.

Hochschild, A.R. 1979. 'Emotion Work, Feeling Rules and Social Structure', *American Journal of Sociology* 85, 3: 551–75.

Hochschild, A.R. 1995. 'The Culture of Politics: Traditional, Post-Modern, Cold-Modern and Warm-Modern Ideals of Care', *Social Politics* 2, 3: 331–46.

Johnson, M. 1995. 'Interdependency and the Generational Compact', *Ageing and Society* 15: 243–65.

Jordan, J.V., A.G. Kaplan, J. Baker Miller, I.P. Stiver, and J.L. Surrey, eds. 1991. *Women's Growth in Connection*. New York: Guilford Press.

Lewis, J., and B. Meredith. 1988. *Daughters Who Care: Daughters Who Care For Mothers at Home*. London: Routledge.

Lightman, E., and D. Baines. 1996. 'White Men in Blue Suits: Women's Policy in Conservative Ontario', *Canadian Review of Social Policy* 38: 145–52.

MacDonald, B., with C. Rich. 1984. *Look Me in the Eye: Old Women, Aging and Ageism*. London: The Women's Press.

Manitoba Government Employees' Union (MGEU). 1996. *We Are Workers Just Like You: The 1996 Manitoba Home Care Strike*. Winnipeg: MGEU.

Marshall, D. 1987. *Silver Threads: Critical Reflections on Growing Old*. Toronto: Between the Lines.

Morris, J. 1993. '"Us" and "Them"? Feminist Research and Community Care', in J. Bornat, C. Pereira, D. Pilgrim, and F. Williams, eds, *Community Care: A Reader*. London: Macmillan: 156–66.

Morris, J. 1995. 'Creating a Space for Absent Voices: Disabled Women's Experience of Receiving Assistance with Daily Living Activities', *Feminist Review* 51: 68–93.

National Council of Welfare. 1997. *Poverty Profile 1995*. Ottawa: Ministry of Supply and Services.

Neysmith, S.M. 1981. 'Parental Care: Another Female Family Function?', *Canadian Journal of Social Work Education* 7.

Neysmith, S.M., and J. Aronson. 1997. 'Working Conditions in Home Care: Negotiating Race and Class Boundaries in Gendered Work', *International Journal of Health Services* 27, 3.

O'Connor, D.L. 1996. 'Living With a Memory-Impaired Spouse: (Re)cognizing the Experience, (Re)storying Support', DSW thesis, Wilfrid Laurier University.

Ontario Ministry of Community and Social Services, Ministry of Health, and Ministry of Citizenship. 1991. *Redirection of Long-Term Care and Support Services in Ontario: A Public Consultation Paper*. Toronto.

Ontario Office for Senior Citizens' Affairs. 1986. *A New Agenda: Health and Social Service Strategies for Ontario's Seniors*. Toronto.

Opie, A. 1992. *There's Nobody There: Community Care of Confused Older People*. Philadelphia: University of Pennsylvania Press.

Peace, S. 1986. 'The Forgotten Female: Social Policy and Older Women', in C. Phillipson and A. Walker, eds, *Aging and Social Policy: A Critical Assessment*. Aldershot: Gower: 61–86.

Qureshi, H., and A. Walker. 1989. *The Caring Relationship: Elderly People and Their Families*. London: Macmillan.

Rich, C. 1989. *Desert Years: Undreaming the American Dream*. San Francisco: Spinsters/Aunt Lute.

Rosenthal, C.J. 1994. 'Long-Term Care Reform and "Family Care": A Worrisome Combination', *Canadian Journal on Aging* 13, 4: 419–22.

Sarton, M. 1988. *After the Stroke*. New York: Norton.

Segal, L. 1987. *Is the Future Female? Troubled Thoughts on Contemporary Feminism*. London: Virago Press.

Shott, S. 1979. 'Emotion and Social Life: A Symbolic Interaction Analysis', *American Journal of Sociology* 84: 1317–34.

Sinding, C. 1994. 'Supporting a Lesbian with Breast Cancer: Weaving Care Outside "Family"', MSW research report, McMaster University.

Smith, D.E. 1979. 'A Sociology For Women', in J.A. Sherman and E. Torton Beck, eds, *The Prism of Sex: Essays in the Sociology of Knowledge*. Madison: University of Wisconsin Press: 135–87.

Smith, D.E. 1986. 'Institutional Ethnography: A Feminist Method', *Resources for Feminist Research* 15, 1: 6–13.

Tarman, V.I. 1989. 'Implications of Public and Private Sector Involvement in Long Term Care: Lessons From Ontario', paper presented at the 18th Annual Scientific-Educational Meeting of the Canadian Association on Gerontology, Ottawa.

Tronto, J.C. 1993. *Moral Boundaries: A Political Argument for an Ethic of Care.* New York: Routledge.

Waerness, K. 1984. 'Caring as Women's Work in the Welfare State', in Harriet Holter, ed., *Patriarchy in a Welfare Society.* Oslo: Universitetsforlaget: 67–87.

Walker, A. 1985. 'From Welfare State to Caring Society? The Promise of Informal Networks', in J.A. Yoder, J.M.L. Jonker and R.A.B. Leaper, eds, *Support Networks in a Caring Community.* Dordrecht: Martinus Nijhoff: 41–58.

Weintraub, L.S. 1995. *No Place Like Home: A Discussion Paper about Living and Working in Ontario's Long-Term Care Facilities.* Toronto: Ontario Federation of Labour.

Willcocks, D., S. Peace, and L. Kellaher. 1987. *Private Lives in Public Places.* London: Tavistock.

ACKNOWLEDGEMENTS

The original research reported in this paper was supported in part by: the National Health Research and Development Program of Health and Welfare Canada through a National Health Fellowship; the Program in Gerontology at the University of Toronto through a seed grant; and the Social Sciences and Humanities Research Council of Canada through a post-doctoral fellowship. The conceptual elaboration included in this revised edition of the chapter has been sustained by an sshrc-funded research network on the changing conditions of women's caring labour (816–94–0003).

7

Caught in Tangled Webs of Care:
Women Abused in Intimate Relationships

JANET MOSHER

INTRODUCTION

The facts are disquieting. One-third of Canadian women have been physically or sexually assaulted by their marital or 'common law' partners, and in one-fifth of these cases the violence occurred following, or during, separation (Rodgers, 1994).[1] Many women endure repeated assaults and sustain multiple physical and psychological injuries.[2] At least 60 per cent (551 of 969) and possibly as high as 78 per cent (691) of the women murdered in Ontario between 1974 and 1990 died at the hands of an intimate partner. The most common motive: an offender's anger or rage over an actual or impending estrangement (Crawford and Gartner, 1992).

For most women, the assaults perpetrated against them are but one of the many weapons of control wielded by their abusive partners. Many men exercise power over and seek to control their intimate partners by resorting to a range of other tactics: coercion and threats; intimidation; emotional abuse (he puts her down in front of others; he humiliates her); isolation (he limits her contact with friends and family); minimizing, denying, and blaming (he minimizes the wrongfulness or harm of his behaviour and/or blames her for it); using the children (he threatens to take them away, or that she will lose custody); exercising male privilege; and economic power (he denies her access to money or to information about finances) (Pence and Paymar, 1986).

Unravelling possible answers to the question of how we ought to understand the reasons for this violence in women's lives—the explanations that might allow us to make sense of these disquieting facts—and whether 'caring' is implicated in this violence are central preoccupations in this chapter. I begin by examining three vantage points, or broad perspectives.[3] Viewed from one vantage point—the 'therapeutic' vantage point—discrete physical and/or sexual assaults are identified as the worrisome behaviour that needs to be understood, explained, and addressed. The explanations offered attribute the violence to the isolated acts of a few men (or women) suffering from some form of psychopathology. The violence is seen as completely detached from male domination or from other systems of domination. From a second vantage point—the 'feminist' vantage point—attention is focused on the full range of tactics of control employed by abusive men. These tactics are understood to draw their sustenance from patriarchal social structures and ideologies and, as such, are integrally connected to a system of male domination. Viewed from this vantage point, these facts reflect a 'sick', patriarchal society. Here, the social construct of 'gender' and the expectations of 'caring' placed upon women, which are central to that construct, hold tremendous explanatory force. From a third vantage point—the 'intersecting oppressions' vantage point—the role of gender just described is overly determinate. While gender is a significant factor, other kinds of oppression, such as that based on race and class, are seen to be equally important. Moreover, from this vantage point, the concepts of 'gender' and of 'care', which are so central to the feminist perspective, are themselves regarded as insufficiently nuanced with respect to race, class, disability, and sexual orientation. In other words, the concepts of 'gender' and 'care', as frequently invoked in feminist accounts, fail to attend to how both 'may refract so very differently when experienced through the lens of race, class, and other forms of socially constructed disadvantage' (see Baines et al.: ch. 1).

The purpose of offering these vantage points is not to attempt to deduce a definitive explanation of violence against women in their intimate relationships.[4] Indeed, I share the view implicit in the third vantage point that no single, definitive meta-theory of violence against women exists and that the quest for such a theory is itself shaped by assumptions that are, at their core, racist, imperialist, etc. This does not mean, however, that all explanations are equally satisfactory, as it is hoped the review of the three vantage points, as well as the discussion in the second part of the chapter, will make clear. Rather, the purpose of offering these vantage points is really twofold: to illuminate the role that caring expectations may play in relation to the abuse of women in their intimate relationships; and to assist in documenting and deciphering some of the many complexities and contradictions—many of which are centred around caring expectations—that permeate the lives of women abused in their intimate relationships (the second major part of the chapter).

Let me briefly foreshadow the discussion of the connections between the three vantage points I have identified and the complexities and contradictions to which I have alluded. Women who are abused in their intimate relationships are frequently subject to multiple, negative, and often contradictory judgements; no matter what a woman does in response to the abuse she is likely to be blamed by others. She may be blamed for causing the abuse, blamed for leaving, blamed for failing in her role as wife and mother (whether she leaves or stays), blamed for staying and labelled a masochist or a manipulative liar, or blamed for putting her needs above those of the children because she stayed or because she left. These judgements are of tremendous import: they are made by friends, family members, and professionals, all of whom she respects; by judges who determine her rights to the custody of her children; by front-line welfare workers; by colleagues; by landlords. These judgements cut deeply not only at the level of the personal psyche, but at her ability to muster the material supports necessary to maintain herself and her dependants. These judgements are themselves grounded in particular understandings of the causes of abuse, and in the second part of the chapter I attempt to show how particular judgements are aligned with each of the three vantage points reviewed in the first part of the chapter.

EXPLAINING THE VIOLENCE IN WOMEN'S LIVES

The Therapeutic Vantage Point[5]

As noted, within this framework isolated acts of physical aggression are understood to be 'the problem' that requires explanation and attention. These discrete acts of aggression are, rather obviously, perpetrated by individual men. While this undisputed fact leads, within other perspectives, to explanations of violence that move beyond the individual, within this framework no such move occurs. Rather, the focus remains resolutely on the individual. Because attention is focused on discrete acts of aggression perpetrated by individuals, the search for an explanation as to why the aggression has occurred is also focused on the individual. It is assumed that 'normal' men do not engage in this 'deviant' or 'abnormal' behaviour. Moreover, plausible links explored in other vantage points between these acts of aggression and other forms of so-called 'normal' behaviours of male dominance go largely unexplored.

Earlier this century it was largely assumed that 'drunken loafers' constituted this class of deviants. So, for example, attribution to the 'drunken loafer' pervaded the debates of the House of Commons in 1909 when an amendment to the Criminal Code, creating an offence of beating one's wife or other female person that was punishable by whipping, was introduced (and passed).[6] W.B. Northrup argued:

> Therefore, on behalf of the inoffensive portion of the community, the women and children of this land, I am prepared to support this legislation. In fact, I would go a step further and say that I have often felt that the provision on the statute-book applicable to this offence is really for the benefit of the lazy loafer. As perhaps every man in this House and every lawyer knows a man unwilling to work is supported by an honest, industrious wife until patience ceases to be a virtue and he is taken to court. She lays a complaint and the husband is punished by sending him to the county jail where, all during the winter, he lives in comfort and luxury, while the poor woman that he has sworn to support is obliged to go out and support herself and her family. If the hon. gentleman would introduce another clause to provide that those men who failed to support their wives and children should not be rewarded by being sent to the county jail where they will not have to work, but would be given an adequate punishment it would have the effect of compelling them to do their duty in this regard. (House of Commons Debates, 4 Feb. 1909)

More recent data have demonstrated that violence cuts across class boundaries, which has forced a shift in explanation. It is now much more common to point to various 'defects', most often psychological in nature but also biological and even nutritional, as the 'cause' of the violence. While it is more common to attribute the cause to defects in the abusive male partner, women do not necessarily escape responsibility for the violence within this framework, for example, when women are described and labelled as masochistic (Stark et al., 1979; Dobash and Dobash, 1992). In either case, faulty individual traits and personalities are understood to be the source of the problem (Dobash and Dobash, 1992).

And in either case, a diagnostic category is assigned, and 'treatment' by a professional therapist (be it social worker, psychologist, or psychiatrist) is understood to be the desired intervention. Acts of physical aggression perpetrated by individual men within their intimate relationships remain completely disconnected from the wider social and political worlds (Dobash and Dobash, 1992).

The Feminist Vantage Point

As with the therapeutic vantage point, there is no single, unified feminist account of the violence in women's intimate relationships. However, several common threads run through 'feminist' accounts, which make it possible to speak of a feminist vantage point or perspective. Within this perspective attention is focused not on discrete acts of physical aggression but on the control (through violence and other tactics) men exercise over women and, more broadly still, on male dominance. The construct of 'gender' and its links to an ideological 'family' are central within this perspective.

Within this framework 'gender' is understood to be a social construct—the attributes socially ascribed to the biological categories of male and female. As Seyla Benhabib (1987) explains, gender is 'the social-historical, symbolic constitution and interpretation of the anatomical differences of the sexes'. Within Western cultures the 'symbolic constitution and interpretation' of these anatomical differences have created two selves: 'woman', who is nurturant, caring, dependent, emotive (irrational), selfless, submissive, passive, and associated with the roles of wife and mother and with the institution of 'the family'; and 'man', who is aggressive, rational, autonomous, independent, and associated with the roles of worker and leader and the institutions of work and politics. Women are constructed as men's opposite and the attributes associated with each are paired in a dichotomous, hierarchical structure.[7] So, for example, the construct of women is one of dependence, and that of men, independence; independence is understood to be antithetical to, the polar opposite of, dependence; independence is valued, dependence is not.[8] Men, and the attributes associated with them, are ranked over and above women and the attributes associated with women. As such women, and the physical and emotive labour (the caring work) they frequently invest in the care of children and of other adults in the household and/or in the labour market, are systematically devalued.

These particular gender constructions are integrally connected to another social construction, the nuclear family. This ideological family is premised on a gendered division of labour according to the role ascriptions of men and women. Men support the family economically through paid employment; women sustain the family by meeting the daily needs of its members for food, cleaning, and emotional support. This image of the family as nurturant, intimate, and based on a gendered division of labour is pervasive. Indeed, to call it a 'cultural image' or 'construct' is to challenge its own projection of timelessness and naturalness.

To claim that 'gender' and 'family' are social constructs is not to suggest that these constructions accurately describe the lived experiences of all men and women. Many, if not most, of our lives depart from these descriptions in multiple and often significant ways (DeVault, 1991; Richie, 1996). They do, however, profoundly, perhaps inescapably, shape our lives. They exert tremendous pull on who we are, who we might aspire to become, and what we might aspire to do in the world (Mosher, 1991). As DeVault (1991) notes, like other cultural images, the cultural image of family both represents and helps to construct social reality.

From a feminist perspective, these normative constructs help us to understand men's violence in intimate relationships. Perhaps most graphically, much abuse centres on the enforcement of these particular role expectations: her performance of her role of wife (submissive, ready to meet his sexual and other needs, house well kept, etc.) and his as the 'ruler of the roost'. Her performance in her role of wife is monitored by her abusive partner and any perceived failure to perform satisfactorily is invoked as a justification for his acts of control, including his physical aggression. He may humiliate her in front of family and friends by criticizing the quality of her food preparation, the cleanliness of the home, the behaviour of the children. His complaints about her meal preparation and service may, as Ellis's (in Murcott, 1983: 164–70) research suggests, trigger his violence. He may prevent her from accessing employment readiness programs, English-language classes—any and every avenue that might decrease her dependence on him and threaten to dislodge the gendered division of labour.[9] He may assault her because he thinks she is flirting with another man or because she is inadequately sexually responsive to him.

Consider, for example, the comments of Mr Maddin, a member of Parliament, when the 1909 amendment to the Criminal Code was being debated in the House of Commons:

> I have no regard or sympathy for the man who hangs about the house, a drunken loafer, living by the earnings of his wife. But what about the diligent hard working man who works eight to ten hours per day, and when he comes home finds his supper not ready, his children not washed and his wife gallivanting about the country. What is sauce for the goose might very well be sauce for the gander, and the mover of this measure might well be asked to incorporate in it husband as well as wife beating. (House of Commons Debates, 4 Feb. 1909)

Role expectations are clearly expressed here—a woman is to be in the home, preparing supper, caring for children. And clearly implicit is the assumption that physical violence is justified should a woman fail to meet these role expectations adequately. These expectations, and the sense of justified violence to enforce them, are also clearly expressed by many abusive men. Ptacek (1988) analysed how men who batter talk about their violence. He found that they use two verbal strategies: excuse ('I lost control') and justification. The justifications centred on finding fault with the woman: she was not a good cook; she was not sexually responsive; she was not sufficiently deferential; she was not faithful. In short, the woman was commonly criticized for not being a good wife. As put by one of his respondents: 'I should just smack you for the lousy wife you've been.' As Ptacek observes, a sense of self-righteousness pervades such comments; the men felt justified because their 'husband rights', to use Adrienne Rich's term, had been violated. As Rich describes, husband rights are those 'rights men are presumed to enjoy simply because of their gender: the "right" to the priority of male over female needs, to sexual and emotional services from women, to women's undivided attention in any and all situations' (Rich, as quoted in Ptacek, 1988).

Given the pervasiveness of these gendered expectations, it is not at all surprising that these same justifications are frequently employed by women to excuse the violence of their partners. For example, in a recent study seeking to identify the needs of immigrant women in the Toronto area, women in focus groups were asked what ideas they had to prevent sexual and physical assaults. Women responded: be a good wife; be a good cook; don't make trouble; be a lady, don't lead them on; don't bother your husband if he's in a bad mood; don't annoy your husband; be submissive (Toronto Advisory Committee on Cultural Approaches to Violence Against Women and Children, 1992: 133).

In DeVault's (1991) work on feeding the family, this sense of 'husband right' pervaded all of her interviews with women. The women she interviewed, including those who stressed that their relationships were grounded in equality, made 'choices' about what to cook, how to prepare the meals, etc. all with a view to the preferences of their husbands. Men's entitlement to good food and to service, and that their preferences should determine women's work, seemed to be taken for granted. Women deferred to men's needs and attempted to meet those needs (Devault 1991: 144–5). While none of her interviewees reported violence in their relationships, as she notes, the assumptions about 'husband rights' that characterized their responses are similar to those in abusive relationships. Food preparation and service, in DeVault's analysis, are ways of 'doing gender' (through the day-to-day preparation and service of food by women within a context where the work is based on, and helps to reinforce, the assumption that this is properly women's work).

It is important to stress that these role expectations are not simply the expression of individual, subjective preferences. Rather, they are embedded in dominant ideologies and social institutions (law, religion, politics). So, for example, the justifications abusive men offer are often heard and reinforced by therapists, lawyers, judges, physicians, and their colleagues at work, precisely because these expectations are pervasively circulated, taught, and transferred within Western culture. As Ptacek notes, the vocabulary of male entitlement has been routinized within the culture at large; the justifications men invoke are socially approved categories for avoiding blame (Ptacek, 1988). Similarly, much in Western law (as written and as interpreted and applied by various legal actors) has been premised upon and has further entrenched these particular role expectations: the denial to women of the right to contract or to hold property; the denial of entry to many professions; the treatment of women as incompetent witnesses; etc. So, too, much in other Western traditions, such as philosophy, reflects views of women's natural irrationality, emotiveness, ability to nurture, etc., rendering them, by 'nature', well suited to (or more strongly, capable only of) the roles of mother and wife (Morgan, 1988; Sherwin, 1992).

From a feminist vantage point, gender operates in a further and related man-

ner to render women vulnerable to abuse. As the gender 'woman' is centrally constructed around the roles of wife and mother, finding and keeping a 'husband'
becomes a pressing preoccupation for many women, since such a figure is necessary, by definition, for the performance of her roles. Adrienne Rich (1986) has
described this as 'compulsory heterosexuality'—the pressure to establish and
maintain a relationship with a man. Susan Pharr (1988) speaks of this as one of
the weapons of sexism. Because a woman's value, both in her own eyes and in the
eyes of many of those who judge her (family, friends, professionals, etc.), is integrally linked to her performance as wife and mother, if she forges a relationship
with a man who becomes violent, one of the reasons why she may find it very difficult to leave is the threat of the loss of this status. Preserving a relationship so
that she continues to hold the status of 'wife' may be paramount, notwithstanding her husband's abuse.

A further significant factor in wife abuse from a feminist vantage point is
women's economic dependence. As many authors have noted, the gendered
expectations and performance of caring labour significantly structure women's
economic marginality. As noted earlier, many acts of violence and of control are
aimed at preventing women from securing any degree of economic independence. And while economic dependence does not in any direct sense cause wife
abuse, it plays an enormously powerful indirect role. In Levinson's (1989) cross-
cultural research the strongest predictor of wife abuse was sexual economic
inequality; wife-beating occurs more often in societies in which husbands have
the economic and ultimate decision-making power in the household.

In light of the many linkages feminists have drawn between gender expectations—including the expectations of caring labour placed upon women—and
men's abuse of women, it is hardly surprising that many feminists are suspicious
of embracing an 'ethic of care' to guide moral deliberations. While recognizing
the limitations of prevalent moral theories that presuppose the nature of persons
to be self-interested, self-sufficient, self-made, and atom-like, and that fail to
attend to relationships and the special obligations to which they give rise, many
feminists worry that an ethic of care that makes fundamentally different—and
more accurate—assumptions about human nature also potentially valorizes
women's subordination. An ethic of care requiring that one see, understand, and
empathize with the vantage point of the one cared for, while potentially a moral-
ly worthy way of being, is also compatible with conditions of oppression. As
Susan Sherwin (1992: 50) notes,

> Within dominance relations, those who are assigned the subordinate position . . .
> have special reason to be sensitive to the emotional pulse of others, to see things in
> relational terms, to be pleasing and compliant. Thus the nurturance and caring at
> which women excel are, among other things, the survival skills of an oppressed group
> that lives in close contact with its oppressors.

Claudia Card (1990) and Barbara Houston (1990) both indicate that care for
the needs of others and the desire to build and maintain relationships often make
it difficult for women to prioritize their own safety in situations of abuse. Indeed,

women frequently protect the men who oppress them. Women abused in their intimate relationships offer many reasons for remaining and being silent about the abuse. These reasons are often directly connected to their sense of what their caring responsibilities entail. Lee Ann Hoff (1990: 43–5) notes that for the women in her study their role included a responsibility to nurture the men who brutalized them. They felt compassion and understanding for the men who abused them and sought to protect them from harm by not exposing the violence and/or by excusing their conduct. They acted on their commitment to make their marriages work and were prepared to blame themselves for the violence. Obviously, what is absent in these situations of 'care' is any mutuality of caring attentiveness and responsiveness. Sherwin (1992: 51) argues, and Card (1990) and Houston (1990) express a similar idea, that we 'need to distinguish the circumstances in which care is appropriately offered and those in which it is better withheld', rather than to reject 'caring' altogether as a guide to moral deliberation. As such, 'an important task . . . is to determine the moral criteria by which we can determine' this. But attempting to discern these criteria is an extremely difficult task.

From a feminist perspective, the therapeutic perspective is deficient. Acts of physical aggression are not the result of individual pathology, but are connected to other tactics of power and control exercised by men and more broadly linked to a system of domination: sexism. The therapeutic perspective is critiqued for decontextualizing, individualizing, and depoliticizing the issue of violence against women in intimate relationships. It conceives of the problem not as a social problem requiring structural change but as faulty individual traits and personalities requiring therapy (Dobash and Dobash, 1992). Yet notwithstanding the critique of the therapeutic perspective by feminists, many feminists have unwittingly pursued arguments and strategies that lend credence and viability to therapeutic discourses and practices (Ferraro, 1996). The clearest example of this is the feminist pursuit of the 'criminalization' of wife assault. In these campaigns (which themselves have become central to feminist agendas), many feminists have come to focus on acts of physical aggression perpetrated by individual men. Increased rates of conviction and incarceration (or sentences mandating therapy) have been problematically equated with improved outcomes for women (Martin and Mosher, 1995). As Ferraro notes, domestic violence discourse establishes parameters of acceptable male domination within relationships; Criminal Code misconduct is used to draw a line separating unacceptable and acceptable male domination in families. Male authority in general is upheld and other forms of domination and control (which many women report are at least as harmful as physical aggression) are ignored. Intervention focuses on individual men, not on structural transformation; attention has drifted from 'male domination and social transformation to criminalized acts' (Ferraro, 1996).

Thus, what we can observe in practice is slippage from the feminist perspective into the therapeutic. As such, many of the important insights of feminists into the realities of women's lives are given little attention—how the construct of gender creates aggressors and passive victims; how the roles of wife and mother and the attendant responsibilities for care of others are policed and enforced by men; how these responsibilities render women vulnerable to abuse.

Intersecting Oppressions Vantage Point

From this vantage point, multiple and intersecting forms of oppression (including sexism) help to explain the violence in women's lives. This perspective suggests that no single account or meta-theory is capable of explaining violence against women. Rather, the account/explanation must vary according to the intersecting forms of oppression present in the life of a woman, and these will be connected to particular historical, cultural, and social factors. For example, violence against Black women will be shaped by racism and its intersections with sexism, and in particular, by how both forms of oppression and their intersections were constructed and practised through slavery. What unifies these explanations is their characterization of both therapeutic and feminist perspectives as inadequate and, more affirmatively, their attention to systems of domination in addition to sexism. This is not to suggest that these other perspectives are rejected; the feminist vantage point in particular is often important within this third vantage point, but its central constructs, such as gender and care, are reinvestigated with attention to how they are shaped by reference to socially constructed disadvantage in addition to sexism.

Beth Richie's work on the gender entrapment of battered African-American women, which led them to participate in criminal activities, illustrates this well. Her work speaks powerfully to the pull of the ideological forces of gender and of family reviewed earlier, but also how they operate within a particular racialized context. The battered African-American women in her study did not grow up in family structures resembling the ideological nuclear family characterized by hegemonic gender roles. Yet they strongly desired, and worked to form, such families. This group of women described experiences of being relatively 'privileged' children, and with this privilege came the responsibility to maintain that status by working to please others. Their identities were wrapped up in pleasing others (not unlike DeVault's research participants) and they experienced love and affection as conditional in nature. But it was not only their gender identity development that propelled them towards the ideological family, but also their racial identity. They assumed 'that "normal" family structure and "normal" gender arrangements would symbolically and materially improve their social status' and would 'provide the protective support that they perceived African American families would need against problems in the future' (Richie, 1996: 135, 139). The women felt that African-American families were discredited because they contradicted the ideological norm, and hence their aspirations to establish such families were driven in part by their desire to improve both their own status and that of their race.

Their desire to create such families was also shaped by their disappointments in the public sphere. Constant rubbing against sexist and racist barriers caused them to modify their expectations of what they could be, or might do, in the 'public' world and led to an intensification of their desire and efforts to create families that perfectly matched the ideological norm. They also desired to create a haven (which the ideological family promised) from the heartlessness of the racist and sexist world they encountered (Richie, 1996: 54, 136–7). When the physical abuse began many of the women first denied it altogether, and later they became ashamed and embarrassed. They went to tremendous lengths to hide the abuse from other family members and friends because they were anxious to continue to portray to the world at large that they had created, and lived within, the cocoon of the nuclear family. And because they perceived that African-American men were disproportionately harmed by racial inequality and discrimination, they were likely to excuse the abuse and unlikely to disclose it for fear of turning their men over to racist authorities. Loyalty to the family meant tolerating the violence, and this loyalty was paramount to their own safety and satisfaction.

Richie's work, like that of other Black women, illustrates many of the limitations in much of the feminist theorizing of gender, family, and care, which arise because of its lack of attention to race, class, disability, and other forms of socially constructed disadvantage (Richie, 1996; Collins, 1990). Her work reveals the enormous investment of caring labour made by Black women in attempting to ensure the survival of Black children and families: battered Black women's loyalty to families was 'a key element in their emotional interest, everyday work, and identities as "Black women trying to create families with Black men"' (Richie, 1996: 68). It also reveals the contradictory space that families may represent for many Black women and the excruciating moral double binds that Black women abused by Black men faced in their intimate relationships (Tong, 1984; Cleage, 1993; Richie, 1996). The centrality of the role of care for one's race and one's community in the lives of Black women generally, and more specifically how it shapes Black women's vulnerability to violence, eludes most feminist accounts. Not surprisingly, Usha George raises similar points with regard to South Asian women in Chapter 4.

The contradictory space of family and the moral double binds facing Black women suggest that the approach offered by Sherwin, Card, Houston, and others—of attempting to discern in which circumstance care is appropriately offered and when best withheld—is perhaps the wrong approach. This attempt seems to imply that caring obligations themselves do not conflict with each other, but the lives of the women Richie interviewed revealed just the opposite. They cared not only for their husbands, but for their children, their communities, their race, and in some ways at least, for themselves. These caring obligations did not all point to a single potential action, but to conflicting courses of action. How is it possible to say that a woman ought to withhold her care of her husband when he inflicts harm upon her, when to withdraw that care may harm him as well as their community? Rather than attempting to discern in what circumstances women's care is appropriately offered, would it not be preferable to discern what would make it possible for her to care for her race, her community, her husband, and herself without having to choose among them?

A further example of a more contextualized approach to the understanding of violence against women, which moves beyond psychopathology and beyond gender, is found in much of the literature authored by Aboriginal persons in Canada. As noted by the Royal Commission on Aboriginal Peoples (1996, vol. 3: 56–7, 73):

> While family violence experienced by Aboriginal people shares many features with violence in mainstream society, it also has a distinctive face that is important to recognize as we search for understanding of causes and identify solutions . . . . the failure in family functioning can be traced in many cases to interventions of the state deliberately introduced to disrupt or displace the Aboriginal family. . . . [It] is fostered and sustained by a racist social environment that promulgates demeaning stereotypes of Aboriginal women and men and seeks to diminish their value as human beings and their right to be treated with dignity.
>
> . . . the unbalanced power relationships that structure the lives of Aboriginal people are not found primarily in the relationships between men and women. The imbalance lies in the powerlessness of Aboriginal people relative to society as a whole, including the social institutions that dominate every aspect of their lives.

Most Aboriginal authors agree with the Royal Commission that the relationship of domination most central to the violence in the lives of Aboriginal women is that of colonization—a relationship of domination that is, of course, integrally connected to another relationship of domination, racism. This is not to suggest that sexism becomes irrelevant, for as the Royal Commission (1996, vol. 4: 66) noted, Aboriginal society is not free from the sexism that exists in the rest of Canada. As Sharon McIvor (1992) has argued, the relationship of equality of men and women in many Aboriginal societies prior to European contact was part of what was destroyed through the process of colonization.[10] The relationships between men and women, the roles of each, and the role of the extended family were, like other Aboriginal structures and values, the subject of intentional destruction through assimilation. These relationships, roles, and values were attacked and replaced by patriarchal values:

> Aboriginal people emphasize that family violence is not a tradition. Rather, family violence has become a problem following impacts of colonization. For over a century First Nations have been subject to a policy of assimilation, which had as its goal the eradication of aboriginal people as distinct peoples. (Frank, 1992: 7)

> Let me tell you that upon European contact our societies required no prisons, armies, police, judges or lawyers. Prostitution, rape, marital illness, suicides, homicide, child sexual abuse, and family violence were all unheard of. Physical diseases were at such a minimum that our bodies had no immunities to even simple endemic diseases upon contact. It was women that passed on that social order intact from one succeeding generation to the next.
>
> It was through the attack on this power of aboriginal woman, that the disempowerment of our peoples has been achieved, in a dehumanizing process that is one of the cruellest on the face of this earth. In the attack on the core family system, the direct attack on the role of aboriginal women resulted in the disintegration of our peoples towards genocide. (Jeanette Armstrong, in McIvor, 1992: 5–6)

But the destruction of male-female relationships and the forced assimilation to patriarchal values are only one dimension of the colonization process that has implications for violence currently present in Aboriginal communities. Most Aboriginal authors also point to the significant causative role of a particular vehicle of assimilation: residential schools. As Sid Fiddler notes, two to four generations of Aboriginal children were exposed to residential schools from 1880 through to 1960. Children were forcibly removed from their families and their communities. They were denied their culture and their language. They were denied the love, guidance, security, and validation of their families and their communities. Many were physically and sexually abused. They were denied opportunities to learn parenting skills and denied intimate human relationships (Fiddler, 1991). The resultant destruction of culture, and of identity, and the exposure to authoritarian ways of relating (person to person, and nation to nation) are understood to be at the root of violence in Aboriginal families.

It is important also to develop in more detail the observation of the Royal Commission that family violence (an explicit choice of term because violence against women in intimate relationships is understood to be integrally connected to other destructive behaviours, including violence against children, violence against elders, alcohol abuse, and suicide) is fostered and sustained by a racist social environment that promulgates demeaning stereotypes of Aboriginal men and women:

When you are talking about oppression, there is a process that goes on. [First] there is a process that demeans us, that belittles us and makes us believe that we are not worthy, and the oppressed begin to develop what they call cultural self-shame and cultural self-hate, which results in a lot of frustration and a lot of anger. At the same time this is going on, because our ways are put down as Native people, because our cultural values and things are put down, we begin to adopt our oppressors' values and, in a way, we become oppressors ourselves. . . . Because of the resulting self-hate and self-shame we begin to start hurting our own people.

When you talk about things like addiction and daily abuse, elder abuse, sexual abuse, jealousy, gossip, suicide and all the different forms of abuses we seem to be experiencing, it's all based on [the original] violence. It's all a form of internalized violence. . . . [Churches and governments] made us believe that the way we are today is the Dene way. It isn't. That is not the Dene culture. (Roy Fabian, submission to the Royal Commission, 1996, vol. 3: 60)

The Commission report goes on to note that 'the stereotyping and devaluing of Aboriginal women, a combination of racism and sexism, are among the most damaging of attitudes that find expression in Canadian society. These attitudes are not held exclusively by non-Aboriginal peoples':

The portrayal of the squaw is one of the most degrading, most despised and most dehumanizing anywhere in the world. The squaw is the female counterpart of the Indian male savage and, as such, she has no human face. She is lustful, immoral, unfeeling and dirty. It is this grotesque dehumanization that has rendered all Native women and girls vulnerable to gross physical, psychological and sexual violence.

I believe there is a direct relationship between these horrible racist, sexist stereotypes and violence against Native women and girls.

I believe, for example, that Helen Betty Osborne was murdered in 1972 by four young men because these youths grew up with twisted notions of Indian girls as squaws. Racist and sexist stereotypes not only harm Aboriginal women and their sense of self-esteem, but actually encourage abuse, both by Aboriginal men and others. Our family violence programs attempt to help both victims and offenders to see beyond the stereotypes. (Donna Sears, submission to the Royal Commission, 1996, vol. 3: 63)

Most Aboriginal violence is directed at other Aboriginal people, in part because of the devaluation of their lives both in their own eyes and in the view of non-Aboriginals. So, for example, the dehumanization of Aboriginal women through the racist and sexist cultural stereotype of the 'squaw' renders Aboriginal women of little value, justifying both the perpetrator's abuse and the failure of many others to express moral outrage and to take action to protect women and end the violence.

For many Aboriginals attempting to end the violence and other destructive behaviours, intervention is seen holistically, requiring healing of the abused, the abuser (acknowledging that often a person is both of these), the family, the extended family, and, indeed, the community. Such healing requires transformation at the individual, familial, communal, and societal levels. Importantly, it hinges on rebuilding a culture, and a cultural identity, that the White settlers had set out to destroy. In this process of rebuilding and in the restoration of control to Aboriginal persons, gender has emerged as a contentious issue. Concerned by the failure of Aboriginal leaders to pay adequate attention to the violence being perpetrated by men against women in their communities and cognizant of the reality that the process of assimilation has included assimilation to patriarchal norms, many Aboriginal women worry about the devolution of governance from the dominant culture to Aboriginal men (McIvor, 1992; Royal Commission, 1996, vol. 3).[11]

Several threads connect this third vantage point. The concept of 'care' is relevant, both because of its connection to the construct of gender and in a manner that eludes most feminist accounts. Within this perspective the webs of care—the relationships one must heal and sustain—are not solely woven within or around the family. Rather, the web is much wider, encompassing obligations to and feelings for one's extended family, one's community, and one's race. Within this perspective it is also clear that racism plays a role in shaping women's experiences of gender; in other words, gender is socially constructed not only on biological differences between the sexes but also on assumed 'natural' differences between races. Donna Sears's submission to the Royal Commission, quoted above, powerfully captures the racist and sexist ideological construct of 'Aboriginal Woman'. Experiences of gender, of care, and of family will also be shaped by a multitude of other axes of socially constructed disadvantage.

Examining this multiplicity is crucial to an adequate understanding of the violence perpetrated against women in their intimate relationships, and to an adequate understanding of the decisions and actions they take in response to the violence.

(MIS)INTERPRETING WOMEN'S CHOICES

As briefly noted earlier, the decision of an abused woman to stay within, leave, and/or return to an abusive relationship is frequently interpreted and judged by others—family, friends, therapists, lawyers, judges, etc. Yet those who 'judge' frequently fail to consider the multiple types of oppression that create and sustain the violence and shape a woman's responses to it. As such, they frequently misinterpret a woman's actions. The problem of misinterpretation is intertwined with a second problem, that of contradictory interpretations and judgements. For example, a woman might be told by one 'adviser' that it is her duty to remain and by another that it is her duty to leave. The action she takes based on this advice (and other factors) is often subsequently judged by another (or others). Both the persons supplying the advice (and they, too, are likely to judge her) and those who exercise judgement with respect to her action may have failed to understand the full context of her life.

An example might help to illuminate the problem. A woman abused in her marriage asks her priest what she ought to do. He asks what she has done to provoke the violence. He tells her that it is her duty as a wife and mother to remain, to care for her husband and her family. She does indeed care for them. In fact, she not only cares for them, but cares deeply about them. While she wishes the violence to stop, she loves her husband and does not want the relationship to end. She also sees a counsellor who tells her that her husband will never stop, that the violence will only get worse. Moreover, she is told that her love for her husband is really the internalization of patriarchal oppression. She is told that the only thing to do is to leave her husband and that she must do this for the sake of the children. She decides to remain: she has no marketable employment skills or employment history, and her English-language skills are limited, so she worries about her ability to care for her children; moreover, he has threatened to take the children should she leave; and besides, she loves her husband and wants the relationship to continue.

When the counsellor learns of the woman's decision she calls a child protection agency because she believes the children have witnessed the violence and may be in need of protection. She also forms the opinion that the mother is suffering from 'learned helplessness'. The children are taken into care and a protection hearing follows. The judge believes that the violence has occurred and is appalled that the woman expresses love for her husband. He suggests that she has placed her own (perhaps masochistic) needs above those of the children. From the judge's position as an economically secure, White man who has never been subjected to violence, he fails to see any risks to her or the children in leaving the relationship. This, of course, only reinforces his view that she remained in the relationship out of some perverse form of self-interest, in complete disregard for the welfare of the children. In response to her testimony that it is her duty as a wife and mother to make the relationship work and to ensure that the children have a father (she is not oblivious to society's condemnation of single mothers), the judge expresses the view that it is a woman's duty to make a relationship work, but only when there is no violence. Thus, he contradicts both the priest, who said it was always a woman's duty to remain, and the counsellor, who would never claim a woman had an obligation to remain in a relationship. Contradictory expectations and misinterpretations wreak havoc on her life; she is blamed by all involved.

As Hoff (1990) notes, people have difficulty being non-judgemental about the decisions made by a woman abused in an intimate relationship. Commonly, as the judge does in our hypothetical case, the woman is blamed and the violence is attributed to pathology (her masochistic tendencies). Her tenacity in trying to meet societal expectations of her as a mother and wife is not rewarded or admired but condemned, and her concern for her children is completely overlooked. Interpretations of this sort are grounded in the therapeutic vantage point, which individualizes, privatizes, decontextualizes. She may also be blamed, as by the priest, for her failure to perform adequately the roles of wife and mother, which simply reinforces the concept of husband rights and the legitimacy of violence to uphold such rights. Here the interpreter completely fails to see her struggle to perform these roles well and assumes that the violence indicates a failure on her part. The constraints that may limit her capacity to meet the ideological norms to which she aspires and the harm that the violence itself causes to her (and that may affect her ability to care for her children as she wishes she could) are completely overlooked.

So, too, the interpretation of her life and the judgement formed by the counsellor are inadequate. While attentive to the role of patriarchal social norms in shaping her decision-making, the counsellor seems to assume that these can simply be discarded without cost. Moreover, the counsellor fails to see the threat to the safety of the woman and her children should they leave, a threat generated both by her economic insecurity and by his explicit threats. Her attribution of 'learned helplessness' is similarly problematic. The counsellor equates women's strength, courage, and agency with leaving the relationship; those who remain or return are assumed to be helpless, passive, unable to discern or to act in their own interests, and unable to seize the (assumed) opportunities for exit. As Martha Mahoney (1994) argues, however, this view obscures the reality that, for many women, remaining in or returning to an abusive relationship is a rational choice in circumstances in which 'choice' is incredibly constrained. This view also obscures the fact that women who remain often act with tremendous courage and seek ways to end the violence, sometimes successfully. In addition, for many women there are no options, or those that exist are indeed worse than living with the violence.

Each of these judgements, then, is fundamentally flawed; each misses crucial dimensions of women's lives. They miss that a mother must weigh 'the benefits of leaving with the children against the consequences her children will suffer on their departure. She must balance her own safety against the harm to the children from inadequate housing, loss of economic security, and the absence of father's companionship' (Roberts, 1993). So, too, she must consider the very real potential for post-separation violence, including lethal violence, which the data reviewed at the outset make clear. The batterer's threats to take the children are not to be taken lightly. (Other threats often made by abusive men include threats to kill her and/or the children should she leave, to abduct the children, and to fight her to the bitter end over custody.) The judgements fail to attend to the risk of economic insecurity, a risk that is very much connected to her own, and other women's, caring labour and to the general devaluation of women. While children may also be harmed by their mother's decision to remain—the evidence seems clear that if the children witness the violence they may be indirectly harmed, and it may be likely that one day, if not already, the father's violence will be directed towards the children—it still does not follow axiomatically that these harms are worse than those visited upon them by leaving.

These judgements also miss yet other potentially relevant considerations that are brought into relief by the third vantage point. As Roberts points out, a woman may not be able to protect her child unless she is protected, but if she asks for protection or assistance for herself, her child may be removed from her care by child welfare authorities. This is a grave concern for Aboriginal women, for whom:

> Fear of child welfare authorities snatching children away, as was largely practised in native communities in the 1950's and 1960's, is a memory many still live with. For that reason, abuse or any other difficulties being experienced in the family may be hidden at great lengths. ('A Broken Silence', in Frank, 1992: 16)

At issue is no less than the survival of group identity. The removal of Aboriginal children threatens the tenuous beginnings of the reconstruction of Aboriginal culture and identity, which, as discussed earlier, is central to the task of eradicating family violence.

In other ways as well, care for one's community confounds the choice of what to do in situations of violence. A strong cultural norm requiring respect for older people may clash with the responsibility to protect victims from abuse, and reconciling these competing norms is not always easy (Royal Commission, 1996, vol. 3: 68). Many racial minority women fear that if they leave the relationship and expose the violence they will further entrench negative stereotypes of their culture or community. In the context of many cultural communities a woman and her family face great humiliation and shame if a marriage fails. And for some, the breaking of marriage vows results in ostracism from one's community and the loss of the comfort and connection that come from that sense of belonging. As Richie's (1996) work documents, this is a particularly acute loss given not only the profound lack of care for or about racial minority women, but also the outright hostility and racism that exist outside their families and communities.

Let me end by discussing an actual case in which the state sought custody of four children. The 'facts' set out by the judge hearing this protection application are as follows. This was an application for the permanent transfer of parental rights and responsibilities of four children, ranging in age from five months to four years. Their mother, V.B., appeared at the hearing with counsel to contest the application. The father, D.C., did not appear. The deputy chief of police stated that this was a serious case of 'domestic violence', one of the worst he had ever seen. V.B. was the subject of frequent assaults by D.C., who was sentenced to nine months in jail for one of these assaults:

> One of the more difficult aspects of this case is that she continued the relationship with Mr C. after these continued serious assaults against her over a lengthy period. There is some evidence that she was afraid to terminate or was powerless to prevent the continuation of the relationship. There is better evidence, and I find as a fact, that in spite of the violent assaults against her personally, V.B. permitted and even encouraged the continuation of her relationship with D.C. The evidence indicates that she wants and even needs this relationship to continue. . . . There is a definite risk that V.B. holds her relationship with D.C. as more important than the interests of her children and I find it probable on the basis of the evidence that she would continue this relationship regardless of the interests of the children. (*Minister of Health and Community Services v. V.B. and D.C.*)

Evidence indicated that the children had witnessed the violent assaults of their mother. The court also heard evidence of V.B.'s supposed 'emotional instability', and negative inferences were made about her 'need' for the relationship. There was also some evidence of possible abuse of the children. V.B. adequately fed and clothed her children, and the trial judge found that she loved them. The state's application for custody was granted and all four children were placed on a permanent basis in care. The trial judge concluded that V.B. would place her interests above those of the children and continue her relationship with D.C., notwithstanding her promise to end the relationship should the custody of her children not be taken away from her.

It may well be the case that the only avenue the trial judge had open to him to protect the children was to make the order that he did, and of course, he was appropriately concerned with their interests. Yet, the 'facts' as presented invite many questions. While it is obviously not possible to answer these questions, it is worth asking them and speculating about possible answers. Was the judge right in his conclusion that V.B. placed her interests ahead of her children? And what were her 'interests' in returning? Why did she return to this abusive relationship? Why did the judge reject her claims about fear and powerlessness? And why did the trial judge conclude that fear and powerlessness were inconsistent with permitting, even encouraging, the relationship? Is it not possible that V.B. feared for her life and the lives of her children and that this fear was the reason she continued the relationship? Is it not plausible that V.B. saw keeping her relationship as the only way to keep her children, the only way to try to preserve her children's interests? She may not have been able to support four preschool children on her own; she may have lacked any other supports; she may have feared that if she left and failed to meet her children's basic needs she would lose them to a child welfare authority. Over the course of her life she may have been told by many persons, many times, that it was her responsibility as a wife and mother to keep her family together.

And what if she were an Aboriginal woman and feared the loss of her children to non-Aboriginal families? And is it not possible that she might have loved her partner, notwithstanding the grave harm he had done to her? As bell hooks (1984) argues, the links between love and violence are drawn for us all the time in popular culture and in lessons we learn as children (this will hurt, but I'm only doing it because I love you). Could V.B. be the woman I described at the outset of this section, the woman whom the White, middle-class judge fails to understand? Deepening our understanding of V.B. does not necessarily mean that the result here was in error. But it may have been; and certainly the reasoning may have been. And routinely asking these sorts of questions and other questions that deepen our understanding of the multiple intersecting axes of oppression in women's lives would lead us to a very different approach in dealing with women and children caught in abusive relationships.

NOTES

1. In 1993 Statistics Canada conducted a nationwide survey, the *Violence Against Women Survey*, of 12,300 women over the age of 18. Women were asked, among other things, about their experiences from the age of 16 of physical and sexual assault as defined by the Criminal Code. Other studies, though less methodologically rigorous, suggest that the rates of Criminal Code violence may well be higher for women with disabilities and Aboriginal women (Disabled Women's Network, n.d.; Ontario Native Women's Association, 1989). The Royal Commission on Aboriginal Persons in its report noted the difficulty in trying to piece together an accurate picture of the extent of violence against Aboriginal women (Royal Commission, 1996: 57–8).

2. Some American authors have concluded that physical abuse in intimate relationships is the leading cause of serious injury to women, accounting for more trauma than automobile accidents, muggings, and sexual assault combined (Sassetti, 1992).

3. Here I am describing broad approaches to the understanding of abuse against women in their intimate relationships. In some respects, the sketch I offer of these approaches is artificial in that the approaches of particular authors frequently embrace features or characteristics of more than one of the 'vantage points' I describe.

4. Nor is it my goal to create a framework for the sorting or classification of the multitude of theories of the etiology of violence against women.

5. Portions of this section and of the subsequent section, 'The Feminist Vantage Point', draw on an article I co-authored with M. Bell: '(Re)fashioning Medicine's Response to Wife Abuse', in S. Sherwin and the Feminist Health Care Ethics Research Network, *The Politics of Women's Health: Exploring Agency and Autonomy* (Philadelphia: Temple University Press, forthcoming).

6. The provision being debated, which was passed and in effect until 1953–4, read as follows: s.292. Every one is guilty of an indictable offence and liable to two years' imprisonment, and to be whipped, who a) indecently assaults any female; or b) does anything to any female by her consent which but for such consent would be an indecent assault, if such consent is obtained by false and fraudulent representations as to the nature and quality of the act; or c) assaults and beats his wife or any other female and thereby occasions her actual bodily harm. R.S., c.146, s.292; 1909, c.9, s.2.

7. The *Concise Oxford Dictionary* includes in its definition of opposite, '2. of contrary kind, diametrically different to and from, being the other of a contrasted pair . . . ; the opposite sex, men in relation to women and vice versa'. Men and women are thus described as diametrically different to and from each other—as opposites (*Concise Oxford Dictionary*, 1982).

8. For an excellent discussion of how the concept of dependence and the connotations associated with it have changed over time, see Fraser and Gordon (1997: 121).

9. Jody Raphael (1995) provides a shocking account of the extent to which abusive male partners will go in preventing women's participation in employment or educational programs, participation that is often mandated as part of their continued eligibility for Aid to Families with Dependent Children. She suggests that male coercion probably accounts for a large proportion of program failures.

10. The Royal Commission on Aboriginal Persons (1996, vol. 2: 122–4) notes that in many Aboriginal societies women's roles were significantly different from those of men in governance and politics, as in other areas of life, and that these differences were the 'subject of widely varying interpretations and comments among interveners' who appeared before the commission. Some argued that this did not mean a lack of respect for women, while others argued the contrary. Women's groups in their submissions also differed in their views about the relative power of Aboriginal women in their communities today by comparison to pre-contact times. Many said that they had more power pre-contact, yet some argued that they have a more powerful voice today. It is possible that each of these accounts is true, since there were, and are, many First Nations.

11. During the 1992 constitutional talks, Aboriginal women were divided on the issue of self-government. Many Aboriginal women expressed concern about self-government because of the failure of male Aboriginal leadership to address family violence in their communities. In *Her Majesty the Queen v. Native Women's Association et al.*, [1994] 3 R.S.C. 627, the Native Women's Association of Canada argued that its exclusion from direct funding by the federal government for constitutional matters and from direct participation in the constitutional discussions threatened the equality of Aboriginal women. The Association expressed its concern that the Canadian Charter of Rights and Freedoms be made applicable to any form of Aboriginal self-government negotiated between the government and the Aboriginal organizations that had been invited and funded to participate. The Association perceived that the national Aboriginal organizations were male-dominated and that there was little likelihood the male majority would adopt the pro-Charter view of the NWAC. The Supreme Court of Canada found that there was no violation of section 2(b) (freedom of expression) or section 15 (equality) of the Charter.

REFERENCES

Benhabib, S. 1987. 'The Generalized and Concrete Other', in S. Benhabib and D. Cornell, eds, *Feminism as Critique*. Minneapolis: University of Minnesota Press.

Card, C. 1990. 'Caring and Evil', *Hypatia* 5, 1: 101–8.

Cleage, P. 1993. *Deals with the Devil and Other Reasons to Riot*. New York: Ballantine.

Collins, P. 1990. *Black Feminist Thought*. London: HarperCollins.

Crawford, M., and R. Gartner. 1992. *Woman Killing: Intimate Femicide in Ontario 1974–1990*. Toronto: Women We Honour Action Committee.

DeVault, M. 1991. *Feeding the Family*. Chicago: University of Chicago Press.

Disabled Women's Network. n.d. *Violence Against Women Fact Sheet*. Toronto.

Dobash, E.D., and R.P. Dobash. 1992. *Women, Violence and Social Change*. New York: Routledge.

Ellis, R. 1983. 'The Way to a Man's Heart: Food in the Violent Home', in A. Murcott, ed., *The Sociology of Food and Eating*. Aldershot: Gower.

Ferraro, K. 1996. 'The Dance of Dependency: A Genealogy of Domestic Violence Discourse', *Hypatia* 11, 4: 77–91.

Fiddler, S. 1991. 'Genesis of Family Violence in Native Society', paper presented as part of the Visiting Lectureship in Native Health, University of Toronto, Oct.

Frank, S. 1992. *Family Violence in Aboriginal Communities, A First Nations Report*. British Columbia Task Force on Family Violence: Queen's Printer for British Columbia.

Fraser, N., and L. Gordon. 1997. 'A Genealogy of "Dependency", Tracing a Keyword of the U.S. Welfare State', in N. Fraser, ed., *Justice Interruptus, Critical Reflections on the Postsocialist Condition*. New York: Routledge.

Her Majesty the Queen v. Native Women's Association of Canada et al., [1994] 3 R.S.C. 627.

Hoff, L.A. 1990. *Battered Women as Survivors*. London: Routledge.

hooks, b. 1984. *Feminist Theory: From Margin to Centre*. Boston: South End Press.

House of Commons Debates, 4 Feb. 1909.

Houston, B. 1990. 'Caring and Exploitation', *Hypatia* 5, 1: 115–19.

Levinson, D. 1989. *Family Violence in Cross-Cultural Perspective*. Newbury Park, Calif.: Sage Publications.

Mahoney, M. 1994. 'Victimization or Oppression? Women's Lives, Violence and Agency', in M. Fineman and R. Mykitiuk, eds, *The Public Nature of Private Violence*. New York: Routledge.

Martin, D., and J. Mosher. 1995. 'Unkept Promises: The Experiences of Immigrant Women with the Neo-Criminalization of Wife Abuse', *Canadian Journal of Women and the Law* 8: 3–44.

McIvor, S. 1992. 'Aboriginal Justice, Women and Violence', paper presented to the British Columbia Indian Homemakers Association, Aug.

Minister of Health & Community Services v. V.B. and D.C. (1987), 6 R.F.L. (3d) 180.

Morgan, K. 1988. 'Women and Moral Madness', in L. Code, S. Mullett, and C. Overall, eds, *Feminist Perspectives*. Toronto: University of Toronto Press.

Mosher, J. 1991. 'The Harms of Dichotomy: Access to Welfare Benefits as a Case in Point', *Canadian Journal of Family Law* 9, 2: 97–156.

Ontario Native Women's Association. 1989. *Breaking Free: A Proposal for Change to Aboriginal Family Violence*. Thunder Bay: Ontario Native Women's Association.

Pence, E., and M. Paymar. 1986. *Power and Control: Tactics of Men Who Batter*. Duluth: Duluth Minnesota Program Development Inc.

Pharr, S. 1988. *Homophobia: A Weapon of Sexism*. New York: Chardon Press.

Ptacek, J. 1988. 'Why Do Men Batter Their Wives?' in K. Yllo and M. Bograd, eds, *Feminist Perspectives on Wife Abuse*. London: Sage Publications.

Raphael, J. 1995. 'Domestic Violence and Welfare Receipt: The Unexplored Barrier to Employment', *Georgetown Journal of Fighting Poverty* 3: 29.

Rich, A. 1986. 'Compulsory Heterosexuality and Lesbian Existence', in *Rich, Blood, Bread, and Poetry: Selected Prose 1979–1985*. New York: Norton.

Richie, B. 1996. *Compelled to Crime: The Gender Entrapment of Battered Black Women*. New York: Routledge.

Roberts, D. 1993. 'Motherhood and Crime', *Iowa Law Journal*: 95–141.

Rodgers, K. 1994. 'Wife Assault: The Findings of a National Survey', *Juristat* 14, 9: 1–22.

Royal Commission on Aboriginal Peoples. 1996. *Report of the Royal Commission on Aboriginal Peoples*, vols 2, 3, and 4.

Sassetti, M. 1992. 'Domestic Violence', *Family Violence and Abusive Relationships* 20, 2: 289–305.

Sherwin, S. 1992. *No Longer Patient: Feminist Ethics and Health Care*. Philadelphia: Temple University Press.

Stark, E., et al. 1979. 'Medicine and Patriarchal Violence: The Social Construction of a "Private" Event', *International Journal of Health Services* 9, 3: 461–93.

Tong, R. 1984. *Women, Sex and the Law*. London: Rowman and Allanheld.

Toronto Advisory Committee on Cultural Approaches to Violence Against Women and Children. 1992. *Our Ways: Anti-Racist and Culturally Appropriate Approaches to Combatting Women Assault*. Toronto.

8

Contradictions in Child Welfare: Neglect and Responsibility

Karen Swift

INTRODUCTION

This chapter deals with the issue of caring for children. It examines both the concept of child neglect and the caring work performed by women that has remained a hidden reality of the issue of child neglect. I will explore ways in which caring has come to be discounted and ignored in the public and professional discourse about child neglect and examine the problems faced by mothers receiving child welfare in caring for their children. The analysis focuses on two themes. Firstly, the traditional relationship between the state and the private family is shown to be crucial to the way we think about caring for children. The social work response to neglect, characterized by contradictory mandates both to help the family and to exercise authority over negligent mothers, is a reflection of this relationship. The second, and closely related, theme is the gendered division of labour in our society through which mothers become the primary and often the only providers of care for children. Through an examination of these themes, I will propose how we might learn to understand and to address the issues of neglect and caring very differently.

The analysis presented here is based partly on a research project carried out in a Canadian child welfare agency. The study is an example of 'institutional ethnography', a research design that facilitates an understanding of the actual operation of an organizational setting (Smith, 1987). The project focused on verified cases of child neglect and involved a detailed study of the case files of selected families, followed by interviews with workers about these families. I wanted to find out how child welfare workers come to identify and understand neglectful behaviour in the context of an organizational setting.

The analysis was accomplished through an alternate view of understanding and developing knowledge about child neglect from that which has ordinarily been employed in child welfare research. This approach is grounded in the writing of Marx and Engels (1846), has been expanded through the work of ethnomethodologists (Garfinkel, 1967; Cicourel, 1976), and more recently has been used in research on gender, organizations, and power relations (Smith, 1987; Campbell and Manicom, 1995). In this approach, reality is not viewed as obvious. Instead, it contains surface realities, which appear to us as self-evident, as well as hidden realities that enter into and organize what appears on the surface. With respect to child neglect, the case material upon which so much knowledge about neglect has been based can be viewed as the surface reality. An exploration of the underlying processes through which case material is produced can suggest new understandings of the surface realities and the social purposes they serve. In this chapter, the underlying realities are represented by two central themes: state-family relationships and the gendered division of labour.

The value of this approach is that it allows us to perceive and examine features of experience that otherwise remain submerged under the rubric of 'fact', and it directs us to use this knowledge for change. We read many 'facts' about child neglect, and we are encouraged to understand social policies and programs as the logical responses to these facts. My purpose is to probe the realities underneath the apparent facts in order to understand the effects of our policies and to identify new directions. I will briefly sketch the 'facts' of neglect as they are usually presented in child welfare literature and review the main components of the social policy response to it. I will pose this view against an analysis based on the model described. Finally, I will propose some ideas for change in our current social response to the care of children.

CHILD NEGLECT: A BRIEF HISTORY

The concept of child neglect reflects a historical relationship between the state and the family. The fundamental concept shaping this relationship is known as *parens patriae*, literally meaning 'parent of the nation'. *Parens patriae* is deeply rooted in English history, with its origins in the medieval reign of Edward I (Custer, 1978). The doctrine was codified in English law in 1765 and later became part of both the American and Canadian legal structures. It is a doctrine that can be used with the humanitarian intent of protecting children from the excesses of their parents, but it also provides a power and rationale for considerable state intervention into private family life. This doctrine and the power of the state provide the framework for child welfare as we know it, and the concept underlies the legislation and social policy that have developed to deal with neglect and other child welfare issues (Farina,1982).

Linda Gordon (1988) notes that child neglect as we currently think of it was 'discovered' in North America around the turn of the century. The issue of neglect in Canada, however, has its roots in the poverty and abandonment of large numbers of children in the earliest years of industrialization. Although many children were an asset to their parents in the early years of settlement, by 1799 sufficient numbers of children had been orphaned or abandoned in Upper Canada that legislation for their protection was thought to be necessary. The first legislation was the Act for the Education and Support of Orphans or Children Deserted by their Parents, and it provided for the binding out of children as apprentices. Through this Act, public responsibility for protecting children outside the family was established in Canada.

Towards the end of the nineteenth century, several sets of conditions conspired to produce organizational and legislative action for more explicit measures to protect children. During these years, thousands of homeless children were sent to Canada from the United Kingdom and placed as apprentices. Some placements did not work out and many of these children eventually made their way to urban centres, especially Toronto, where their poverty became a visible problem (Sutherland, 1976). In addition, the intensity of the processes of industrialization during the 1880s and 1890s produced conditions of homelessness and exploitation for many Canadian children of the working class. These same processes also produced a new middle class whose standard of living rapidly increased. The social climate for this group, especially for women with increased leisure, provided time and energy for social change. The efforts of these women to effect change are explored by Carol Baines in Chapter 2.

Out of these conditions grew a social reform movement directed towards improving the living conditions of deprived children, known at the time as 'child saving' (Jones and Rutman, 1981). This movement helped to establish the first Children's Aid Society in Canada in 1891 and was instrumental in promoting legislation in Ontario that applied to children living with their own families as well as to those who were abandoned or orphaned. Ontario legislation in 1888 articulated the principle of the state's right to evaluate the suitability of a child's environment and allowed for the removal of a child from that environment if this is deemed to be in the child's interests. This Act laid the groundwork for more specific child welfare legislation in Ontario, passed in 1893, addressing the Prevention of Cruelty To and Better Protection of Children. A neglected child was defined by this legislation in the following ways:

- a child who is found begging or receiving alms;
- a child who is found wandering about without any home or proper guardianship;
- a child who is found associating or dwelling with a thief, drunkard, or vagrant and growing up without salutary parental control;
- a child who is found in any house of ill-fame or the company of a reputed prostitute;
- a child who is found destitute, being an orphan or having a surviving parent undergoing punishment for crime.

Assumed in these definitions is that children require safe and stable living conditions and that these conditions should be provided by parents or suitable guardians. The role of the state is to ensure that this occurs. In this we see an important feature in the relation of state and family codified in law: that the first responsibility of the state is not that of supplying care for children but of enforcing needed care through the medium of the family. This perception of the role of the state grew out of ideas firmly embedded in English common law identifying parental responsibilities for the maintenance, protection, and education of their children. As Farina (1982) notes, these ideas, published by Blackstone, who codified English common law in the latter half of the eighteenth century, produced the framework for subsequent family law in Canada.

The 1893 legislation also established several of the cornerstones of child welfare practice designed to protect children when parents failed to provide adequately. The newly formed Children's Aid Societies, the administrative arm of the law, were charged with enforcement of standards of care and parental behaviour. Thus, the focus for the societies was from the beginning organized around the case-by-case supervision of particular families. Also, the reformers believed, along with their American counterparts, that the family was the proper source of nurture for children (Falconer and Swift, 1983). They opposed group and institutional care and fought successfully for the incorporation into the legislation of a foster care model of substitute care for children who could not or did not live in families of their own. Finally, although poverty and exploitation became relevant issues in the fight for Mothers' Allowances early in the twentieth century, the early reformers did not include these 'social' issues in their reform agenda. Consequently, built into the legislation and organizational policy from the beginning was the idea that the family was primarily responsible for its own destiny and the state was responsible for the enforcement of this ideal.

The traditions of the 'friendly visitors' inherited by the first child welfare workers perpetuated and elaborated this approach (Lubove, 1965). The duties of visitors were spelled out early on. They were to 'visit each applicant, to examine particularly into her moral character, her situation, her habits and modes of life, her wants, and the best means of affording relief' (Treudley, 1980: 136). Child welfare workers retained the investigative functions of the early visitors along with some discretion to establish the eligibility of clients for whatever resources might be available. In the early years of child welfare, extra resources were rarely available, and often consisted of personal contributions from the workers themselves.[1] Nevertheless, in principle, the responses established through the original legislation, and by the first child welfare workers, represent the same three elements of service that Kadushin (1967: 23) outlined decades later as the basis of child welfare: (1) protection, to help parents 'enact their roles in a more socially acceptable manner' and the 'apprehension' or removal of children from homes found to be unsuitable; (2) supplementary services, the 'second line of defence'; and (3) substitute services, both temporary and permanent.

Other provinces (except Quebec) and the two territories developed child welfare legislation around the turn of the century, modelled to a great extent on Ontario's, which in turn was based on English roots and traditions (Swift, 1997). Thus, even at this early stage, the contradictory roles of enforcement and help were enshrined in Canadian child welfare practice.

CURRENT ISSUES

The stage set by the first legislation and reformers remains a framework for understanding child neglect in contemporary times. The emphases on the moral attributes of individual parents, especially mothers, and on enforcing and improving care of children within the family have continued to be primary issues for the attention of child welfare authorities (Swift, 1995c).

Neglect was the issue around which child welfare legislative and administrative activity revolved until the 1960s. In the last three decades, physical and sexual abuse have become more prominent issues than neglect, although the largest single kind of day-to-day work in child welfare still falls into the category of neglect (Swift, 1997; Trocme, Tam, and McPhee, 1995). Diminished attention to neglect is reflected by the fact that this term seldom appears in provincial legislation, as well as by the small amount of recent child welfare literature dealing with this topic. When neglect is examined, the debate generally centres on how intrusive the power of *parens patriae* should be.

The discretionary use of this power by social workers has been strenuously criticized. The basic dispute, in an era characterized by rights movements of all kinds, has been whether state intrusion into private family life has occurred too frequently and too extensively. In the 1970s, legal critics such as Wald (1976) and Mnookin (1973) suggested that social workers were imposing middle-class values of child care on poor and culturally different populations. They suggested a criterion of actual and demonstrable harm to a child as the minimum grounds necessary to justify child welfare intrusion into the family. The definition of harm as 'physical injury' and 'emotional disability' contained in recent provincial legislation indicates that legislators have moved to the position of stronger protection of family autonomy. Manitoba's legislation states, for example, that families and children have a right to the 'least interference' with their affairs compatible with 'the best interests of children', a phrasing that emphasizes the role of enforcement rather than one of support and assistance. One of the less prominent features of this trend is its gendered nature. What has appeared on the surface as an issue of rights has also been a successful attack by the male-dominated law profession on the female arena of social work, with the 'subjectivity' of women's judgements as its primary target (Swift, 1995b).

In Canada, the 'rights' issue has been sharpened and expanded by critics from the Native community. Although Aboriginal families complained for many years about the treatment they received from child welfare agencies and workers, only in the 1970s and 1980s did these complaints become political issues. Studies by Hepworth (1980) and Johnston (1983) conclusively demonstrated the high numbers of Native children in care across Canada, many of whom were permanently removed from their families, often on charges of neglect. Native leaders criticized authorities for failing to understand the cultural differences in family life and child care between Native people and the dominant culture, and also for failing to realize the difficulties of caring for children under the conditions of poverty and dislocation experienced in so many Native communities. The politicization of these issues has resulted in specific legislative changes aimed at protecting the rights of Native families and children, and in some cases has also led to the development of child welfare organizations run by and for Native people. Many 'tripartite agreements' among bands and provincial and federal governments have been developed, involving various degrees of devolution of authority to bands (Timpson, 1990; Satzewich and Wotherspoon, 1993). Although there are problems in these arrangements (Wharf, 1989; Armitage, 1993), the transfer of authority and decision-making power represents a significant achievement and an important step in the direction of self-government by Native people.

DEFINING NEGLECT

Closely related to the rights question is the issue of defining neglect. A more precise definition, it is suggested, would provide child welfare workers with clear guidelines as to when intrusion into the family is necessary. Consequently, a good portion of scholarly discussion of neglect over the past three decades has been taken up with definitional problems. Typically, neglect is referred to in the social work literature as a 'problem of omission', whereas abuse is viewed as a 'crime of commission'. Neglect is usually characterized descriptively: 'the child is found to be living in filth, malnourished, without proper clothing, unattended and unsupervised' (Kadushin, 1967: 210). Such descriptions generally distinguish among the different 'types' of neglect identified in child welfare literature: physical, emotional, moral, and educational. Beyond these basic understandings, according to Hutchinson (1990), 'significant disagreements' continue to exist.

One major debate is whether neglect should be broadly understood to allow for discretion in protecting children or narrowly defined to protect families from the intrusions of the state. In this debate, as previously noted, legal voices have often argued for more narrowly defined concepts, while social workers have tended to support broader definitions. A related issue has been whether a standardized version of neglect can be developed, or whether flexibility in defining such a concept should be promoted. Craft and Staudt (1991) favour standardizing the definition, basing their conclusion on a study showing that workers often use resource availability, not personal values, as the basis for their definitions. A similar finding was also demonstrated in Austin's earlier study (1981). When resources are scarce, these studies suggest, fewer situations are defined as neglect. Standardizing the concepts, it is argued, would encourage workers to identify neglect even when it is organizationally inconvenient.

Others have argued against a standardized definition on the basis that social norms are intrinsic to the definition of neglect. This idea is sometimes expressed in child welfare literature as the 'relative' nature of neglect, meaning that what is considered as neglect in one context may not be perceived as neglect in another context. This phenomenon has been well documented, for instance by Garbarino (1981), who based his work on an 'ecological' model emphasizing interaction between the family and its surroundings. He defined maltreatment of children as a violation of community or scientific standards of the expected development of children, an approach that explicitly relies on social norms as a feature of the problem definition. Wolock's 1982 study appeared to confirm that workers in practice do use flexible standards by rating specific cases of neglect in relation to the prevailing norms in their area. Korbin (1980) discusses neglect from a cultural perspective, showing that not only do North Americans judge some other culturally accepted behaviours as child neglect, but that child-care practices considered normal by North American parents are considered neglectful by parents of other cultures.

Another arena of debate has been whether parents or children should be the focus of these definitions. Historically, the characteristics of parents have been the focal point of definitions (Swift, 1995c). In practice, however, researchers have shown that harm to children is the critical criterion used by workers to determine neglect. The study conducted by Giovannoni and Becerra (1979), for instance, demonstrated that professionals rely on harm and risk of harm to children as a defining criterion. In a recent study, Trocme, Tam, and McPhee (1995) demonstrated that workers in Ontario used harm to children as a primary test in substantiating claims of abuse and neglect.

In summary, a great deal of energy has been devoted to determining what constitutes neglect in order to clarify for social workers appropriate grounds for intervention into the private family. Both the definitional and the rights debates are closely related to and in fact grow out of the framework established by the original child welfare legislation, which relies on the investigation of individual families to ensure that specific parental duties are carried out. Although the academic debates continue, the recent legislative trend has been towards establishing narrow definitions, articulated in standardized legal language, in order to protect parents from undue intrusion by the state. Criteria are focused ostensibly on children, but, as we shall see, the class, race, and gender characteristics of parents provide prior screening devices, and whatever standards of care are invoked often result in minimal care of children being contrasted against idealized standards of parenting.

THE CAUSES AND CURES OF NEGLECT

Although not often explicitly expressed, discussions of neglect always imply that mothers are responsible. Fathers are rarely mentioned in this literature. When fathers are mentioned, it is usually to exonerate them (McCord, 1983) or to connect them to the mothers' inadequacy in choosing them (Polansky et al., 1981). Mothers are seen as so central to the issue of neglect that some definitions of the problem specifically name them. David Gil (1970: 31), for instance, defines neglect as a 'breakdown in the ability to mother'.

The dominant perspective on causation in the child welfare literature is that neglect is caused by the immaturity of particular mothers. Traditionally, neglecting mothers have been described as 'children themselves' (Young, 1964); 'childlike, pleasure-seeking, irresponsible and impulsive' (Katz, 1971); and 'infantile' (Polansky et al., 1972, 1981). Mothers have also been implicated as key figures in the so-called 'cycles' of abuse and neglect, through which they supposedly pass on their deficiencies to their children (Breines and Gordon, 1983; Swift, 1995a). Since mothers are so heavily implicated in the causes of neglect, the literature on treatment is generally aimed at changing the behaviour of mothers and improving their performance in the mothering role (Swift, 1988). Suggestions over the past two decades have focused on meeting the mother's emotional needs and, more recently, have concentrated on upgrading the mother's 'parenting skills' (Swift, 1995a).

Nearly invisible in the literature on cause is the question of minority status of mothers and children. A growing number of studies suggest, however, that children who are members of minority groups stand a much better chance of being apprehended by child welfare authorities than others. Hepworth (1980) established that as of 1971, 20 per cent of all children in care in Canada were of Native origin. This amounted to 3.5 per cent of all Native children, as compared to 1.35

per cent of all Canadian children. The publication of these figures was a key reason that substitute care has been re-examined recently. Although substitute care has been reduced overall across Canada (Swift, 1997), Rosenbluth's (1995) recent study in Saskatchewan shows a continued trend towards the frequent apprehension of Native children and shows, as well, disturbing trends towards repeat placements for Native children as well as apprehension at earlier ages than for children overall. Similar findings were reported by Barkwell et al. (1989) concerning Métis children and by McKenzie et al. (1995) with respect to Native children in Manitoba. In Quebec, a recent study showed the overrepresentation of Black children in care (Hutchinson et al., 1992).

THE STATE'S RESPONSE TO CHILD NEGLECT

Social work has become more professionalized and bureaucratized during the past century. However, agencies continue to be directed by the three basic functions of protection, supplementary care, and substitute care. The primary feature of the state's response to child neglect continues to be one of 'protecting' children through enforcement of parental duty, with support and substitute care available in some measure when the family's care is deemed to be inadequate. Social workers continue to investigate, supervise, counsel, and provide advice and resources.

During the 1970s, substitute care was quite prominent as a feature of child welfare service (Hepworth, 1980), but in the ensuing decades, supplementary in-home forms of care have come to predominate (Swift, 1997). An array of support services can be made available to clients of child welfare agencies, including income support, medical services, recreational groups, child care, educational resources, housing, homemakers, and institutional settings for disturbed children. Among the main tasks of workers, especially in the present era of substantial budget cuts, are to ration these services and to account for their distribution to particular clients. Over time, consequently, resource provision has become more prominent, based on what we believe is needed to assist parents in their own homes.

Substitute care, when it is offered, continues to be based primarily on the foster care model. The legal processes through which children may be removed temporarily or permanently from their homes have become complex. Court procedures and the worker's role in bringing a case to court require considerable time and effort. The 'least intrusive' principle has been incorporated into most recent child welfare law and signifies the importance of 'family autonomy' in our society and the political intent of present governments to preserve it. As Gillian Dalley (1988) points out, the growing conservatism of Western governments promotes the idea of family life as a buttress against the intrusions of the state. In child welfare, this principle means that workers are obligated to provide the least intrusive assistance compatible with protection of the child in the home, with removal only as a last resort. Thus, the time of workers is increasingly consumed by the legal process, and often there is little left over to devote to 'helping' clients.

RECONCEPTUALIZING CHILD NEGLECT

The account of neglect outlined above covers the main themes, issues, and problems described in the literature. This usual presentation of neglect, including its current interpretations, debates appearing in academic literature, and the state apparatus designed to address the issue, is ideological in form. By 'ideological', I mean that the account masks and distorts the reality of everyday lived experience; society and social relations are instead represented 'from the standpoint of their ruling and from the standpoint of men who do that ruling' (Smith, 1987: 2). This traditional account depends on acceptance of the concepts and 'facts' of neglect forming the 'official view', and on acceptance of state and professional responses as more or less appropriate, since they follow from this perspective.

Beneath these official views and responses, however, lies a world remaining to be explored. This is the often contradictory world of women, of mothers, of their work and caring activities, and of the context within which this occurs. This is a world organized by social, economic, and political forces of which we are usually aware, which are sometimes invoked by the relevant literature but are not ordinarily brought into the debates and discussions of child neglect. In this section the images and 'instructions' for understanding that underlie this meaning of child neglect are examined. These socially structured images distort or direct our attention away from social forces that shape reality, and they are sustained through the discourse about neglect, that is, the 'ongoing interchanges among "experts" doing research and developing theories' (Griffith and Smith, 1987: 96). Discourse is not confined to academia or to the formal literature, but also provides ideas for newspapers, magazines, and television. In addition, it supplies links to educational material, so that ideas receive wide public dissemination, not only among adults but also among school-age children. Discourse on child neglect intersects and interacts with related discourses, for instance, on the family and on mothering. I will examine two methods through which the usual presentation of neglect glosses over significant portions of reality. The first is through use of language, the second, closely related, is through the presence of an implicit underlying schema for understanding both the issue itself and the state's response to it.

THE LANGUAGE OF NEGLECT

In discourse, neglect is characterized by contradictory presentations of reality. For the most part, the usual language of research is employed. Such language assumes a fact-finding tone suggesting a disciplined search for truth. Polansky et al. (1972), in studying neglected children, asked the question why some children 'come to live so poorly'. To 'advance theory' on this issue and to bring about change, the researchers considered a range of possible causes of neglect, which were eventually narrowed to two—poverty and the 'pervasive inadequacy in the maternal personality'. Mothers were then identified as the 'crucial variable' in neglect.

Posed against this neutral language is the human face of suffering revealed in the descriptive language of the case example, as we see in this social worker's description of neglected children:

> They had sore crusts on their arms and legs. They were indescribably dirty, hair matted, body and hands stained and covered with spilled food particles. Sitting on a urine soaked and soiled mattress in a baby carriage behind them was a younger child. (Kadushin, 1967: 212)

Such a presentation invokes in the reader an immediately sympathetic response, and sometimes outrage. Most of us are touched by such suffering, and our sense of outrage is quite naturally directed at the responsible parties. We may notice that while the official research language directs our attention to mothers, the descriptive language evoking sympathy is usually about children. This contrast provides implicit instructions to readers as to how to regard mothers. We do not feel sympathetic towards them as we do towards the children; instead, we hold them responsible for the children's suffering. Often, explicit reasons for doing so are provided, as in this example from my research taken from the notes of a night-duty worker:

> Mom is drinking again. There was a passed-out male in the house, and a fire almost started as he was cooking when he collapsed. Kids say mom is drinking and they are 'afraid of the guy'. Place was a mess, empty beer bottles were scattered all over. Kids appeared neglected, baby was soaked, not changed for some time, and reeked of stale urine. No diapers in the house. Kids anxious to go with worker and were apprehended.

The mandates and organizational structures of child welfare agencies, which produce case material, also provide basic instructions for the way child neglect can be spoken about. Along with other child welfare issues, neglect is perceived and examined on a case-by-case basis. Investigations take place in the private domain, with particular families as their focus. It is important to recognize that these processes necessarily produce a particular view of the issue. The case-by-case approach instructs us to see the problem as individualized; our attention is directed to the unique circumstances and behaviours occurring in this particular family and to the specific effects on particular children. The legislative mandate tells us that neglect is an issue demanding intervention into these individual families by some system of justice. This way of organizing child welfare moves the social and economic issues affecting these families to the background. The tasks of workers are structured around determining the culpability of individual families and acting on those determinations. An issue such as poverty is not made actionable in such a system; data about its existence and effects are not gathered, and workers have no organizational or legal mandate to act on poverty as a problem. What becomes visible through this system must inevitably be questionable behaviours of individuals, and the language of case files reflects this.

As we have also seen, neglect of children always implicates parents, usually mothers. As Gerald DeMontigny (1980) points out, the mandate of child welfare does not entitle workers to protect children from environmentally caused dangers or from violence in the streets. This fact alone substantially narrows the mandate for protecting children. It suggests no social responsibility for the well-being of children, but rather, as we have seen, social responsibility only for enforcing minimal care by parents.

Further, while the category of neglect may appear on the surface to be gender-free, implicating 'parents' as responsible for care, we can easily see that almost all people accused of neglecting their children, both historically and at present, are mothers (Gordon, 1988; Polansky and Polansky, 1975). It is interesting that although this fact is 'common knowledge' among researchers, few of us writing about neglect have examined the issue from the perspective of women's lives.[2] Instead, we almost always speak of the neglect of children by their 'parents'. Use of the gender-free term 'parent' performs at least two functions in directing our thoughts. The word 'parent' suggests a non-sexist and fair approach, and its frequent use implies that our concern is equally with fathers and mothers. When coupled with research findings that mothers are the 'crucial variable', the implication is that fathers and mothers have been submitted to identical scrutiny, and it is the mothers who are clearly 'causal variables'.

The language of neglect also emphasizes certain aspects of the parent-child relationship at the expense of others. The term 'to parent' is relatively new. It refers us to complex, modern images of tasks involved in child care: providing consistency, teaching the child to behave appropriately, co-ordinating the child's relationship with schools and day care, supervising diet and television viewing, careful discipline, and so on. In this construction, the affective component of the relationship is valued and expressed largely through carrying out these tasks. Thus, a worker is able to say of a loving but inconsistent mother, 'she can't parent her children'. Carried into the processes of legal adjudication, this thought process has important implications, for it means that the evidence collected by workers focuses on the completion of those parenting tasks that can be observed and measured. The resulting evaluation can then be seen as a reflection of the quality of affection a mother feels for her children.[3]

Finally, the category 'neglect' carries explicit instructions, formalized by definitions in the discourse of child welfare, to see the problem as one of passivity, as 'omission' of some kind of necessary care (Kadushin, 1967). Polansky et al. (1972: 81) solidify this idea with their extensive work on the 'apathetic-futile mother', a term conjuring images of ragged children in the care of a depressed and hopeless mother. The reality beneath the surface for many of these mothers, however, is a life of violence and abuse by fathers, husbands, and lovers, of poverty and marginalization, of racism and discrimination.

The concept of neglect, however, does not take account of these experiences as factors in the lives of children or in the quality of care provided by the mother. Protection of the children is seen as the responsibility of the mother, and the instructions of neglect tell us to perceive problems experienced by the children as a sign of her apathy or incompetence. Any serious dilemma experienced by the mother herself may be viewed, as one worker commented, as 'just another crisis on a list of many for her', and the problem for the mother of producing consistent, quality care of children in violent, poverty-ridden, racialized situations is ignored. A judge in one neglect case shows clearly how these instructions are incorporated into the legal mandate:

> Always remember this: the Court is not concerned so much with your problems . . . the Court's paramount concern is with respect to the welfare of the child. . . . the whole objective of the law [is] to ensure that the child receives a decent upbringing and is looked after carefully. . . . So if you people don't, somebody else will.

THE UNDERLYING SCHEMA

Upon what foundation are such directives built? These 'instructions of neglect' may be more easily understood if the concept is placed in its historic and social context. The concept of 'the family' is a necessary basis for understanding the surface reality of neglect. As we have seen, responsibility for the care of children on a day-to-day basis has been relegated almost exclusively to 'the family', which has come to mean the nuclear family in modern times. We are familiar with the idea that this outcome has occurred through processes of urbanization and industrialization, which have fragmented the extended family and produced a separation between this private domain of caring and the public domain of paid work. The notion of parents as the usually exclusive caregivers for their children is closely wedded to the individualistic philosophy so basic to our social and economic life. The consequences of this for women and our models of child care are spelled out by Evelyn Ferguson in Chapter 9. Individualism provides the logic and moral force supporting the delegation of caring responsibilities to individual parents and families, regardless of the resources needed to carry them out. Self-reliance is the 'dominating virtue' that 'justifies the shutting of doors firmly in the faces of those unable to be self-reliant' (Dalley, 1988: 118).

Embedded in assumptions about mothers' suitability to care is also the obverse: that fathers (and men generally) are not suited for 'caring' and therefore need not be responsible for the tasks involved in the care of children. Their role, it is assumed, should primarily be the more removed and distant one of breadwinning. Although it is often supposed that these spheres are to some extent merging, studies show that actual parenting provided by fathers (La Rossa, 1992) is of a different quality and order than that expected of mothers and that fathers are significantly less accountable for it. When we speak of the nuclear family, then, we refer not only to the configuration of two parents living in a private dwelling with their children; a gender-based division of labour is also implied.

This nuclear family as an ideal of adult life and child-rearing, as Michele Barrett and Mary McIntosh (1982) forcefully show, has become all-encompassing. The ideal of the family provides the underlying schema for understanding neglect, because the image of the nuclear family provides us with the standards against which care can and should be measured. It dictates the division of labour in the family and tells us precisely what mothers ought to be doing with and for their children.

WHAT DOES IT MEAN TO CARE?

While the tasks of modern motherhood are very specifically covered in the discourse of parenting, the everyday realities of caring for children remain hidden, only now coming to light in feminist discourse. That this is so is especially ironic, given the enormous attention paid to mothers in the literature of child neglect. This almost exclusive focus on mothers makes it appropriate and in fact essential to take up the issue of neglect from the perspective of women, the lives they lead, and their actual capacity to do the work of caring.

Efforts to examine the concept of caring usually begin with the idea that caring involves both feelings and activities (Waerness, 1984) or 'caring about' and 'caring for' (Dalley, 1988). According to Dalley, these two aspects of caring merge in modern motherhood. They are thought of as inseparable, probably because of our strongly held belief that it is 'natural' for mothers to both love and labour for their children. Mothers who attempt to separate these aspects of caring—and this is often the case in neglect—are seen as deviant. Thus, as Dalley (1988: 8) notes, 'cleaning the lavatory and washing the kitchen floor are invested with as much significance as is reading a bedtime story.' Examples of neglect complaints show that we ordinarily do take this to be the case. Two contrasting images from case files from my research make the point: 'Apartment reeked of stale urine; dirty diaper lying around'; 'Mom lives with kids in a tiny apartment which she keeps clean.' Although neither observation relates directly to care of children, we are easily able to infer the quality of a mother's care of the children from comments about cleanliness. Not only do the writer and the reader understand this to be so, but the mother herself knows that a clean apartment reflects well on her capacity to mother.

Fathers, it must be noted, will not be assessed by virtue of clean kitchens. In accordance with the ideological model posited by the nuclear family, they may be judged by their efforts at provision. However, they will not be judged at all unless they are present. If they are not living with the mother and children, it is a simple step to expand our expectation of the mother to both provide and care. We do not often explore in any detail how she goes about achieving a reasonable standard of living for her children or how the work of caring is affected by the disappearance of the father. 'The prevailing ethos of family-based care suggests that normal tasks are being performed, that the roles enacted are straightforward, expected and unproblematic' (Dalley, 1988: 10).

Arlene Kaplan Daniels (1987) suggests that the activities of 'caring for' children are invisible because in our society only paid activities are classified as 'work'. Work in the labour market has 'moral force and dignity', while unpaid work does not and thus remains unnoticed and uncredited (Leira, 1994). Caring involves both the obvious physical activities such as feeding and diapering babies, but also the minutiae of caring such as finding lost mittens, fetching drinks of water, and bandaging wounds. Caring also involves the considerable 'emotional work' of attempting to meet the needs of others. Daniels (1987) suggests some of the components of emotional work include tailoring tasks to meet special circumstances, meeting others' deadlines, and lobbying on behalf of family members. These tasks are carried out in a particular context that, depending on the circumstances, may promote or hinder their successful completion.

When we examine cases of neglect, circumstances often must be inferred because written records usually omit all descriptions of the work of caring, as well as the context of its occurrence. In one case record, for instance, medical personnel are repeatedly critical of a mother of six for her failure to visit one of the children who is in hospital. The lack of visits forms part of an argument that is being built in the written record to show the mother as unconcerned for the welfare of the child. Although it is noted at one point that the mother did visit when supplied with transportation money, no further notice is taken of poverty as a possible explanation for her failure to visit, nor is it anywhere discussed how her other children could be cared for should she attempt to make the visits. This is a fairly typical example of how practical problems of caring are treated in the written files of child welfare. The actual tasks remain unexamined and may instead be construed as having psychological significance.

Since the child welfare mandate involves a search for problematic care, it is not surprising to find that successful efforts to care are usually missing from case files. If no problems are perceived, this is likely to be noted in such phrases as 'no immediate concerns'; 'family does not require assistance of this agency'; or 'other support systems are in place.' How the mother does the work of caring not only remains unrecorded, but it may be assumed that it is accomplished through institutionalized services rather than by the mother herself. This does not mean that workers fail to see resourceful efforts of the mother—often they do. However, it is not the worker's job to account for good mothering but to attend to those features of a mother's behaviour that are relevant to establishing the existence of neglect. The child welfare mandate directs the attention of the worker to the issue of neglect through a variety of organizational routes, including the layout of reporting forms and instructions, the principles of the legislation the caseworker is authorized to enforce, exposure to child welfare literature and training opportunities, and so on. As a result of these processes, neither the case records nor the academic literature about neglect includes discussion of how successful caring is managed by these mothers.

BREADWINNING AND THE SINGLE MOTHER

From the outset, as Gordon's (1988) work clearly shows, single mothers have been greatly overrepresented in the population of neglecting mothers, and this remains the case today. At times, these women have been charged with neglect because they could not, simultaneously, work for pay outside the home and be at home with their children, but neither could they afford to pay others to care for their children (Spearly and Lauderdale, 1983). Prior to the existence of accessible welfare for single mothers in Western industrialized countries, the death or abdication of the father inevitably put women in this precarious position unless they had extended family or inherited wealth to rely on.

With the advent of Mothers' Allowances in Canada, this contradictory experience for mothers was reduced, as they were usually able to apply for some form of welfare. This program has provided some small independence for single mothers, although the help they receive has recently been diminished in several provinces, and access curtailed. One of the effects of financial aid may be that a mother is dependent on her children for her income, and often for her housing as well. If the children of a single mother are apprehended by child welfare authorities, she loses the benefits she receives on their behalf and frequently her housing, since she needs those benefits to pay the rent. Sometimes she loses her belongings, too: 'When the workers come to pick the kids up out of the home, they just pick up the kids. And if the mum is sort of transient and sort of down and out, the belongings get sent to some Salvation Army by the landlord.' If she is not pursuing the return of her children, the mother may also lose contact with her Children's Aid worker and whatever resources that contact has represented, since the mandate of the agency is not to offer support to women but to offer help in keeping families together.

If children remain in agency care for any length of time, then, a mother may find herself in the position of starting over, looking for housing, re-establishing her benefits, and creating a new set of relationships with various workers. In line with the individualist ethic underlying the ideal of the nuclear family, the onus is on her. Child welfare workers encourage her to recognize that she has to achieve independence if she is to have the children back. 'She's going to have to learn to be very strong for herself, because she is going to have to ask for service, she won't be able to handle all her children herself, so it's a skill that she's going to have to acquire.' Workers do this because they recognize the social reality that awaits the mother, a reality based on the belief that individuals in our society can and must 'make it on their own'. The proof of self-reliance in the context of child welfare is a mother caring for her children with minimal or no assistance; failure to achieve this goal will have drastic consequences for all concerned.

WHEN CARING IS IMPOSSIBLE

The care of children by single mothers poses potentially serious problems, since there is no automatic or immediate backup should the mother become incapacitated. Specific issues, not uncommon in neglect caseloads, are alcohol and drug addictions. Professional literature on alcoholism usually alludes to this condition as a disease. For child welfare workers, however, an alcoholic mother means poor care for kids. Even if the father is present, the mother is still expected to be the primary caregiver, and the onus for recovery will be on her. She will be expected to choose a recovery program, to follow through, and to maintain sobriety. The worker may have difficulty understanding how a mother could fail in this attempt, given that her children's lives are at stake, and ask, as did one worker from my study: 'How many times do your children have to be in care before you decide to stop drinking?'

Child welfare workers are quite naturally upset and frustrated by such a situation, for they see the anguish of the children as they are shuttled back and forth to foster placements, and they are aware of the risk and harm children sustain as dependants of an addict. As onlookers, we yearn for such a mother to right herself and get the family back together. Behind this yearning is again the image of 'the family'—happy children at home with their mother. When the problem is constructed in this way, the work of caring merges into affect and becomes invisible. We assume that the mother can be cured if she chooses and that the joys of children, the rewards for a mother of having them with her, should constitute sufficient motivation to overcome addiction.

If we look at the mother's problem from the perspective of her caring work, however, we see a different picture. We see the children increasingly upset and perhaps difficult to manage as they move back and forth from home to foster care, each move accompanied by attendant strains of loss of friends, schools, belongings, and so on. To maintain the support services the mother receives through her status as a child welfare client, she has to submit to ongoing scrutiny and criticism when the children are in her care. In fact, the support staff who help her will also act as scrutineers and may testify in court against her. The mother may often be required to make 'contracts' with the worker imposing conditions on her lifestyle and relationships. If she has relatives with similar addictions, she may be asked to sever ties with them, which means cutting herself off from the very family we are taught to revere, and she will then be even more reliant on the agency to supply needed supports for her child-caring responsibilities.

The reality for such a mother if she keeps her children with her is a difficult life, involving attempts to manage several children on resources below the poverty line, often living in barren cold quarters, possibly in an unsafe neighbourhood. The children will share this poverty-ridden existence with her, based on the rationale that she has a right to the 'least intrusive' alternative. Such a case will be seen as having a 'successful' outcome on the grounds that the family is together. Since the child welfare mandate does not include protecting children from poverty and racism or helping the mother enrich her own life, the case will likely be closed—until the next crisis. The rewards of sobriety, in short, may come to seem doubtful.

When addiction produces repeated placements of the children, court proceedings to determine the mother's fitness may eventually be invoked. In this instance, the workers involved must choose between the mother's right to her children and the rights of the children to be protected from her problematic behaviour. A decision will be made based on the 'best interests' of the children.[4] When the mother has been seen to fail repeatedly, foster care or adoption may seem the desirable options. Although the failures of the foster care system have been well documented (Johnston, 1983; Hepworth, 1980), we will likely perceive this outcome as a successful 'rescue' operation because we witness a solution to the immediate problem. The children then disappear into another system, their 'case' as victims of neglect is closed, and their fate as foster or adopted children is not pursued.

THE LITERATURE REVISITED

Having explored some of the hidden realities beneath the surface of neglect, I now return to issues posed by the literature to suggest how we might view them differently. Literature on neglect represents the problem primarily as a failure in mothering, although this failure has not been defined in clear and unequivocal terms. The resulting ambiguity, it is argued, has permitted social workers and the child welfare system to impose White, middle-class standards on the poor and culturally different.

While this argument has some merit, it is oversimplified and ideologically based. Social workers do recognize the problems of poverty faced by clients. As the critique developed by and about Native children has begun to expose, the work of caring has been concealed and consequently not examined for the kinds of standards we assume can and ought to be carried out. In addition, these standards include a growing number of components, as the social sciences develop and test methods of measuring 'appropriate' child development. The assumptions of class and the dominant culture embedded in our ideas of caring for children and assumptions about the division of labour, both within the family and in the society in general, need to be revealed if a less ideological understanding of neglect is to be achieved.

With these divisions in mind, prominent research problems, such as predicting who is most likely to neglect their children and what factors are most likely to be associated with neglect, are rendered unimportant. If the underlying schema of neglect rests on the ideal of a two-parent, middle-class, dominant-culture family, it is quite logical that parents not matching this ideal are the most likely to become clients of the child welfare system—the poor, single mothers and those who are culturally and racially different. And—no surprise—this has traditionally been the caseload (Johnston, 1983; Horowitz and Wolock, 1981; Gordon, 1988; Swift, 1995a).

Also important to note is the liberal form of arguments concerning the definition of neglect. The heavy focus on 'rights', with the contradictory and seemingly unsolvable tensions between the rights of children and the rights of parents (read mothers), has reduced the issue of child neglect to the question of determining specific harms to a child. Further, narrow and standardized definitions of neglect close out questions of resources and cultural values that underlie the surface realities of care. Such a framing of the question does not address, and therefore conceals, the issues of care: who performs caring work, what resources are required, what problems are faced by caregivers, what traditions of care are drawn upon. At the same time, the intersection of two discourses, one on neglect and one on parenting, produces two vastly different pictures of child care, with the effect of pushing the ideal 'standards' of care ever higher. The picture of the maltreatment of children suggests dirty, ragged, underfed, unhealthy children in the care of an apathetic mother. In contrast, the large and growing discourse on parenting provides detailed images of excellent care, including attention to every facet of a child's development by two engaged and loving middle-class parents.

Preparing nutritious meals, attending home-and-school meetings, reading at bedtime, giving birthday parties, and soothing a sick child are examples of the images of good parenting we receive on a daily basis through women's magazines, advertising, and television programs. Many of the recommended activities, it will be noticed, not only reflect values of the dominant group but also require considerable material resources to execute. Thus the job of child welfare workers appears more contradictory as time goes by. On the one hand, they are dealing with a legal mandate reduced to proving harmful effects on children. On the other, they are exhorted to move 'neglecting' parents towards standards of parenting that even those families conforming to the outlines of the mainstream nuclear family find difficult to approach. Of course, simple failure to match the ideal does not bring the child welfare worker to the door. However, once a mother is under suspicion, her departures from these ideals can and will be used as evidence in court.

When children are removed from the care of their mothers, the proposed remedy is the 'rescue' of the child(ren) from the mother, usually leading to the substitution of another mother for the original deficient mother. That the work and responsibility are passed on to another woman is seldom questioned. As White (1986, cited in Dalley, 1988) notes, any number of failures in foster care will be tolerated so that the image of family care can be produced and reproduced. The child welfare system as it stands today has set the parameters for caring, in effect pitting women against each other, competing to provide 'the best' individual care of children (Swift, 1995b). While the nuclear family model suggests the presence of an active and caring father, this is not often the case even in two-parent families, and rarely is this so in families on child welfare caseloads. The current professional focus on treatment of deficient mothers has successfully directed attention away not only from the foster care system but also from fathers, both individually and collectively. It has also concealed the effort required and the resources needed to perform caring work in the home, as well as ignored many structural obstacles, such as the high cost of housing, that women confront in their efforts to provide care.

Nor are the needs of the women themselves legitimated in current approaches. While the standard of the nuclear family requires the woman to be dependent, this does not mean she will be cared for:

> for women, the experience of dependency is contradictory. Their dependent status—
> as housewives, mothers, dutiful daughters—is not absolute, but is conditional upon
> their being simultaneously depended upon by others. Thus for many women, being
> a dependent is synonymous not with receiving care but with giving it. (Graham,
> 1983: 24–5)

A RECONFIGURATION

It is essential to recognize that children do need good and consistent care. The 'rights' debate of the 1970s and 1980s, while claiming concern, actually ignored the quality of the care that children received. The defence of families against state intrusion inevitably operates to deny many children access to badly needed services. Debates based exclusively on protection of class and cultural rights may also operate to deny children needed care, although this has not necessarily been the intent. Reconceptualizing the issue of child neglect means understanding the components of care and a willingness to rethink how responsibility for needed care is distributed. Current political and economic conditions in Canada suggest very negative indicators for the success of such a project. The neo-conservative agenda dominating the political scene is making life even more difficult for low-income single mothers. A recent study in Toronto (Cohen-Schlanger et al., 1993) confirms that children continue to be brought into care as the result of economic hardships such as inadequate housing. Given the reduction of welfare benefits in recent years in some provinces and cuts to all kinds of support programs for women, we may expect to see an increasing number of cases labelled as child neglect. The gradual erosion of our social safety net and the virtual disappearance of the concept of universality of social programs are likely to exacerbate this effect. Child welfare agencies and departments themselves are likely to experience reductions in already scarce funding in the process. Further, as governments divest themselves of service responsibilities, it is likely that caregiving work will increasingly fall on the shoulders of women in the unpaid private domain. At the same time, as Leira (1994) points out, unpaid caring work does not provide the social and political entitlements that paid labour does. The result may be that the poorest and most marginalized women will see an increase in their caring responsibilities but simultaneous reductions in their already meagre entitlements.

The analysis in this chapter, on the other hand, suggests that improved care for children can only be achieved by allocating less responsibility and more entitlements and resources to mothers, especially those who clearly do not have the resources to manage. In fact, the serious erosion of social support for Canadian mothers, and especially for the poorest mothers, suggests that the need to challenge old directions and create new ones has never been greater. This is indeed a time for social workers to initiate and engage in the strongest possible advocacy efforts to assist vulnerable women and their children. In this section, some proposals and initiatives that may be helpful to consider are reviewed in relation to the two themes of the chapter: the relationship between the family and the state, and the gendered divisions of labour.

Our traditional view of child neglect has resulted in targeting particular poor, minority, and otherwise marginalized mothers as deficient, but it has not resulted in improved care for Canada's vulnerable children (Swift, 1995a). Consequently, the child welfare mandate and services require review. To gather information for such a project, Gorlick (1995) proposes a system of national data collection designed to measure both child well-being and risk indicators such as poverty levels. Child welfare workers and administrators are well placed to collect and publicize data about the material deprivation experienced by their clients and about the social structures that oppress them. These workers are aware of, and sympathetic to, the problems faced by their clients, but they must work to create the organizational means to make this knowledge visible and actionable—

a difficult but exciting task. As the recent history of political action by Aboriginal groups shows, it is possible to use information as the basis for initiating important legal and administrative changes in child welfare.

Wharf (1993) proposes a variety of program and policy strategies, including universal payments for children, to support the actual costs of care for children. He further recommends that provinces get out of the business of service delivery. Wharf suggests instead the formation of partnerships between provinces and communities for purposes of service delivery, with 'community governance' as a mechanism to reflect the community's values and responsibilities for children.

The child welfare mandate itself, currently based on an outworn set of social relations and on European traditions, could and should be changed. Callahan (1993), speaking from a feminist perspective, proposes the removal of 'neglect' altogether from the mandate, on the basis that neglect so clearly reflects social rather than personal problems. Instead, she suggests, actual negligence by parents can be prosecuted under the Criminal Code, leaving the creative arena of supportive work with clients to child welfare workers. This proposal suggests a radical shift in the child welfare mandate from scrutiny of individual mothers to the protection of children from social forces that negatively affect well-being. This approach requires a reversal of the recent trend towards narrow, legalized definitions of neglect to a broader social view. We might consider a return to Gil's (1981: 295) universal definition of abuse and neglect as those 'human-created or tolerated conditions that inhibit or preclude unfolding development of inherent potential of children'.

In creating new strategies, it will be important to take account of the hidden realities of caring work and to reconsider how this labour can be accomplished in the interests of children and their mothers. Developing needed changes depends on questioning the very foundations of child care in our society. As Kari Waerness (1984) points out, caring for children within the confines of individual families is relatively new. For those of us who have never experienced child-rearing differently, it seems the only possible way. It is risky to propose something else, for of all our social directives the call to motherhood is surely the most powerful and dangerous to challenge. Further, it is not clear that many women themselves wish to challenge it.

However, for many cultural groups, allocating care exclusively to mothers remains an alien concept. Traditions of kinship and community networks sharing care and responsibilities for children remain strong and useful in some cultural communities. In others, kinship relations have been damaged through processes of colonialization (Bourgeault, 1988; Swift, 1995a) but remain within the community's cultural value base. Some feminist literature addressing the reallocation of responsibility for care has emerged. Caroline New and Miriam David (1985), for instance, challenge the mystique of mothering, citing a wide variety of collective forms of child care in the present as well as in the past. Along with Gillian Dalley (1988), they argue that collective forms of care not only free mothers from the exclusively held responsibilities that now exist, but can help to shield children from unnecessary threat and produce high-quality care for the many children who are not living in the ideal nuclear family.

Until the components of care are made visible and until caring work is legitimized as a social value, the issue of child neglect will continue to be viewed from traditional and individualistic perspectives. Many social workers have recognized that the visible signs of child neglect represent a serious social problem. However, the attention to punishment and treatment encouraged by our legal and medical approach to child welfare has served to obscure rather than to reveal the fundamental nature of the problem. It has become increasingly clear that in failing to address the material circumstances of life for the caregiver, neither legal nor medical approaches can work.

The current deconstruction of the welfare state represents a devolution of care from the public to the private arena. It is in this context that social and 'collective' forms of care must be developed. Rather than trying to reconstruct the past, it may be well to remember our own criticisms of care under the welfare state, which often provided the appearance but not the fact of social responsibility. However, in that model, care is provided on the basis of 'charity', rationed according to principles of deservedness (Dalley, 1988). This model has repeatedly led to individualized solutions to problems of caregiving, delivered in the private sphere. Social or 'collective' forms of care, on the other hand, presuppose that those who provide care and those who receive care are part of a reciprocal network. Such a model stands in opposition to the charity approach, in which the carer (i.e., the welfare agency) is invested with moral virtue while the virtue of the one cared for (i.e., the mother) automatically comes up for review. Collective caring suggests a greater emphasis on group living and group interactions. Group interaction allows carers and cared-for to come to know each other personally and to develop concern for each other. This model of caring also allows for those being cared for to move eventually into roles of assisting in caregiving, rather than being consigned forever to a position of moral inferiority. Smith and Smith (1990), for example, studied a child welfare project based on a collegial rather than hierarchical model of fostering. Their study shows that when the agency encouraged this approach, foster mothers adopted a 'familial' and sympathetic attitude towards natural mothers.

These ideas, of course, run counter to our beliefs in privacy and individualism, yet they hold possibilities for much more effective kinds of care for children currently at risk without inevitably causing damage to both mother and children. To illustrate, I return to the case of an addicted mother to examine how we might treat this differently. At present, treatment programs house the mother for set periods of time to help her through withdrawal and to provide some counselling and support. During this time, the children must be placed in substitute care, and the household is likely to be dismantled. Upon release, the mother begins again. She is probably homeless and penniless as she attempts to reclaim her children. Can we imagine collective forms of living that provide children with ongoing care when their mothers are in trouble, in which mothers and fathers can help each other through crises and receive ongoing support and treatment in their living situations following release from treatment? Collective forms of living can mean that children have ties to other caretakers, based in their own communities and cultures, which obviates the need to leave their homes, schools, belongings, and friends should their mother require further treatment. Finally, collectives can allow the mother a socially useful role in helping others through problems she has experienced.

A collective approach allows us to face the fact that in some situations the work of caring cannot or will not be done by the natural mother. It requires courage and honesty to begin to challenge the centrality of the mother in the North American family. Many women fear a loss of importance within the family circle, and we fear that giving permission for a few mothers to 'resign' from or reduce their caring labour may lead to desertion of responsibility on a massive scale. Perhaps we believe that only ideology keeps mothers firmly fixed in their responsibilities. If this is so, our fears should lead us to a deeper examination of the actual experience of caregiving in the mothering role, and to the collective responsibility for improving that experience.

The concept of caring can be used to re-evaluate how we view a mother in distress and what the state response might be. At present, repeated failures to 'care for' mean a potential decision to remove the children, often with permanent cutting of ties, regardless of whatever feelings of 'caring about' exist between mother and child. By separating caring for from caring about, we can begin to give value to affection, recognizing that caring about has value for children even when caring for is sporadic or impossible. Both children and their mothers are paying a high price for our failure to make this distinction.

And what of fathers? Missing almost completely from the picture of 'parenting' to date is a clear analysis of the abdication of so many fathers.[5] We must begin to address this issue in child welfare planning, not only in the interests of the immediate care of children, but to help to prevent reproducing traditional gender roles into the future. In utterly ignoring the disappearance of fathers, the message we give to these children, most assuredly, is that fathers count for nothing, a message that fathers themselves may also have received. For girls, this is a prediction of the responsibilities they may expect when they become mothers; for boys, this picture provides a script for avoiding responsibility in the future. As many child welfare workers know, taking an active interest in an absent father sometimes produces an unexpected resource for children and may produce a new and important life interest for the father. Certainly if we wish to socialize and share the work of caregiving, we must begin to consider how fathers can play a part in this different configuration of responsibility.

The kinds of resources we typically deploy in child welfare must also be questioned. The value of our 'professional' help has rightly been questioned by critics of the current system. We may need research to demonstrate what we already know: the resources we put in are largely ineffective, and are primarily used for purposes of evidence-gathering, management, and control. We must also question the cultural appropriateness of many services now provided. Parenting classes, alcohol treatment programs, and other staples of service provision may often fail because they are based on a Eurocentric model of individualism considered irrelevant or even damaging to the many minority mothers involved with child welfare authorities. Cross-racial foster care has also come under fire as not just inappropriate but damaging to the racial identities of children. In addition, our present allocation of resources carries a very strong moral message that stigmatizes mothers for requiring help. Even well-intentioned individuals providing care cannot overcome the moral divisiveness implicit in present models of care. In explicating the actual work involved in doing a good job of caring for children we provide ourselves with some direction, but we must go further, to ask how this caring is to be supplied, thus raising the issue of care for the caregivers. Studies of neglect typically show that these mothers lead impoverished lives, emotionally as well as physically. They often have no one to care for them, and may have never had the experience of being cared for. Instead of supplying support as a way to improve their child-caring capacities, we must legitimize the needs of mothers for care and self-care as having value in their own right. Mothers can be helped towards both self-care and mutual care, as demonstrated by guided self-help projects (Lovell, Reid, and Richey, 1988; Keresit and St-Amand, 1995). Recent projects have demonstrated the usefulness of strengthening informal networks (Fuchs, 1995; Cameron, 1995), employing the extended family in healing and caring processes (Burford and Pennell, 1995), and employing the traditions of cultural communities (McKenzie et al., 1995) in programs. These efforts should not remain as marginal or demonstration efforts but should be added to and adapted for the regular repertoire of service provision.

Revealing some of the hidden realities of child neglect helps to outline a way of changing and expanding old debates. While the critique of child welfare practices has been necessary and useful, it has proven insufficient. Timpson (1990) argues that these debates have tended to reduce the problem to 'cultural ignorance and frivolous workers' while overlooking the arduous and underfunded nature of child welfare work and the serious inattention to issues such as health, education, and employment that affect child welfare clients and make the work of caring so difficult. As Durst (1995) asks, how much control do First Nations really have, even with tripartite agreements, given the conditions of poverty, unemployment, addiction, etc. that exist on reserves as a residue of colonial relations? A different strategy is needed for deploying resources to those families who are already having difficulties in providing adequate care. We will have achieved some success in child welfare, I would argue, when a reasonable standard of care can be provided children without the necessity of continuing colonial relations, and of impoverishing, stigmatizing, and coercing mothers to do the caring work.

NOTES

1. Jones and Rutman (1981) describe in detail the budget shortages that plagued Ontario Children's Aid Societies from their beginnings.
2. See Breines and Gordon (1983) for an excellent review and discussion of the attribution and responsibility for family problems to the mother. Linda Gordon (1988) also

deals extensively with this theme as it relates historically to child neglect. For Canadian perspectives on this issue, see Martin (1985), Callahan (1993), and Swift (1995a).
3. This is not to suggest that social workers fail to distinguish between affection and parenting tasks. Data from my study show that workers are well aware of this distinction. However, the evidence that counts in court involves the completion of identifiable tasks. Workers are therefore required to turn attention to that issue.
4. For discussion of the complexity of meanings attached to the phrase 'best interests of the child', see Goldstein, Freud, and Solnit (1973, 1979).
5. An exception is Barbara Ehrenreich's (1983) examination of the 'flight from commitment' of American men in the past few decades.

REFERENCES

Armitage, A. 1993. 'Family and Child Welfare in First Nation Communities', in Brian Wharf, ed., *Rethinking Child Welfare in Canada*. Toronto: McClelland & Stewart.

Austin, Carol D. 1981. 'Client Assessment in Context', *Social Work Research and Abstracts*, 17, 1: 4–12.

Barkwell, L.J., L. Longclaws, and D. Chartrand. 1989. 'Status of Métis Children within the Child Welfare System', *Canadian Journal of Native Studies* 9, 1: 33–5.

Barrett, Michele, and Mary McIntosh. 1982. *The Anti-Social Family*. London: Verso.

Bourgeault, R.G. 1988. 'Race and Class Under Mercantilism: Indigenous People in Nineteenth-Century Canada', in B.S. Bolaria and P.S. Li, eds, *Racial Oppression in Canada*, 2nd edn. Toronto: Garamond Press.

Breines, W., and Linda Gordon. 1983. 'The New Scholarship on Family Violence', *Signs* 8, 3: 491–531.

Burford, G., and J. Pennell. 1995. 'Family Group Decision Making: An Innovation in Child and Family Welfare', in J. Hudson and B. Galaway, eds, *Child Welfare in Canada: Research and Policy Implications*. Toronto: Thompson Educational Publishing.

Callahan, Marilyn. 1993. 'Feminist Approaches: Women Recreate Child Welfare', in Brian Wharf, ed., *Rethinking Child Welfare in Canada*. Toronto: McClelland & Stewart.

Cameron, G. 1995. 'The Nature and Effectiveness of Parent Mutual Aid Organizations in Child Welfare', in J. Hudson and B. Galaway, eds, *Child Welfare in Canada: Research and Policy Implications*. Toronto: Thompson Educational Publishing.

Campbell, M., and A. Manicom. 1995. *Knowledge, Experience, and Ruling Relations*. Toronto: University of Toronto Press.

Cicourel, A.V. 1976. *The Social Organization of Juvenile Justice*. London: Heinemann.

Cohen, N., ed. 1992. *Child Welfare: A Multicultural Focus*. Boston: Allyn and Bacon.

Cohen-Schlanger, M., A. Fitzpatrick, J.D. Hulchanski, and D. Raphael. 1992. 'Housing as a Factor in Child Admission to Temporary Care'. Toronto: Joint Research Report of the Faculty of Social Work, University of Toronto, and the Children's Aid Society of Metropolitan Toronto.

Craft, J., and M. Staudt. 1991. 'Reporting and Founding of Child Neglect in Urban and Rural Communities', *Child Welfare*: 359–70.

Custer, Lawrence B. 1978. 'The Origins of the Doctrine of Parens Patriae', *Emory Law Journal* 27, 2: 195–208.

Dalley, Gillian. 1988. *Ideologies of Caring*. London: Macmillan.

Daniels, A. 1987. 'Invisible Work', *Social Problems* 34, 5: 403–15.

DeMontigny, Gerald. 1980. 'The Social Organization of Social Workers' Practice', Master's thesis, Ontario Institute for Studies in Education.

Durst, D. 1995. 'Aboriginal Government of Child Welfare Services: Hobson's Choice?', in J. Hudson and B. Galaway, eds, *Child Welfare in Canada: Research and Policy Implications*. Toronto: Thompson Educational Publishing.

Ehrenreich, Barbara. 1983. *The Hearts of Men: American Dreams and the Flight from Commitment*. Garden City, NY: Anchor Books.

Falconer, Nancy, and Karen Swift. 1983. *Preparing for Practice*. Toronto: Children's Aid Society of Metropolitan Toronto.

Farina, Margaret R. 1982. 'The Relationship of the State to the Family in Ontario: State Intervention in the Family on Behalf of Children', Ph.D. thesis, Ontario Institute for Studies in Education.

Fuchs, D. 1995. 'Preserving and Strengthening Families and Protecting Children: Social Network Intervention, a Balanced Approach to the Prevention of Child Maltreatment', in J. Hudson and B. Galaway, eds, *Child Welfare in Canada: Research and Policy Implications*. Toronto: Thompson Educational Publishing.

Garbarino, James. 1981. 'An Ecological Approach to Child Maltreatment', in L. Pelton, ed., *Social Context of Child Abuse and Neglect*. New York: Human Sciences Press.

Garfinkel, Harold. 1967. *Studies in Ethnomethodology*. Englewood Cliffs, NJ: Prentice-Hall.

Gil, D. 1970. *Violence Against Children*. Cambridge, Mass.: Harvard University Press.

Gil, D. 1981. 'The United States versus Child Abuse', in L. Pelton, ed., *The Social Context of Child Abuse and Neglect*. New York: Human Sciences Press.

Giovannoni, Jeanne, and Rosina Becerra. 1979. *Defining Child Abuse*. New York: Free Press.

Goldstein, J., Anna Freud, and A. Solnit. 1973. *Beyond the Best Interests of the Child*. New York: Free Press.

Goldstein, J., Anna Freud, and A. Solnit. 1979. *Before the Best Interests of the Child*. New York: Free Press.

Gordon, Linda. 1988. *Heroes in Their Own Lives*. New York: Penguin.

Gorlick, C. 1995. 'Listening to Low Income Children and Single Mothers: Policy Implications Related to Child Welfare', in J. Hudson and B. Galaway, eds, *Child Welfare in Canada: Research and Policy Implications*. Toronto: Thompson Educational Publishing.

Graham, H. 1983. 'Caring: A Labour of Love', in J. Finch and D. Groves, eds, *A Labour of Love: Women, Work and Caring*. London: Routledge & Kegan Paul.

Griffith, Alison, and Dorothy E. Smith. 1987. 'Constructing Cultural Knowledge: Mothering as Discourse', in J. Gaskell and A. McLaren, eds, *Women and Education*. Calgary: Detselig.

Hepworth, Philip. 1980. *Foster Care and Adoption in Canada.* Ottawa: Canadian Council on Social Development.

Horowitz, Bernard, and Isabel Wolock. 1981. 'Material Deprivation, Child Maltreatment and Agency Interventions Among Poor Families', in L. Pelton, ed., *Social Context of Child Abuse and Neglect.* New York: Human Sciences Press.

Hutchinson, S. 1990. 'Child Maltreatment, Can it be Defined?', *Social Service Review* 64: 60–78.

Hutchinson, Y., et al. 1992. *Profile of Clients in the Anglophone Youth Network: Examining the Situation of the Black Child.* Montreal: Joint Report of Ville Marie Social Service Centre and McGill University School of Social Work.

Johnston, Patrick. 1983. *Native Children and the Child Welfare System.* Toronto: Canadian Council on Social Development in association with James Lorimer and Company.

Jones, Andrew, and Leonard Rutman. 1981. *In the Children's Aid.* Toronto: University of Toronto Press.

Kadushin, Alfred. 1967. *Child Welfare Services.* New York: Macmillan.

Katz, S. 1971. *When Parents Fail.* Boston: Beacon Press.

Keresit, M., and N. St-Amand. 1995. 'Taking Risks with Families at Risk: Some Alternative Approaches with Poor Families in Canada', in J. Hudson and B. Galaway, eds, *Child Welfare in Canada: Research and Policy Implications.* Toronto: Thompson Educational Publishing.

Korbin, Jill. 1980. 'The Cultural Context of Child Abuse and Neglect', *Child Abuse and Neglect*: 3–13.

La Rossa, R. 1992. 'Fatherhood and Social Change', in M. Kimmel and M. Messner, eds, *Men's Lives.* Toronto: Macmillan.

Leira, A. 1994. 'Concepts of Caring: Loving, Thinking, and Doing', *Social Service Review* 68, 2: 185–201.

Lovell, M., K. Reid, and C. Richey. 1988. 'Social Support Training for Abusive Mothers', in J. Garland, ed., *Social Group Work Reaching Out: People, Places, and Power.* Binghamton, NY: Haworth Press.

Lubove, Roy. 1965. *The Professional Altruist.* Cambridge, Mass.: Harvard University Press.

McCord, Joan. 1983. 'A Forty Year Perspective on Effects of Child Abuse and Neglect', *Child Abuse and Neglect* 7, 3: 265–78.

McKenzie, B., E. Seidl, and N. Bone. 1995. 'Child Welfare Standards in First Nations: A Community-based Study', in J. Hudson and B. Galaway, eds, *Child Welfare in Canada: Research and Policy Implications.* Toronto: Thompson Educational Publishing.

Martin, Marjorie. 1985. 'Poverty and Child Welfare', in K. Levitt and B. Wharf, eds, *The Challenge of Child Welfare.* Vancouver: University of British Columbia Press.

Marx, K., and F. Engels. 1846, trans. 1947. *The German Ideology, Parts I and III.* New York: International Publishers.

Mnookin, Robert. 1973. 'Foster Care—In Whose Best Interests?', *Harvard Educational Review* 43: 599–638.

New, Caroline, and Miriam David. 1985. *For the Children's Sake.* Harmondsworth, Middlesex: Penguin.

186 Living the Realities of Care

Noddings, Nell. 1984. *Caring: A Feminine Approach to Ethics and Moral Education.* Berkeley: University of California Press.

Polansky, N., D. Bergman, and C. De Saix. 1972. *Roots of Futility.* San Francisco: Jossey-Bass.

Polansky, N., and N. Polansky. 1975. *Profile of Neglect: A Survey of the State of Knowledge of Child Neglect.* Washington: US Department of Health, Education and Welfare.

Polansky, N., M.S. Chalmers, E. Buttenweiser, and D. Williams. 1981. *Damaged Parents: An Anatomy of Child Neglect.* Chicago: University of Chicago Press.

Rosenbluth, D. 1995. 'Foster Care in Saskatchewan: Drift or Revolving Door?', in J. Hudson and B. Galaway, eds, *Child Welfare in Canada: Research and Policy Implications.* Toronto: Thompson Educational Publishing.

Satzewich, V., and T. Wotherspoon. 1993. *First Nations: Race, Class, and Gender Relations.* Toronto: Nelson Canada.

Smith, Brenda, and Tina Smith. 1990. 'For Love and Money: Women as Foster Mothers', *Affilia* 5, 1 (Spring): 66–80.

Smith, Dorothy E. 1987. *The Everyday World as Problematic: A Feminist Sociology.* Toronto: University of Toronto Press.

Spearly, J.L., and M. Lauderdale. 1983. 'Community Characteristics and Ethnicity in the Prediction of Child Maltreatment Rates', *Child Abuse and Neglect* 7, 1: 91–105.

Sutherland, Neil. 1976. *Children in English Canadian Society.* Toronto: University of Toronto Press.

Swift, Karen. 1988. *Knowledge about Neglect: A Critical Review of the Literature.* Working Papers on Social Welfare, Faculty of Social Work, University of Toronto.

Swift, Karen. 1995a. *Manufacturing 'Bad Mothers': A Critical Perspective on Child Neglect.* Toronto: University of Toronto Press.

Swift, Karen. 1995b. 'Missing Persons: Women in Child Welfare', *Child Welfare* 74, 3: 486–502.

Swift, Karen. 1995c. 'An Outrage to Common Decency', *Child Welfare* 74, 4.

Swift, Karen. 1997. 'Canadian Child Welfare: Trends and Issues in Placement and Reporting', in Neil Gilbert, ed., *Combating Child Abuse: An International Perspective on Reporting Systems.* Toronto: Oxford University Press.

Timpson, Joyce B. 1990. 'Indian and Native Special Status in Ontario's Child Welfare Legislation', *Canadian Social Work Review* 7: 49–68.

Treudley, Mary. 1980. 'The "Benevolent Fair": A Study of Charitable Organizations Among American Women in the First Third of the Nineteenth Century', in F.R. Breul and S.J. Diner, eds, *Compassion and Responsibility.* Chicago: University of Chicago Press.

Trocme, N., K.K. Tam, and D. McPhee. 1995. 'Correlates of Substantiation of Maltreatment in Child Welfare Investigations', in J. Hudson and B. Galaway, eds, *Child Welfare in Canada: Research and Policy Implications.* Toronto: Thompson Educational Publishing.

Waerness, Kari. 1984. 'Caring as Women's Work in the Welfare State', in H. Holter, ed., *Patriarchy in a Welfare Society.* Oslo: Universitetsforlaget.

Wald, Michael. 1976. 'State Intervention on Behalf of Neglected Children: A Search for

Realistic Answers', in M.K. Rosenheim, ed., *Pursuing Justice for the Child*. Chicago: University of Chicago Press.

Wharf, B. 1989. *Toward First Nation Control of Child Welfare: A Review of Emerging Developments in B.C.* Victoria: University of Victoria.

Wharf, B., ed. 1993. *Rethinking Child Welfare in Canada*. Toronto: McClelland & Stewart.

Wolock, I. 1982. 'Community Characteristics and Staff Judgments in Child Abuse and Neglect Cases', *Social Work Research and Abstracts* 18, 2: 9–15.

Young, L. 1964. *Wednesday's Children*. New York: McGraw-Hill.

Part Three

Policy Directions and Caring Expectations

9

The Child-Care Debate: Fading Hopes and Shifting Sands

EVELYN FERGUSON

INTRODUCTION

> Canada's failure to develop a sound national child care policy and appropriate fund-
> ing mechanisms is having serious effects on this generation of children and their par-
> ents, and may have longer-term impacts on our economy and social cohesion. (Lero,
> 1997: 38)

Over 10 years ago a major Canadian task force sounded an alarm that our child-
care situation was in a state of crisis (Status of Women, 1986: 279). Unfortunately, after a flurry of activity in the late 1980s, including another major
federal task force (House of Commons, 1987), numerous provincial government
policy papers, and countless academic and professional research studies, our
child-care policy remains much the same in 1998 as it did a decade earlier. While
our hopes fade for a comprehensive, high-quality Canadian child-care system to
meet the needs of working women and their children, shifting sands on the policy front portend new changes and reveal new contradictions.

This ongoing child-care crisis is directly related to women's caring. As women
have swelled the ranks of the paid labour force during the past three decades, our
traditional 'mother at home' model of child care has ceased to provide an adequate response to the needs of most Canadian families (Lero et al., 1992; Baker,
1995). Parents are scrambling to create acceptable child-care arrangements from
every available resource: formal, licensed day-care services; informal, unlicensed
paid care such as 'sitters' and 'nannies'; and unpaid services usually provided by
family members.[1] Parents, child-care professionals, service providers, and
women's groups have sought solutions ranging from more government intervention for licensed non-profit services (Status of Women, 1986; Canadian Child
Care Federation, 1993) to appeals to women to stay at home with their children
(Maynard, 1985; Fraiberg, 1977; REAL Women, n.d.).

Most of the issues surrounding the child-care question, however, have centred
on controversies over non-familial care, including profit or non-profit care
(Prentice, 1997), licensed or unlicensed care (House of Commons, 1987), and the
acceptable degree of government involvement (Friendly, 1997; Krashinsky and
Cleveland, 1997). Missing from the debate has been a theoretical perspective that
highlights the centrality of the work of caring in all child-care situations, including those within the family. With the largest amount of care being provided by
family members, especially mothers, and women in other informal settings, a
central controversy is the extent and nature of the public role for child care.

This chapter explores some of the common realities underlying preschool
child-care arrangements and the implications for women, whether they are
mothers, grandmothers, babysitters, nannies, family home providers, or day-care

teachers. While many of these issues affect children of all ages, the particular dependency of preschoolers and women's primary responsibility in caring for them are the reasons why this chapter focuses on the care for the under-sixes. By examining the similarities in the child-care work carried out in different settings, we gain an understanding of the ways an ideology of caring underpins the under-valuing and the invisible nature of this work. It also helps us to formulate options that would benefit all women and acknowledge the critical importance of all child care.

Three issues provide the cornerstone of the present analysis. The first is that whatever the setting, it is overwhelmingly women, not men, who care for depen-dent children, and this work is not adequately recognized or remunerated. Secondly, the conception of children as a private responsibility has an important influence on the way we organize child care. Social policies reinforce the assump-tion that child care is women's work in both the private and public spheres. Finally, while there are differences in child-care work, this analysis also recog-nizes that whatever the setting, they are all based on an ideology of women's car-ing. By stressing the differences, public discourse has divided women, diminish-ing their opportunities to work together to change our social organization of child care.

The care of very young children is a demanding but rewarding job that women in all settings describe with conflicting and contradictory feelings. Marni Jackson, a journalist and mother, states that 'interruption, contradiction, and ambivalence are the soul of motherhood' (1989: 34). In a letter to a federal task force on day care, a family home caregiver graphically describes the tasks and the feelings associated with her work:

> The job involves being a maid, a cook, a child psychologist, a teacher, and a mother to these children—from getting a baby onto solid foods, to toilet training, to teach-ing him to walk, talk, do's and don't, to the basics of the alphabet, counting, colours, body health and body grooming, to the day to day trivia and hassle of learning to be—what a deal. . . . With such enormous output and so little recognition or recom-pense, you'd have to be a lunatic to want to be a Day Care mother. But I do. (Status of Women, 1986: 108)

The chapter begins by describing the variety of locations where women care for preschool children, emphasizing, in particular, the monetary value accorded to child care in each setting. Secondly, some realities shaping the context in which women care for children are explored. Finally, principles for restructuring our child-care system are discussed.

CHILD-CARE SETTINGS

Preschool Canadian children receive care in a wide variety of situations. These range from informal settings with family, neighbours, and friends, where there is no outside support or monitoring, to formal licensed care regulated by provincial governments or their agents. The latter form meets only a small percentage of the need for child care. Recent reports estimate that the informal sector provides 80 to 90 per cent of all care given to Canadian children (Friendly, 1994; Baker, 1987: 13). All non-familial settings reflect an assumption that the primary responsibility for preschool children rests with parents. These settings provide care for a specific number of hours per day and assume parents, usually mothers, will provide the balance of care.

The most common type of formal care is the group day-care centre, which employs trained day-care teachers and is licensed to care for as few as 10 children in some centres to more than 100 children in others. The sponsorship of these centres includes municipal governments, private non-profit groups such as churches, service clubs, and parent co-ops, and independent and franchised businesses. Licensed forms of care can also include individual women, usually referred to as family home caregivers, who care for a small number of children in their homes. Although they represent only a very small share of licensed child care, family homes can be licensed in almost all provinces and territories (Friendly, 1994: 88).

Group size, child/staff ratios, qualifications of staff, and condition of facilities are some of the factors regulated by provincial statute in all licensed settings. The fundamental mandate of all child-care services is to provide care for preschool children for all or part of their parents' working day. Trained early childhood educators, family care providers, and others provide supervision, meals, snacks, places for the children to nap, toys, and various kinds of activities. Licensed settings are typically open only during normal working hours, from 8 a.m. to 6 p.m., Monday to Friday, although more centres are now providing after-hours care (Friendly, 1994: 89).

A final category of licensed care is the nursery school or kindergarten, mandated to provide education for preschool children. These use trained teachers and the programs are focused on the educational needs of children rather than 'care' needs of working parents. They are usually available only a few hours per day and working parents employed full-time must make additional arrangements for their children's care. Local boards of education as well as private organizations offer kindergarten and junior kindergarten programs in a number of provinces (Friendly, 1994). However, by far the largest amount of care provided to our preschool children is by parents at home and by others in informal settings. These include unlicensed family home caregivers who babysit in their own homes, and relatives, nannies, and other paid caregivers providing care in the child's home. Services are similar to those found in licensed settings, but the hours of care may be more flexible, and those providing care may do additional housekeeping work for the family. As these are not formally regulated, little is known about the nature and quality of the care provided in these settings (Status of Women, 1986: 125; Lero et al., 1992).

As McWatt and Neysmith describe in Chapter 10, many of these care providers are foreign domestic workers and/or women of colour who, while theoretically guaranteed certain minimal working conditions through Citizenship and Immigration Canada, are frequently subject to exploitation (see also Arat-

Koc, 1990). Financial remuneration varies among these settings, but in almost all cases it is abysmally low (Status of Women, 1986). The report of the Canadian Commission for the International Year of the Child (1979) argued that child-care workers and other caregivers are chronically underpaid because they replace parents, particularly mothers, who are paid nothing for their work as caregivers; 20 years later this has not changed. At the opposite end of the continuum are teachers in nursery schools and kindergartens, who are the most highly paid. Unlike the payment for child care, teachers' salaries, particularly in the public sector, suggest that society is more prepared to recognize education as a child's right and an important form of public labour, although the age at which this begins appears somewhat arbitrary and the differences in salary can be substantial (Friendly, 1994: 223–6). The level of teachers' salaries is a function of a universal education system, strengthened by professional organizations and unions fighting for better wages and working conditions. Because these services are not primarily designed to meet the needs of working parents they are often excluded in discussions of child care. Lero and Kyle (1989) and Doherty-Derkowski (1994) remind us, however, that the historical divisions between preschool education and child care are disappearing as the educational components and qualifications of child-care workers increase.

Those caring for young children in licensed group child-care centres earn far less than their counterparts in education. Considered child care, not education, their services are not universally available or state financed, and as a result their funding arrangements are less secure. Provincial and federal governments partially subsidize low-income parents and provide start-up funds, maintenance, and salary enhancement grants, but child care is substantially financed through parent fees and some private contributions (Friendly, 1994; Doherty-Derkowski, 1994).

Two major national studies of wages and working conditions of regulated child-care workers have taken place in Canada since the mid-1980s (Canadian Day Care Advocacy Association/Canadian Child Care Federation, 1993; Schom-Moffat, 1985). Both found that the type of centre, the presence or absence of a union, the nature of its sponsorship, and the provincial location are important influences on the wages and working conditions offered by licensed centres. Schom-Moffat (1985: 131) found that the most poorly paid are those in family day-care homes who received in 1984 an average net wage of $2.26 per hour. Unfortunately, family day-care homes were not included in the more recent study, but there is no reason to believe their wages have substantially increased. Municipal government day-care workers are all unionized, as are some private non-profit centres, such as parent co-ops, churches, and service organizations, but workers in for-profit child care are rarely unionized.

The presence of a union has an important effect on wage levels: in 1991, the hourly rate for unionized staff was 33 per cent higher than for staff not represented by a union (Canadian Day Care Advocacy Association/Canadian Child Care Federation, 1993; Friendly, 1994: 224). However, in 1984, only 8 per cent of all Canadian child-care workers were union members (Schom-Moffat, 1985:

101). The poorest wages and benefits are found in the commercial centres, which usually receive fewer government subsidies and private donations than the non-profit sector, while the highest wages and most favourable benefits are paid in the unionized government-run centres, confined almost exclusively to Ontario and Quebec (Prentice, 1997: 44; Friendly, 1994: 224). Figures for 1991 indicated the mean hourly wage in municipal centres was $13.88 compared to $10.07 in non-profit centres and $8.07 in commercial centres (Canadian Day Care Advocacy Association/Canadian Child Care Federation, 1993; Friendly, 1994: 223–6). Finally, there is a wide provincial variation in average wages. In 1991, for example, pay for a day-care teacher ranged from $6.03 per hour in Newfoundland to $11.51 per hour in Ontario (Canadian Day Care Advocacy Association/ Canadian Child Care Federation, 1993; Friendly, 1994: 225). Pay differences are also partially influenced by sponsorship. The for-profit sector provides the majority of day-care spaces in Newfoundland and Alberta ($6.76 per hour) while the higher wages in Ontario reflect the greater presence of municipal centres and the smaller percentage of commercial centres.

The most commonly used but lowest-paid caregivers are in the informal sector (Status of Women, 1986; Friendly, 1994). Nannies and others who provide care in the child's home usually earn more per child, while babysitters in their own homes earn proportionally less per child but often care for a larger number of children. Not surprisingly, studies indicate that the latter form of care is most common because it is the most accessible and least expensive form of child care (Friendly, 1994; Status of Women, 1986; Lero et al., 1992). Parents, child-care professionals, journalists, and day-care lobby groups have expressed concerns about the quality of care in the informal sector (Lero, 1997; Friendly, 1997; Canadian Child Care Federation, 1993; Status of Women, 1986; Johnson and Dineen, 1981). Because they are unregulated, specific figures about wages and working conditions are not available, but the Status of Women task force concluded that the earnings of these workers are similar to those of the licensed family home caregivers but tend to be lower (1986: 117).

Informal care settings, unlike licensed centres, do not receive favourable tax subsidies. Parents, whatever the non-familial setting, may deduct some child-care expenses from their income tax if the caregiver provides receipts. In 1996, parents could claim up to $5,000 for each eligible child age six or under, $5,000 for each child over the age of six who had 'a severe and prolonged mental and physical impairment', and $3,000 for each eligible child from 7 to 14 years of age (Revenue Canada Taxation, 1996). In addition, parents are allowed to deduct $8,000 per year for a child with special needs. However, many informal caregivers do not declare this income or provide tax receipts, so many parents are unable to take advantage of the deduction (Power and Brown, 1985; Baker, 1995: 203). Tax deductions, because they reduce the amount of tax an individual is required to pay, are worth more at higher levels of income. As a result, they have a regressive impact and will be of least benefit to lower-income families.

The lowest-paid but generally least controversial form of preschool child care is parental care, which is almost always provided by the mother. Historically, the only direct remuneration Canada has provided to recognize the costs of children was a nominal universal Family Allowance benefit and a refundable Child Tax Credit that assisted low- and middle-income families. In 1989, the Child Tax Credit was supplemented by $200 per year for each child, provided that no child-care expenses were claimed (Baker, 1995; Revenue Canada Taxation, 1989). Unlike tax deductions and exemptions, a tax credit has a progressive impact because it is worth more at lower levels of income. In 1992 this tax credit was rolled into a new Child Tax Benefit targeted to families with low or middle incomes, and parents claiming child-care deductions were included (Baker, 1995). However, the most recent changes to the Canada Child Tax Benefit, announced in the February 1997 federal budget, indicate a clear direction away from acknowledging parental care by the mother (Pulkingham and Ternowetsky, 1997). Benefits are enhanced for mothers moving into the labour force. These changes, while ostensibly targeted towards alleviating child poverty, in fact become income supplements for working poor families and further incentives for parents to move off financial assistance and into the labour market. Mothers not claiming the tax benefit through the tax system are left a token $200 annual child-care supplement.

In addition to Family Allowances, Child Tax Credits, and Child Tax Benefits, low-income single mothers have received financial benefits to enable them to care for their children; Manitoba became the first province to usher in legislation in 1916. These means-tested and stigmatizing benefits are variously referred to as 'mothers' allowances', 'family benefits', or 'public welfare'. Recently, these benefits have been under major attack, as Patricia Evans discusses in detail in Chapter 3. The economic recession in the early 1990s and the rising costs of welfare for the state have led to increased pressures on single mothers to become financially independent from the state by working in the labour market. Not only are mothers being encouraged to work but in some jurisdictions they are being pressured or coerced into 'workfare' or training programs (Low, 1996).

Ironically, these changes have led to an enhanced policy focus on child-care provision in provinces, a trend that the day-care community has seen as being in their self-interest (Friendly, 1997: 5; Krashinsky and Cleveland, 1997: 19). As provinces have either encouraged or pressured single mothers to leave welfare, many programs, such as 'Taking Charge' in Manitoba and 'NB Works' in New Brunswick, have built child-care provision into the program planning, although not always successfully (McFarland and Mullaly, 1996). While the day-care lobby remains committed to universal provision, they are caught in a dilemma when child-care provision targeted to single mothers on social assistance receives enhanced monetary and policy support from these sources (Friendly, 1997: 5).

At the same time, the day-care community has also supported the renewed interest in the compensatory model of child care for low-income disadvantaged children (Friendly, 1997: 4). In the 1960s in the US, Head Start programs, high-quality day-care programs targeted to low-income preschoolers, many of whom were Black, became popular as a model to enhance children's long-term educational achievements. These early intervention programs for 'at risk' children have become popular now in Canada for Aboriginal children and others from poor and disadvantaged families, many of whom are led by single mothers (Tremblay and Japel, 1997: 7). The emphasis on compensatory child care and the increasing popularity of workfare are two trends that have served to undermine the legitimacy of single mothers looking after their children while receiving benefits from the state.

The continuing shortage of affordable child care, the lack of decent paying jobs, and the complexities of juggling poorly paid work with caring for children frequently mean that women are either confronted with an unpalatable choice—struggling on a low income from work or a minimal benefit from welfare—or they are effectively given no choice at all. All of these alternatives pay little attention to the value of child-care work and serve to highlight the class-based double standard for mothers. When mothers are potentially dependent on the state and their children are perceived as disadvantaged or at risk, the 'mother at home' model is unacceptable and children are seen as better off in day care. Yet when mothers depend on husbands or partners within private families, the traditional 'mother at home' model of child care is still often presented as preferable for children and families.

REALITIES SHAPING THE CONTEXT OF CARE

Feminist theorists who focus on the centrality of caring in women's lives have argued that we must make the realities about caring for young children explicit before we can seriously challenge the dilemmas inherent in our child-care structure (Pascall, 1986). This section explores four important realities that shape the context within which women care for preschool children.

Many realities surrounding the care of preschool Canadian children also shape the care of other vulnerable groups, such as the frail elderly and the disabled, whose care is also invisible and undervalued (Pascall, 1986). Some factors, however, are unique. These include: the degree to which the expectation of 'mothering' defines many Canadian women's lives (Hutter and Williams, 1981); the changing nature of this care as children grow and become more independent; the political nature of the caring as women instil norms and values in our future Canadian citizens and the subsequent value judgements attached to 'inadequate' care (Waerness, 1984); and the public debate about child care during election campaigns (House of Commons, 1987; Cleveland and Hyatt, 1997; Lero, 1997). An exploration of the dilemmas and contradictions inherent in the current models of child care should help to suggest changes that will be more supportive to women and children.

Reality 1. Caring for children is a very important part of the work Canadian women do, but it is invisible and undervalued.

The first reality to be made explicit is the invisibility and low value attached to the work of caring for preschool children. These characteristics have an important influence on the women who provide the care and on the organization of child-care services. The most obvious reason for the invisibility of women's care to children is the reality that much of it occurs in the private domestic sphere or in the informal market where it is not recognized as an occupation (Graham, 1983; Johnson, 1987; Status of Women, 1986). Even when acknowledged, caring in the domestic sphere is frequently subsumed under 'unpaid household work' or 'domestic labour' that incorporates many other tasks (Eichler, 1988). Child care is considered an occupation only in the labour market, which comprises a small percentage of the child-care labour in Canadian society (Armstrong and Armstrong, 1990; Goelman et al., 1993).

A second aspect of this reality is that caring for children is only part of the work women do. Powell (1997: 11) notes that labour force participation rates for married and single mothers with preschool children reached 64 per cent and 47 per cent, respectively, by 1995. Since caring for children is considered women's work, the reality that women have at least two jobs is not acknowledged. For many women, child care is their 'hidden' work while their paid occupation defines their public profile. In addition, this 'invisible' work constitutes a very demanding 24-hour responsibility. Women who work in the paid labour force are also confronted with arguments from some child development specialists who suggest that care of preschool children, or at least those under three, should be a mother's only occupation (White, 1980; Maynard, 1985). While this position is extremely controversial and typically is argued in relation to the developmental needs of children, it does highlight the importance and demands made by this work. Failing to acknowledge the significance of this work not only distorts the reality of many women's lives and vastly underestimates their working hours and conditions, but it also undervalues the importance of the child-care component of their work.

Another facet of this reality is that women, not men, are the primary caregivers for most very young children. Most professional child-care workers and informal care providers are women, and in families in which one parent works in the home caring for children it is unusual for the father to be that parent (Baker, 1995; Eichler, 1988). In single-parent families, custody of children is overwhelmingly the mothers' responsibility (Lero and Brockman 1993; Foote, 1988), and it is more often mothers who collect social assistance while caring for children at home (Gorlicke and Pomfret, 1993; Gorlick, 1988). Any research that explores the gender breakdown of work within the home shows that women assume most domestic responsibilities regardless of paid outside employment (Eichler, 1988; Baker, 1995). While some fathers are now more involved in rearing their children, there is as yet no indication of a broad-based gender restructuring of child care.

The devaluing of women's child-care work in the private sphere influences the structure of our public child-care services. As we compare the value of the labour across all types of child care, several factors emerge. Firstly, all child care is undervalued. The most highly valued is that which is labelled as education and lodged within schools. However, the educational component in child-care settings is not acknowledged, nor is the child-care component in 'educational' settings recognized. As the differences in mandate and purpose of these two major service streams diminish, the wage gap between them becomes more apparent and pressure could grow to improve the child-care sector's wages and working conditions (Friendly, 1994; Lero and Kyle, 1989). Unfortunately, over the last 10 years this wage gap has seemed stubbornly impervious to change, although the child-care community has lobbied extensively to enhance wages and working conditions and has increasingly emphasized the educational elements of their work (Friendly, 1994). At the same time, as child-care workers seek to improve the status of their work through an emphasis on its educational component, there is a real risk that the 'care' component may be devalued and the distinctions between education and care will increase rather than diminish. As Carol Baines illustrates in Chapter 2, models of professionalization have sometimes served to render more invisible the significance of women's caring.

The second important aspect that emerges as we compare the value given to the work of child care across settings is that these divisions in the delivery of child care and the differing monetary values attached to caring for children fail to provide women with a common understanding of women's caring. Resentment and hostility often emerge between different groups of women: between mothers in the paid labour force and caretakers who care for their children; between mothers who are employed and those whose work is confined to the home; and between licensed and unlicensed, trained and untrained caregivers. Child-care workers, for example, may resent mothers they perceive as spending insufficient time with their children; mothers working at home are angry about the public subsidies received by employed mothers using child-care centres; and untrained workers take offence at the implication that they have limited skills when compared to child-care workers with professional degrees. These divisions also reinforce competition between settings and their supporters, which further undermines efforts to provide a united front for developing mutual help and support and for negotiating and advocating solutions together. Thus, we have advocacy groups appearing to support licensed care over unlicensed care, non-profit care over for-profit care, and mother-at-home care over day care (Canadian Day Care Advocacy Association, 1990; REAL Women, n.d.). These divisions make it easier to avoid the issue of the underfunding and undervaluing of all child-care labour in the political arena.

Thirdly, this undervaluing of child care has psychological implications. 'Mothers go through so much, every day, that is never acknowledged' (Jackson, 1989: 36). Mothers and other caregivers experience the contradictory messages accorded to their work. They receive society's moral message that caring for young children is a virtuous activity and neglecting it is a grave sin (Hutter and Williams, 1981). Financially, they derive little monetary reward, which leaves many dependent on and vulnerable to both men and the state. Dependent on men, they and their children risk physical and emotional abuse, and dependent on the state, they risk the stigma of charity or welfare. In both cases they always face the possibility of loss of income. Whether caring for her own children full or part time, or looking after someone else's child, each woman is likely to experience the undervaluing of an important part of her life.

In summary, the invisibility and undervaluing of child-care work pose a dilemma for women. They experience financial and physical vulnerability. At the same time, women's commitment to caring is reinforced by love and the moral importance accorded this work. This commitment is also supported by a belief system, another reality of women's lives.

Reality 2.   Women's caregiving is supported by the belief that it is 'normal' and 'natural'.

A second reality about women's caring for young children is the belief that it is 'normal' and 'natural'. As New and David (1985: 13) put it: 'Women are given caring work on the grounds that they are mothers, or may become mothers, or should have been mothers.' Hutter and Williams (1981) conclude that women who, through choice or necessity, do not bear children are considered deviant.

Reinforced by this belief, the public has remained relatively unconcerned about the gender imbalance so apparent in our child-care structure. Studies concerned about mother-child attachment have dominated the child development literature, but there is a striking lack of concern about paternal bonding (Doherty-Derkowski, 1994; Rutter, 1981). Even in the 1990s, a different form of caring is expected from fathers than mothers. Mothers continue to be the primary caregivers to their children, while fathers remain chiefly responsible for earning money to provide material resources. This breadwinner model of the family dictates that women provide physical and emotional care for children while they and their children depend materially on spouses or the state.

These expectations translate into Canadian social policies. Fathers who wish to look after their children receive far less state support than mothers. Only recently, in 1990, under the Unemployment Insurance program (currently the Employment Insurance program) a parental leave plan was established that entitled fathers or mothers to care for their children for a 10-week period, supplementing the 17-week maternity leave. Maternity leave is still restricted to mothers except under very specific circumstances (Baker, 1995). Traditionally, as well, it has been more difficult for single fathers to receive social assistance to care for their children at home (Eichler, 1988).

At the same time a double standard has been established for different groups of women. Nelson (1996) and Cossman (1996) both demonstrate how lesbian mothers face social, legal, and economic discrimination in collecting benefits, obtaining custody and support, and having partners acknowledged as spouses. As mentioned earlier, mothers' dependent status is still an acceptable norm for those with breadwinner spouses, but recent family law and public welfare changes have pushed single mothers to be independent and both physically and materially care for their children (Low, 1996; Hurl, 1989; Foote, 1988). These changes most affect the poorest mothers on social assistance and those who are separated and divorced.

The belief that it is the normal and natural role for women to be mothers has important implications for men as well as for women in that it limits choices available to both sexes. But 'different' mothers, such as lesbian mothers, as well as single and poor women who possess the least control, have the fewest child-care options and bear the brunt of society's judgements of their parenting. With our present undervaluing of caring work, these women and their children pay most dearly for the current organization of our child care.

Reality 3.   Care for preschool children is primarily a private responsibility of those parents who bear or raise those children.

Parents must plan, provide, and pay for child-care services unless their inability to do so is demonstrated and they are deemed financially 'in need' or their children emotionally or physically 'neglected'. If parents are in financial need, provincial governments subsidize care if the parents use licensed day-care facilities, and the federal government may contribute through the Canadian Health and Social Transfer and the income tax system (Friendly and Oloman, 1996; Cleveland and Hyatt, 1997). If mothers are deemed neglectful, child welfare authorities may recommend substitute care to counteract what they have identified as poor parenting (Swift, 1995).

'Normal' families not deemed in financial or emotional need receive minimal government help, and what is available occurs primarily through tax deductions. As discussed earlier, these deductions provide a larger benefit to higher-income Canadians and are therefore regressive in their impact.

The implications of the privacy of child care can be contrasted to the public responsibility assumed for education. Child care is supposed to be available through a child's family, typically provided by the mother, whereas education is universally provided in the public domain once a child reaches the age of four or five. Each begins with different perceptions of the child. Child care assumes that the child belongs to a parent, while education assumes that the child is a citizen in his or her own right.

The welfare state, therefore, is not totally absent from our system of child care. The support it provides 'normal' families, however, is minimal and is regressive in impact, giving greater support to high-income families and those who purchase care in the child-care market. This, however, is not the only role the welfare state plays in our organization of child care. As Wilson (1977) emphasized years ago in her analysis of women and the welfare state, the state also controls the lives of women and children.

Reality 4.   While women provide the daily care of preschool children, the state intervenes by controlling important aspects of this care.

Caring for young children involves socializing and preparing them to assume productive roles in society. This task is ultimately political, and partially explains the protective or compensatory perspective that pervades the literature on child-care provision (Pascall, 1986). For instance, if a young Aboriginal mother is perceived to be neglecting her preschool child, the state, through its child welfare agents, may recommend or insist that her child be enrolled in a licensed day-care centre. Control by the state is also apparent in the provincial regulations imposed on licensed child-care centres establishing the numbers and qualifications of the caregivers and the standards of care.

Feminists raise concerns about the sources of this control, including the professionalization of child care. Some argue that the state's interest in socialization has resulted in mothers and other caregivers losing control over children's care while they continue to do most of the labour (Maroney, 1985). While child-care workers' wages have increased as they expanded into the public sphere, concomitantly child-care experts, many of them men or women not providing daily care, have established standards of care. The danger is that women's authority and respect have subsequently been eroded. Not only does this risk undermining women's confidence in their caring abilities, but by focusing state action on educating mothers and regulating caregivers, it diverts attention and resources from economic supports and public services offering relief and practical support (Waerness, 1984).

The state's control and the professionalization of child care have divided women. Professionals too often judge young, low-income, and/or single mothers as neglectful (Swift, 1995), and expect mothers to be educated child-care service consumers (Browne, 1984; Prentice and Ferguson, 1997; Ferguson and Prentice, 1998). 'It is usually other women—health visitors, social workers, teachers, relatives—who approve or disapprove of the way mothers manage their children. In this way divisions form between mothers and women who look after children in different ways' (New and David, 1985: 22).

Whether they stem from a feminist or traditional perspective, these political implications lend a moral and ideological tone to the child-care debate, often delivering contradictory messages. Pascall notes the 'ludicrous outcome' of some of our social policies and gives the example of the sudden shift in what is considered best for our four- and five-year-old children: four-year-olds are believed best cared for at home by mother, but 'woe betide any parent who decides thereafter that she would prefer to keep her child at home' (Pascall, 1986: 84).

POSSIBLE SOLUTIONS TO THE CHILD-CARE PROBLEM

The challenge we face as we explore alternatives to the current child-care system is how to respect the integral aspects of care while acknowledging and enhancing the value of this labour. Pascall (1986) notes that those bearing the child-care burden are not clamouring to give others this work. Yet women and their children remain vulnerable, dependent, and poor, at least partly as a result of our present system.

To face this challenge, it is critical to examine how the private and public worlds intersect. Our view of the family places responsibility for child care within the private sphere of the home. This does not limit care exclusively to the home, but it does mean that the family, and usually the mother, has ultimate responsibility for care. She plans and organizes the care she does not personally provide, and when these plans break down, the responsibility for caring generally reverts to her.

The public nature of the debate suggests that the individual contradictions and conflicts confronting mothers are pushing the boundaries of child care increasingly into the public sphere. Children are cared for in the formal market and the government has started to provide tax deductions for the purchase of child care. On the surface it appears that over the last three decades the boundaries of child care have been pushed from the private sphere of the home into the public sphere. During the late 1980s there was considerable optimism that changes in child-care policy were on the leading edge of public policy. At that time, the highly public and political nature of the child-care dilemma, with its attendant task force reports and studies, prominence in party leaders' debates, even with its contradictory messages, was seen as an important development because it moved the caring debate into the political arena.

By 1997, however, observers of child-care policy were more concerned. As Martha Friendly, a long-time advocate for child care, has noted:

> In 1997, Canada still has no coherent strategy to ensure child care/early childhood development services are available to meet contemporary needs. Indeed, after an optimistic phase in the 1980's, the child care situation has been deteriorating throughout the 1990's from both public policy and service delivery perspectives. (Friendly, 1997: 3)

Worrisome trends include: financial debts and cutbacks in many provinces resulting in either a loss of licensed child-care spaces or very minimal growth while demand continues to increase (Friendly, 1997; Prentice, 1997); federal funding changes from the Canada Assistance Plan to a block funding arrangement, the Canada Health and Social Transfer, that in no way protects the funding of child care compared to other social programs (Friendly and Oloman, 1996); an increased emphasis on a residual approach targeting child care rather than a universal model directed to meet the needs of all children and families (Friendly, 1997); a continued policy focus on tax deductions that benefit higher-income families over lower-income families and indirectly support informal and commercial care (Prentice, 1997); and unfulfilled promises by the most recent federal government even when they gave child care some support during the last election campaign (Lero, 1997).

These trends have tempered advocates' optimism, although not their commitment to change. Along with progressive policy changes, such as recently in Quebec (Berthiaume, 1997), and a growing appreciation for children with special needs (Hope Irwin, 1997), the child-care field offers policy advocates a model for community organizing. For three decades, organized federal voices for child care, including the Canadian Day Care Advocacy Association and the Canadian Child Care Federation, as well as groups and individuals in every province and territory, have consistently pressured both provincial and federal governments. This effort has greatly facilitated progressive changes during times such as the 1980s, but of equal importance, it has helped protect aspects of these changes when they are under attack, as is the case in the current political climate. The outcomes of these changes are contradictory and the impacts at times unjust, but in the long term they may portend movement from child care being seen as a private responsibility to the recognition that the well-being of children is a public issue.

A similar trend occurred when day nurseries were established during World War II, but the direction was reversed after the war. It remains to be seen whether contemporary changes will benefit women in the long run. Ten years ago indications such as the steady increase of mothers with preschool children moving into the paid labour force, the increasing professionalization of child-care workers, two federal task forces on child care, and the profile of the child-care debate during provincial and federal elections suggested that this issue would no longer be pushed back into the privacy of the home and women's lives. But in 1998 children still are primarily cared for in informal settings, those caring for children in most settings continue to be woefully underpaid, the issue is no longer the subject of federal task forces, and concerns are being raised about the stress on families and children in current arrangements (Lero, 1997; Friendly, 1997).

We have also learned that changes don't move quickly or in a manner that equally benefits all women. Changes to date have benefited upper-income women at the expense of poor and middle-income women, particularly single mothers, poorly paid providers, immigrant women, and Aboriginal mothers. Higher-income women have the resources to purchase child care and they have the most to gain from tax deductions that partially offset these private costs. Clearly, the education, experience, and skills of these women to the paid labour force are valued, not their caring labour within the home. Their gains, it can be argued, have been made at the expense of lower-income women, including those who care for children on a live-in basis, as is discussed in more detail in Chapter 10.

The challenge is to change our child-care system in ways that will benefit all women. The following principles for doing this acknowledge the centrality of caring in women's lives. These principles outline major issues to be addressed in altering our structure of preschool child care. The discussion of each principle suggests a variety of concrete systemic changes as well as some of the difficulties and dynamics working against such changes.

Fundamental to each of these principles is one imperative: the need to acknowledge and enhance the labour value of child care in all settings. This means we must recognize all child care, whether it occurs in the formal market, the informal market, or the private sphere of the home. Dividing our support to neglect any one sector undermines the long-term goal of change that would benefit all women. Wages and working conditions of child-care staff must remain priorities, even when policy-makers and politicians offer a choice between more spaces to meet need or improvements in staff salaries. At the same time we cannot ignore the abysmal working conditions found in the informal market. This labour must be brought into the public sphere for evaluation and financial reward. As discussed by Sue McWatt and Sheila Neysmith in Chapter 10, the racist and exploitative working conditions imposed on immigrant women working as nannies in Canadian homes must be challenged. Finally, we must directly confront the difficulties of defining women's child-care work in the private sphere of the home as public labour. This is a long-term task, but steps need to be taken now to move our child-care system in this direction. Defining what is integral to caring is critical to ensuring that we protect it. We can begin by examining our conceptualization of caring.

Principle 1.   The conceptualization of caring underlying our system of child care needs to integrate both physical and emotional dimensions.

This principle is based on the recognition that caring has two separate but interconnected dimensions: caring 'for' children—the physical dimension, and caring 'about' children—the emotional or affective dimension (Graham, 1983; Pascall, 1986). This conceptualization highlights a critical but often ignored distinction in our current arrangements for child care and gets lost if caring for children is subsumed under the framework of domestic labour or unpaid work.

All types of caregiving contain an aspect of the physical dimension of care, what is often called custodial care—for example, feeding, supervising, and changing diapers. Regulations of licensed centres usually deal with these factors to ensure that children are in buildings with a sufficient number of caretakers so that they are safe and well cared for. However, the emotional or affective dimension—the idea that one's child is loved and cared 'about'—is not always present. While regulations ensure adequate supervision and physical care, the emotional part of caring cannot be so easily regulated.

Arguments about the comparative strengths and weaknesses of various child-care settings often focus on the affective component and debate the greater benefits of 'mother care' or 'substitute mother care'. In a study on parents' preferences for child care, the second most influential factor after availability and reliability was satisfaction with the amount of affection and attention for the child in care (Lero et al., 1985). Other studies have found that parents who prefer family home and informal care value most highly the individualized affection given to their children (Johnson, 1977; Lero, 1981; Stevens, 1984). This concern is not limited to those who prefer 'mother' or 'mother substitute' care. In another study on parents' preferences for licensed group care, parents ranked low staff turnover as the most important of 33 factors affecting quality of care (Ferguson, 1989).

Ironically, settings that provide the most individualized affection also provide the lowest remuneration to staff (Canadian Day Care Advocacy Association/ Canadian Child Care Federation, 1993; Schom-Moffat, 1985). This appears to mirror the lack of value we attach to child care provided by mothers. We need to legitimate the affective dimension of caregiving, make it more visible, and include it in monetary assessments along with other factors such as professional qualifications and experience.

This principle implies that it is essential to connect the caring 'for' to the caring 'about' in all settings. This requires an emphasis on low worker-child ratios, reduced turnover, and the fostering of close child-carer relationships in any child-care setting. It also includes supportive training in child development and increased remuneration for family home caregivers. The result would be increased value and visibility for child-care work. Such an orientation would weaken a persistent argument against publicly provided child care that suggests that 'the impersonal and fragmental character of the public health and social services means that they lose the very qualities of personal commitment which transform a service into caring' (Waerness, 1984: 74). As long as the affectional component in child care is believed to be exclusively the domain of the unpaid mother or poorly paid mother substitute, parents will undermine public calls for universal child care and women's labour will be exploited in the name of love.

Assigning monetary value to the affectional dimension of caring is neither an easy nor a straightforward task. One of the factors working against such an evaluation is the trend towards professionalization. The professionalization of child care in the public sphere is producing highly educated experts who enjoy high status in the child-care community and are considerably better paid for their labour than child-care workers. As well, the organizational structure of publicly funded child care has produced managers, supervisors, and other administrative support workers who receive higher wages than direct service workers. The contradiction is that the professionalization of child care has been largely responsible for the greater recognition and pay it receives. This has been made possible, however, because child care has been increasingly perceived as a form of pre-school education and caregivers have received professional degrees and diplomas.

Any solution to the child-care problem must combine the benefits of professionalization with a recognition of the value of the affective dimension across the child-care spectrum. To assume child care is simply another form of education ignores one of caring's critical dimensions. We need, therefore, to integrate the affective dimension into our professional expectations while offsetting those aspects of professionalization that devalue daily child-care delivery. This will necessitate conscious efforts to protect the value of child care by paying workers good salaries commensurate with those of experts and administrators. It may also include assessing skills and knowledge gained from child-care experience as well as from formal training.

A role might be played by unions in this situation. Unionized workers already have the highest wages and best working conditions in the child-care field. Only a small proportion of workers in the formal market are unionized, however, and most women have been in public-sector unions, a sector that is in decline (Friendly, 1994; Fudge, 1996). Unions, too, must understand the importance of the affective dimension in assessing the value of child care. It could be integrated into classification systems re-evaluating women's work as governments and unions attempt to enhance women's labour. However, this process, including various pay equity programs, has come under serious attack in our restructured economy (Edgecombe-Dobb, 1987; Fudge, 1996).

Government and workplaces need to be encouraged to implement more generous maternity and paternity leave policies to facilitate parental care of newborn infants. Canadian policies are not nearly as well developed as those found in other industrialized nations. In most European countries the duration of the leave is longer, the income replacement is higher, and a greater proportion of the population is eligible for benefits (Baker, 1995; Baker 1997). The odds for improving these policies in the short term may not be great, however. Even in European countries, the international impact of restructuring is putting pressure on them, and as Baker (1997: 68) argues, no programs, even the most success-ful, will be effective for women without other measures to promote gender equity.

Finally, changes are long overdue in the way we conceptualize our research. The distinction between the physical and emotional dimensions of care predi-cates the research that informs our policy. Pascall (1986) notes that the disci-plines fragment and obscure the meaning and importance of caring. Our child-care studies are conducted by academics who historically have divided the material care and emotional care into separate disciplines. For instance, social policy analysts and economists have focused on the physical aspects of care, 'emphasizing the material constraints within which women make choices about caring and the material effects on women's lives flowing from these responsibili-ties' (Pascall, 1986: 71). The psychological and clinical literature, on the other hand, has stressed the emotional and affective dimensions of caring. Few studies cross those boundaries, and less often do they explore the interconnectedness of the physical and affective dimensions of caring.

Principle 2.   Changes in the child-care system should be directed towards integrating men into the primary caretaking roles and shifting the system's present gender imbalance.

The second principle is directed towards sharing the demands and rewards of caring for children more equitably between men and women in both the private and public spheres. Motivating men's participation in child care would likely be easier if the financial rewards attached to the work increased. If our organization of child care respected both women and men as carers and rewarded them ade-quately, the inherent fascination and joy of this work that has motivated women for centuries should attract a proportion of our male workforce.

Feminists emphasize the importance of the child-care system for influencing society's gender structure (Chodorow, 1978; O'Brien, 1981). Currently, socializa-tion encourages young girls to see themselves as potential paid workers as well as caregivers, but there is no converse for our young boys, whose socialization con-tinues to dictate their future roles as task-oriented workforce participants. Unlike the socialization of young girls, the importance of co-operative relationships and honouring the affective dimensions of people's lives remains secondary for boys (Gilligan, 1982). The present gender imbalance in our child-care arrangements reinforces and perpetuates these socialization patterns. If men began to partici-pate in the child-care system, both girls and boys could see a broader range of role models, thus expanding the life choices of all children.

Without an increase in the value we attach to caring for children, it is unlike-ly that men will ever participate in significant numbers as primary carers of young children. People rarely change in a way that threatens their own self-interest. As women's vulnerability in their homes and their poverty are more publicly linked to their devalued work, men's incentive for giving up the status and rewards asso-ciated with male models of paid labour will be no stronger than it has ever been. We can expose them in our school system to a greater variety of work options and attempt to model greater gender equality in our homes and workplaces, but the likelihood of major changes occurring will remain slim.

An inherent risk in increasing the value of child care and encouraging men to participate more equitably is that they may eventually control and dominate it, bringing with them administrative, organizational, and professional criteria for quality care. As Baines argues in Chapter 2, this patriarchal model has already influenced other female-dominated professions. Feminists have already demonstrated how the movement of child care into the public sphere has been accompanied by a weakening of women's control over the practice and the establishment of standards of care. While women have remained undervalued carers, they continue to be responsible for the day-to-day work of child care. Any significant movement by men into the field, without a serious challenge to the patriarchal model, risks a further erosion of women's power and influence. Any change in the gender structure of child care must therefore mitigate against this.

> *Principle 3.   Changes in the child-care system should build on the strengths of the child-care arrangements already established by women.*

While we need to recognize the extent to which parents' preferences for child care are constrained by the options available to them, we should not ignore some of the strengths of the current system. Parents use the informal market because of its low cost and availability as well as the emotional care that children may receive. In addition, such arrangements are usually accessible and can be flexible, for example, about hours of service and care for mildly ill children (Goelman et al., 1993; Status of Women, 1986).

Studies of parental preferences in child-care arrangements indicate that parents' wishes vary for their children. Some prefer group care with more structure and professionalized input, others value the family home model's personal attention and flexibility, and still others choose to provide most of the care themselves. Factors such as age, health, and personality of the child also influence preferences. For example, parents may prefer mother care or family home care for infants while preferring group care for a toddler (Lero et al., 1992; Lero et al., 1985; Stevens, 1984; Lero, 1981).

In private homes, however, and in settings modelling family homes, women are particularly exploited over wages and working conditions. Children are most at risk in some of the informal settings because the system offers no regulation or supports to carers. Parents express a preference for regulated care if available and affordable (Lero et al., 1992; Status of Women, 1986). This suggests that informal market care should be integrated into the formal market through licensing, which would more effectively protect children, promote good wages and working conditions, and potentially provide training and concrete physical supports such as backup staff. It would respect many of the strengths in these settings while minimizing some risks.

Changes should also focus on the expansion of group centre care. Long waiting lists indicate that many parents now using informal care might prefer group centre care. Government, non-profit agencies, and small and large businesses currently sponsor these centres. Expansion of both government and non-profit sectors is the position taken by the major national lobbying group, the Child Care Advocacy Association of Canada (1995). The low wages and poor working conditions so prevalent in the commercial sector need to be addressed (Prentice, 1997). In addition, a variety of studies and task force reports determined a substantial proportion of parents and Canadians generally raise questions about the appropriateness of profit involvement in child care (Prentice 1997; Status of Women, 1986; Ferguson, 1989; Friendly, Mathien, and Willis, 1987; National Council of Welfare, 1988).

The organization of child care should acknowledge that mothers are caring for children in private homes. One of the challenges facing us is the development of some system to compensate them. This process should first separate the care of young children and other dependent populations from what we now call 'domestic labour' (Eichler, 1988). While some theorists have advocated private arrangements within families to compensate mothers, many others realize the limitations to leaving this issue to the private sphere of the family (Scott, 1978; Riley, 1983). Giving serious consideration to some form of payment to mothers caring for children at home necessitates greater acceptance of an active role by the state in the delivery of child care. Specifically, it requires greater involvement from the welfare state, the topic discussed below.

Principle 4.   The responsibility for child care must be shared more collectively by families and the welfare state.

The value of child-care work can only be enhanced if the responsibility for care is shared more collectively between families and the welfare state. The state's increasingly residual role, in which help is provided only if parents are deemed in need or inadequate, does not ensure support for 'normal' families and reinforces the perception that child care is the primary responsibility of women who work in the private sphere of the home. While a tax deduction is a step towards the state sharing in child care, the impact is regressive, with the greater benefit to higher-income families. Subsidies for low-income families are stigmatizing and limited to those most in need. Middle-income families are left with very little help with the cost of child care.

If we are ever to challenge seriously our current model of child care, it is imperative that the state take a more active institutional role in the delivery of services by providing more direct funding towards a system and/or by providing more direct financial support to families/women who provide or buy that care. Families cannot bear the cost of a reasonable child-care system without funding help. Ideally, this funding would be provided for the care of every child regardless of financial need. It would bring child care more fully into the public sphere. Only then would women's undervalued labour be made public and its worth re-evaluated. In the process, children would be seen as citizens with a right to quality care, not left poor and vulnerable because society does not financially value their mothers' work. Given the realities of government/private-sector restructuring within the last decade, such an ideal model is unlikely to be realized in the near future. Pressures to privatize, refamilialize, and limit state funding are echoing throughout our social welfare system (Brodie, 1996: 21–2). Nevertheless, we must challenge current discourse and not lose sight of our goal. This means protecting what positive changes have been made in the more recent past while pushing the state to go further.

Collectively sharing the responsibility for child care between families and the state facilitates greater integration of the public and private spheres. The state would have a much clearer mandate than it does now to use public money to subsidize the system. This is what the Status of Women task force (1986) and various lobby groups such as the Child Care Advocacy Association of Canada mean when they recommend movement towards provision of a universal child-care system.

This would ease the problem of financially rewarding all those doing child care, including mothers in the home. There are a number of options, some of which directly target child care while others more generally subsidize parents. One is to increase direct grants to child-care centres for maintenance or directly to increase workers' salaries. A second option is to use the tax system, either through tax deductions that lower taxable income and benefit higher-income Canadians, or through refundable tax credits available to anyone who files an income tax form whether or not they owe any tax. Such tax credits are designed to advantage lower-income Canadians. Similar to this last option is a child benefit, an income-tested benefit for low-income parents (Battle, 1997; Pulkingham and Ternowetsky, 1997). A fourth idea is a demogrant, a universal payment like Family Allowances, sent directly to a mother or parent providing or purchasing care. A final option is the provision of a state-provided voucher that would be comparable to the cost of child care for one child.

The last four options, which involve paying parents of children using child care or providing care themselves rather than directly subsidizing the system itself, have the advantage of maximizing parental choice and could be used to pay mothers who care in the home. However, if direct payment to parents is the only method of subsidy, this assumes that the private market will provide adequate and accessible child care for parents to purchase. Many observers of the child-care system in the United States and Canada have raised serious concerns about this assumption (Friendly, 1997; Rose, 1997).

The first option, directly subsidizing the system, has been supported by day-care lobby groups to ensure that a high-quality accessible system is available to parents (Canadian Day Care Advocacy Association, 1990). Direct payments to parents do not ensure a licensed system or reasonable wages to workers. On their own, such payments are likely to reinforce the use of an informal system in which parents use their payments or vouchers to support it. In addition, it is difficult to provide direct subsidies to the informal system or mothers at home unless they can be formally integrated into a child-care system.

Many possible strategies could be developed by combining a number of these options or by using one or more along with a licensing system. The level of financial support attached to any of these options is a critical issue and would influence the usefulness of any one or combination of strategies. For example, our current system combines direct subsidy to day-care workers and child-care centres, tax deductions, a licensing system, and an income-tested child benefit. However, the child benefit is minimal and discriminates against families whose sole income is social assistance, and the bulk of support to parents is through tax deductions and subsidies to low-income parents. The subsidies to day-care centres and workers vary by province but nowhere provide a licensed system that comes close to meeting need. The result is a very large and active informal system, an inadequate licensed system with poor wages for workers and subsidies for some low-income parents, stigmatizing low incomes for mothers at home on social assistance, and the bulk of direct subsidy to parents with the highest incomes.

Any single strategy must be assessed in the context of a total package of changes. Organizations such as the National Council of Welfare (1988), the Canadian Child Care Federation (1993), the Child Care Advocacy Association of Canada (1995), the National Commission on Aboriginal Child Care (Jette and Dumont-Smith, 1994), and the Canadian Advisory Council on the Status of Women (Doherty at al., 1995) have all recommended different combinations of these options for enhancing government involvement (see also Status of Women, 1986; House of Commons, 1987). Establishing criteria for assessing such proposals has been part of the purpose in developing these principles. The final principle presents one further essential criterion.

Principle 5.   Reforms should always be assessed in terms of their implications for women of all classes, races, sexual orientations, and geographical locations.

Although reforms should be considered in light of all the foregoing principles, it is particularly important that this final principle be made explicit. Changes in recent times have been of more benefit to higher-income women, who are usually White and urban. Tax deductions benefit higher-income women, while tax credits are only minimally employed. The new Child Tax Benefit discriminates against women whose sole income is social assistance. Lesbian mothers face many kinds of overt and less obvious discrimination. Licensed child-care facilities are in scarce supply all over Canada, but are particularly limited in rural areas and in First Nation communities.

The child-care concerns of Aboriginal women have much in common with those of other women, but also require an understanding of unique cultural contexts (Jette and Dumont-Smith, 1994). Several jurisdictions have instituted First Nations control over child welfare; control over their child-care system would be an appropriate parallel service. The child-care concerns of rural women are also different from those of urban women and need special consideration (National Coalition for Rural Child Care, 1995). As Chapter 10 describes, our 'nannies' and informal caregivers are often immigrant women who may be exploited. As well, immigrant parents may have special child-care needs and preferences.

To assess changes as they impact on different groups of women as providers and mothers, the particular effects of different options must be examined. For example, First Nations mothers are among the poorest groups in Canadian society, so tax deductions are of limited benefit to them. A system using tax credits or a non-discriminating and generous child benefit would give them more support. These tax credits or benefits would be particularly useful if they were available to all mothers of children and were not dependent on a particular form of child care. Aboriginal mothers would also benefit from a licensed system directly funded by government if it was available to them.

In contrast, the option offering the greatest support for a double-income family with a professional mother using a nanny would be an unlimited tax deduction allowing the family to choose high-priced care in the informal sector and to be subsidized in the process. Such a family would not benefit from a tax credit or child benefit program, and a licensed day-care system would be of limited help if they specifically wanted a care provider to come to their home.

From the point of view of carers, reasonable salaries, benefits, and protected working conditions are available only in the licensed formal sector. Direct grants to a licensed system would therefore provide the best form of support if the informal sector were to be integrated into this system. If mothers at home are not included in a licensed system, direct payments in the form of a demogrant would be more supportive. For lower-income mothers at home a refundable tax credit system or child benefit would be at least as helpful as a demogrant.

These examples illustrate how particular strategies benefit specific groups of women. By placing emphasis on the use of tax deductions, the federal government's child-care strategy supports upper-income families and reinforces the use of the informal system. Low-income mothers in the labour market receive the Child Tax Benefit and subsidized licensed care if they can find a space. Those caring at home receive stigmatizing social assistance if they have no other means of support, and virtually nothing if they are of middle or higher income and depend on partners' incomes. Workers' wages and working conditions are not given any direct priority. Unfortunately, there are no simple or straightforward solutions to our child-care dilemma. However, many of the options presented above would provide greater equity within our child-care system than what we have now.

CONCLUSIONS

These principles suggest guidelines for examining and reorganizing our present child-care system. Each emphasizes the critical importance of caring in women's lives. While this discussion focuses on child care, a number of principles apply equally to the reorganization of society's care of other vulnerable persons. The importance of protecting the affective dimension in caring as our services become professionalized, of bringing private caring into the public sphere, and, most critically, of acknowledging and enhancing the economic value of caring labour, applies also to those caring for persons with disabilities and for the frail elderly.

We must not lose sight of the similarities of much of our caring work, despite our tendency to divide socially dependent groups by factors such as age, income, and the degree and nature of their dependency. Women, with their devalued labour, are members of these groups as well as providers of care to others. As we struggle to formulate options and convince politicians and other Canadians that change must occur, we should not forget that political will can make possible any alternative.

NOTE

1. The term 'formal market' refers to all the varieties of care licensed by a level of government or mandated agency. This includes group day-care centres in neighbourhoods, schools, and workplaces as well as family home child-care centres. 'Informal market' refers to unlicensed non-parental child-care arrangements. These include paid and unpaid babysitting in the homes of parents as well as neighbours, friends, family, and strangers.

REFERENCES

Arat-Koc, S. 1990. 'Non-Citizen Domestic Workers and the Crisis of the Domestic Sphere in Canada', in M. Luxton, H. Rosenberg, S. Arat-Koc, eds, *Through the Kitchen Window: The Politics of Home and Family*, 2nd edn. Toronto: Garamond Press: 81–104.

Armstrong, P., and H. Armstrong. 1990. *Theorizing Women's Work*. Toronto: Garamond Press.

Bagley, C. 1986. 'Day Care in Alberta: A Review with National Implications', paper delivered at Sharing Our Future Conference.

Baker, M. 1987. *Child Care Services in Canada*. Ottawa: Library of Parliament.

Baker, M. 1995. *Canadian Family Policies, Cross-National Comparisons*. Toronto: University of Toronto Press.

Baker, M. 1997. 'Parental Benefit Policies and the Gendered Division of Labor', *Social Service Review* 71, 1: 51–71.

Battle, K. 1997. 'National Child Benefit', *Policy Options* 18, 1: 20–3.

Berthiaume, D. 1997. 'The Development of Early Childhood Services in Quebec', *Interaction* 11, 2: 4–5.

Browne, A. 1984. 'The Mixed Economy of Day Care: Consumer Versus Professional Assessments', *Journal of Social Policy* 13, 3: 321–31.

Canadian Child Care Federation. 1993. *Quality Childcare: Contextual Factors*. Ottawa.

Canadian Commission for the International Year of the Child. 1979. *For Canada's Children*. Ottawa.

Canadian Day Care Advocacy Association. 1990. *Vision*. Ottawa.

Canadian Day Care Advocacy Association/Canadian Child Care Federation. 1993. *Caring for a Living: A Study on Wages and Working Conditions in Canadian Child Care*. Ottawa.

Child Care Advocacy Association of Canada. 1995. *Child Care: An Investment in Canada's Future*. A Brief to the Standing Committee on Human Resources Development. Ottawa.

Chodorow, N. 1978. *Mothering: Psychoanalysis and the Sociology of Gender.* Berkeley: University of California Press.

Cleveland, G., and D. Hyatt. 1997. 'Assessing Federal Child Care Policy: Does the Arrow Reach Its Target', *Policy Options* 18, 1: 20–3.

Cossman, B. 1996. 'Same-Sex Couples and the Politics of Family Status', in J. Brodie, ed., *Women and Canadian Public Policy.* Toronto: Harcourt and Brace.

Doherty-Derkowski, G. 1994. *Quality Matters: Excellence in Early Childhood Programs.* Don Mills, Ont.: Addison-Wesley.

Doherty, G., R. Rose, M. Friendly, S.H. Irwin, and D.S. Lero. 1995. *Child Care: Canada Can't Work Without It.* Report commissioned by the Canadian Advisory Council on the Status of Women. Toronto: Childcare Resource and Research Unit, Centre for Urban and Community Studies, University of Toronto.

Edgecombe-Dobb, R. 1987. 'Equal Pay for Work of Equal Value: Issues and Policies', *Canadian Public Policy* 4: 445.

Eichler, M. 1988. *Families in Canada Today: Recent Changes and Their Policy Consequences.* Toronto: Gage.

Ferguson, E. 1989. 'Private or Public? Profit or Non-Profit? The Preferences of a Sample of Day-Care Consumers in Ontario', paper delivered at the 4th National Conference on Social Welfare Policy, Toronto.

Ferguson, E., and S. Prentice. 1998. 'Exploring Parental Involvement in Canada: An Ideological Maze', in J. Hayden, ed., *Landscapes in Early Childhood Services: Cross National Perspectives on Empowerment and Restraint.* Sydney: Peter Lang Publishing.

Foote, C. 1988. 'Recent State Responses to Separation and Divorce in Canada', *Canadian Social Work Review* 5: 28–43.

Fraiberg, S. 1977. *Every Child's Birthright: In Defense of Mothering.* New York: Basic Books.

Friendly, M. 1994. *Child Care Policy in Canada: Putting the Pieces Together.* Don Mills, Ont.: Addison-Wesley.

Friendly, M. 1997. 'What is the Public Interest in Child Care?', *Policy Options* 18, 1: 3–6.

Friendly, M., J. Mathien, and T. Willis. 1987. *Childcare—What the Public Said: An analysis of the transcripts of hearings held across Canada by the parliamentary Special Committee on Child Care* (March-June, 1986). Ottawa: Canadian Day Care Advocacy Association.

Friendly, M., and M. Oloman. 1996. 'Child Care at the Centre: Child Care on the Social Economic and Political Agenda in the 1990's', in J. Pulkingham and G. Ternowetsky, eds, *Remaking Canadian Social Policy: Social Security in the Late 1990's.* Halifax: Fernwood: 273–85.

Fudge, J. 1996. 'Fragmentation and Feminization: The Challenge of Equity for Labour-Relations Policy', in J. Brodie, ed., *Women and Canadian Public Policy.* Toronto: Harcourt and Brace.

Gilligan, C. 1982. *In a Different Voice: Psychological Theory and Women's Development.* Cambridge, Mass.: Harvard University Press.

Goelman, H., A.R. Pence, D.S. Lero, L.M. Brockman, N. Glick, and J. Berkowitz. 1993. *Where Are the Children? An Overview of Child Care Arrangements in Canada. Canadian National Child Care Study.* Ottawa: Statistics Canada and Health and Welfare Canada.

Gorlick, C. 1988. 'Economic Stress, Social Support, and Female Single Parents', *Canadian Social Work Review* 5: 194–205.

Gorlicke, C., and D.A. Pomfret. 1993. 'Hope and Circumstances: Single Mothers Exiting Social Assistance', in J. Hudson and B. Galloway, eds, *Single Parent Families: Perspectives on Research and the Family*. Toronto: Thompson Educational Publishing: 253–70.

Graham, H. 1983. 'Caring: A Labour of Love', in J. Finch and D. Groves, eds, *A Labour of Love: Women, Work, and Caring*. London: Routledge & Kegan Paul.

Hope Irwin, S. 1997. 'Including All Children', *Interaction* 10, 4: 15–16.

House of Commons. 1987. *Sharing the Responsibility*. Ottawa: Special Committee on Child Care.

Hurl, L. 1989. 'The Value of Policy Dynamics: Pattern of Change and Stability in a Social Assistance Program', paper delivered at the 4th National Conference on Social Welfare Policy, Toronto.

Hutter, B., and G. Williams. 1981. *Controlling Women: The Normal and the Deviant*. London: Croom Helm.

Jackson, M. 1989. 'Bringing Up Baby', *Saturday Night* 104, 12 (Dec.): 30–9.

Jette, D., and Dumont-Smith, C. 1994. *National Commission on Aboriginal Child Care: Our Children—Our Responsibility: Blueprint for Action*. Ottawa: Native Council of Canada.

Johnson, L. 1977. *Who Cares? A Report of the Project Child Care Survey of Parents and Their Child Care Arrangements*. Toronto: Social Planning Council of Metro Toronto.

Johnson, L., and J. Dineen. 1981. *The Kin Trade: The Day Care Crisis in Canada*. Toronto: McGraw-Hill.

Johnson, N. 1987. *The Welfare State in Transition*. Amherst, Mass.: University of Massachusetts Press.

Krashinsky, M., and G. Cleveland. 1997. 'Rethinking the Rationales for Public Funding of Child Care', *Policy Options* 18, 1: 16–19.

Lero, D. 1981. *Factors Influencing Parents' Preferences For and Use of Alternative Child Care Arrangements for Preschool Age Children*. Guelph, Ont.: University of Guelph College of Family and Consumer Studies.

Lero, D. 1997. 'Principles for sound child care policy', *Policy Options* 18, 1: 38–41.

Lero, D., et al. 1985. *Parents' Needs, Preferences, and Concerns about Child Care: Case Studies of 336 Canadian Families*. Report delivered to the Task Force on Child Care. Ottawa: Canadian Government Publishing Centre.

Lero, D., and I. Kyle. 1989. *Families and Children in Ontario: Supporting the Parenting Role*. Toronto: Child, Youth and Family Policy Research Centre.

Lero, D., H. Goelman, A. Pence, L. Brockman, and S. Nuthall. 1992. *Canadian National Child Care Study: Parental Work Patterns and Child Care Needs*. Ottawa: Statistics Canada.

Lero, D., and L. Brockman. 1993. 'Single Parent Families in Canada: A Closer Look', in J. Hudson and B. Galloway, eds, *Single Parent Families: Perspectives on Research and the Family*. Toronto: Thompson Educational Publishing.

Low, W. 1996. 'Using "Targeting" and Work Incentives to Direct Social Assistance to

Single Parents', in J. Pulkingham and G. Ternowetsky, eds, *Remaking Canadian Social Policy: Social Security in the Late 1990's*. Halifax: Fernwood: 188–201.

McFarland, J., and R. Mullaly. 1996. 'NB Works: Image vs. Reality', in J. Pulkingham and G. Ternowetsky, eds, *Remaking Canadian Social Policy: Social Security in the Late 1990's*. Halifax: Fernwood: 202–19.

Maroney, H. 1985. 'Embracing Motherhood: New Feminist Theory', *Canadian Journal of Political and Social Theory* 9, 1–2: 40–64.

Maynard, F. 1985. *The Child Care Crisis: The Real Costs of Day Care for You and Your Child*. Markham, Ont.: Penguin.

National Coalition for Rural Child Care. 1995. *Presentation to the Standing Committee on Human Resources Development*. Langruth, Manitoba.

National Council of Welfare. 1988. *Child Care: A Better Alternative*. Ottawa.

Nelson, F. 1996. *Lesbian Motherhood: An Exploration of Canadian Lesbian Families*. Toronto: University of Toronto Press.

New, C., and M. David. 1985. *For the Children's Sake: Making Childcare More Than Women's Business*. Markham, Ont.: Penguin.

O'Brien, M. 1981. *The Politics of Reproduction*. London: Routledge & Kegan Paul.

Pascall, G. 1986. *Social Policy: A Feminist Analysis*. London: Tavistock.

Powell, L. 1997. 'Family Behaviour and Child Care Costs: Policy Implications', *Policy Options* 18, 1: 11–15.

Power, D., and M. Brown. 1985. *Child Care and Taxation in Canada: Who Pays?* Report delivered to the Task Force on Child Care, Series 1. Ottawa: Canadian Government Publishing Centre.

Prentice, S. 1997. 'The deficiencies of commercial day care', *Policy Options* 18, 1: 42–5.

Prentice, S., and E. Ferguson. 1997. 'My Kids Come First: The Contradictions of Mothers' Involvement in Childcare Delivery', in J. Pulkingham and G. Ternowetsky, eds, *Child and Family Policies: Struggles, Strategies and Options*. Halifax: Fernwood.

Pulkingham, J., and G. Ternowetsky. 1997. 'The New Canada Child Tax Benefit: Discriminating Between the "Deserving" and "Undeserving" Among Poor Families with Children', in Pulkingham and Ternowetsky, eds, *Child and Family Policies: Struggles, Strategies, and Options*. Halifax: Fernwood.

REAL Women. n.d. *Universal Day Care* (pamphlet).

Revenue Canada Taxation. 1996. *General Tax Guide*. Ottawa: Canadian Government Publishing Centre.

Riley, D. 1983. 'The Serious Burdens of Love? Some Questions on Childcare, Feminism, and Socialism', in L. Segal, ed., *What Is To Be Done about the Family?* Harmondsworth: Penguin.

Rose, R. 1997. 'For Direct Public Funding of Child Care', *Policy Options* 18, 1: 31–3.

Rutter, M. 1981. *Maternal Deprivation Reassessed*. Harmondsworth: Penguin.

Schom-Moffat, P. 1985. *The Bottom Line: Wages and Working Conditions of Workers in the Formal Day Care Market*. Report delivered to the Task Force on Child Care, Series 1. Ottawa: Canadian Government Publishing Centre.

Scott, A.C. 1978. 'The Value of Housework', in A. Jaggar and P. Struhl, eds, *Feminist Frameworks: Alternative Theoretical Accounts of the Relations between Women and Men*. New York: McGraw-Hill.

Status of Women Canada. 1986. *Report of the Task Force on Child Care*. Ottawa: Canadian Government Publishing Centre.

Stevens, H. 1984. *Child Care Needs and Realities in Winnipeg—1984*. Winnipeg: Social Planning Council of Winnipeg.

Swift, K.J. 1995. *Manufacturing 'Bad Mothers': A Critical Perspective on Child Neglect*. Toronto: University of Toronto Press.

Tremblay, R., and C. Japel. 1997. 'The Long-Term Impact of Quality Early Child Care', *Policy Options* 18, 1: 7–10.

Waerness, K. 1984. 'Caring as Women's Work in the Welfare State', in H. Holter, ed., *Patriarchy in a Welfare Society*. Oslo: Universitetsforlaget.

White, B. 1980. *A Parent's Guide to the First Three Years*. Englewood Cliffs, NJ: Prentice-Hall.

Wilson, E. 1977. *Women and the Welfare State*. London: Tavistock.

10

Enter the Filipina Nanny:
An Examination of Canada's Live-In Caregiver Policy

SUE McWATT AND SHEILA NEYSMITH

INTRODUCTION

In the opening chapter of this book the multiple threads of the current discourse on care are laid out. This exercise revealed that until quite recently feminist writing on care tended to assume that components of care are provided by female kin who 'care about' the family members they are 'caring for'. This focus, it was suggested, reflected the interests and social location of the feminist writers who were theorizing this new area of scholarship. This concentration on kin-based caring ignored the widespread provision of care by poorer and/or racialized women that benefits upper-income households (Graham, 1993). White First World/Black Third World dichotomies are misleading because women such as Filipina nannies, who are the focus of this chapter, provide this labour to wealthy households in Hong Kong and the Middle East, as well as in Canada. This chapter argues that the history and structure of Canada's Live-In Caregiver Program (LCP) is most clearly understood as a policy attempt to resolve a Canadian 'crisis in the domestic sphere'. Our analysis locates the LCP within a transnational discourse about the value of caring labour and its relationship to citizenship entitlements for all women (Pittman, 1996). Thus, in the discussion that follows, we will be moving our analysis among the fragmented domains of immigration, labour, child care, and foreign affairs policy.

The Live-In Caregiver Program was established to meet a labour market need for live-in caregiving in Canada (Marchi, 1994: 2). This policy, like its predecessor, the Federal Domestic Movement (FDM) program, continues a century-long tradition of recruiting women from other countries to fill this Canadian supply/demand problem (see Calliste, 1991; Daenzer, 1993; Macklin, 1992; Silvera, 1989). Almost all (98 per cent) live-in caregivers are women (Daenzer, 1993: 2). Over 75 per cent come from Third World countries such as the Philippines (Macklin, 1992: 693). In the following pages we show how the LCP works against the interests of several groups of women and thus represents an extremely problematic response to a perceived shortage of caregivers and domestic workers.

As noted in Chapter 1, Western welfare states have been structured on a patriarchal distinction wherein men make claims as workers in the labour market while women's claims are made as wives and mothers in the domestic sphere of the home (Evans, 1997; Orloff, 1993: 315–16; Pateman, 1988: 241–2). In fact, women work both inside and outside the home. The LCP is an example of how the Canadian state continues to deny this dual reality of women's lives, while the gender-neutral language of the policy hides the fact that it positions groups of women in antagonistic stances. In this chapter we examine the history of the LCP and argue that it serves today as a child-care strategy for those Canadian house-holds with the resources to participate. As such, many Canadian households are excluded from this particular child-care option. The result is to reinforce dispar-ities within and among Canadian families at the same time that the policy con-tributes to the debasement of caring labour. However, the existence of the LCP also implicates Canada in an international flow of labour that is part of a response by Third World countries to the restructuring demands made on their economies in order to service their international debt. The percentage of women in these migrations has increased and their experiences are different from those of men. The perception of domestic work as non-productive work means that women are not as protected by labour legislation and are subject to provisions that can lead to abuse. The migration of women has also meant separation from families that remain in the home countries. We end the chapter by raising questions that fem-inists need to address as they challenge some of the assumptions that underlie the continued existence of policies like the Live-In Caregiver Program.

THE HISTORICAL CONSTRUCTION OF CAREGIVERS IN CANADIAN IMMIGRATION POLICY

The Live-In Caregiver Program remains unchanged since 1994. Its regulations state that a person must have the equivalent of a Canadian secondary school leav-ing certificate, must have completed six months of full-time child-care training in a classroom setting or one year of full-time paid employment, including six months of continuous employment with one employer, and be proficient in one of the two official languages before she will be granted authorization to seek employment in Canada as a live-in caregiver. A person may apply for landed immigrant status after two years of full-time employment as a live-in caregiver or a foreign domestic (Marrocco and Goslett, 1994). The LCP is the culmination of a century-long discourse on the place of immigrant women in resolving Canada's 'servant problem'. Canada has a history of racist immigration policies[1] reflecting gender and class cleavages and delineating the boundaries of social cit-izenship. These dynamics are particularly visible in the different policies about foreign domestic workers that have emerged over the years, even though the par-ticular regulations of these schemes change in relationship to the shifting racial and ethnic demography of target groups. The 'Empire-building' agenda, where-in poor White women were brought in to do domestic work but also to serve as stand-ins for the scarcity of immigrant middle-class women, was transformed into the 'good enough to work, not good enough to stay' ideology that marked the postwar indenture of increasing numbers of women of colour on temporary work authorizations (see Macklin, 1992; Arat-Koc, 1990; Calliste, 1991; Bakan and Stasiulis, 1994; Daenzer, 1993; Silvera, 1989).

The regulation that caregivers must live in the home of the employer is a hall-mark of the LCP and its predecessors. This obliterates the distinction between public and private spaces; work and leisure; paid and unpaid labour; pay cheque and rent cheque. A caregiver's live-in status results in unpaid overtime because she is seen to be available during off-time hours. INTERCEDE, an advocacy orga-nization for domestic workers, conducted a survey of 576 live-in domestics in the

Toronto area and found that 65 per cent of women surveyed worked more than 44 hours per week, with an astonishing 44 per cent stating that they received no compensation for these extra hours (Arat-Koc and Villasin, 1990: 6). Employers often have limited definitions of what constitutes tangible work. According to INTERCEDE's survey, 'work' does not include such things as watching over sleeping children or staying at home to let in a repair person. A second area of concern with the live-in arrangement is the lack of privacy, such as not having a lock on the bedroom door, having phone and mail monitored, and sharing a room with a baby or family pet (also see Silvera, 1989: 12). The quality of room and board is mediated by an employer, and this can mean substandard living quarters, insufficient amounts of food, the necessity of complying with the employer's diet, or having to pay for food outside. Exercising tenancy rights is highly unlikely under live-in conditions. In Ontario, boarders are covered under the provisions of the Residents' Rights Act (1994). However, the slippage between workplace and home, between pay cheque and rent cheque, effectively minimizes the exercise of tenancy rights. Finally, vulnerability to sexual harassment and abuse has been well documented (Arat-Koc and Villasin, 1990: 8; 'Hyacinth' in Silvera, 1989: 53–62). In sum, the program allows for the replication of relations of power along gender, class, racial, and ethnic lines and undermines a woman's ability to exercise the few rights she may have.

The FDM/LCP rules require that women remain in live-in service with a specific employer. This restriction to occupation mobility is highly problematic. Although a change of employer may occur if a complaint is lodged with Canada Employment officials, complaint-driven policies rely totally on the initiative of those who experienced the harm. This procedure is especially intimidating to women who have recently arrived in Canada, and hence they remain silent or endure deplorable living and working conditions in order not to risk losing their job/housing or receiving an unfavourable assessment (Silvera, 1989: 3; Arat-Koc and Villasin, 1990: 12). The need to produce a release letter from the employer was Department of Immigration policy up until 1992, when the standard 'record of employment' was required instead. The release letter requirement compounded the vulnerability of women wanting to leave detrimental working/living situations. Marina, a Filipina participant, shares her experience of the working conditions of the program in this way:

> The salary is okay. . . . I am doing light housekeeping, cooking, laundry, taking care of one child. . . . [Regarding the hours] I am live-in so this is the problem. I eat with them, then I have to clean up, so maybe I finish around 7 p.m. . . . They [the government] need to change the hours. Some employers want to take more of your time—it is unfair. If you work from 8 a.m. to 8 p.m. this is not good [with respect to living arrangements]. Like me, I go to my room—before, my room was in the basement. We just moved in the new house and I have a room on the third floor.

Joanne, a White British live-in caregiver, describes the vulnerability associated with the overlapping spheres of citizenship, home, and work:

You agree on an employment contract and you battle it out with them. But you can really get locked in. If you leave or get fired you're in trouble—you have to find housing and have to find another job with no backup from the government. Because there are situations where you just don't get on, or it's personality stuff, or their expectations are different from the contract. They think like I'm Mary Poppins. Maybe they don't like how I look, my music, or something else like if they found out [about my being a lesbian]. There's no hostel for homeless nannies—you don't know anybody in those first few months. It's a tough time anyway—you've left everybody you know, your family, everything you know. It's tough.

The problems associated with the eligibility criteria, live-in requirement, temporary status, and program administration witnessed in the FDM program were exacerbated in subsequent changes introduced in 1992, when it was renamed the Live-In Caregiver Program. The government, in fact, initially set out tighter controls in 1992, which then were rescinded in 1994 because of public outcry. There was a significant drop in participation rates since the establishment of the LCP, from 10,000 under the FDM in 1991 to 5,000 under FDM/LCP in 1992 and 3,000 under the LCP in 1993 (Citizenship and Immigration Canada, 1995a: 23). This decline was attributed to the program's eligibility criteria and stringent screening of job offers (*Canada Gazette*, 6 Apr. 1994: 1408). However, the eligibility criteria in the LCP outlined earlier still discriminate against women from the South. In comparison to women of the upper classes or those from Anglo-European countries, poorer women in Third World countries have limited access to the necessary education and training. The official rationale for the educational requirement is that the labour force of the 1990s requires as a minimum a grade 12 education, and 'the more education a caregiver has, the more able that individual is to understand his or her rights and seek redress should those rights be violated' (Valcourt, 1992: 3). The embedded contradiction is the acknowledgement that these women will leave live-in positions as soon as the residency requirement is fulfilled to seek other types of jobs. Instead of attempting to fill the demand based on the applicant's future employability in other fields, advocates argue that the state should turn its attention to protection of workers and to elevating the status of caregiving and domestic labour (INTERCEDE, 1992: 2).

THE LIVE-IN CAREGIVER PROGRAM AS CANADA'S NATIONAL CHILD-CARE STRATEGY

If the LCP is not an immigration policy, as persistently maintained by Immigration Canada, it is also not a labour force policy, as policy-makers claim it to be. The continued existence of a live-in caregiver program can only be understood if it is seen as a substitute for a national child-care strategy. The changing definition of 'participant' can be traced from a generic conception of private-sphere labourers in earlier schemes into a more defined articulation of child-care workers in the LCP. This shift in policy has a material basis that directly connects to an increase in Canadian women's participation in paid labour and the absence of structural supports to bridge the gap in unpaid labour in the home.

The LCP becomes a viable primary care option for some families and in the process erodes pressure for a national care strategy as a welfare state provision for all women.

This and other feminist analyses of Canadian foreign domestic worker schemes focus on some of the aspects of women's un(der)paid labour that give rise to the rationale for the LCP's existence: the linkage of women's increased labour force participation, the inflexibility of workforce structures to accommodate workers' commitments to family, the reality of household work, the refusal of men to take up the slack, and the failure of the state to establish a universal, accessible, high-quality child-care system. (Arat-Koc, 1990; Macklin, 1992; Bakan and Stasiulis, 1994; Murdock, 1992). When considering caregiving aspects of the LCP/FDM most analysts focus on the care of children. The LCP objectives, however, also include live-in care of the elderly and the disabled. This important aspect is discussed in Chapter 11.

We want to draw attention first to how policy reform reflects an ideological shift from a general concern with social reproduction towards a more specific concern with care labour in the private sphere. This is seen in how participants, the policy term used to describe women who enter Canada under the program, were redefined as the Temporary Employment Authorization system (1973) became the Foreign Domestic Movement Program (1981), which preceded the current Live-In Caregiver Program (1992). Under the Temporary Employment Authorization system, participants were incorporated into a wide rubric of occupational categories: housekeeper, maid, domestic, babysitter, and parent helper (Canada, 1981: 53). In 1981, under the Federal Domestic Movement Program, participants were classified as housekeepers, companions, servant-domestics, babysitters, nannies, and parent's helpers (Canada, 1981: 1). By 1992, the language narrowed the definition of participant to live-in caregiver, defined as 'a person who provides, without supervision, in a private household in Canada in which the person resides, child care, senior home support care or care of the disabled' (Marrocco and Goslett, 1995: 464–5). Regardless of job title, the range of activities women actually undertake are enormous. For instance, housekeeping has not disappeared, even if a change in policy language makes it seem that way. The type of activities that can be required seems to be limited only by the way that relations of power in the household are played out and by how an employer chooses to define work and/or caregiving. In addition, the nature of work activities undertaken is informed by a racialized discourse that reproduces stereotypes of what particular women should do. Thus, as we were told in interviews, White British nannies 'don't clean' whereas Filipina nannies 'have to clean'.

The shift in policy language that resulted in the Live-In Caregiver Program, reflects a political reorientation towards a 'Canadians first' ideology. This occurs both in the *caregiver* sense, because state policy is about taking care of vulnerable Canadians, not houses, and in the *live-in* sense, that is, living-in is what no Canadian will do (Smith, 1994: A9). The invisibility of housework in the new language of caregiving elides the whole question of the difference between housework and caregiving and who will do the work in both areas. When housework is dropped from the discourse, or subsumed under caregiving, a certain elasticity of women's labour is being called upon.

The introduction of the LCP opened up a new care labour discourse just as women, the caregivers of children, were establishing themselves in the labour force in record numbers as citizen workers. In linking women's labour force participation with the need for live-in nannies, we place a preferential value on the labour of particular women in particular locations within a highly stratified social structure. Women's choices are contingent not only upon gendered work but also are channelled through class, race, citizenship, and nationality (Williams, 1995). Women of colour and working-class women have always been in paid labour in higher proportions than higher-income White women (Calliste, 1991), frequently doubling as maids for the latter (Silvera 1989).

As social policy evolves in a context of global restructuring, retention of the two most repressive elements of the LCP/FDM, the live-in requirement and temporary residency status, continues to situate the contemporary caregiver in a precarious position. These requirements remain in effect under the premise that there is no shortage of Canadian workers willing to do live-out work and if foreign domestics arrived with landed status they would not 'fill the jobs they came to Canada to do' (Valcourt, 1992: 4–5). This statement is an ironic recognition of the degradation of care labour and the proper place of immigrant women of colour in the social reproduction of Canadian citizens.

Caring labour is devalued by the degrading regulations of the program (the live-in requirement, temporary residency status, and restricted occupational mobility), which apply to no other class of immigrant or Canadian worker, and were only introduced in concert with the active recruitment of women of colour into the schemes. The government has still not resolved its 1961 dilemma about the schemes' intent: whether it is to select [Black] women who will be good domestics on a career basis or to select 'a girl who will not stay in domestic service any longer than necessary but will move out after a year into an occupation for which she is best suited, and be in the long-run a greater credit to herself, her race and to Canada?' (Calliste, 1991: 157). This 1961 statement captures the discourse of burden within which Third World immigrant women struggle to redefine themselves into images that will project them as more citizen-like beings.

THE ORGANIZATION OF THE LIVE-IN CAREGIVER PROGRAM AS AN INTERNATIONAL LABOUR MARKET

In examining the situation of migrant female domestic workers from Southeast Asia, Heyzer and Wee (1995) argue that the international trade in domestic workers is a global business encompassing recruitment networks spanning villages in sending countries and cities in receiving countries with profits generated at every level of recruitment.[2] Canada enters this international ring by way of

the Live-In Caregiver Program. The program encompasses an extensive recruitment, selection, and regulation network involving Citizenship and Immigration
Canada, Canadian overseas embassies, Human Resource Development Canada
(CECs), private recruitment and placement agencies within Canada and sending
countries, the governments of labour-exporting nations/World Bank clients,
Canadian citizens/families/employers, women/families/employees from other
countries, and employer and employee advocacy organizations. In the following
pages we explore the gatekeeper roles of the Canadian state, the agencies, and
sending countries embedded in the labour market need discourse of the LCP.

The Role of the Canadian State

How the state talks about its role is an important starting point for examining
how the discourse slips between the LCP as a statement of labour policy, caregiving policy, and immigration policy. It is simultaneously all of these and none
of these. Framing the LCP in the needs of an ungendered labour market language allows the state to abdicate responsibility for creating policies friendly to
women as employees, family members, and migrants. We see this most clearly
in the Immigration Minister's response to criticisms when the LCP was first
introduced:

> The Live-In Caregiver Program is, as I indicated at the outset, a program designed
> to meet a specific labour market need. Immigration plays a facilitation role. However,
> I believe that the program is seen by some as an immigration program, and that may
> be how misunderstandings arise. For those who have perceived the program in this
> way, any attempts to modify its provisions are mistakenly seen as affecting the abili-
> ty of Third World women to immigrate to Canada. (Valcourt, 1992: 4)

In this reply, the role of the state is perceived as that of facilitator (responding
to a market demand), arbitrator[3] (mediating between the interests of employ-
ers/families/citizens and employees/immigrant women/non-citizens); and regu-
lator (delineating the terms of employee mobility and citizenship). The common
good is redefined from a language about social welfare to a language about market efficiency in an increasingly competitive global economy. Within such a
framework, the LCP targets recruitment of populations of women who can be
brought in cheaply to fulfil a need for labour. In doing so, the state meets the
immediate demands of a privileged sector of society and ensures that the language of, and responsibility for, caregiving remains in the private sphere.
Confining the discourse to the boundaries of private market arrangements
ensures that common and disparate interests are obscured between Canadian
women who are making social benefit claims at the national level for a child-care
policy and 'Other' women who are making claims at the international level about
the need for the redistribution of North/South wealth. Finally, the state regulates
the development of responsible 'Canadians first'[4] policies so that immigrants do
not take the jobs of 'citizens'. Restricting the occupational, housing, and citizenship mobility of LCP caregivers, while requiring employers to prove that they cannot find a Canadian to do this work, alleviates a xenophobic concern that the

state is undercutting the indigenous citizen and market. The existence of the Live-In Caregiver Program, and its surrounding discourse, distracts from the more fundamental discussion that would consider the alternatives the Canadian state might take in developing social and fiscal policies to begin to redefine what is productive activity, i.e., activity that contributes to human well-being, and whether that production takes place in the context of family, community, the commercial sector, or government bureaucracy.

The Role of Private Canadian Agencies

In Canada, private agencies also play a facilitative role in screening applicants from abroad and linking them with employers. These agencies function as brokers, charging a fee to both parties to filter the demand for, and the supply of, live-in caregivers. They are translators, assisting clientele with state bureaucracy. Sometimes they are mediators in conflict resolution between employers and employees. They can be trainers. For example, one west coast agency has extended its services by setting up a nanny school in the Philippines (Macklin, 1992). Such agencies, as well as the state, play a pivotal part in delineating the spheres of home and work and the power differentials between employers and live-in caregiver employees. Racism often structures these constructions.

Three images of domestic workers currently exist in Canada: the figure of the dedicated, pliant Filipina nanny who is 'naturally' good with children; the image of the Black Caribbean domestic worker as mammy/whore/welfare mother (see Calliste, 1991); the figure of the British nanny as Mary Poppins (see Bakan and Stasiulis, 1994: 23–4). Private agencies engage these racist constructions in meeting a market demand for particularistic features of caregivers. Most agencies are run as small businesses. Not to cater to client preferences means forgoing revenue (Bakan and Stasiulis, 1994). LCP/FDM participants Joanne and Marina describe the prevalence of racism in the Toronto industry. As Joanne, from Great Britain, explains:

> Most of the Filipinas I know made the same as me but they had to do a whole lot more work . . . [Why?] Well, the race thing. Like you call up one of these agencies and they will ask questions about what you're looking for. Housekeeping or cleaning is for Filipinas. They might not say it explicitly like that but they say it. Like with me, they assumed that I *wouldn't* clean, that I was qualified to take care of children. Driver's licences is another thing that affects the sort of job you'll get—all the Filipina women I know don't have them. Language is another barrier. . . . It's really stereotyped. All of my White friends who are British (and one from Newfoundland) won't clean.

Marina, from the Philippines, notes the same distinction in tasks expected:

> There is racism here, too, but it is like this everywhere. We [Filipina women] are trained to do cleaning, cooking, all sorts of things—it is in our upbringing—we *have* to do this. Some of the British nannies, if they finish at 6:00 p.m. they do; they don't work past that time. But for me, I have to finish my work.

Immigrant women may share concerns arising out of working conditions, the live-in requirement, settlement issues, and immigration bureaucracy, but racism and nationalism structure their experiences. Racist constructions of foreign domestic workers are not limited to Canada; they are well-documented in other OECD countries and high-growth areas in Southeast Asia (Heyzer and Wee, 1995). The LCP reflects and reinforces deeply ingrained race, gender, and class stratifications, which, as Romero aptly suggests, 'so typif[y] domestic service that social expectations may relegate all lower class women of colour to the status of domestic' (Romero, 1992: 71).

The Role of World Bank Clients: The Sending Countries

The effect of international debt politics on the South significantly influences sending countries' willingness to export female domestic workers to Canada (Macklin, 1992; Calliste, 1991; Bakan and Stasiulis, 1994). For instance, the active role of West Indian governments during the years of Canada's Caribbean Domestic Scheme (1955) was clearly influenced by inequities in wealth between the Caribbean and Canada (Calliste, 1991). During that same period, however, a number of countries refused to participate in group recruitment schemes because of the exploitive nature of the foreign domestic system in Canada.[5]

It is important to place Canadian policy within the debates about economic restructuring that form part of the current globalization discourse. Economic restructuring to repay foreign debt in low-growth countries creates social and economic conditions in the South that encourage the migration of female labour. Power is exercised in international financial institutions through control over resources. Voting is weighted, based on levels of capital contribution. Industrial economies make up more than half of the weighted decision-making process in the International Monetary Fund (IMF) and the World Bank (Kabeer, 1994: 70).

Our discussion focuses on the Philippines since it is now the major source country for Canada's LCP (Grandea, 1996). IMF directives resulted in the Philippine government adopting fiscal policies that reduced health, social service, and education budgets, intensified poverty, and transformed market structures (Anastacio, 1996; Eviota, 1992). One outcome is that the Philippines has become a massive export-producing zone within an international division of labour. The effects on women are particularly acute in the transformation from subsistence agricultural production to export cash crops and manufacturing—women are employed in the lower echelons of these exporting sectors at subsistence wages (Anastacio, 1996).

Directly relevant to our argument is the fact that these adjustment policies have also caused a 'warm body' export in the Philippines. Migratory flows from the Philippines are the result of industrialization, patterns of urbanization, state social policies, and the position of labour-exporting and -importing countries in the international economy. However, the categories of people who leave are determined by sex, age, position in the household, and the household's position in the economy (Eviota, 1992: 142–3). It is estimated that 4 per cent of the

Philippines' total population is involved in overseas contract work and that 70 per cent of the people in this group are female domestic workers (Vincent, 1996: A6). The majority of migrant Filipina domestic workers are motivated to work abroad by subsistence and survival concerns (Cruz and Paganoni, 1989: 29). Women who are forced to emigrate under such conditions do so at great risk. It is now well documented that the international trade in women is responsible for gross human rights violations against Filipina domestic workers, such as Singapore's execution of Flor Contemplacion in March 1995 (INTERCEDE, 1995: 2) and Sarah Balabagan's (commuted) death sentence in the United Arab Emirates. Emigration patterns from the Philippines indicate other significant social and economic consequences for women. Studies of Filipina domestic workers show that most are between 25 and 34 years of age and are well educated (Heyzer and Wee, 1995: 98). This kind of de-skilling of the labour force marks a serious concern for developing countries. In addition, the lack of legitimation of foreign professional and academic credentials poses a structural barrier that maintains their 'underqualified' occupational status in Canada.

The women who migrate, however, are also mothers, daughters, wives, caregivers. Of the women who emigrate from the Philippines to take up foreign domestic labour, 48 per cent are married with children (Heyzer and Wee, 1995). When women migrate from household economies marked by a sexual division of labour, someone still needs to provide the caring labour in the sending household/country. Migrant women working abroad are subjected to pressures from families (and from themselves) to send their earnings home to support un(der)employed male relatives, children, and elderly kin (Heyzer and Wee, 1995: 99). These women are also under great pressure to sponsor immigration of their dependants and partners to Canada (Arat-Koc and Villasin, 1990; Vincent, 1996: A6). Yet their low pay, discriminatory immigration requirements, such as the right-of-landing fee, and the low-income cut-off of $15,452 per annum for sponsorship eligibility[6] create significant barriers to family sponsorship as a survival strategy. If they do put together the required resources, they then face the onerous burdens of sponsorship regulations if the relationship breaks down.

The economic contributions of female domestic workers to the household are also contributions to the national economies of both the sending and receiving countries (Heyzer and Wee, 1995). Canadian consumers can import cheap Philippine products (food, clothes, appliances) *and* the women to transform these goods into the (re)production of Canadian citizens. Remittances by Filipina domestic workers are that country's largest single source of foreign revenue, estimated at $2 billion to $6 billion per year (Vincent, 1996: A6). Recent IMF-imposed structural adjustment policies have encouraged the Philippine government, under President Fidel Ramos, to implement educational measures to turn out more overseas contract workers (Anastacio, 1996) in order to increase the flow of foreign currency needed to finance the country's huge foreign debt. The Philippine government's new economic blueprint proposes private schools to prepare a labour force directed at the export market for work in domestic/caregiving occupations and the tourism industries of receiving countries. In other words, instead of teaching mathematics and science, some schools will start to teach First World home economics.

The Live-In Caregiver system provides economic gains to Canada. Some of these include: CPP, UIC, and income tax revenues collected from domestic workers for benefits they are unlikely to receive; the appropriation of the labour of workers whose training has been financed by sending countries; the savings generated because the LCP reduces pressure to provide an accessible, social child-care system; the remittances sent back to debtor countries, which, in turn, buy Canadian imports and services. These factors implicate Canada in sustaining women in poverty in both the North and the South. At the same time, this system exonerates Canada from the responsibility for developing a healthy, sustainable labour force and of supporting migrant workers during unemployment, old age, and illness (Arat-Koc, 1990: 93). When these women do remain in Canada, the prospects of social citizenship entitlements in old age are precarious. Calliste (1991) has underscored the plight of the single women who were part of the Caribbean Domestic Scheme and who are now seniors in Canada. Foreign-born elderly women are at great risk of poverty in old age because structured inequalities in the labour force dovetail with inequities in the structure of the income retirement system (see Boyd, 1992; O'Connell, 1996).

CONCLUSION

The LCP policy refuses to recognize that upwardly mobile women workers from the North and the South are also bound, as caregivers, into relationships of power in families and nations. Secondly, the LCP embodies the patriarchal notion of the worker/citizen in its central premise that care labour is not citizenship-appropriate labour. It seems that it is 'uncitizen-like' to need or to do dependent care work in either the private or the public domain. This stigma on dependent care work affects those women who want someone to relieve them of care responsibilities (thus the dearth of non-familial care for children and other persons needing help with the activities of daily living), as well as those women who actually do the work as unpaid family help or low-paid market work. Thirdly, the LCP discourse is textured by a racism that paints immigrants and jobs as an uncitizen-like oxymoron. Citizens work and jobs are for citizens. Nevertheless, immigrants should be self-sufficient, which means that they should work but not take citizen-type jobs. Fourthly, sometimes utterances about women, dependent care, immigrants, and jobs bring citizens and the state into patriarchal and racist conversations about welfare burdens. The LCP is one such conversation. Seen in this way, some of the ongoing features of Canada's domestic workers policies become understandable.

The 'household' for the live-in caregiver contains overlapping socio-economic spheres of citizenship, workplace, and home. The blurring of these boundaries structurally supports the possibilities of her exploitation and abuse. It requires that women of colour from the South accept working conditions that Canadian citizens refuse, even in depressed labour market conditions. The risks of losing her job, losing her housing, and facing deportation are inextricably connected. Exercising the few rights she may have is tempered by fear. This fear is inscribed in the consciousness of all women. However, the fear is reinforced when the terms of the LCP encourage the women workers to remain silent and thus relinquish the freedoms guaranteed all other classes of immigrants, women, and workers—for a chance at gaining fully citizened personhood. The fear suggested by Joanne's apt remark—'There's no hostel for homeless nannies'[7]—underscores the urgency for radical shifts in the mechanisms that displace the inadequacies of Canada's social policy onto the backs of immigrant women caregivers.

In this chapter we have tried to delineate how the Live-In Caregiver Program is ultimately a discourse about how the Canadian state differentiates (un)paid care labour from other forms of market labour in relationship to citizenship, gender, race, and class under the shift of global capital. The LCP shifts care labour into the official market economy as waged work. In this respect it calls attention to caregiving and household labour as *economic* activities that women do in the family economy. The program's existence also recognizes that alleviation of women's simultaneity as worker/caregiver has to be addressed if they hope to participate equitably in the labour force. However, the LCP acts to re-privatize care provision.

Like many policies, the LCP is contradictory. If it were eliminated tomorrow, there would be a public outcry not only from employing households but also from sender countries and women migrants, and from their families back home who depend on their wages. Without such a program these women would be competing for immigration under criteria that would devalue their skills. At the national level, the Live-In Caregiver Program's *raison d'être* will only disappear when there is a redistribution of responsibilities for social reproduction across the sexes, and when a comprehensive child-care policy framework is put into place. At the international level, concerted challenges are required in the area of Canadian foreign economic policies that contribute to the increasing disparities between North and South.

Feminist reframing of the 'crisis in the domestic sphere' will be a significant challenge to First World women who engage private Third World solutions to this public issue. The underlying premises and exclusions in the sexual, racial, and international divisions of labour that give rise to the rationale for and maintenance of the LCP must be confronted. We are under no illusion about the difficulty of this task. However, a first step would be to eliminate the live-in component. This would not only eliminate some of the vulnerability arising from this requirement but would also set the stage for negotiating a living wage for the caring labour performed by various groups of women. This, in turn, would eliminate some of the socially constructed disparities that currently exist between immigrant women caregivers and the women in whose households they seek employment. In the longer term, it would provide the political space to mount pressure for a national child-care policy that all Canadian women support.

NOTES

1. For an overview of divergent theoretical positions on the historical shifts in overtly racist Canadian immigration policy, see Taylor (1991). With respect to the experiences of Black, Chinese, Japanese, and South Asian Canadians as a captive, cheap labour pool, see Henry et al. (1995), who note such legislative immigration devices as the Continuous Passage Act (1908), the Chinese Exclusion Act (1923), the Chinese Head Tax (1888 and 1903), the requirement that South Asian immigrants possess $200 upon landing (1907), and the widely exclusionary provisions within the 1910 Immigration Act. Within an international context, 'White Canada' immigration policies linked to labour migration are elaborated in Stalker (1994: 139–40).

2. Loans are often provided to women who cannot pay the array of fees to recruiters. Women are then forced to find ways of financing these loans either through direct deduction from their salaries or through sale of property or taking loans from other sources (Heyzer and Wee, 1995: 98). This is reminiscent of the Canadian government's practice of providing 'assisted passage' to women during the early twentieth century. This practice was racially constructed since British women were given passage assistance loans and Caribbean women were not (see Daenzer, 1993).

3. In response to INTERCEDE on the shift from the FDM program to the LCP, Immigration Minister Bernard Valcourt stated: 'Most of the changes to the program are in response to submissions made by the groups consulted and strike a balance between the needs of the employer and the live-in caregiver' (1992: 1).

4. In response to the call from Sunera Thobani of the National Action Committee on the Status of Women for removing the live-in requirement, the Minister of Citizenship and Immigration, Sergio Marchi, used a 'Canadians first' rationale for its continuation: 'There are sufficient numbers of Canadian workers to provide caregiving on a live-out basis. The objective of the program could not be met if participants were allowed to live-out and job opportunities for Canadians would be compromised' (Marchi, 1994: 2).

5. In the 1950s the German government intervened on behalf of German domestics who were widely reporting abuse and discrimination. In the 1960s the Japanese and Guyanese governments flatly refused to participate because of the well-known exploitations taking place (Daenzer, 1993: 78).

6. This is the low-income cut-off for one person in a metropolitan city (Citizenship and Immigration Canada, 1995b: 38).

7. Heyzer and Wee (1995) note that Bethune House Women's Shelter, in Hong Kong, is a non-profit shelter specifically for Filipina migrant workers experiencing difficulties.

REFERENCES

Anastacio, Rina. 1996. 'Impact of Structural Adjustment Programs on Women and Children in the Philippines', radio interview, Radioactive Feminism Program, CKLN, Ryerson University, Toronto, 15 Apr.

Arat-Koc, Sedef. 1990. 'Non-Citizen Domestic Workers and the Crisis of the Domestic Sphere in Canada', in M. Luxton, H. Rosenberg, and S. Arat-Koc, eds, *Through the Kitchen Window: The Politics of Home and Family*, 2nd edn. Toronto: Garamond Press: 81–104.

Arat-Koc, Sedef. 1992. 'In the Privacy of Our Own Home: Foreign Domestic Workers as Solution to the Crisis of the Domestic Sphere in Canada', in P. Connelly and P. Armstrong, eds, *Feminism in Action*. Toronto: Scholars' Press: 149–74.

Arat-Koc, Sedef, and Fely Villasin. 1990. *Report and Recommendations on the Foreign Domestic Movement Program*. Toronto: INTERCEDE.

Bakan, Abigail, and Daiva Stasiulis. 1994. 'Foreign Domestic Worker Policy in Canada and the Social Boundaries of Modern Citizenship', *Science and Society* 58, 1: 7–33.

Boyd, Monica. 1992. 'Foreign-Born, Female, Old and Poor', *Canadian Woman Studies* 12, 4: 50–2.

Calliste, Agnes. 1991. 'Canada's Immigration Policy and Domestics from the Caribbean: The Second Domestic Scheme', in J. Vorst et al., 'Race, Class, Gender: Bonds and Barriers', special issue of *Socialist Studies* 5: 136–68.

Canada, Task Force on Immigration Practices and Procedures. 1981. *Domestic Workers on Employment Authorizations: A Report of the Task Force on Immigration Practices and Procedures*. Ottawa: Minister of Supply and Services Canada.

Canadian Council on Social Development, Centre for International Statistics. 1993. 'Focus on Child Care', *Centre for International Statistics Newsletter* 2 (July): 1–15.

Citizenship and Immigration Canada. 1995a. *A Broader Vision: Immigration Plan. 1996 Report to Parliament*. Hull: Minister of Supply and Services Canada.

Citizenship and Immigration Canada. 1995b. *Immigration Reference Manual*. Hull: Information Systems and Technologies Branch, CIC.

Cruz, Victoria, and Anthony Paganoni. 1989. *Filipinas in Migration: Big Bills and Small Change*. Quezon City, Philippines: Scalabrini Migration Center.

Daenzer, Patricia. 1993. *Regulating Class Privilege: Immigrant Servants in Canada, 1940s–1950s*. Toronto: Canadian Scholars' Press.

Evans, Patricia. 1997. 'Divided Citizenship? Gender, Income Security and the Welfare State', in P. Evans and G. Weberle, eds, *Women and the Canadian Welfare State: Challenges and Change*. Toronto: University of Toronto Press: 91–116.

Eviota, Elizabeth. 1992. *The Political Economy of Gender: Women and the Sexual Division of Labour in the Philippines*. London: Zed Books.

Graham, H. 1993. 'Social Divisions in Caring', *Women's Studies International Forum* 16, 5: 461–70.

Grandea, Nona. 1996. *Uneven Gains: Filipina Domestic Workers in Canada*. Ottawa: North-South Institute.

Henry, Francis, C. Tator, W. Mattis, and T. Rees. 1995. *The Colour of Democracy: Racism in Canadian Society*. Toronto: Harcourt Brace.

Heyzer, Noeleen, and Vivienne Wee. 1995. 'Domestic Workers in Transient Overseas Employment', *Canadian Woman Studies* 15, 2–3: 98–103.

INTERCEDE. 1992. 'INTERCEDE's Response to the Announcement of "Improvements to the Foreign Domestic Program" by Minister Bernard Valcourt: Presentation to the Standing Committee on Labour, Employment and Immigration, House of Commons, Ottawa'. Toronto: INTERCEDE, 26 Feb.

INTERCEDE. 1995. 'Angry Protest Against Hanging of Domestic Worker', *Domestics' Cross-Cultural News* 2 (May).

Kabeer, Naila. 1994. *Reversed Realities: Gender Hierarchies in Development Thought*. London: Verso.

Lero, Donna, Hillel Goelman, Alan Pence, Lois Brockman, and Sandra Nuthall. 1992. *Canadian National Child Care Study: Parental Work Patterns and Child Care Needs*. Ottawa: Statistics Canada and Health and Welfare Canada.

Macklin, Audrey. 1992. 'Foreign Domestic Worker: Surrogate Housewife or Mail Order Servant?', *McGill Law Journal* 37, 3: 681–766.

Marchi, Sergio, Minister of Citizenship and Immigration Canada. 1994. Letter to Sunera Thobani, National Action Committee on the Status of Women. Toronto: INTERCEDE Office, 5 May.

Marrocco, Frank, and Henry Goslett, eds. 1994. *The 1995 Annotated Immigration Act of Canada.* Toronto: Carswell.

Murdock, Rebecca. 1992. 'Cross-Border Shopping for Domestic Labour', *Canadian Woman Studies* 12, 4: 60–3.

O'Connell, Anne. 1996. 'Public Pensions and Immigrant Women: Restricted Access', unpublished manuscript. Toronto: Faculty of Social Work, University of Toronto.

Orloff, Ann. 1993. 'Gender and the Social Rights of Citizenship: The Comparative Analysis of Gender Relations and Welfare States', *American Sociological Review* 58, 3: 303–28.

Pateman, Carole. 1988. 'The Patriarchal Welfare State', in A. Gutman, ed., *Democracy and the Welfare State.* Princeton, NJ: Princeton University Press: 231–60.

Pittman, J. 1996. *Worlding Women: A Feminist International Politics.* St Leonards, NSW, Australia: Allen & Unwin.

Romero, Mary. 1992. *Made in the U.S.A.* New York: Routledge, Chapman and Hall.

Silvera, Makeda. 1989. *Silenced: Talks with Working Class Caribbean Women About Their Lives and Struggles as Domestics in Canada*, 2nd edn. Toronto: Sister Vision, Black Women and Women of Colour Press.

Smith, Vivian. 1994. 'Rules Yield to Need for Nannies', *Toronto Star*, 4 Mar.: A1.

Soja, Edward. 1989. *Postmodern Geographies.* London: Verso.

Stalker, Peter. 1994. *The Work of Strangers: A Survey of International Labour Migration.* Geneva: International Labour Organization.

Taylor, K.W. 1991. 'Racism in Canadian Immigration Policy', *Canadian Ethnic Studies* 23, 1: 1–20.

Valcourt, Bernard, Minister of Employment and Immigration Canada. 1992. Letter to Pura Velasco et al., INTERCEDE. Toronto: INTERCEDE Office, 2 July.

Vincent, Isabel. 1996. 'Canada Beckons Cream of Nannies', *Globe and Mail*, 20 Jan.: A1, A6.

Williams, Fiona. 1995. 'Race/Ethnicity, Gender, and Class in Welfare States: A Framework for Comparative Analysis', *Social Politics: International Studies in Gender, State and Society* 2, 2: 127–59.

11

From Home Care to Social Care: The Value of a Vision

SHEILA M. NEYSMITH

INTRODUCTION

The emotional and physical work inherent in responding to the needs of others characterizes much of the paid and unpaid labour that women do. The under-valuing of this work has a negative impact on the quality of life enjoyed by women both in the domestic arena and in the labour force, whether they work as low-paid service-sector employees or as members of female-dominated professions such as social work, teaching, and nursing. It is even suggested that the commitment that women have to caring contributes to social problems: the persistence of high poverty rates among single mothers, separated and divorced older women, and widows is explained as resulting from their interrupted employment patterns; women are raised on patriarchal notions of an ideal family and then are blamed for not leaving violent partners. Finally, in direct contradiction to earlier messages, women who have been caring for others all their lives are expected to be independent and self-sufficient and to make few demands on state and familial resources in their old age.

The conceptual separation of family life, labour market activity, and state responsibility has resulted in segmented, fractured discussions of caring. Bits and pieces get addressed by policy-makers, academics, and service professionals, each using different languages and varying theoretical frameworks for analysing the issues. One of the purposes of this book has been to expand our understanding of how caring shapes the experiences of all women, recognizing that these effects will vary by the structured location of individual women in Canadian society, as well as by their stage in the life cycle. Both the diversity and the continuity of caring in women's lives become obscured as academic disciplines delineate specialized areas of interest for detailed examination and/or social policies and services are restricted to specific population groups.

The preceding chapters highlight the contradictions that women face as they provide instrumental and emotional support to those around them. However, contradictions can present opportunities and conceptual spaces for mapping out pathways to change. In different ways each chapter has shown that women recognize the importance of the various types of caring they do for those around them. The problem is that this assessment by women is not reflected in public policy. There has been little change since World War II in the redistribution of caring responsibilities between men and women, minimal recognition by employers that workers are citizens with non-market responsibilities, and a dearth of child-care and elder-care policy development at both federal and provincial levels. Not surprisingly, then, the research that underpins discussions in this book documents the high price that women pay to ensure that their loved ones receive the care they need. The expectation that it is women's responsibility to provide care is unjust because this work is undervalued, less is asked and expected of men, the earning capacity of women is diminished, and the well-being of persons in need of care is entrenched as a familial rather than a social responsibility. These caring arrangements result in women and the dependent persons they care for being cast as victims or victimizers when they are neither.

In this chapter my aim is to gather together these seemingly unrelated threads in the process of arguing for a degendered, collective approach to caring. However, in reframing the argument, we must recognize conflicting interests if strategies for change are to have any hope of surmounting the numerous obstacles that lie ahead. The ongoing debate on the purpose and organization of long-term care for elderly persons will be used to illustrate the extent and nature of this challenge. The analysis serves as a springboard for considering structural features of existing caring arrangements that will need to be altered if the risks, as well as the benefits, of caring are to be more equitably distributed in Canadian society. Thus, the discussion will be rooted in a constant assessment of the relationship of the domestic sphere, the world of paid work, and the state. It is my assumption that the nature of these bonds produces many of the contradictions facing women.

THE ILLUSION OF COMMUNITY-BASED CARE VERSUS THE REALITY OF FAMILY-BASED CARE

Long-term care is an excellent arena for examining how assumptions about women's caring get reflected in social policy. National surveys show that both men and women care for others, but men provide care mainly to their spouses while women provide it to a variety of other persons (Health and Welfare Canada, 1993: 70, Table 2; Statistics Canada, 1997). We also know that the physical and cognitive condition of an elderly person does not predict whether she will actually receive services. Need for care is also no predictor of caregiver response. The heaviest of care can be seen as relatively easy in some situations, while relatively light care can become intolerable. Finally, informal caregiving is relationship-based but this is no predictor of quality—as the elder abuse literature amply documents (MacLean, 1995). These well-known facts raise questions about the ethical underpinnings of home-care policies that ration their scarce resources according to the apparent presence of kin, who are assumed to be able and willing to provide day-to-day care.

Horl (1992), reviewing the situation in Austria, a demographically old country, is one of a handful of policy writers who directly challenge assumptions about family that underlie most European and North American home-care policy. He argues that a policy encouraging family care is no policy because family members are already the dominant source of help, and there will be fewer, not more, female kin available in the future. The roles of mother, wife, and daughter will be partialized as individuals go through several family constellations over a lifetime. Who is responsible for whom at any given moment will become an increasingly moot point.

Today, when people talk about long-term care, they are referring to care provided within a person's home. Across countries, financial pressures driving the restructuring of long-term care have resulted in institutionally based care being minimally available, while home care has expanded. These same pressures have resulted in a purchaser/provider split wherein governments use public funds to buy services from a range of providers who are encouraged to compete for contracts. In such a model, governments define their role as that of enabler in the market for social care. Quality assurance is frequently devolved to a local authority responsible for purchasing services from available providers. In Ontario, for example, this takes the form of 43 Community Care Access Centres governed by community boards. Whatever the attractiveness of such models in terms of responding to local needs, province-wide standards will be difficult to enforce. In the US the high costs associated with its private health care system have resulted in a focus on minimizing organization and delivery costs. Health Management Organizations (HMOs) have sprung up offering service packages under an insurance model called 'managed care'. Although the language of client need and consumer choice is used, there is very little focus on the elderly person. Advocates note that charters of patients' rights seem to be the only form of empowerment available to consumers. Such mechanisms, however, would seem to be quite unenforceable in situations where services are being received from the very organization against which one is bringing a claim.

In Canada, all provinces expanded their home-care programs during the 1990s, although considerable variation exists because there is no federal legislation comparable to the Canada Health Act, which stipulates certain conditions for federal dollars. In fact, the federal government has been withdrawing steadily from providing policy-specific funding in the areas of health, social services, and education, thus diminishing the policy clout that can come with 'the power of the purse'. Most important was the elimination of the Canada Assistance Plan (CAP) and the emergence of the new Canada Health and Social Transfer arrangements, which also incorporated spending on medicare and post-secondary education. Under CAP, provincial expenditures on community care were shared with the federal government. The financial incentive for provinces to maintain and develop services now disappears because cost-sharing has been replaced by a fixed 'megatransfer'.[1]

At the provincial level, community care budgets usually sit within ministries of health, where they must jostle for resources alongside the powerful interests that represent acute care. Ontario, for instance, was in the process of reforming its long-term care for over a decade. Various arguments advanced for organizing community-based programs came and went across three changes in government. Their merits, whatever they may have been, seem unimportant when we consider that while home care was in turmoil, nursing home fees and daily care rates rose, the for-profit sector was encouraged to expand in order to respond to so-called market demand, and massive hospital restructuring resulted in early discharge and a leap in the demand for home care by acute-care patients. For instance, in 1996 for the first time some home-care services in Toronto were pro-

viding around-the-clock service to patients because they were still too incapacitated to care for themselves when discharged from hospital (Metro Consumers,
1997). Such intensive use of resources was not factored into home-care planning
and budgets. The dollars being infused slowly into home care have limited capacity to do more than respond to rapidly increasing numbers. It seems that the
greatest influence on home-care policy is hospital budget decisions.

The Ontario experience in developing a long-term care policy is also infor-
mative in that it reveals the power imbalances among the various players in the
long-term care drama and the illusiveness of such concepts as community and
participation (Aronson, 1993; Deber and Williams, 1995). For instance, if participation is measured in numbers, then there was massive public participation in
the various versions of long-term care reform. However, this view of participation appears to rely, in part, on the myth of a 'community' view. For many issues
there is no such thing as a homogeneous, non-differentiated community. As the
chapters in this book emphasize, the caring responsibilities of women vary greatly depending on their social location. Most of the recipients in long-term care are
women and although some of these women are cared for by their frail elderly
spouses, other female family members frequently assume the responsibility.
Women, too, are primarily employed in the lower echelons of caring work. There
is no reason to believe that these key players in home-care delivery share the same
priorities. The latter group, to which I now turn, has received minimal attention
in the feminist literature.

The bulk of home-care work is classified as semi-skilled labour performed by
large numbers of low-paid workers who perform tasks under the supervision of a
small, relatively well-paid cadre of health care professionals. In large metropolitan centres like Toronto and Vancouver this new labour force of home-care workers is increasingly composed of immigrant women. Hugman (1994) paints a similar picture following the implementation of community care in Britain. The case
management model proposed in the UK legislation, and tested in large demonstration experiments, was operationalized into care management where relatively few social work professionals supervise diploma-level practitioners who develop individual care plans but have little authority over resource allocations. Thus,
care managers actually become resource managers as they desperately seek to
ration the limited budgets available for purchasing services. In the United States
the scenario is somewhat different. In that country, the terms of Medicare and
Medicaid reimbursement schemes encouraged managers to use professional
health care personnel such as physiotherapists, visiting nurses, and podiatrists
even when home-care workers, were they covered, could have done the work
(Estes, Swan, and Associates, 1993; Szasz, 1990). The financing guidelines of
Canadian home-care programs in most provinces seem to have avoided these
types of budget distortions.

This observation is not intended to stifle important debates about the boundaries of professional-paraprofessional care. Rather, my point is that funding formulae, not client need or professional expertise, influence which type of labour is
used. Under such circumstances, tensions between these groups of women work-

ers are exacerbated. We know that the effects of home-care policies and programs are not experienced equitably across the many groups of women who both give and receive care. Tracing the specifics of how this happens in a policy arena peopled by women reveals the power embedded in the structures and the social relations that undergird the visible workings of public policy. Social policies are gendered, but they are also enacted in a society with class and race cleavages. Thus, seemingly universal social policies can actually pit different groups of women against each other.

Finally, reconceptualizing community-based care might provide a space for elderly women, the primary receivers of care, to have a voice and escape being categorized as victim and/or oppressor. Jane Aronson develops this theme in Chapter 6. In her review of the feminist literature on care, Jackie Barry (1995) concludes that care receivers are silenced by their position both in the community and in the family. She notes how care receivers are treated as a homogeneous group in policy and in practice, how limited services foreclose options for *not* relying on family, and how burdensome the knowledge can be that one is perceived as a burden.

VALUES SHAPING THE DISCOURSE ON CARING

Caring is pivotal to keeping the human enterprise going, yet its function is invisible in the organization of our daily lives. When aspects of it do break into the public domain, only the task component is seen, defined as unskilled labour, and paid accordingly. Each chapter has shown how caring is made up of hard practicalities as well as personal attention, warmth, involvement, and empathic understanding. The effects of caring are recognized not when the outcome is right but on those occasions when it goes wrong. Like prevention, the product is invisible; it exists in the negative form of distress rather than in the positive form of adjustment. Furthermore, when emotional and mental labour go unrecognized, the work gets defined as concrete tasks, ensuring that it remains hidden. The results are predictable. As resources become scarce, visible work is given priority. For example, caring labour is reduced to counting the number of meals delivered, baths given, sheets changed, etc. The emotional and mental work that underpins the tasks is slotted as time allows but not considered essential. Ironically, although women may be hired for these jobs because of their skills in dealing with people's feelings, they are given no credit for these skills (James, 1992).

The boundary between paid and unpaid work in women's lives continues to exist but it is extremely permeable. Social policies such as home care not only affect both types of work but also redefine the public/private boundary of caring responsibilities and, consequently, of expectations about the labour of women. As care work seeps through the above-mentioned permeable membrane dividing the public and private lives of Canadian women, language becomes muddy. Concepts of domestic labour and social reproduction draw from a tradition built on the production of commodities and thus hide the fact that caring always involves relating personally to another human being. Such language encourages an

emphasis on task performance rather than relationship skills—a work transformation process now occurring in the job descriptions of home-care workers
(Aronson and Neysmith, 1996; Neysmith and Aronson, 1996). Providing care
differs fundamentally from the production of objects, a difference that lies not in
the hierarchical organization of the work, or of wages, but in the skills or accom-
plishments required by the different tasks, the normative requirements and the
social experiences that each entails (Leira, 1994: 188). Care is both public and
private. It is not evident that better or more adequate care is provided if one set
of emotions accompanies or is integrated with the activities rather than another;
it is just different (Leira, 1994: 190). If we could accept that care provision can,
quite appropriately, entail different degrees of attachment, we could then rethink
ways of assessing the work involved and the proper compensation for whoever
does it, no matter what the caregiver's relationship to the care recipient (Thomas,
1993: 663). Thus, focusing too much on personal relationships may underplay
the considerable collective interests with the provision of care and further contain it as 'women's domain'.

At the beginning of this chapter I suggested that the family, the state, and the
labour market all have an interest in defining community care. The concept of
community care implies a collective responsibility for protecting the welfare of
vulnerable groups in our society, which is at odds with assumptions about the private family, a market-based economy, and a non-interventionist government.
Caring for others is seen by Canadian policy-makers as a private responsibility.
Occasionally it is expanded to include informal helping networks, self-help
groups, volunteers, and even neighbours. This remains so even when the term
'community care' is used. A social care model, outlined in the next section, would
provide explicit recognition that care of vulnerable persons is not a family responsibility, but rather that public services are made available to people who need
them as part of a social security system based on the rights of citizenship. The
state would be actively involved in the development of a range of services and
would guarantee that financial impediments did not discriminate against their
use. Labour force policies would reflect the fact that employees have family
responsibilities.

Recognition that such policies do not fit neatly into current assumptions about
the respective responsibilities of our major social institutions does not automatically assign them to the realm of unworkable possibilities based on naïve idealism. Rather, the parameters of such policies are laid out with the intent of challenging the status quo and making explicit the premise that change has to be seen
as a long-term endeavour that will be riddled with compromises. History also
suggests that progress towards such goals may be more feasible in certain periods
than in others. Let me hasten to add, however, that this is quite a different stance
from one that argues that the national debt must be eliminated or that Canada
must be competitive within a changing global economy before we can start to
address the inequities that women bear because caring is seen as a private responsibility. The following dimensions of a social model of care can be put in place
tomorrow without affecting these national and international goals. What would

be needed, however, is a change in how and where resources available today are allocated.

A SOCIAL MODEL OF CARE: CONSIDERING THE ESSENTIALS

Degendering Caring

As women moved into the labour force some services and resources were made available to aid them with their domestic responsibilities. Day care, maternity leave, pay and employment equity legislation, and family care provisions are responses to some of the obstacles facing women employees. It is important to note, however, that not all women benefit equally from these types of policies. Pay equity helped primarily middle-income women employed in public-sector jobs. Employment equity did break down some of the racial and class obstacles that women faced. However, both operate within the parameters of a labour market designed by men for men. These programs, now disappearing, helped some women obtain a better deal within current models of paid employment, but they could not address the problem that women face in blending family and employment responsibilities. Having entered the private realm of the home, caregiving becomes invisible. It runs on a different clock than the world of employment. Both these characteristics make it difficult to see it as work when the definition of work is so firmly market-related. It is, after all, work that isn't seen and isn't valued except when it isn't done! The unequal allocation between men and women of opportunities and responsibilities in the public world of employment and the private world of family life continues.

Men, when they care for others, are often viewed with sympathy and praised for going beyond the call of duty. Women, although they may be lauded for doing their duty, are expected to care. This reflects not only our differing expectations of men and women, but also our assessment that the actions of such men are particularily praiseworthy because the decision is usually more costly for the male carer in terms of forgone earnings. Because women are expected to care, the element of choice in decision-making is removed, as is any consequent claim to moral worth. Women have fewer opportunities in the labour market and thus have less to lose by withdrawing. To choose to care for a dependent family member under these circumstances is seen as less costly. Thus, both moral and financial claims are weakened. The result is that a person's worth in the labour market influences the assessed value of his or her contributions in other spheres of life.

The option that men have of leaving caring to women is commonly considered an essential element in women's structurally inferior position in modern welfare societies (Connell, 1994). That women would care for dependants was an assumption in the design of all welfare states, even in the more socially egalitarian Scandinavian countries, where citizenship claims also are modelled on the 'waged' worker (Orloff, 1993). Caring obligation was resolved along gender lines, neatly avoiding the necessity to deal with inherent inequities. Entitlements and rights continue to be associated with wage, not care, labour. In other words, an individual's access to social benefits differs according to: the context of the work, that is, whether it is outside or inside formal employment; the decision by most welfare states to leave a considerable share of caring as a private responsibility; the gendered division of labour—caring is, for the most part, ascribed to women (Leira, 1994: 198). What matters when entitlements are adjudicated is not the hours or the significance of the work; what matters is the existence of a formal work contract and wage. Access to the full range of entitlements and to a better pension income upon retirement is accorded only to those who are attached full time to the labour market in their adult years.

Degendered employment practices would not penalize those who assume family responsibilities; rather, they would ensure that both men and women had equal freedom and responsibility in decision-making about who does what in caring. In such a woman-friendly society, federal and provincial guidelines would be in place setting out timetables for employers to define jobs and career ladders that do not discriminate against employees with caring responsibilities. Although, to the best of my knowledge, such policies do not yet exist, one can think of guidelines that would parallel those developed for pay equity.

Changing Managed Care into Social Care
The organization of care in the domestic sphere is marked by flexibility and attention to individual preferences; criteria for receiving services are particularistic, e.g., claims are made on the basis of a relationship (Ferguson, 1984). Moving care into the public domain allows us to look at what it means to be a client, consumer, and service provider. Women populate all three of these positions today and the same person might occupy each at different points in her life cycle. Services, whether public, voluntary, or for profit, are housed in organizations that, by definition, rationalize, delegate authority, are hierarchical, and stress efficiency and effectiveness. Criteria for receiving service are established and assessments become the basis for allocating available resources. The content and organization of formal services seldom fit smoothly with the particular needs of individuals. These well-documented delivery problems are frequently seen as resulting from fragmented services that need to be co-ordinated.

One suggestion, gaining in popularity, is that families become the case managers for services received in the home. The initial attractiveness of such schemes in terms of resource control and empowerment of family caregivers fades as one examines the dynamics of co-ordination. Such an approach would simply leave female kin carers with a new set of problems. Female kin expend time and energy in finding the relevant services for their elderly family members and then use considerable creativity in adapting what is available to the needs of the particular person they care for. Becoming a case manager would not decrease the amount of time or energy required to do this work because there would continue to be a discrepancy between available programs and the particular needs of individuals. It should be noted that this work by kin would not disappear even if Canada-wide standards and common delivery criteria were enacted—not a likely scenario in the foreseeable future.

In addition to the normal customizing of standard services to particular needs, in the 'family as case manager' scenario family members would be working in relative isolation as they try to steer their way through a myriad of services, each characterized by its own set of rules and regulations. Any potential client empowerment envisioned by this suggestion has to be weighed against the cost of time and energy to kin carers. As well, there is the assumption that kin have the knowledge, experience, skill, and will to perform this function in a way that would maximize benefits to the elderly person. Such a model leaves much to the vagaries of individual families. The same arguments can be made in terms of models that position the elderly person as her/his own case manager. My own position on the foregoing proposals is one of extreme scepticism. Information and contacts are a form of knowledge and a source of power that professionals have and families do not. A family carer may be able to modify what is available, but it is truly a professional skill to advocate and manoeuvre in a complex system of health and social services.

The most common service approach presently in use is some kind of case management model attached to a single point of entry that begins with assessments. Ideally, this allows local organizations to deliver services and avoids the depersonalizing and expensive attributes of large bureaucracies, while decreasing the number of applications and repeated assessments that an elderly person or his/her family carer has to make. However, these efforts at co-ordination and reducing fragmentation are occurring at the same time that provinces are introducing quasi-markets through competitive tendering and contracting of services and changing the funding formulae, as discussed in the previous section. Although occurring together in the daily practice of community care service providers, advocates for elderly persons and their family carers need to monitor them as separate entities. For instance, 'one-stop access' cannot increase an inadequte flow of resources to community-based programs. Community boards can reflect local priorities, but they have little ability to monitor the services delivered by the organizations that they contract.

The organizational issues sketched above are inherent to a mixed-economy-of-care policy model. Social workers and nurses will frequently be the ones doing assessments and making recommendations for services. It therefore behooves us to look at the models of professionalism that exist today. In Chapter 2, Carol Baines documented how professionalism has been a contested arena among members of the helping professions throughout their histories. Authoritative relationships seem to be inherent to Western models of professionalism. Authority is granted on the basis of claims to special knowledge and skills. Practice is regulated by codes of ethics designed to control self-interest and define acceptable behaviour between colleagues and in interactions with clients. However, beyond these questions about the ethical behaviour of individuals are issues about the structure of professional organizations. Professional models reflect the values of a market economy that rewards individuals who possess certain skills, knowledge, education, and experience, what economists refer to as 'human capital'. Professional credentials have a financial value to the person possessing them. As the US Medicare example used earlier illustrates, prestigious professions are usually more successful in ensuring that the services they provide are defined as essential, and thus are given priority in funding decisions. Whatever the financial benefits such professional 'turf-guarding' might have for particular groups of women, it is an obstacle to developing programs that envision a more egalitarian and collective approach to caring for others.

In a case management model the rights of elderly persons are conditional on the discretion of professionals. To phrase the issue more bluntly, the claims of a service user are pitted against the assessment of need by experts in care provision. The latter control information and resources in ways that the former cannot. Some of the contradictions inherent in the case management model have been recognized, but they tend to get picked up as ethical dilemmas facing professional staff who must simultaneously act as advocate and resource gatekeeper (Kane et al., 1993). Less heard are the ethical concerns facing families (Hasselkus and Stetson, 1991). Likewise, paraprofessionals, who deliver daily care in isolated work settings to vulnerable elderly people, face conflicting allegiances as they negotiate relationships across class, race, and gender lines (Neysmith and Aronson, 1997).

Guaranteeing Services
In Canada the growth of day-care centres for children and home-care services for elderly and disabled persons has been agonizingly slow, and the form they have taken has often aggravated existent class and race disparities among women. A paucity of services means that they are targeted to certain groups: child-care spaces are reserved for single mothers; scarce home-care workers give priority to persons who are living alone or where no female family carer is apparent. I am not suggesting that today's high-risk groups should *not* receive service, but two-parent low-income families and elderly persons who have a relative judged capable of providing care are pushed further back in the service queue based on accidents of family structure. In situations of such rationing, to talk of a mother or daughter *choosing* to stay home to care for a dependent family member ignores the fact that choice assumes the existence of options. An increasingly common response to expanding choice is to point to a commercial market that consumers can access for some services. Obviously, this option is only available to those who can pay. Another popular policy route is to have certain services staffed by volunteers. This means that their existence rises or falls on the availability of people, usually women, who fit volunteer work into days that are already crammed with responsibilities. The mixed-economy-of-care scenario can result too easily in different income groups and family types becoming pawns as service providers jockey to position themselves better in the rapidly changing world of health care funding.

If voluntary and proprietary services continue to be seen as major components of our future community service structure, the welfare of all women will be affected. Volunteers cannot staff services to which people have a right by virtue of being Canadian citizens. Similarly, proprietary agencies are in business to make a profit. They are not concerned with guaranteeing that services are universally available to those needing them. Thus, unless a funding mechanism for community-based care is developed that is like that underlying the Canada Health Act—one that guarantees universal access while disallowing individuals or organizations from receiving both public and private fees for service—we can anticipate the continued development of a two-tiered long-term care system. Such a system will consist of underfunded minimum-level public services for those with limited incomes and a multichoice private market of services available to those who can pay.

The necessity for a public model of home care was voiced in the final report of the National Forum on Health (1997: 20).

> Preserving medicare, however, also means adapting to new realities by:
> * expanding publicly funded services to include all medically necessary services and, in the first instance, home care and drugs; and
> * reforming primary care funding, organization and delivery.

After an initial flurry of newspaper editorials there has been remarkably little response to these recommendations. Currently, a number of demonstration projects are under way. Experience in countries such as Australia, which has a commonwealth-state structure not unlike Canada's federal-provincial system, suggests that a national home-care policy would be quite feasible in the Canadian context (Neysmith, 1995). A national home and community care policy will not resolve the gendered nature of caring, but it would go a long way towards guaranteeing minimum services, the institution of national standards, and, perhaps most importantly, access to low levels of home help so valued by many elderly persons (Turvey and Fine, 1996).

In countries with a mixed economy of care such as Canada, four sectors are involved: public or state, market, voluntary, and informal sectors (Evers, 1993; Johnson, 1993; Walker, 1993). To develop a social model of care, Canadians would have to reject an interest group model wherein all players are assumed able to make their claims heard and then the state arbitrates with an eye to ensuring that due process is observed and equal opportunity is available to the various stakeholders. In a state committed to promoting policies that take the starting positions of various groups into account, policy questions would be formulated from the standpoint of those groups defined as experiencing unchosen effects of group membership, whether these result from class, gender, race, sexual orientation, or any other social inequity that riddles Canadian society. In other words, claims arising from groups in positions of privilege would be seen as irrelevant to understanding and eventually addressing such harms. Thus, the policy-making model would not be one of competing interests gathered around a table, but rather one of putting processes in place that can turn up the volume on the voices of those who belong to segments of society seen as vulnerable to the impact of a given policy. This model assumes conflict and challenges the legitimacy of arguments positing that particular policy issues, whether deficit reduction or saving the current model of medicare, somehow can take precedence over other issues such as a national child-care or home-care policy (Harrington, 1992: 77).

Which Comes First—Consumers or Citizens?

In recent years Canadian long-term care policy has adopted market language. Service users are no longer called clients but are positioned as consumers with a right to choice. While the existence of such a demand by elderly persons may be a moot point, of greater concern is the equating of choice with empowerment of service users. It is important to ask if this new language designates a change in the way we think of service recipients, as discussed in the preceding section. Does it reflect a material change in the social conditions of these women's lives? Does changing a client into a consumer indicate that the person has more choice or autonomy over what services she uses? Or is it another instance where language is co-opted but business proceeds as usual? Is the expression 'consumer' any more meaningful than that of 'community care', which, as noted earlier, only meant that people were no longer being housed in institutions, not that an alternative system of services was being actively built?

The consumer model is accurate insofar as it makes clear that elderly persons can choose from what is available. However, one of the tenets of a market model is that products are determined by producers, not consumers. Under a policy of so-called 'consumer sovereignty' elderly people would, at best, be able to choose from among those goods and services that providers make available, subject to the terms and conditions defined by providers. The usual test of whether products meet consumer needs is whether or not they sell. Empowerment, however, means that consumers would affect the shape and content of services. To accomplish this, service users would be involved, for instance, in developing assessment criteria upon which need is determined and services allocated. As well, service users would be central to the development, management, and organization of future long-term care policy. Most long-term care legislation, however, does not provide for more than a consultative role in these areas. Rather than being positioned as protagonists whose well-being is critically affected by long-term care policy, service users and their informal carers in the mixed-economy-of-care drama being played out in Canada today become merely part of the stage setting.

If, as a result of advocacy, research, and public debate, Canadians invigorate the tradition of an active state presence, such as we see reflected in the framing of the Canada Health Act, what might the long-term care policy debate look like? At the level of discourse, policy concerns would centre on ensuring equity across various groups of Canadians. It would put the lie to a consumer model by recognizing oppression resulting from conditions over which people have little choice. The debate would be on how to reduce or redress the resultant harms of social disparities. In such a policy, attention would be paid to guaranteeing access to a minimum level of specified services. For instance, in the Canada Health Act a choice of physician is granted but the guarantees are for service, not consumer choice. Choice is not one of the five principles that frame the Act. Thus, in a parallel long-term care policy there would be less focus on encouraging a range of services and providers than on guaranteeing a minimum level of service to old people and/or their kin carers.

CONCLUSION

Much social policy discussion presupposes the separation of the public from the private, the family from the state, production from reproduction, even when our daily experience leads us to reject the concept of separate spheres. Change is hampered by the discourses available to us. An examination of the relationship of the family, the paid labour force, and the state as it is being played out in the development of community care services for elderly persons illustrates how this occurs. It was argued that the contradictions that this examination revealed can open up possibilities for resistance and change. The notion of resistance emerged in Jane Aronson's chapter on aging women and Marge Reitsma-Street's chapter on girl delinquents. Current community care and delinquency discourses, how-ever, offer little opportunity for either group to define themselves differently from a dominant view of them as dependent old women or sexually promiscuous females.

In contrast, as Janet Mosher illustrates in Chapter 7, the discourse around vio-lence has undergone considerable modification in the last decade. This area is an example of how a change in language (wife abuse, marital rape) allowed women to restructure their experiences, think about them in a new way, and suggest alternatives that were not possible before. However, as this newly legitimized social problem of violence against women demanded responses in the form of resources to meet the needs of these women, the language and structure of the 'problem' again changed. For instance, in order for the legal system to respond, charges had to be laid against a husband/partner and women were expected to leave violent relationships—as if this would guarantee safety! To obtain funding, shelters had to fit into funding categories originally designed for hostels—thus the need for housing was seen as temporary until 'something' could be worked out. To access counselling services wife abuse was renamed to fit into the profes-sional categories of 'domestic' or 'family' violence. These descriptions of the phe-nomenon, however, make invisible again the source of the abuse. Both terms return it to the private sphere of the family, unhooking its link to other types of violence that exist in our society (Walker, 1990).

Thinking about something in a different way can initiate change—it is a nec-essary step to action. Understanding state/family/market relations is central to understanding how caring is socially constructed in Canada. The emotional and physical work is done in both private and public spheres and permeates all aspects of women's lives. The state, as an active participant, can influence how costs and benefits accrue to different groups of women. Equally, an analysis of caring high-lights the importance of crossing the micro/macro schisms that permeate both theory and practice in the helping professions. A perspective is needed that jux-taposes contradictions more sharply than is possible using traditional separatist approaches to policy and clinical practice. The realities of women's lives do not fit neatly into these professional categories.

Canadians have policy options available to them, albeit alternative voices may have trouble being heard in the current rhetoric of restructuring and global competition. The alternatives mentioned in this chapter will require, however, an active state presence in the development of social policy. The challenge is made greater because an activist state has been subject to attacks from the left as well as from the right. It has been critiqued, with justification, as frequently supportive of market forces and organized interests rather than promoting the well-being of oppressed groups. However, assuming an anti-state position in response can actually increase the vulnerability of women. For instance, federal and provincial legislation, despite resistance from the market sector, initiated pay and employment equity policies, property splitting upon divorce, anti-violence programs, and welfare schemes that have benefited different groups of women. Women may have a contradictory relationship with the state, but in countries like Sweden and Denmark, where a more active state exists, women have registered real gains from policies that recognized the social benefits of child-care and elder-care programs. These effects are summarized by Daatland (1994: 188–9) in his recent review of trends in aging policy:

> The great expansion of care and services for the aged was not a more or less reluctant response to increased demands for public services due to the growing number of old people and changes in family structure. The expansion was part of a general trend of increased ambition in the welfare state itself. The war years produced political agreement and popular support for an active state role in the provision of welfare . . . .

While other welfare states gave priority to private consumption and/or early retirement, Scandinavian countries became *service welfare states*. These services are labour-intensive, hence public employment expanded greatly and came to be the main arena for the inclusion of women in the labour market. The expanding public sector in Scandinavia can be credited for the high employment rates of women, who most often moved into the health and social sector, into jobs they earlier had performed without pay in the family setting. Public services were not expanded to compensate for women moving into paid labour; rather, the contrary was true—women found paid work in an expanding public sector.

The above observations are not offered to evoke nostalgia for past achievements of welfare states but rather to give some social context to current debates about policy options that so often seem to be ahistorical. Canadians have exemplars upon which to fashion 'made in Canada' responses to fiscal constraints, restructuring, and globalization. It is important, however, to articulate the costs associated with different options. Whatever their limitations, legislators and public policy-makers have a different relationship to the citizenry than bond markets or the International Monetary Fund. This relationship means that the state can disrupt economic and patriarchal power (Harrington, 1992). This is most evident in national programs such as the Canada Health Act, where the delivery of health care disrupts class privilege, or in the Canada Pension Plan, where child-rearing drop-out clauses and contribution rates have the potential for disrupting gender- and class-specific employment patterns not found in private pension schemes. In a similar vein, pay and employment equity legislation disrupts privileges of class, sexual orientation, and race. As welfare pluralism is debated and constructed within the Canadian political economy, the starting point for the compromises and alternatives is critical to determining their outcome. The current emphasis on the expansion of the market and informal sectors in long-term care provision will result in very different consequences for women who reside in differing social locations in Canada.

NOTE

1. It is also important to keep in mind that community care is only one of a number of programs undergoing fundamental reforms in financing approaches. The Canada Pension Plan contribution rules are being changed and a Seniors Benefit will replace Old Age Security, the Guaranteed Income Supplement, and pension income tax credits in 2001. There are conflicting projections about how these separately, and together, will affect aging women. The very poor elderly will be protected, but those just above the poverty line, which is the case of many women because of their employment histories, will be less secure. What there seems to be a silent consensus on is that it will be women who are most affected (Caledon Institute of Social Policy, 1996).

REFERENCES

Aronson, J. 1993. 'Giving Consumers a Say in Policy Development: Influencing Policy or Just Being Heard?', *Canadian Public Policy* 19, 4: 367–78.

Aronson, J., and S. Neysmith. 1996. '"You're not just in there to do the work": Depersonalizing Policies and the Exploitation of Home Care Workers' Labor', *Gender and Society* 10, 1: 59–77.

Barry, J. 1995. 'Care-Need and Care-Receivers: Views from the Margins', *Women's Studies International Forum* 18, 3: 361–74.

Caledon Institute of Social Policy. 1996. *Round Table on Canada Pension Plan Reform: Gender Implications*. Ottawa.

Connell, R.W. 1994. 'The State, Gender and Sexual Politics: Theory and Appraisal', in H.L. Radke and H.J. Stam, eds, *Power/Gender Social Relations in Theory and Practice*. London: Sage Publications: 136–73.

Daatland, S. 1994. 'Recent Trends and Future Prospects for the Elderly in Scandinavia', *Journal of Aging and Social Policy* 6, 1–2: 181–97.

Deber, R., and A.P. Williams. 1995. 'Policy, Payment and Participation: Long-Term Care Reform in Ontario', *Canadian Journal on Aging* 14, 2: 294–318.

Estes, C., J. Swan, and Associates. 1993. *The Long-Term Care Crisis: Elders Trapped in the No-Care Zone*. Newbury Park, Calif.: Sage.

Evers, A. 1993. 'The Welfare Mix Approach: Understanding the Pluralism of Welfare Systems', in A. Evers and I. Svetlik, eds, *Balancing Pluralism: New Welfare Mixes in Care for the Elderly*. Aldershot: Avebury: 3–31.

Ferguson, K. 1984. *The Feminist Case Against Bureaucracy.* Philadelphia: Temple University Press.

Harrington, M. 1992. 'What Exactly is Wrong with the Liberal State as an Agent of Change?', in V. Spike Peterson, ed., *Theory Gendered States: Feminist (Re)Visions of International Relations.* Boulder, Colo: Lynne Reinner: 65–82.

Hasselkus, B., and S. Stetson. 1991. 'Ethical Dilemmas: The Organization of Family Caregiving for the Elderly', *Journal of Aging Studies* 5, 1: 99–110.

Health and Welfare Canada, Seniors Secretariat. 1993. *Ageing and Independence: Overview of a National Survey.* Ottawa: Minister of Supply and Services Canada.

Horl, J. 1992. 'Family Care of the Elderly in Austria', in J. Kosberg, ed., *Family Care of the Elderly: Social and Cultural Changes.* Newbury Park, Calif.: Sage: 235–51.

Hugman, R. 1994. 'Social Work and Case Management in the U.K.: Models of Professionalism and Elderly People', *Ageing and Society* 14, 2: 237–53.

James, N. 1992. 'Care = organization + physical labour + emotional labour', *Sociology of Health and Illness* 14: 488–509.

Johnson, N. 1993. 'Welfare Pluralism: Opportunities and Risks', in A. Evers and I. Svetlik, eds, *Balancing Pluralism: New Welfare Mixes in Care for the Elderly.* Aldershot: Avebury: 51–66.

Kane, R., A. Caplan, and C. Thomas. 1993. 'Conclusion: Toward an Ethic of Case Management', in R. Kane and A. Caplan, eds, *Ethical Conflicts in the Management of Home Care: The Case Manager's Dilemma.* New York: Springer Publishing: 249–62.

Leira, A. 1994. 'Concepts of Caring: Loving, Thinking, Doing', *Social Service Review* 68, 2: 185–201.

MacLean, M., ed. 1995. *Abuse and Neglect of Older Canadians: Strategies for Change.* Toronto: Thompson Educational Publishing.

Metro Consumers for Community-Based Long Term Care. 1997. 'Will There Be Enough Money?', *Network News* 6: 1–4.

National Forum on Health. 1997. *Canada Health Action: Building on the Legacy. Final Report of the National Forum on Health.* Ottawa.

Neysmith, S. 1995. 'Would a National Information System Promote the Development of a Canadian Home and Community Care System? An Examination of the Australian Experience', *Canadian Public Policy* 21, 2: 159–73.

Neysmith, S., and J. Aronson. 1996. 'Home Care Workers Discuss Their Work: The Skills Required to "Use Your Common Sense"', *Journal of Aging Studies* 10, 1: 1–14.

Neysmith, S., and J. Aronson. 1997. 'Working Conditions in Home Care: Negotiating Race and Class Boundaries in Gendered Work', *International Journal of Health Services* 27, 3: 479–99.

Orloff, A. 1993. 'Gender and the Social Rights of Citizenship: The Comparative Analysis of Gender Relations and Welfare States', *American Sociological Review* 58, 30: 303–28.

Statistics Canada. 1997. *Who Cares? Caregiving in the 1990's.* Ottawa.

Szasz, A. 1990. 'The Labour Impacts of Policy Change in Health Care: How Federal Policy Transformed Home Health Organizations and Their Labour Practices', *Journal of Health Politics, Policy and Law* 15, 1: 191–210.

Thomas, C. 1993. 'De-Constructing Concepts of Care', *Sociology* 27, 4: 549–669.

Turvey, K., and M. Fine. 1996. *Community Care: The Effects of Low Levels of Service Use.* SPRC Reports and Proceedings No. 130. Sydney, Australia: Social Policy Research Centre.

Walker, A. 1993. 'A Cultural Revolution? Shifting the UK's Welfare Mix in the Care of Older People', in A. Evers and I. Svetlik, eds, *Balancing Pluralism: New Welfare Mixes in Care for the Elderly.* Aldershot: Avebury: 67–88.

Walker, G. 1990. *Family Violence and the Women's Movement: The Conceptual Politics of Struggle.* Toronto: University of Toronto Press.

Subject Index

Aboriginal people: abuse of women, 149–52, 154–6; colonization, 149–50; communities, 17–18; families and child welfare, 154–6, 164, 166–7, 182; poverty of women, 48

Abuse of women: Aboriginal people, 149–52, 154–6; Black women, 147–8; criminal acts or social problem, 146, 245; dependence of women, 145, 154, 155–6; effects on children, 150, 152–3, 154, 155; female excuses, 144, 146; feminist perspective, 139–40, 142–7; incidence, 139; increased awareness of, 163; interpretations of victim's responses, 152–6; 'intersecting oppressions' viewpoint, 140, 147–52; male justification, 143–4; relationship to caring, 145–6, 148, 151; role expectations, 142, 143, 144, 145, 146–7; therapeutic perspective, 139, 141–2, 146, 153

Activist groups, 18–19

Adolescent girls: costs of caring, 94–8; dependence or poverty, 96–8, 103; physical vulnerability, 93, 95–6; resistance to male expectations, 104–7; sister study, 88–9; social control of, 88, 98–102, 103; socialization to caring, 88, 89–94, 102–3; see also Delinquent girls

Aging. See Elderly

Alcoholism and child neglect, 169, 174–5, 180

Black women, 10–11; abuse, 147–8; poverty, 48, 52

Breadwinner model of the family, 64

Bureaucracy, 7, 43, 241

Canada Health Act, 235, 243, 244–5, 246–7

Canada Health and Social Transfer (CHST), 55, 203, 235

Canada/Quebec Pension Plan (C/QPP), 61, 62, 63, 247

Caring: 'burden of care', 8, 12, 78, 237; children, see Child care; community, see Community care; consumer model, 244; costs, 94–8, 127–9; cutbacks, see Government cutbacks; definition, 3;

devaluation of, 8, 234; dimensions, 5–6; for disabled, 11–12, 17, 52; for elderly, see Elderly; and employment, 52–4; expected of women, 8, 89–94, 102–3, 124–5, 131, 139–40, 168–77, 182, 233–4, 239; health care, see Health care in Canada; 'labour' and 'love', 5, 205–7, 237–8; professionalization, see Professionalization; public, see Social services; Welfare state; social care model, 238, 239–45; and women of colour, 69–79

Case management model, 241, 242

Child care: advocacy groups, 203, 209, 210; collective responsibility, 179–80, 181, 182, 209–11; early intervention programs, 196–7; expected of women, 191–2, 200–1; foster care, 167, 175, 177, 180, 182; gender imbalance, 207–8; informal sector, 195; invisibility and undervaluing of, 197–200, 204; licensed day-care centres, 192, 193; national policy needed, 16, 17, 191; physical and emotional dimensions, 205–7; private and public spheres, 201, 202–3; professionalization, 206; reforms should benefit all, 211–12; settings, 192–7; spaces limited, 55, 203; strengths of current system, 208–9; in Sweden, 64–5; wages for workers, 194–5; welfare state and, 201–2, 209–11; see also Live-in Caregiver Program

Child neglect: alcohol or drug abuse, 169, 174–5, 180; cultural context, 165, 179; definitions, 162, 164–6; diminished attention to, 163–4; focus on mother, 14–15, 166, 168–77, 179; hidden realities, 160–1, 172–3, 175, 182; history, 161–3; individualization of problems, 169, 171, 174; language, 168–71; and poverty, 170, 171, 173, 175, 176, 182; rights vs intervention, 164, 176, 177–8; social responsibility, 169–70, 171, 173, 175, 176, 179, 182; and women's care, 168, 172–3, 175, 176–7, 182

Children: effects of poverty, 55–6, 175–6;

Author Index